The Oracle8i™ DBA: Architecture and Administration Cram Sheet

This Cram Sheet contains the distilled, key facts about Oracle8i architecture and administration. Review this information immediately before you enter the test room, paying special attention to those areas that you feel you need to review the most. Once you are seated in the exam room, you can transfer any of these facts from your short-term memory onto a blank piece of paper.

ORACLE ARCHITECTURAL COMPONENTS

1. Know the following Oracle8i structures:
   - *Control files*—Track database structures and ensure synchronicity of all database files via the log sequence number.
   - *Datafiles*—Make up the physical side of tablespaces. Each tablespace has one or more datafiles. A datafile can belong to only one tablespace.
   - *Parameter file*—Contains the initialization parameters that tell the Oracle server how to configure memory and internal resources. Also contains external file locations and process configurations.
   - *Redo log files*—Contain changes made to data. The redo log files are the only place that Oracle guarantees to have this information, so they are critical for database recovery. Redo log files that are copied to an archive destination if archive logging is enabled are called archived redo logs.

GETTING STARTED WITH THE ORACLE SERVER

2. SQL*Plus is used to perform database administration tasks. Database startup, shutdown, and recovery are all performed through SQL*Plus.

3. Oracle Enterprise Manager (OEM) is Oracle's management tool that uses a graphical user interface (GUI) to simplify database management. It eliminates the need to memorize syntax for DBA tasks.

MANAGING AN ORACLE INSTANCE

4. The system global area (SGA) is made up of the data buffer cache, the shared pool, and the log buffer cache.

5. The data buffer cache is where data is stored in memory to improve access times to the data.

6. The shared pool stores the library cache, the data dictionary cache, and control structures.

7. The log buffer cache is used to store redo log entries prior to their being written to disk.

8. An instance is composed of the SGA and a set of background processes. The five mandatory processes are DBW*n*, LGWR, PMON, SMON, and CKPT.

9. The DBW*n* process(es) (also known as Database Writer) writes dirty or changed buffers from the data buffer cache to disk.

10. The LGWR process (also known as Log Writer) writes redo log entries from the log buffers to the redo logs.

11. The PMON process (also known as Process Monitor) cleans up failed processes by rolling back uncompleted transactions, and releasing locks and resources held by the failed process.

SQL*Loader, the Export and Import utilities, or transportable tablespaces.

50. Direct-load inserts can be used to copy data from one table to another table within the same database. They bypass the buffer cache completely and write directly into the datafiles, thus considerably speeding up the insert operation.

51. SQL*Loader is used to load data from external files. It can be loaded either in conventional path (using the normal SQL engine) or direct path (writing directly to the datafiles above the high-water mark).

52. SQL*Loader uses five file types: the control file (contains information on how to load the data), the log file (contains detailed information about the load), the bad file (contains rejected records), the discard file (contains records that did not match the selection criteria specified in the control file), and the data file (contains the data to be loaded).

53. The Export and Import utilities are used to reorganize data or move database objects from one schema to another (or one database to another). Export extracts the data from an Oracle database to a binary dump file that the Import utility can then read to reload the data.

54. Objects can be exported and imported in table mode, user mode, or full database mode.

55. The Export and Import utilities are also used to transport tablespaces from one database to another.

MANAGING SECURITY

56. Users can be created, altered, and dropped using the **CREATE**, **ALTER**, and **DROP** commands.

57. Users are granted profiles, roles, and privileges.

58. Profiles are used to limit resource usage and can be used to enforce password limitations.

59. Roles are used to group a collection of privileges, roles, and grants that can then be granted en masse to a user or another role.

60. Grants and privileges are given at the system, table, or column level.

CORIOLIS™
Certification Insider Press

USING NATIONAL LANGUAGE SUPPORT

61. National Language Support (NLS) is the functionality in Oracle databases that allows you to store, process, and retrieve data in languages other than English.

62. You can specify both a database character set (using the **CHARACTER SET** clause of the **CREATE DATABASE** command) and a national character set (using the **NATIONAL CHARACTER SET** clause). The national character set tells Oracle which character set to use specifically for **NCHAR**, **NVARCHAR2**, and **NCLOB** columns.

63. To create a database using a character set other than US7ASCII, you must have set up the **ORA_NLS33** environment variable.

64. You can specify NLS parameters in three different ways:

- The default values for the database can be set as initialization parameters. (This will affect only the server-side settings, not the client-side settings.)

- You can override the default settings for the server by setting environment variables at the client.

- You can override both the default settings and the environment variable settings with an **ALTER SESSION** command.

65. The two initialization parameters used to derive other initialization parameters are:

- **NLS_LANGUAGE**—Sets the values of language-dependent behavior, such as the language that Oracle error messages are sent in.

- **NLS_TERRITORY**—Sets the values of territory-dependent behavior, such as the default date format, the decimal character, the thousands separator, and currency symbols.

66. The environment variable that is used to override the two parameters just mentioned is **NLS_LANG**. The format of this environment variable is *language_territory.characterset* (*language* overrides **NLS_LANGUAGE**, *territory* overrides **NLS_TERRITORY**, and *characterset* specifies the character encoding scheme used by the terminal where data is being entered.

31. The **ALTER TABLESPACE** command can be used to relocate tablespaces while the database is up (except for the SYSTEM tablespace and tablespaces containing active rollback segments). The SYSTEM tablespace can be moved while the database is mounted but not open using the **ALTER DATABASE** command.

32. Datafiles are the physical representation on disk of a permanent tablespace. Tempfiles are the physical representation on disk of a temporary tablespace.

STORAGE STRUCTURES AND RELATIONSHIPS

33. Oracle stores data in data blocks, extents, and segments within a tablespace (or tablespaces for partitioned segments).

34. The block is the smallest unit of I/O performed by the database. It is sized by the **DB_BLOCK_SIZE** parameter. A set of contiguous blocks is called an *extent*, and a segment can be made up of many extents.

35. The different segment types are data (tables and clusters), index, rollback, temporary, index-organized tables, and the bootstrap segment.

36. A block is composed of the common and variable header, the table directory, and the row directory. The remaining part of the block is composed of free space and the actual row data.

37. Block space usage is controlled by four parameters: **INITRANS** (initial number of transaction slots), **MAXTRANS** (maximum number of transaction slots), **PCTUSED** (amount of space set aside in a block for inserts), and **PCTFREE** (amount of space set aside for updates to rows that are already in the block).

MANAGING ROLLBACK SEGMENTS

38. Rollback segments are used for transaction rollback, read-consistency, and instance recovery. They are created using the **CREATE ROLLBACK SEGMENT** command and dropped with the **DROP ROLLBACK SEGMENT** command.

39. Rollback segments should have **OPTIMAL** set so that they can shrink back to an optimal size after growing due to long-running transactions. You can shrink a rollback segment manually as well.

40. Rollback segments need to be sized properly for the database environment in which they are used, and you need to have the right number for the type of environment.

41. Rollback segments should be stored in their own tablespace, not with other objects.

42. **INITIAL** should be set to the same value as **NEXT** for rollback segments. **PCTINCREASE** cannot be set at all, and **MINEXTENTS** must be at least 2 for rollback segments.

MANAGING TABLES, INDEXES, AND INTEGRITY CONSTRAINTS

43. Tables and indexes are managed by the **CREATE, ALTER, DROP**, and **TRUNCATE** commands. The **TRUNCATE** command removes all rows from a table without creating rollback information.

44. From a DBA perspective, the most important settings when creating tables and indexes are for the **STORAGE** clause and the **TABLESPACE** clause.

45. Indexes can be of several different types: B-tree, bitmap, reverse key, and function-based. They can be on a single column or multiple columns (composite). Composite indexes (also known as *concatenated*) can have up to 32 columns (except for bitmap indexes, which can have up to only 30 columns). Indexes can also be unique or nonunique.

46. Data integrity can be enforced by integrity constraints—**NOT NULL, PRIMARY KEY, FOREIGN KEY, UNIQUE KEY**, and **CHECK**.

47. Constraints can be in one of four states: **DISABLE NOVALIDATE** (not checked at all), **DISABLE VALIDATE** (modifications to columns are not allowed in this state), **ENABLE NOVALIDATE** (new data is checked but existing data in the table is not), or **ENABLE VALIDATE** (both new and existing data are checked).

48. Constraints can be enforced at the end of each statement (**INITIALLY IMMDEDIATE**) or at the end of a transaction (**INITIALLY DEFERRED**).

LOADING AND REORGANIZING DATA

49. Data can be loaded and reorganized in an Oracle database using direct-load insert,

2. The SMON process (also known as System Monitor) cleans up temporary segments, performs instance recovery, and coalesces contiguous chunks of free space in datafiles.

3. The CKPT process (also known as Checkpoint) signals DBW*n* at checkpoints and updates all the datafiles and control files with current checkpoint information.

4. Other optional processes include ARC*n*, RECO, D*nnn*, S*nnn*, SNP*n*, and QMN*n*. The most important of these to be aware of for the exam is the ARC*n* process(es) (or Archiver), which archives copies of the redo logs to an archive destination when the database is in **ARCHIVELOG** mode.

15. To start up an Oracle instance, use the **STARTUP** command with one of these options: **NOMOUNT**, **MOUNT**, or **OPEN**. To shut down an Oracle instance, use the **SHUTDOWN** command with one of these options: **NORMAL**, **IMMEDIATE**, **TRANSACTIONAL**, or **ABORT**.

CREATING A DATABASE

16. Create the database with the optimal **DB_ BLOCK_SIZE** setting for your environment (OLTP or DSS). The database must be re-created to change the block size.

17. In addition to the SYSTEM tablespace, create tablespaces for temporary segments, rollback segments, application data segments, and application index segments.

18. File placement (of control files, log files, datafiles, and archive log files) is critical to performance. Distribute input/output (I/O) evenly.

CREATING DATA DICTIONARY VIEWS AND PACKAGES

19. The base data dictionary tables are not meant to be accessed by normal users. Oracle provides a set of data dictionary views, created by the catalog.sql script, to access the data in the base data dictionary tables.

20. The data dictionary views are divided into three categories: **USER_*** views that contain information about objects owned by a user, **ALL_*** views that contain information about objects that a user owns or has been granted access to, and **DBA_*** views that contain information about all database objects.

21. Oracle also provides a set of dynamic performance views, the **V$** views, that are used for performance monitoring and diagnostics.

22. Standard packages provide much of the functionality needed by DBAs to maintain the Oracle database. These packages are created by the DBMS_*.SQL scripts located under the $ORACLE_HOME/rdbms/admin directory.

MAINTAINING CONTROL FILES AND REDO LOG FILES

23. Control files are critical to the operation of an Oracle database and should be mirrored across multiple devices at the operating system level.

24. Redo log files are also critical to the operation of an Oracle database and should be mirrored across multiple devices at either the operating system level or the database level.

25. An Oracle database must have at least two redo log groups of one member each to be functional. However, in most cases, a group should have multiple members to provide for redundancy.

26. Nearly all production databases should be run in **ARCHIVELOG** mode, in which redo logs are copied to an archive destination by the ARC*n* process(es) before they can be reused.

MANAGING TABLESPACES AND DATAFILES

27. Tablespaces are logical structures for storing either permanent or temporary data. They are created with the **CREATE TABLESPACE** command and dropped using the **DROP TABLESPACE** command.

28. Tablespaces can be set to use a bitmap (locally managed) or to use data dictionary tables (dictionary managed) to manage free space within the tablespace. Locally managed tablespaces are advantageous because fragmentation can be less of a problem than with dictionary-managed tablespaces.

29. Tablespaces can be set to automatically grow by using the **AUTOEXTEND** clause, or they can be manually increased in size either by resizing or by adding another datafile to the tablespace.

30. Tablespaces can be either online (the default) or offline, and they can be toggled from read-write to read-only.

Oracle8i™ DBA: Architecture and Administration

Peter Sharman

Oracle8i™ DBA: Architecture and Administration Exam Cram

Limits of Liability and Disclaimer of Warranty

Trademarks

The Coriolis Group, LLC
14455 N. Hayden Road
Suite 220
Scottsdale, Arizona 85260

(480)483-0192
FAX (480)483-0193
www.coriolis.com

Library of Congress Cataloging-in-Publication Data
Sharman, Peter.
    Oracle8i DBA : architecture and administration / by Peter Sharman.
        p.   cm. -- (Exam cram)
    Includes index.
    ISBN 1-58880-036-9
    1. Relational databases.   2. Oracle (Computer file)   I. Title.
II. Series.
QA76.9.D3 S515   2001
005.75'85--dc21   2001042412
                                                        CIP

President and CEO
Roland Elgey

Publisher
Steve Sayre

Associate Publisher
Katherine R. Hartlove

Acquisitions Editor
Sharon Linsenbach

Director of Marketing
Susan Hughes

Project Editor
Meredith Brittain

Technical Reviewer
Robert Freeman

Production Coordinator
Todd Halvorsen

Cover Designer
Laura Wellander

Layout Designer
April Nielsen

Printed in the United States of America
10 9 8 7 6 5 4 3 2 1

The Coriolis Group, LLC • 14455 North Hayden Road, Suite 220 • Scottsdale, Arizona 85260

A Note from Coriolis

Our goal has always been to provide you with the best study tools on the planet to help you achieve your certification in record time. Time is so valuable these days that none of us can afford to waste a second of it, especially when it comes to exam preparation.

Over the past few years, we've created an extensive line of *Exam Cram* and *Exam Prep* study guides, practice exams, and interactive training. To help you study even better, we have now created an e-learning and certification destination called **ExamCram.com**. (You can access the site at **www.examcram.com**.) Now, with every study product you purchase from us, you'll be connected to a large community of people like yourself who are actively studying for their certifications, developing their careers, seeking advice, and sharing their insights and stories.

We believe that the future is all about collaborative learning. Our **ExamCram.com** destination is our approach to creating a highly interactive, easily accessible collaborative environment, where you can take practice exams and discuss your experiences with others, sign up for features like "Questions of the Day," plan your certifications using our interactive planners, create your own personal study pages, and keep up with all of the latest study tips and techniques.

We hope that whatever study products you purchase from us—*Exam Cram* or *Exam Prep* study guides, *Personal Trainers, Personal Test Centers*, or one of our interactive Web courses—will make your studying fun and productive. Our commitment is to build the kind of learning tools that will allow you to study the way you want to, whenever you want to.

Help us continue to provide the very best certification study materials possible. Write us or email us at

Visit ExamCram.com now to enhance your study program.

learn@examcram.com and let us know how our study products have helped you study. Tell us about new features that you'd like us to add. Send us a story about how we've helped you. We're listening!

Good luck with your certification exam and your career. Thank you for allowing us to help you achieve your goals.

ExamCram.com Connects You to the Ultimate Study Center!

Look for these other products from The Coriolis Group:

Oracle8i DBA: Backup and Recovery Exam Cram
by Debbie Wong

Oracle8i DBA: Performance and Tuning Exam Cram
by Zulfiqer Habeeb

Oracle8i DBA: SQL and PL/SQL Exam Cram
by Michael R. Ault

Oracle8i DBA: Network Administration Exam Cram
by Barbara Ann Pascavage

Java 2 Exam Cram, Second Edition
by Bill Brogden

MCSE SQL 2000 Administration Exam Cram
by Kirk Hausman

This book is dedicated to my family.
I know that writing this book was harder on them than it was on me
because it meant that they didn't get to see as much of me as they wanted,
and when they did see me, I was likely to be grumpy from lack of sleep.
So to Emma, Kit, and Sandi—my love and thanks for your understanding.

A special word of dedication to my wife, Ann.
Without her love and understanding,
and all her hard work keeping the family together
while I was slaving on this book,
none of this would have been remotely possible.

❧

About the Author

Peter Sharman is an Oracle consultant with Advanced Technology Solutions in Oracle Consulting, and he is currently the global Oracle9i Consulting lead. With more than 14 years of Oracle experience, Pete has been a speaker at a number of Oracle OpenWorld conferences. He has been part of the development team of many of the Oracle Education database administration courses and has trained hundreds of people both internally and externally on advanced functionality of the Oracle database. Pete is OCP certified for Oracle7.3, Oracle8, and Oracle8i. He lives in San Mateo, California, with his wife and three children, but he hopes to return home to Australia soon!

Acknowledgments

I would like to acknowledge the team that helped me to write this book. Their expertise has helped me immensely, and they improved the quality of the book significantly. Thanks to Sharon Linsenbach, acquisitions editor, for her professionalism; Meredith Brittain, project editor, who kept me on track with my deadlines; Robert Freeman, technical reviewer, who did a great job of finding all my mistakes; Tom Gillen, copyeditor; and Sarah Call and Mark Janousek, the proofreaders who corrected everything else. Thanks also to the rest of the team for their excellent work: production coordinator Todd Halvorsen, cover designer Laura Wellander, and layout designer April Nielsen.

I'd also like to thank all those people who got me where I am—Rob DeNardi, who first taught me what a **ROLLBACK** command was; Kevin Barry, who gave me the opportunity to move into DBA work; Marcel Kratochvil, who showed me how broad a knowledge level I needed to go forward; Surinder Randhawa, who gave me the opportunity to join Oracle in the Education group; Mike Cohen, who taught me all about the realities of Consulting; Mark Dochtermann, who smoothed the waters of a migration from Australia to the United States; and my current management team, Paul Cross and Paul Silverstein, for giving me the opportunity to write this book and to work on the Oracle9i technology.

A special thanks to Bruce Pihlamae, DBA extraordinaire, who was sadly taken from this life at the early age of 37. Bruce taught me how to be a DBA, and look where it's gotten me now, mate!

Contents at a Glance

Chapter 1   Oracle OCP Certification Exams   1

Chapter 2   Oracle Architectural Components   13

Chapter 3   Getting Started with the Oracle Server   39

Chapter 4   Managing an Oracle Instance   61

Chapter 5   Creating a Database   91

Chapter 6   Data Dictionary Views, Standard Packages, and Trigger Types   107

Chapter 7   Managing Control Files and Redo Log Files   129

Chapter 8   Managing Tablespaces and Datafiles   159

Chapter 9   Storage Structure and Relationships   183

Chapter 10   Managing Rollback Segments   201

Chapter 11   Managing Tables, Indexes, and Integrity Constraints   223

Chapter 12   Loading and Reorganizing Data   261

Chapter 13   Managing Security   289

Chapter 14   Using National Language Support   329

Chapter 15   Sample Test   341

Chapter 16   Answer Key   361

Table of Contents

Introduction xix

Self-Assessment xxix

Chapter 1
Oracle OCP Certification Exams 1
    Assessing Exam-Readiness 2
    The Testing Situation 3
    Test Layout and Design 4
    Using Oracle's Test Software Effectively 6
    Taking Testing Seriously 6
    Question-Handling Strategies 7
    Mastering the Inner Game 8
    Additional Resources 9

Chapter 2
Oracle Architectural Components 13
    The Oracle Database 14
        Physical Database Structure 14
        Logical Structure 16
    The Oracle Instance 18
        The System Global Area 19
        Background Processes 23
        User Processes 28
        The Program Global Area 28
    Commit Processing 28
    Practice Questions **30**
    Need to Know More? 37

Chapter 3
Getting Started with the Oracle Server 39

Features of the Oracle Universal Installer   40

Setting Up Operating System and Password File Authentication   42

The SYS and SYSTEM Accounts   42

Authentication Methods   43

Using SQL*Plus and Server Manager   45

Oracle Enterprise Manager   46

First Tier: OEM Console   47

Second Tier: OMS, Common Services, and
OEM Repository   51

DBA Management Pack   52

Practice Questions   54

Need to Know More?   58

Chapter 4
Managing an Oracle Instance 61

Creating the Parameter File   62

Starting an Oracle Instance and Opening the Database   69

Closing a Database and Shutting Down an Instance   72

Getting and Setting Parameter Values   74

Dynamic Initialization Parameters   78

Managing Sessions   80

Enabling **RESTRICTED SESSION**   80

Terminating User Sessions   81

Disabling **RESTRICTED SESSION**   82

Monitoring Alert and Trace Files   82

Practice Questions   84

Need to Know More?   89

Chapter 5
Creating a Database 91

Before You Create a Database   92

Creating a Database   92

The Database Configuration Assistant (DBCA)   92

Creating a Database Manually   94

Dropping a Database   100

Practice Questions   101

Need to Know More?   106

Chapter 6
Data Dictionary Views, Standard Packages, and Trigger Types 107

Constructing the Data Dictionary Views   108

Querying the Data Dictionary   109

Preparing the PL/SQL Environment   117

Administering Stored Procedures and Packages   119

Listing Database Event Trigger Types   121

Practice Questions   123

Need to Know More?   127

Chapter 7
Managing Control Files and Redo Log Files 129

The Uses of the Control File   130

The Contents of the Control File   130

Multiplexing the Control File   131

Obtaining Control File Information   132

The Uses of the Online Redo Log Files   135

Archiving Redo Log Files   138

Obtaining Log and Archive Information   138

Controlling Log Switches and Checkpoints   142

Multiplexing and Maintaining Online Redo Log Files   143

Adding Redo Log Files and Groups   143

Renaming and Relocating Redo Log Files   145

Dropping Redo Log Files   146

Clearing Redo Log Files   147

Planning Online Redo Log Files   148

Troubleshooting Common Redo Log File Problems   149

Analyzing Online and Archived Redo Logs   150

Using LogMiner   150

Practice Questions   153

Need to Know More?   158

Chapter 8
Managing Tablespaces and Datafiles 159

Creating Tablespaces   160

Changing the Size of Tablespaces   165

Automatic Datafile Resizing   165

Manually Resizing Datafiles   167
Adding Datafiles to an Existing Tablespace   167
Allocating Space for Temporary Segments   168
Changing the Status of Tablespaces   169
Changing the Storage Settings of Tablespaces   171
Relocating Tablespaces   173
Dropping Tablespaces   174
Obtaining Tablespace Information   175
Practice Questions   176
Need to Know More?   181

Chapter 9
Storage Structure and Relationships 183

Segment Types and Their Uses   184
    Tables   184
    Partitioned Tables   184
    Nested Tables   184
    LOB Segments   185
    Index Clusters   185
    Hash Clusters   185
    Indexes   186
    Partitioned Indexes   186
    LOB Indexes   187
    Index-Organized Tables   187
    Rollback Segments   188
    Temporary Segments   188
    Bootstrap Segment   189
Controlling Block Space Usage   189
Obtaining Information about Storage Structures from the
  Data Dictionary   191
Criteria for Separating Segments   194
Practice Questions   196
Need to Know More?   200

Chapter 10
Managing Rollback Segments 201

Overview of Rollback Segments   202
    Read-Consistency   202
    Types of Rollback Segments   203

Using Rollback Segments with Transactions   204

Growth of Rollback Segments   204

Shrinkage of Rollback Segments   204

Creating Rollback Segments Using Appropriate Storage Settings   205

Maintaining Rollback Segments   208

Changing Storage Parameters   208

Deallocating Unused Space   208

Taking a Rollback Segment Offline   209

Dropping a Rollback Segment   211

Planning the Number and Size of Rollback Segments   212

Obtaining Rollback Segment Information from the
Data Dictionary   213

Troubleshooting Common Rollback Segment Problems   214

Insufficient Space for Transactions   214

Read-Consistency Errors   214

Blocking Session Problems   215

Taking a Tablespace Offline   215

Practice Questions   217

Need to Know More?   222

Chapter 11
Managing Tables, Indexes, and Integrity Constraints 223

Creating Tables Using Appropriate
Storage Settings   224

Structure of a Row   224

Oracle **ROWID**s   225

Creating a Table   228

Guidelines for Creating Tables   230

Setting **PCTFREE** and **PCTUSED**   231

Controlling the Space Used by Tables   232

Manually Allocating Extents   235

Relocating a Table   235

The High-Water Mark   236

Truncating a Table   238

Dropping Columns from a Table   239

Retrieving Table Information from the Data Dictionary   240

Listing Index Types and Their Uses   242

Logical Classifications   242

Physical Classifications   242

Creating B-Tree and Bitmap Indexes 243
B-Tree Indexes 243
Bitmap Indexes 244
Comparing Bitmap and B-Tree Indexes 245
Guidelines for Creating Indexes 245
Reorganizing Indexes 246
Allocating and Deallocating Index Space 246
Rebuilding Indexes 247
Getting Index Information from the Data Dictionary 248
Implementing Data Integrity Constraints 249
Constraint States 249
Constraint Enforcement Modes 250
Maintaining Integrity Constraints 251
Obtaining Constraint Information from the Data Dictionary 254
Practice Questions 255
Need to Know More? 260

Chapter 12
Loading and Reorganizing Data 261
Loading Data Using Direct-Load Insert 262
Loading Data Using SQL*Loader 263
Conventional and Direct Path Loads 264
Parallel Direct Loads 266
Ways to Execute SQL*Loader 266
SQL*Loader Usage Guidelines 270
Reorganizing Data Using the Export and Import Utilities 270
Uses of Export and Import 270
Export Modes 271
Conventional and Direct Path Exports 272
Using the Export Utility 272
Using the Import Utility 276
Export and Import Guidelines 279
Moving Data Using Transportable Tablespaces 279
Transportable Tablespace Process 279
Transportable Tablespace Restrictions 281
Practice Questions 282
Need to Know More? 287

. . . .

Chapter 13
Managing Security 289

Creating, Altering, and Dropping Users   290
    Creating a User   291
    Altering a User   294
    Dropping a User   296
Monitoring Information about Users   297
Identifying System and Object Privileges   297
    System Privileges   298
    Object Privileges   301
Identifying Auditing Capabilities   305
    Using Database Auditing   305
    Auditing Guidelines   307
    Displaying Auditing Information   307
Creating, Altering, and Dropping Roles   308
    Creating a Role   309
    Altering a Role   310
    Granting and Revoking Roles to Users or Other Roles   311
    Dropping A Role   312
Controlling Availability of Roles   312
    Enabling and Disabling Roles   313
Using Predefined Roles   313
Displaying Role Information from the Data Dictionary   314
Administering Profiles   315
    Creating a Profile   316
    Altering a Profile   317
    Dropping a Profile   318
Managing Passwords Using Profiles   319
Controlling Resource Usage with Profiles   320
Obtaining Information about Profiles, Password Management,
    and Resources   321
Practice Questions   322
Need to Know More?   328

Chapter 14
Using National Language Support 329

Choosing the Database Character Set and the National
    Character Set   330

Specifying Language-Dependent Behavior   331

    Database Default Settings   331

    Environment Variable Settings   332

    Session Settings   332

Using the Different Types of NLS Parameters   333

Obtaining Information about NLS Usage   334

Practice Questions   336

Need to Know More?   340

Chapter 15
Sample Test 341

Chapter 16
Answer Key 361

Glossary 379

Index 389

Introduction

Welcome to *Oracle8i DBA: Architecture and Administration Exam Cram*! This book will help you get ready to take—and pass—the second of the five-part series of exams for Oracle Certified Professional-Oracle8i Certified Database Administrator (OCP-DBA) certification. In this Introduction, I talk about Oracle's certification programs in general and how the *Exam Cram* series can help you prepare for Oracle's certification exams.

Exam Cram books help you understand and appreciate the subjects and materials you need to pass Oracle certification exams. The books are aimed strictly at test preparation and review. They do not teach you everything you need to know about a topic, nor are they designed to make you competent DBAs by themselves. Instead, I present and dissect the questions and problems that you're likely to encounter on a test. If you are a beginning-level reader, I suggest you start instead with the excellent *Oracle DBA 101* book by Marlene Theriault et al. (McGraw-Hill, Berkeley, CA, 2000; ISBN 0-07-212120-3) and then read this Exam Cram book before taking the exam.

Nevertheless, to completely prepare yourself for any Oracle test, I recommend that you begin by taking the Self-Assessment included in this book immediately following this Introduction. This tool will help you evaluate your knowledge base against the requirements for an OCP-DBA under both ideal and real circumstances.

Based on what you learn from that exercise, you might decide to begin your studies with some classroom training or by reading one of the many DBA guides available from Oracle and third-party vendors. I also strongly recommend that you install, configure, and experiment with the software or environment that you'll be tested on, because nothing beats hands-on experience and familiarity when it comes to understanding the questions you're likely to encounter on a certification test. Book learning is essential, but hands-on experience is the best teacher of all!

The Oracle Certified Professional (OCP) Program

The OCP program for DBA certification currently includes five separate tests, as shown in Table 1 and in the following bulleted list. You do not have to take the tests in any particular order. However, it is usually better to take the examinations in the order shown in this list because the knowledge tested builds from each exam. Here is a brief description of each test required:

➤ *Introduction to Oracle: SQL and PL/SQL (Exam 1Z0-001)*—Test 1 is the base test for the series. Knowledge tested in Test 1 will also be required in all other tests in the DBA series. Besides testing knowledge of SQL and PL/SQL language constructs, syntax, and usage, Test 1 covers Data Definition Language (DDL), Data Manipulation Language (DML), and Data Control Language (DCL).

➤ *Oracle8i: Architecture and Administration (Exam 1Z0-023)*—Test 2 deals with all levels of database administration in Oracle8i (primarily version 8.1.5 and above). Topics include architecture, startup and shutdown, database creation, managing database internal and external constructs (such as redo logs, rollback segments, and tablespaces), and all other Oracle structures. This test also covers database auditing, use of National Language Support (NLS) features, and use of SQL*Loader and other utilities.

➤ *Oracle8i: Backup and Recovery (Exam 1Z0-025)*—Test 3 covers one of the most important parts of the Oracle DBA's job: database backup and recovery operations. Test 3 tests knowledge in backup and recovery motives, architecture as it relates to backup and recovery, backup methods, failure scenarios, recovery methodologies, archive logging, supporting 24×7 shops, troubleshooting, and use of Oracle8i's standby database features. The test also covers the use of the Recovery Manager (RMAN) product from Oracle.

➤ *Oracle8i: Performance and Tuning (Exam 1Z0-024)*—Test 4 covers all aspects of tuning an Oracle8i database; topics in both application and database tuning are covered. The exam tests knowledge in diagnosis of tuning problems; database optimal configuration; shared pool tuning; buffer cache tuning; Oracle block usage; tuning rollback segments and redo mechanisms; monitoring and detecting lock contention; tuning sorts; load optimization; the Resource Manager; tuning with Oracle Expert; and tuning in OLTP, DSS, and mixed environments.

➤ *Oracle8i: Network Administration (Exam 1Z0-026)*—Test 5 covers all parts of the Net8 product: Net8, Oracle Names Server, the listener process, lsnrctl (the listener control utility), Multithreaded Server and Connection Manager

Table 1 Oracle8i OCP-DBA Requirements

Oracle8i

All 5 of these tests are required	
Exam 1Z0-001	Introduction to Oracle: SQL and PL/SQL
Exam 1Z0-023	Oracle8i: Architecture and Administration
Exam 1Z0-024	Oracle8i: Performance and Tuning
Exam 1Z0-025	Oracle8i: Backup and Recovery
Exam 1Z0-026	Oracle8i: Network Administration

If you are currently an OCP certified in Oracle8, you need take only the upgrade exam (Oracle8i: New Features for Administrators, Exam 1Z0-020) to be certified in Oracle8i. If you have passed Introduction to Oracle: SQL and PL/SQL during your pursuit of Oracle8 certification, you do not need to retake it for Oracle8i certification.

usage and configuration, and the Net8 configuration files (sqlnet.ora, tnsnames.ora, and listener.ora).

To obtain an OCP certificate in database administration, an individual must pass all five exams. The core exams require individuals to demonstrate competence with all phases of Oracle8i database lifetime activities. If you already have your Oracle8 certification, you need to take only one exam—Exam 1Z0-020: "Oracle8i: New Features for Administrators"—to upgrade your status.

With the Oracle8i release of the OCP exams, it is now possible to take another path to become an Oracle8i certified DBA. Oracle now allows you to take what they call the Mixed Release Path, containing six exams. This path starts with the standard introductory exam, Exam 1Z0-001: "Introduction to Oracle: SQL and PL/SQL"; then you can take *either* the Oracle8 or the Oracle8i exams for administration, backup and recovery, performance tuning, and network administration, followed by Exam 1Z0-020: "Oracle8i: New Features for Administrators." (If you are currently certified in Oracle7.3, there is also an upgrade exam from 7.3 to Oracle8, which can then be upgraded to the Oracle8i release.)

Whichever path you take (the Upgrade Path of new features exams, the standard DBA Core Path or the Mixed Release Path), the result is the same—you end up as an Oracle Certified Professional DBA. If you are just starting the OCP path, I would suggest you take the DBA Core Path (after all, five exams has to be better than six!). However, if you're partway through the Oracle8 exams, the Mixed Release Path allows you to easily switch over to the Oracle8i exams and end up as an Oracle8i OCP.

It's not uncommon for the entire process to take a year or so, and many individuals find that they must take a test more than once to pass. The primary goal of the *Exam Cram* series is to make it possible, given proper study and preparation, to pass all of the OCP-DBA tests on the first try.

Certification is an ongoing activity. Once an Oracle version becomes obsolete, OCP-DBAs (and other OCPs) typically have a six-month time frame in which they can become recertified on current product versions. (If an individual does not get recertified within the specified time period, his or her certification becomes invalid.) Because technology keeps changing and new products continually supplant old ones, this should come as no surprise.

The best place to keep tabs on the OCP program and its various certifications is on the Oracle Web site. The current root URL for the OCP program is at **www.oracle.com/education/certification**. Oracle's certification Web site can change frequently, so if this URL doesn't work, try using the Search tool on Oracle's site (**www.oracle.com**) with either "OCP" or the quoted phrase "Oracle Certified Professional Program" as the search string. This will help you find the latest and most accurate information about the company's certification programs.

Taking a Certification Exam

Alas, testing is not free. You'll be charged $125 for each test you take, whether you pass or fail. In the United States and Canada, tests are administered by Prometric. Prometric can be reached at 1-800-891-3926, any time from 7:00 A.M. to 6:00 P.M., central time, Monday through Friday. If you can't get through at this number, try 1-612-896-7000 or 1-612-820-5707. If you are disabled and require special assistance when completing your exam, call Prometric at 1-800-443-1684 before taking the exam. They will be able to answer any questions you might have about accommodations that can be made for people with disabilities. If you are not located in the United States or Canada, go to **www.2test.com** to locate the testing center nearest you. This site can also be used to register for the exams, regardless of your location.

To schedule an exam, call at least one day in advance. To cancel or reschedule an exam, you must call at least one day before the scheduled test time (or you may be charged the $125 fee). The cancellation policy varies by region, so please be sure to check what the local cancellation policy is. When calling Prometric, have the following information ready for the telesales staffer who handles your call:

➤ Your contact details.

➤ The number and title of the exam you want to take.

➤ A method of payment. (The most convenient approach is to supply a valid credit card number with sufficient available credit. Otherwise, payments by check, money order, or purchase order must be received before a test can be scheduled. If the latter methods are required, ask your order-taker for more details.)

An appointment confirmation will be sent to you by mail if you register more than five days before an exam, or it will be sent by fax if less than five days before the exam. A Candidate Agreement letter, which you must sign to take the examination, will also be provided.

On the day of the test, try to arrive at least 15 minutes before the scheduled time slot. You must supply two forms of identification, one of which must be a photo ID.

All exams are completely closed book. In fact, you will not be permitted to take anything with you into the testing area. I suggest that you review the most critical information about the test you're taking just before the test. (*Exam Cram* books provide a brief reference—The Cram Sheet, located inside the front of the book— that lists the essential information from the book in distilled form.) You will have some time to compose yourself, to mentally review this critical information, and even to take a sample orientation exam before you begin the real thing. I suggest you take the orientation test before taking your first exam; they're all more or less identical in layout, behavior, and controls, so you probably won't need to do this more than once.

When you complete an Oracle8i certification exam, you will be given an exam score report so you know whether you've passed or failed. Results are broken into several topical areas. Whether you pass or fail, I suggest you ask for—and keep— the report that the test administrator prints for you. You can use the report to help you prepare for another go-round, if necessary, and even if you pass, the report shows areas you may need to review to keep your edge. If you need to retake an exam, you'll have to call Prometric, schedule a new test date, and pay another $125.

Tracking OCP Status

Oracle generates transcripts that indicate the exams you have passed and your corresponding test scores. After you pass the necessary set of exams, you'll be certified as an Oracle8i DBA. Official certification normally takes anywhere from four to six weeks (generally within 30 days), so don't expect to get your credentials overnight. Once certified, you will receive a package with a Welcome Kit that contains a number of elements:

➤ An OCP-DBA certificate, suitable for framing (along with information on purchasing officially authorized frames).

➤ OCP logo usage requirements. You are allowed to use the logo for business cards and resumes, as stated in the OCP Candidate Agreement that you must agree to before taking an OCP exam. Information on how to download electronic copies of the logo is also included (unfortunately, the URL provided is no longer valid, but you can access the material off the certification home page mentioned previously).

➤ Information on how to register for other Oracle benefits and tools, such as the Oracle Technology Network and the just-released Oracle Learning Network, as well as Oracle Magazine.

Many people believe that the benefits of OCP certification go well beyond the perks that Oracle provides to newly anointed members of this elite group. I am starting to see more job listings that request or require applicants to have an OCP-DBA certification, and many individuals who complete the program can qualify for increases in pay and/or responsibility. As an official recognition of hard work and broad knowledge, OCP certification is a badge of honor in many IT organizations.

How to Prepare for an Exam

At a minimum, preparing for OCP-DBA exams requires that you obtain and study the following materials:

➤ The Oracle8i Server version 8.1.6 Documentation Set on CD-ROM (Oracle8i version 8.1.7 did not include a complete documentation set, so use the 8.1.6 Documentation Set).

➤ The exam preparation materials, practice tests, and self-assessment exams on the Oracle certification page (**www.oracle.com/education/certification**). Find the materials, download them, and use them!

➤ This *Exam Cram* book. It's the first and last thing you should read before taking the exam.

In addition, you'll probably find any or all of the following materials useful in your quest for Oracle8i DBA expertise:

➤ *OCP resource kits*—Oracle Corporation has a CD-ROM with example questions and materials to help with the exam; generally, these are provided free by requesting them from your Oracle representative. They have also been offered free for the taking at most Oracle conventions, such as IOUGA-Alive! and Oracle Open World.

➤ *Classroom training*—Oracle, TUSC, LearningTree, and many others offer classroom and computer-based training materials that you will find useful to help you prepare for the exam. But a word of warning: These classes are fairly expensive (in the range of $500 per day of training). However, they do offer a condensed form of learning to help you brush up on your Oracle knowledge.

The tests are closely tied to the classroom training provided by Oracle, so I would suggest taking at least the introductory classes to get the Oracle-specific (and classroom-specific) terminology under your belt.

➤ *Other publications*—You'll find direct references to other publications and resources in this book, and there's no shortage of materials available about Oracle8i DBA topics. To help you sift through some of the publications out there, I end each chapter with a "Need to Know More?" section that provides pointers to more complete and exhaustive resources covering the chapter's subject matter.

➤ *The RevealNet Knowledge Base for Oracle and the RevealNet Knowledge Base for Active PL/SQL*—These online references from RevealNet, Inc., an Oracle database online reference provider, allow instant lookup on thousands of database and developmental topics and are invaluable resources for study and learning about Oracle. Demo copies can be downloaded from **www.revealnet.com**. Also available at the RevealNet Web site are the DBA and PL/SQL Pipelines (also called Knowledge Groups), which are online discussion groups where you can obtain expert information from Oracle DBAs worldwide. The cost of these applications run about $400 each (current pricing is available on the Web site) and are worth every cent.

These required and recommended materials represent a nonpareil collection of sources and resources for Oracle8i DBA topics and software. In the section that follows, I explain how this book works and give you some good reasons why this book should also be on your required and recommended materials list.

About this Book

Each topical *Exam Cram* chapter follows a regular structure, along with graphical cues about especially important or useful material. Here's the structure of a typical chapter:

➤ *Opening hotlists*—Each chapter begins with lists of the terms, tools, and techniques that you must learn and understand before you can be fully conversant with the chapter's subject matter. I follow the hotlists with one or two introductory paragraphs to set the stage for the rest of the chapter.

➤ *Topical coverage*—After the opening hotlists, each chapter covers a series of topics related to the chapter's subject. Throughout this section, I highlight material most likely to appear on a test using a special Exam Alert layout, like this:

This is what an Exam Alert looks like. Normally, an Exam Alert stresses concepts, terms, software, or activities that will most likely appear in one or more certification test questions. For that reason, any information found offset in Exam Alert format is worthy of unusual attentiveness on your part. Indeed, most of the facts appearing in The Cram Sheet appear as Exam Alerts within the text.

Even if material isn't flagged as an Exam Alert, *all* the contents of this book are associated, at least tangentially, to something test-related. This book is tightly focused for quick test preparation, so you'll find that what appears in the meat of each chapter is critical knowledge.

I have also provided tips that will help build a better foundation of database administration knowledge. Although the information may not be on the exam, it is highly relevant and will help you become a better test-taker.

This is how tips are formatted. Keep your eyes open for these, and you'll become a test guru in no time!

➤ *Practice questions*—A section at the end of each chapter presents a series of mock test questions and explanations of both correct and incorrect answers.

➤ *Details and resources*—Every chapter ends with a section titled "Need to Know More?". This section provides direct pointers to Oracle and third-party resources that offer further details on the chapter's subject matter. In addition, this section tries to rate the quality and thoroughness of each topic's coverage. If you find a resource you like in this collection, use it, but don't feel compelled to use all these resources. On the other hand, I recommend only resources I use on a regular basis, so none of my recommendations will be a waste of your time or money.

The bulk of the book follows this chapter structure slavishly, but there are a few other elements that I would like to point out. Chapter 15 is a sample test that provides a good review of the material presented throughout the book to ensure you're ready for the exam. Chapter 16 provides an answer key to the sample test. In addition, you'll find a handy glossary and an index.

Finally, look for The Cram Sheet, which appears inside the front of this *Exam Cram* book. It is a valuable tool that represents a condensed collection of facts, figures, and tips that I think you should memorize before taking the test. Because you can dump this information out of your head onto a piece of paper before answering any exam questions, you can master this information by brute force—

you need to remember it only long enough to write it down when you walk into the test room. You might even want to look at it in the car or in the lobby of the testing center just before you walk in to take the test.

How to Use this Book

If you're prepping for a first-time test, I've structured the topics in this book to build on one another. Therefore, some topics in later chapters make more sense after you've read earlier chapters. That's why I suggest you read this book from front to back for your initial test preparation.

If you need to brush up on a topic or you have to bone up for a second try, use the index or table of contents to go straight to the topics and questions that you need to study. Beyond the tests, I think you'll find this book useful as a tightly focused reference to some of the most important aspects of topics associated with being a DBA, as implemented under Oracle8i.

Given all the book's elements and its specialized focus, I've tried to create a tool that you can use to prepare for—and pass—the "Oracle8i: Architecture and Administration" exam. Please share your feedback on the book, especially if you have ideas about how I can improve it for future test-takers.

Send your questions or comments to **learn@examcram.com**. Please remember to include the title of the book in your message. Also, be sure to check out the Web pages at **www.examcram.com**, where you'll find information updates, commentary, and certification information.

Thanks, and enjoy the book!

Self-Assessment

I've included a Self-Assessment in this *Exam Cram* to help you evaluate your readiness to tackle Oracle Certified Professional-Oracle8i Certified Database Administrator (OCP-DBA) certification. It should also help you understand what you need to master the topic of this book—namely, Exam 1Z0-023 (Test 2), "Oracle8i: Architecture and Administration." But before you tackle this Self-Assessment, let's talk about the concerns you may face when pursuing an Oracle8i OCP-DBA certification, and what an ideal Oracle8i OCP-DBA candidate might look like.

Oracle8i OCP-DBAs in the Real World

In the next section, I describe an ideal Oracle8i OCP-DBA candidate, knowing full well that only a few actual candidates meet this ideal. In fact, my description of that ideal candidate might seem downright scary. But take heart, because although the requirements to obtain an Oracle8i OCP-DBA may seem pretty formidable, they are by no means impossible to meet. However, you should be keenly aware that it does take time, requires some expense, and consumes a substantial effort.

You can get all the real-world motivation you need from knowing that many others have gone before you. You can follow in their footsteps. If you're willing to tackle the process seriously and do what it takes to obtain the necessary experience and knowledge, you can take—and pass—the certification tests. In fact, the *Exam Crams* are designed to make it as easy as possible for you to prepare for these exams. But prepare you must!

The same, of course, is true for other Oracle certifications, including:

➤ Oracle8 OCP-DBA, which, like the Oracle8i OCP-DBA certification, requires five core exams.

➤ Application Developer, Oracle Developer Rel 1 OCP, which is aimed at software developers and requires five exams.

➤ Application Developer, Oracle Developer Rel 2 OCP, which is aimed at software developers and requires five exams.

➤ Internet Application Developers OCP, which is the upgrade to the previous two certifications and requires four exams if taken from scratch.

➤ Oracle8 Database Operators OCP, which is aimed at database operators and requires only one exam.

➤ Oracle Internet Database Operator OCP, which is the Oracle8i version of the previous exam.

➤ Oracle Java Technology Certification OCP, which is aimed at Java developers and requires five exams.

➤ Oracle Certified Applications Consultant, Procurement and Order Fulfillment Release 11 OCP, which is aimed at Oracle Financial Application Consultants and requires four exams.

The Ideal Oracle8i OCP-DBA Candidate

Just to give you some idea of what an ideal Oracle8i OCP-DBA candidate is like, here are some relevant statistics about the background and experience such an individual might have. Don't worry if you don't meet these qualifications (or, indeed, if you don't even come close), because this world is far from ideal, and where you fall short is simply where you'll have more work to do. The ideal candidate will have:

➤ Academic or professional training in relational databases, Structured Query Language (SQL), performance tuning, backup and recovery, and Net8 administration

➤ Three-plus years of professional database administration experience, including experience installing and upgrading Oracle executables, creating and tuning databases, troubleshooting connection problems, creating users, and managing backup and recovery scenarios

I believe that well under half of all certification candidates meet these requirements. In fact, most probably meet less than half of these requirements (that is, at least when they begin the certification process). But, because all those who have their certifications already survived this ordeal, you can survive it, too—especially if you heed what this Self-Assessment can tell you about what you already know and what you need to learn.

Put Yourself to the Test

The following series of questions and observations is designed to help you figure out how much work you'll face in pursuing Oracle certification and what kinds of resources you may consult on your quest. Be absolutely honest in your answers, or you'll end up wasting money on exams you're not ready to take. There are no right or wrong answers, only steps along the path to certification. Only you can decide where you really belong in the broad spectrum of aspiring candidates.

Two things should be clear from the outset, however:

➤ Even a modest background in computer science will be helpful.

➤ Hands-on experience with Oracle products and technologies is an essential ingredient to certification success.

Educational Background

1. Have you ever taken any computer-related classes? [Yes or No]

   If Yes, proceed to question 2; if no, proceed to question 4.

2. Have you taken any classes on relational databases? [Yes or No]

   If Yes, you will probably be able to handle Oracle's architecture and network administration discussions. If you're rusty, brush up on the basic concepts of databases and networks.

   If No, consider some basic reading in this area. I strongly recommend a good Oracle database administration book such as *Oracle8i DBA Handbook* by Kevin Loney and Marlene Theriault (McGraw-Hill, 2000). Or, if this title doesn't appeal to you, check out reviews for other, similar titles at your favorite online bookstore.

3. Have you taken any database administration classes? [Yes or No]

   If Yes, you will probably be able to handle Oracle's terminology, concepts, and technologies (but brace yourself for frequent departures from normal usage). If you're rusty, brush up on basic concepts and terminology.

   If No, you might want to check out the Oracle technet Web site (**http://technet.oracle.com**) and read some of the white papers on Oracle8i. If you have access to the technet Web site, download the Oracle8i database administration manual.

4. Have you done any reading on relational databases? [Yes or No]

   If Yes, review the requirements from questions 2 and 3. If you meet those, move to the next section, "Hands-on Experience."

   If No, consult the recommended reading for both topics. This kind of strong background will be of great help in preparing you for the Oracle exams.

Hands-on Experience

Another important key to success on all of the Oracle tests is hands-on experience. If I leave you with only one realization after taking this Self-Assessment, it should be that there's no substitute for time spent installing, configuring, and using the various Oracle products upon which you'll be tested repeatedly and in depth.

5. Have you installed, configured, and worked with Oracle8i? [Yes or No]

   If Yes, make sure you understand basic concepts as covered in Exam 1Z0-023, "Oracle8i: Architecture and Administration" (Test 2) and advanced concepts as covered in Exam 1Z0-024, "Oracle8i: Performance and Tuning" (Test 4). You should also study for Exam 1Z0-001 (Test 1), "Introduction to Oracle: SQL and PL/SQL."

You can download the candidate certification guide, objectives, practice exams, and other information about Oracle exams from the certification page on the Web at **www.oracle.com/education/certification**.

   If No, you must obtain a copy of Oracle8i or Personal Oracle8i. Then, learn about Oracle databases, not just by reading up on them, but by actually experimenting with them as well.

For any and all of these Oracle exams, the candidate guides for the topics involved are a good study resource. You can download them free from the Oracle Web site (**www.oracle.com/education**). You can also download information on purchasing additional practice tests.

   Before you even think about taking any Oracle exam, make sure you've spent enough time with Oracle8i to understand how it may be installed and configured, how to maintain such an installation, and how to troubleshoot the software when things go wrong. This will help you in the exam—as well as in real life.

If you have the funds or your employer will pay your way, consider taking a class at an Oracle training and education center.

Testing Your Exam-Readiness

Whether you attend a formal class on a specific topic to get ready for an exam or use written materials to study on your own, some preparation for the Oracle certification exams is essential. At $125 a try, pass or fail, you want to do everything you can to pass on your first try. That's where studying comes in.

I have included in this book several practice exam questions for each chapter and a sample test, so if you don't score well on the chapter questions, you can study more and then tackle the sample test at the end of the book. If you don't earn a score of at least 80 percent after this test, you'll want to investigate the other practice test resources I mention in this section.

For any given subject, consider taking a class if you've tackled self-study materials, taken the test, and failed anyway. If you can afford the privilege, the opportunity to interact with an instructor and fellow students can make all the difference in the world. For information about Oracle classes, visit the certification page at **www.oracle.com/education/certification**.

If you can't afford to take a class, visit Oracle's certification page anyway, because it also includes free practice exams that you can download. Even if you can't afford to spend much at all, you should still invest in some low-cost practice exams from commercial vendors, because they can help you assess your readiness to pass a test better than any other tool. In addition, check out **www.examcram.com**, which features exam information, questions of the day, and practice exams.

6. Have you taken a practice exam on your chosen test subject? [Yes or No]

   If Yes—and you scored 80 percent or better—you're probably ready to tackle the real thing. If your score isn't above that crucial threshold, keep at it until you break that barrier. If you answered no, obtain all the free and low-budget practice tests you can find (or afford) and get to work. Keep at it until you can comfortably break the passing threshold.

There is no better way to assess your test readiness than to take a good-quality practice exam and pass with a score of 80 percent or better. When I'm preparing, I shoot for 85-plus percent, just to leave room for the "weirdness factor" that sometimes shows up on exams.

Assessing Your Readiness For Exam 1Z0-023 (Test 2)

In addition to the general exam-readiness information in the previous section, other resources are available to help you prepare for Exam 1Z0-023, "Oracle8i: Architecture and Administration." For starters, visit **http://technet.oracle.com**. This is a great place to ask questions and get good answers, or simply to observe the questions that others ask (along with the answers, of course).

Oracle exam mavens also recommend checking the Oracle Knowledge Base from RevealNet. You can get information on purchasing the RevealNet software at **www.revealnet.com**.

To prepare for this exam in particular, I'd also like to recommend that you check out one or more of these books as you prepare to take the exam:

➤ Loney, Kevin, and Marlene Theriault. *Oracle8i DBA Handbook*. McGraw-Hill, Berkeley, CA, 2000.

➤ Scherer, Douglas, William Gaynor, Arlene Valentinsen, Sue Mavris, and Xerxes Cursetjee. *Oracle8i Tips and Techniques*. McGraw-Hill, Berkeley, CA, 1999.

Visit your favorite bookstore or online bookseller to check out one or more of these books. These books are—in my opinion—among the best general all-around references on Oracle8i available.

One last note: Hopefully, it makes sense to stress the importance of hands-on experience in the context of the "Oracle8i: Architecture and Administration" exam. As you review the material for that exam, you'll realize that hands-on experience with Oracle8i commands, tools, and utilities is invaluable.

Onward, through the Fog!

Once you've assessed your readiness, undertaken the right background studies, obtained the hands-on experience that will help you understand the products and technologies at work, and reviewed the many sources of information to help you prepare for a test, you'll be ready to take a round of practice tests. When your scores come back positive enough to get you through the exam, you're ready to go after the real thing. If you follow my assessment regime, you'll not only know what you need to study, but when you're ready to make a test date at Prometric. Good luck!

Oracle OCP
Certification Exams

Terms you'll need to understand:
✓ Radio button
✓ Checkbox
✓ Exhibit
✓ Multiple-choice question formats
✓ Careful reading
✓ Process of elimination

Techniques you'll need to master:
✓ Assessing your exam-readiness
✓ Preparing to take a certification exam
✓ Practicing (to make perfect)
✓ Making the best use of the testing software
✓ Budgeting your time
✓ Saving the hardest questions until last
✓ Guessing (as a last resort)

As experiences go, test taking is not something that most people anticipate eagerly, no matter how well they're prepared. In most cases, familiarity helps relieve test anxiety. This means you probably won't be as nervous when you take your fourth or fifth Oracle certification exam as you will be when you take your first one.

But no matter whether it's your first test or your tenth, understanding the exam-taking particulars (how much time to spend on questions, the setting you'll be in, and so on) and the testing software will help you concentrate on the material rather than on the environment. Likewise, mastering a few basic test-taking skills should help you recognize—and perhaps even outfox—some of the tricks and gotchas you're bound to find in some of the Oracle test questions.

In this chapter, I'll explain the testing environment and software, as well as describe some proven test-taking strategies you should be able to use to your advantage.

Assessing Exam-Readiness

Before you take any Oracle exam, I strongly recommend that you read through and take the Self-Assessment included with this book (it appears just before this chapter, in fact). This will help you compare your knowledge base to the requirements for obtaining an OCP, and it will also help you identify parts of your background or experience that may be in need of improvement, enhancement, or further learning. If you get the right set of basics under your belt, obtaining Oracle certification will be that much easier.

Once you've gone through the Self-Assessment, you can remedy those topical areas where your background or experience may not measure up to an ideal certification candidate. But you can also tackle subject matter for individual tests at the same time, so you can continue making progress while you're catching up in some areas.

Once you've worked through an *Exam Cram*, read the supplementary materials, and taken the practice test at the end of the book, you'll have a pretty clear idea of when you should be ready to take the real exam. Although I strongly recommend that you keep practicing until your scores top the 80 percent mark, 85 percent would be a good goal to give yourself some margin for error in a real exam situation (where stress will play more of a role than when you practice). Once you hit that point, you should be ready to go. But if you get through the practice exam in this book without attaining that score, you should keep taking practice tests and studying the materials until you get there. Check out **ExamCram.com**, where you can find practice tests, study tips, and questions of the day. You'll find even more pointers on how to study and prepare in the Self-Assessment. But now, on to the exam itself!

The Testing Situation

When you arrive at the Prometric Testing Center where you scheduled your test, you'll need to sign in with a test coordinator. He or she will ask you to produce two forms of identification, one of which must be a photo ID. Once you've signed in and your time slot arrives, you'll be asked to leave any books, bags, or other items you brought with you (including your cell phone!), and you'll be escorted into a closed room. Typically, that room will be furnished with anywhere from one to half a dozen computers, and each workstation is separated from the others by dividers designed to keep you from seeing what's happening on someone else's computer.

You'll be furnished with a pen or pencil and a blank sheet of paper. You're allowed to write down any information you want on this sheet, and you can write on both sides of the page. I suggest that you memorize as much as possible of the material that appears on The Cram Sheet (inside the front of this book), and then write that information on the blank sheet as soon as you sit down in front of the test machine. You can refer to the sheet any time you like during the test, but you'll have to surrender it when you leave the room.

Usually, the test coordinator monitors the test room, to prevent test-takers from talking to one another, and to observe anything out of the ordinary that might go on. This may be via a wall with a large window, or a series of video cameras spread around the room. The test coordinator will have preloaded the Oracle certification test you've signed up for, and you'll be permitted to start as soon as you're seated in front of the machine.

All Oracle certification exams permit you to take up to a certain maximum amount of time (usually 90 minutes, which is the case for Exam 1Z0-023) to complete the test (the test itself will tell you, and it maintains an on-screen counter/clock so you can check the time remaining any time you like). Exam 1Z0-023, "Oracle8i: Architecture and Administration," consists of 65 questions, randomly selected from a pool of questions.

Note: The passing score varies depending on the exam. For Exam 1Z0-023, the passing score is 65 percent. Also note that if you take the same exam multiple times, you don't get the same questions each time.

All Oracle certification exams are computer generated and largely multiple-choice in format (a few questions may be fill-in-the-blank questions instead). Although this might sound easy, the questions are constructed not just to check your mastery of basic facts and figures on topics that an Oracle8i database administrator (DBA) should know, but they also require you to evaluate one or more sets of circumstances or requirements. Often, you'll be asked to give more than one answer to a question; likewise, you may be asked to select the best or most effective solution to a problem from a range of choices, all of which technically are correct. The tests are quite an adventure, and they involve real thinking. This book will show you what to expect and how to deal with the problems, puzzles, and predicaments you're likely to find on the tests—in particular, Exam 1Z0-023 (Test 2), "Oracle8i: Architecture and Administration."

Test Layout and Design

A typical test question is depicted in Question 1. It's a multiple-choice question that requires you to select a single correct answer. (A small percentage of these questions will be fill-in-the-blank statements, where you'll be expected to choose from the multiple-choice answers which word belongs in the blank.) Following the question is a brief summary of each potential answer and why it is either right or wrong.

Question 1

If an instance fails, which type of segment is used to recover uncommitted transactions?

○ a. Table

○ b. Index

○ c. Rollback

○ d. Temporary

Answer c is correct. Transaction recovery occurs after an instance failure. All uncommitted transactions are rolled back using the redo log files and the before images stored in rollback segments. Answer a is incorrect because table is a data segment and is not used in recovery. Answer b is incorrect because index is an index segment and is not used in recovery either. Answer d is incorrect because temporary segments are used for sorting, not for recovery.

This sample question corresponds closely to those you'll see on Oracle certification tests. To select the correct answer during the test, you would position the cursor over the radio button next to answer c and click the mouse to select that particular choice. The only difference between the certification test and this question is that the real questions are not immediately followed by the answers.

Next, I'll examine a question where one or more answers are possible. This type of question provides checkboxes, rather than radio buttons, for marking all appropriate selections.

Question 2

Which dynamic performance views would you join to display the current size of the R03 rollback segment? [Choose two]

- ❏ a. **V$SESSION**
- ❏ b. **V$ROLLNAME**
- ❏ c. **V$ROLLSTAT**
- ❏ d. **V$PARAMETER**
- ❏ e. **V$DATAFILE**
- ❏ f. **V$TRANSACTION**
- ❏ g. **V$DATAFILE_HEADER**

Answers b and c are correct. **V$ROLLNAME** displays the name and USN (undo segment number) of each rollback segment. **V$ROLLSTAT** displays the USN, status, optimal size, current size, high-water mark, and the current and active extent of each rollback segment. Answer a is incorrect because **V$SESSION** shows session information for each current session. Answer d is incorrect because **V$PARAMETER** shows information about initialization parameters. Answer e is incorrect because **V$DATAFILE** shows datafile information from the control file. Answer f is incorrect because **V$TRANSACTION** shows the active transactions in the system. Answer g is incorrect because **V$DATAFILE_HEADER** shows datafile information from the datafile headers.

For this type of question, one or more answers must be selected to answer the question correctly. For Question 2, you would have to select the checkboxes next to items b and c to obtain credit for a correct answer.

These two basic types of questions constitute the foundation on which all Oracle certification exam questions rest. More complex questions may include so-called "exhibits," which are usually tables or data-content layouts of one form or another. You'll be expected to use the information displayed in the exhibit to guide your answer to the question.

Other questions involving exhibits may use charts or diagrams to help document a workplace scenario that you'll be asked to troubleshoot or configure. Paying careful attention to such exhibits is the key to success; be prepared to toggle between the picture and the question as you work. Often, both are complex enough that you might not be able to remember all of either one.

Using Oracle's Test Software Effectively

A well-known test-taking principle is to read over the entire test from start to finish first, but to answer only those questions that you feel absolutely sure of on the first pass. On subsequent passes, you can dive into more complex questions, knowing how many such questions you have to deal with.

Fortunately, Oracle test software makes this approach easy to implement. At the bottom of each question, you'll find a checkbox that permits you to mark that question for a later visit. (Note that marking questions makes review easier, but you can return to any question by clicking the Forward and Back buttons repeatedly until you get to the question.) As you read each question, if you answer only those you're sure of and mark for review those that you're not, you can keep going through a decreasing list of open questions.

There's at least one potential benefit to reading the test over completely before answering the trickier questions: Sometimes, you can find information in later questions that sheds more light on earlier ones. Other times, information you read in later questions might jog your memory about Oracle8i DBA facts, figures, or behavior that also will help with earlier questions. Either way, you'll come out ahead if you defer those questions about which you're not absolutely sure of the answer(s).

Keep working on the questions until you are absolutely sure of all your answers or until you have five minutes left. If there are still unanswered questions at that point, you'll want to zip through them and guess. No answer guarantees no credit for a question, and a guess has at least a chance of being correct. (Oracle scores blank answers and incorrect answers as equally wrong.)

At the very end of your test period, you're better off guessing than leaving questions blank or unanswered.

Taking Testing Seriously

The most important advice I can give you about taking any Oracle test is this: Read each question carefully. Some questions are deliberately ambiguous, some use double negatives, and others use terminology in incredibly precise ways. I've taken numerous practice tests and real tests myself, and in nearly every test I've missed at least one question because I didn't read it closely or carefully enough.

Here are some suggestions on how to deal with the tendency to jump to an answer too quickly:

➤ Make sure you read every word in the question. If you find yourself jumping ahead impatiently, go back and start over.

➤ As you read, try to restate the question in your own terms. If you can do this, you should be able to pick the correct answer(s) much more easily.

➤ When returning to a question after your initial read-through, reread every word again—otherwise, the mind falls quickly into a rut. Sometimes, seeing a question afresh after turning your attention elsewhere lets you see something you missed before, but the strong tendency is to see what you've seen before. Try to avoid that tendency at all costs.

➤ If you return to a question more than twice, try to articulate to yourself what you don't understand about the question, why the answers don't appear to make sense, or what appears to be missing. If you chew on the subject for a while, your subconscious might provide the details that are lacking, or you may notice a "trick" that will point to the right answer.

Above all, try to deal with each question by thinking through what you know about being an Oracle8i DBA—utilities, characteristics, behaviors, facts, and figures involved. By reviewing what you know (and what you've written on your information sheet), you'll often recall or understand things sufficiently to determine the answer to the question.

Question-Handling Strategies

Based on the tests I've taken, a couple of interesting trends in the answers have become apparent. For those questions that take only a single answer, usually two or three of the answers will be obviously incorrect, and two of the answers will be plausible. But, of course, only one can be correct. Unless the answer leaps out at you (and if it does, reread the question to look for a trick; sometimes those are the ones you're most likely to get wrong), begin the process of answering by eliminating those answers that are obviously wrong.

Things to look for in the "obviously wrong" category include spurious command choices or table or view names, nonexistent software or command options, and terminology you've never seen before. If you've done your homework for a test, no valid information should be completely new to you. In that case, unfamiliar or bizarre terminology probably indicates a totally bogus answer.

Numerous questions assume that the default behavior of a particular Oracle utility (such as Oracle Enterprise Manager [OEM] or SQL*Loader) is in effect. It's essential, therefore, to know and understand the default settings for OEM, SQL*Loader, and SQL*Plus utilities. If you know the defaults and understand what they mean, this knowledge will help you cut through many Gordian knots.

Likewise, when dealing with questions that require multiple answers, you must know and select all the correct options to get credit. This, too, qualifies as an example of why careful reading is so important.

As you work your way through the test, another counter that Oracle thankfully provides will come in handy—the number of questions completed and questions outstanding. Budget your time by making sure that you've completed one-fourth of the questions one-quarter of the way through the test period. Check again three-quarters of the way through.

If you're not through after 85 minutes, use the last five minutes to guess your way through the remaining questions. Remember, guesses are potentially more valuable than blank answers, because blanks are always wrong, but a guess might turn out to be right. If you haven't a clue with any of the remaining questions, pick answers at random, or choose all a's, b's, and so on. The important thing is to submit a test for scoring that has an answer for every question.

Mastering the Inner Game

In the final analysis, knowledge breeds confidence, and confidence breeds success. If you study the materials in this book carefully and review the questions at the end of each chapter, you should be aware of those areas where additional studying is required.

Next, follow up by reading some or all of the materials recommended in the "Need to Know More?" section at the end of each chapter. The idea is to become knowledgeable enough with the concepts and situations this test covers to be able to answer all the questions in this book, and reason your way through similar situations on a real test. If you know the material, you have every right to be confident that you can pass the test.

Once you've worked your way through the book, take the practice test in Chapter 15. The test will provide a reality check and will help you identify areas you need to study further. Make sure you follow up and review materials related to the questions you miss before scheduling a real test. Only when you've covered all the ground and feel comfortable with the whole scope of the practice test should you take a real test.

If you take the practice test in Chapter 15 and don't score at least 80 percent correct, you'll want to practice further. At a minimum, download the practice tests and the self-assessment tests from the Oracle Education Web site's download page (its location appears in the next section). If you're more ambitious or better funded, you might want to purchase a practice test from a third-party vendor.

Armed with the information in this book and with the determination to augment your knowledge, you should be able to pass the certification exam. But if you don't work at it, you'll spend the $125 test fee more than once before you finally pass. If you prepare seriously, the execution should go flawlessly. Good luck!

Additional Resources

By far the best source of information about Oracle certification tests comes from Oracle itself. Because its products and technologies—and the tests that go with them—change frequently, the best place to go for exam-related information is online.

If you haven't already visited the Oracle certification pages, do so right now. As I'm writing this chapter, the certification home page resides at **www.oracle.com/ education/certification/** (see Figure 1.1).

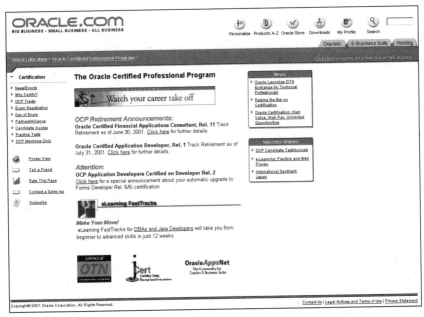

Figure 1.1   The Oracle certification page should be your starting point for further investigation of the most current exam and preparation information.

Note: It might not be there by the time you read this, or it may have been replaced by something new and different, because things change regularly on the Oracle site. Should this happen, please read the sidebar titled "Coping With Change on the Web," later in this section.

The menu options in the left column of the page point to the most important sources of information in the certification pages. Here's what to check out:

➤ *News/Events*—This section provides information on track upgrades, retirements, beta exam opportunities, new exams, and so on. The beta exams are offered at a discounted price in return for your feedback, so they're a good opportunity to get certified if you're short on ready cash!

➤ *Why Certify?*—This link provides information on the advantages of becoming an Oracle Certified Professional.

➤ *OCP Tracks*—Information on all the OCP tracks is provided in more detail here, including the target audience, exam preparation information, test content, and so on.

➤ *Exam Registration*—This section provides information for phone registration and a link to the Prometric Web page for online registration. Also, this section provides a list of testing sites outside of the United States, and if you're feeling really nervous, you can take a virtual tour of a Prometric Test Center to calm those butterflies!

➤ *Day Of Exam*—This link tells you what to do on the actual day of the exam.

➤ *Partners/Alliance*—This link provides information about test discounts and other offers for Oracle Partner Program members.

➤ *Candidate Guides*—Download or view the individual candidate guides for each track off this page.

➤ *Practice Tests*—This section is a source for practice tests that you can purchase.

➤ *OCP Members Only*—This is the link where you can download the OCP logo for use on your business cards. To actually download the logo, you need to provide the username and password provided in your welcome package once you've passed the exams.

Of course, these are just the high points of what's available in the Oracle certification pages. As you browse through them—and I strongly recommend that you do—you'll probably find other things I didn't mention here that are every bit as interesting and compelling.

Coping with Change on the Web

Sooner or later, all the specifics I've shared with you about the Oracle certification pages, and all the other Web-based resources I mention throughout the rest of this book, will go stale or be replaced by newer information. In some cases, the URLs you find here might lead you to their replacements; in other cases, the URLs will go nowhere, leaving you with the dreaded "404 File not found" error message.

When that happens, please don't give up. There's always a way to find what you want on the Web—if you're willing to invest some time and energy. To begin with, most large or complex Web sites—and Oracle's qualifies on both counts—offer a search engine. As long as you can get to Oracle's home page (and I'm sure that it will stay at **www.oracle.com** for a long while yet!), you can use this tool to help you find what you need.

The more particular or focused you can make a search request, the more likely it is that the results will include information you can use. For instance, you can search the string "training and certification" to produce a lot of data about the subject in general, but if you're looking for the Preparation Guide for the Oracle DBA tests, you'll be more likely to get there quickly if you use a search string such as this:

"DBA" AND "preparation guide"

Likewise, if you want to find the training and certification downloads, try a search string such as this one:

"training and certification" AND "download"

Finally, don't be afraid to use general search tools, such as **www.yahoo.com**, **www.google.com**, or **www.excite.com**, to search for related information. Even though Oracle offers the best information about its certification exams online, there are plenty of third-party sources of information, training, and assistance in this area that do not have to follow a party line like Oracle does. Therefore, if you can't find something where this book says it lives, intensify your search.

Oracle Architectural Components

Terms you'll need to understand:

✓ Instance

✓ Database

✓ System global area (SGA)

✓ Background processes

✓ Program global area (PGA)

✓ Redo logs

✓ Control files

✓ Datafiles

✓ Tablespace

✓ Segment

✓ Extent

✓ Data block

Techniques you'll need to master:

✓ Understanding the SGA structures

✓ Explaining the purposes of the Oracle background processes

✓ Describing the physical structure of the database

✓ Understanding commit processing

Understanding the core Oracle architectural components is the key to understanding everything else you will learn about Oracle, so it's a good place to start this book. If you have problems with this area, then you're probably not ready to tackle the OCP exams. In this chapter, I'll explain what Oracle's core architectural components are, the relationships among them, and how a commit is processed.

The Oracle Database

At its core, the Oracle Server has two main components: the *database* and the *instance*. All too often, these terms are confused and misused, even sometimes in the Oracle documentation. Part of the confusion is that, in the majority of cases, there is a one-to-one mapping between a single Oracle database and a single Oracle instance. The exception to this is in Oracle Parallel Server, where multiple instances access a single database. However, because that architecture is not included in the "Oracle8i: Architecture and Administration" exam, I won't cover it any further.

So let's look at the Oracle database in more detail. From a purist perspective, an *Oracle database* is defined as a group of physical files that you can see on disk. However, to really understand how these files work, you need to understand both their physical and logical structure.

Physical Database Structure

The physical database structure is composed of datafiles, redo log files, and control files.

Datafiles

Datafiles are the physical files that contain all the data in the database, both system data and user data. The system data (also known as the *data dictionary*) is contained logically within the SYSTEM tablespace, which is the only datafile that must exist and be accessible in an Oracle database. An attempt to start a database without this datafile will fail. User data can be kept in the SYSTEM tablespace, but this is not the preferred configuration for reasons of both performance and recoverability. We'll discuss the SYSTEM tablespace in the "Logical Structure" section of this chapter.

Modified data is written to the datafiles by the Database Writer (DBWn). DBWn processes are discussed later in this chapter, along with other Oracle background processes. Oracle uses a deferred write model and writes to the datafiles asynchronously. This reduces input/output (I/O) and therefore improves performance.

Redo Log Files

Redo log files contain the redo entries that represent changed data values due to inserts, updates, or deletes (unless an operation is done in **NOLOGGING** mode). Each redo entry contains what are called *change vectors* that make up a single change to the data.

Redo logs are primarily used to recover the database from instance or media failure. Because all changes are recorded in the redo logs, any failure should be recoverable from the information contained in the redo logs.

Obviously, the redo log files fulfill a vital role in an Oracle database. As a result, although all Oracle needs to create a database is two redo logs, there are usually more. To protect against a loss of the redo log itself, Oracle allows you to multiplex, or mirror, the redo log files on different disks. A group of multiplexed redo log files is known as a *redo log group*, and each file within a group is called a *redo log member*. All redo log members contain the same information.

Oracle writes to the redo logs in a circular fashion, filling up one redo log group before moving on to the next. To ensure that there are enough logs to write to, there are often more than two redo log groups. Redo logs are written to synchronously (to ensure recoverability); when a commit is issued, the write must complete before control is returned to the user. When the redo logs are mirrored, both mirrors are written to at the same time. Should one mirror become unavailable, Oracle will continue writing to the available mirror and flag an error in the alert log for the database.

Control Files

Control files are binary files that contain the name and location of all the datafiles and the redo log files in the database, as well as their state (such as online or offline). The control file also contains the database name and creation timestamp, and the log number of the current redo log file. The control file size is variable in Oracle8i, depending on the settings of various database limits (see Chapter 5 for more information) and whether you are using the Recovery Manager (RMAN) utility with the control file as a repository. (RMAN is covered in detail in Exam 1Z0-025, "Oracle8i: Backup and Recovery," but it is not referred to in Exam 1Z0-023, "Oracle8i: Architecture and Administration.")

Control files are used when the database is started to ensure that all the files that make up the database are available. Because the current log number is also kept in the headers of all the datafiles, the control file can also be used to check datafile consistency on database startup.

Control files are important files in the Oracle database, so the control files are usually mirrored. However, rather than being mirrored at the database level, as redo logs are, control files are mirrored at the operating-system level by using operating system copy commands to mirror the files in more than one location.

Note: The datafiles, redo log files, and control files are the only files that are included in the composition of an Oracle database. Although Oracle uses other important files (notably the initialization file and the Net8 files), these are not considered part of the database.

Logical Structure

At the logical level, an Oracle database is composed of a number of different entities: data blocks, extents, segments, and tablespaces.

Data Blocks

An Oracle data block is the smallest unit of I/O that can be performed by the database. In Oracle8i and earlier versions of the database, the block size is specified at the database level when the database is created, and it cannot be changed without re-creating the database. Although the block size is normally specified in bytes at database creation time, it is always referred to in kilobytes. It is generally set by the DBA on the basis of the data size for the application data held in the database. Larger block sizes are normally set for data warehouse environments, and smaller block sizes are used in online transaction processing (OLTP) systems. Although the default Oracle block size is 2KB, most databases are now created with either 4KB or 8KB data block sizes. The maximum block size possible is 32KB, but not all operating systems support a block size this large.

Every data block in an Oracle database has the same format; see Figure 2.1. The common and variable header contains general block information, such as the segment type (table, index, rollback, and so on) and the block address. The table directory is a list of tables that contain data in this block (this is usually relevant

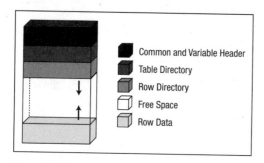

- Common and Variable Header
- Table Directory
- Row Directory
- Free Space
- Row Data

Figure 2.1 Data block format.

only for clusters). The row directory contains information about rows in the block, including pointers to where the rows are. The remaining part of the block is made up of free space and the actual row data. Depending on the size of the rows, a single row may span one or more data blocks.

Extents

A group of contiguous blocks on disk makes up an extent. An object such as a table can contain one or more extents; these extents are allocated to objects such as tables when the objects are created or when they grow (either automatically or manually). In most cases, an extent contains data for a single object. (The exception to this is clusters, in which an extent can hold data for multiple tables.)

Generally, extents for a single object are not stored adjacent to each other on disk, because they are allocated on an as-needed basis.

Segments

A group of extents that make up a particular data structure such as a table or index is called a *segment*. Segments are of four different types:

➤ *Data*—A data segment contains all the rows pertaining to a particular object. That object may be a table that is not clustered or partitioned, a partition of a particular table, or a cluster.

➤ *Index*—An index segment contains pointers to table or cluster data and is used for performance reasons or to ensure uniqueness. An unpartitioned index is composed of a single segment, whereas a partitioned index contains multiple segments.

➤ *Rollback*—Rollback segments contain undo data. They may be needed for statement or database recovery, or for providing read consistency. Generally, an individual rollback segment contains multiple rollback entries, each of which contains block information (to locate the information to be rolled back) and the old values of the data before it was changed. The database always has at least one rollback segment, called the *SYSTEM rollback segment*, located in the SYSTEM tablespace.

Note: Rollback entries are logged in the redo logs. This is necessary for recovery in case of system failure, because the only location Oracle guarantees it will write information to is the redo logs.

➤ *Temporary*—Temporary segments are automatically allocated and deallocated by Oracle to hold the intermediary results of statement processing—for example, sort results. They are not required if sorting can be done in memory, which is the preferred approach from a performance perspective. The types of operations that may need temporary segments are selects with a group clause (for example, **GROUP BY, UNION**), **ORDER BY** clauses, index creation, or temporary table creation.

Tablespaces

Tablespaces are logical storage units. Collectively, the tablespaces that make up a database contain all the data for that database. Tablespaces are used to group objects together for manageability, or for administrative or performance reasons. Datafiles are the physical representation on disk of tablespaces.

Typically, a database is composed of multiple tablespaces. The SYSTEM tablespace contains the data dictionary, and it must be available for the database to be available. Other tablespace names may vary, but you will often see the RBS tablespace used to contain rollback segments, and the TEMP tablespace used to contain temporary tablespaces.In addition to these tablespaces, there may be a USERS tablespace, as well as multiple application tablespaces for application data and indexes.

By default, tablespaces are read-write. However, it is possible to swap any tablespace that does not include an active rollback segment (which, of course, includes the SYSTEM tablespace) to read-only. This is useful for tablespaces that contain historical or unchanging data. A big advantage of read-only tablespaces is their ability to be put on CD-ROM. They also have to be backed up only once, and then can be left out of your backup strategy. The headers of any datafiles for a tablespace that is read-only are frozen, so there is no need to write the current redo log number to them.

The Oracle Instance

As mentioned previously, there is a fundamental difference between the terms *Oracle database* (the physical files on disk) and *Oracle instance*. In this section, I look at the Oracle instance in more detail.

An *Oracle instance* can be defined as the combination of the main memory area that Oracle uses—the system global area (SGA)—and a number of background processes or threads. Processes are used in just about every operating system except NT, which has a multithreaded model instead. The number of these processes will vary depending on your configuration, but there are five that are mandatory: DBWn, LGWR, PMON, SMON, and CKPT. Other processes that you may need to know about for the exam are Archiver (ARCn) processes, Dispatcher (Dnnn) processes, Shared Server (Snnn) processes, and Parallel Query (Pnnn) processes, among others. See the "Background Processes" section later in this chapter for more information.

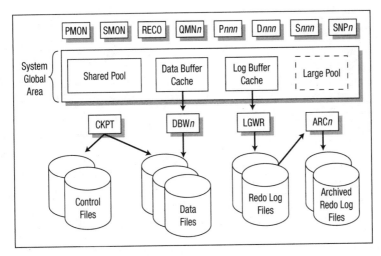

Figure 2.2   Database and instance relationships.

Examine Figure 2.2, which shows the interrelationships among all the different parts of the instance and the database. I'll cover each of these in more detail below. I'll also cover the program global area (PGA), which, although not considered part of the database or the instance, is closely related to both.

The System Global Area

The SGA, as it's more commonly known, is the main memory structure used by Oracle. It is a shared memory structure. All users connected to an Oracle database share the same SGA, so it is also sometimes called the *shared global area*. The three main components of the SGA are the data buffer cache, the shared pool, and the log buffer cache.

Note: Oracle often uses the terms "database buffer cache" and "data buffer cache" interchangeably. Similarly, "redo log buffer cache" and "log buffer cache" are two different ways of saying the same thing. You'll also see the word "cache" left off these terms.

A fourth component, the large pool, is optional, and its presence requires the DBA to set it up. In addition, more information is stored in the SGA when the multithreaded server (MTS) architecture is used. The request and response queues used by MTS are located in the SGA, as is some of the Java pool memory. In a non-MTS environment, the sort extent pool is also contained in the SGA. (It moves to an area called the *user global area* in MTS configurations.) Other control structures are also kept in the SGA, but these are relatively unimportant in the context of the OCP exam.

The SGA is allocated at instance startup, and its size is based on a number of parameters specified by the DBA in the initialization parameter file. (I'll point these out in each of the following sections.) The SGA is deallocated when the instance is shut down.

The SGA is read-write. Everyone connected to the database can read information in the SGA, but only a subset of processes actually write to it. This subset includes server processes, SMON, PMON, and RECO, where it is needed.

The Data Buffer Cache

Sometimes known as the *database buffer cache*, the data buffer cache is used to hold copies of data blocks in memory for performance reasons. Server processes, not DBW*n* processes, read blocks into memory on the user's behalf.

When a user needs to access a piece of data, the block that contains the data may have already been loaded into the data buffer cache by another user. Rather than rereading the block from disk, Oracle can read the in-memory copy of the block. This outcome, called a *cache hit*, is what we want to achieve from a performance perspective. If the block is not already loaded in memory, Oracle will read the block in from disk (a cache miss). Because this requires a disk read (that is, I/O) rather than a memory read, it is much slower.

The size of the data buffer cache is controlled by two initialization parameters set by the DBA: **DB_BLOCK_SIZE** (the database block size, set at database creation time) and **DB_BLOCK_BUFFERS** (the number of buffers assigned to the data buffer cache). Multiplying these two parameters together will give you the size of the data buffer cache. Because **DB_BLOCK_SIZE** is set at database creation time and because **DB_BLOCK_BUFFERS** is not dynamic, changing the size of the data buffer cache requires the instance to be shut down and restarted.

The data buffer cache is divided into two lists: the dirty list and the least recently used (LRU) list. The dirty list contains copies of data blocks that have been changed from the block contents on disk, but which have not yet been written back to the datafiles. (DBW*n* processes write asynchronously for performance reasons.) The LRU list contains buffers that may be either pinned (that is, currently being accessed) or free (buffers that are available for use), as well as dirty buffers that haven't been moved to the dirty list yet. These blocks will be moved to the dirty list when another process searches the LRU list for a free buffer.

As a process attempts to allocate a buffer, it will need to find a free buffer in the LRU list. The process scans the LRU list, searching for a free buffer until it either finds one or a certain threshold is reached. Any dirty buffers it finds are moved to the dirty list while this scan is taking place. If a free buffer is not found, the process signals the DBW*n* processes to wake up and flush the dirty buffers to disk, thus freeing buffers for use.

It's important that you realize that this algorithm actually changed significantly in Oracle8i. The new algorithm is based on a touch count or clock frequency scheme.

However, the Oracle Education Oracle8i Administration courseware (and therefore the OCP exam) does not cover this change, but instead refers to the old mechanism I've described here. This mechanism was valid in releases earlier than Oracle8i.

If you want to find out more about the new algorithm, Steve Adams covered it extremely well in his October 2000 newsletter. The URL for this particular section of the newsletter is **www.ixora.com.au/ newsletter/2000_10.html#cache**.

Normally, a process reads data onto the most recently used end of the LRU list. This is generally not what you want when a full table scan is performed. By default, Oracle will cycle the blocks from a full table scan through the opposite or least recently used end of the list to ensure that other data is not being flushed unnecessarily from the data buffer cache. You can override this default by using the **BUFFER_POOL** clause with the **KEEP** option, or by using the **CACHE** clause with either the **CREATE TABLE** or **ALTER TABLE** statement. Be careful not to do this with large, dynamic tables, because you can flush the buffer cache and cause a performance hit by doing this.

The **CACHE** option is being deprecated in favor of the **KEEP** option, so I recommend that you get comfortable with using the **KEEP** option now.

In Oracle8i, you have the capability of having multiple buffer pools in the data buffer cache. You can load objects into three different pools:

➤ The DEFAULT buffer pool is used for objects that have either not been assigned to a particular buffer pool or have been explicitly assigned to the DEFAULT pool (which isn't something you see too often). The size of the DEFAULT buffer pool isn't explicitly allocated. Rather, whatever's left of the data buffer cache after the KEEP and RECYCLE pools (the other two bullets in this list) are allocated is the size of the DEFAULT buffer pool.

➤ The KEEP buffer pool is used for data that you want to keep in memory. Its size is controlled by the **BUFFER_POOL_KEEP** initialization parameter.

➤ The RECYCLE buffer pool is used for data that you want aged out of memory as soon as it is no longer needed. Its size is controlled by the **BUFFER_POOL_RECYCLE** initialization parameter.

The Shared Pool

The shared pool is largely composed of the library cache and the data dictionary cache. (Although there are also some control structures and reusable runtime memory components, these are much smaller and not covered in the OCP exam.) If you are using MTS, the shared pool will also contain some (if not all) of the private SQL areas. The size of the shared pool is controlled by the **SHARED_POOL_SIZE** parameter, which is set in bytes. The default of 3,500,000 bytes is woefully inadequate for most systems, so you need to change this setting. Like the data buffer cache sizing parameters, **SHARED_POOL_SIZE** is not dynamic, so changing this parameter requires the instance to be restarted before it takes effect.

The library cache is used to contain SQL or PL/SQL statements being issued by users. Each statement issued by a user has a shared SQL area (which includes the parse tree and the execution plan) and a private SQL area (which contains runtime buffers, bind information, and so on). When a statement is issued, Oracle looks through the library cache for an identical statement; it must be exactly identical, including case, white space, line breaks, and so forth. If it finds a duplicated statement, Oracle will reuse the shared SQL area already allocated. Because the MTS architecture requires shared server processes to access the information that is normally in the private SQL area, these are moved from the program global area (PGA, discussed later in this chapter) to the SGA for sessions connected via MTS.

Oracle allocates memory in the shared SQL area when statements are issued. If the shared pool is already full, Oracle cannot automatically extend it to allocate space for the new statement, so older statements need to be removed from the shared pool. This is done using a modified LRU algorithm. Any statements that have been aged out of the shared pool in this way will need to be reparsed and more memory will need to be allocated the next time they are issued. Other operations that can cause statements to be flushed from the library cache include:

➤ *Altering an object*—Invalidates all shared SQL areas that reference it.

➤ *Changing the name of the global database*—Causes the entire shared pool to be flushed.

➤ *Executing the ANALYZE command to gather new statistics for the cost-based optimizer*—Flushes the shared SQL areas that reference the object being analyzed, so the new statistics can be used for better performance.

➤ *Manually flushing the shared pool with an ALTER SYSTEM FLUSH SHARED_POOL command*—Clears the cache before a major change in database use (for example, if different applications use the same database at different times).

The other major part of the shared pool is the data dictionary cache, which holds rows of data dictionary information. The data dictionary is frequently accessed by Oracle when parsing SQL statements, and having this data stored in memory vastly improves the performance of data dictionary access.

Oracle automatically manages the separation of memory allocated to the library cache and the data dictionary cache. You cannot independently size these two caches (or any of the other structures in the shared pool). In addition to not being able to independently size the two caches and the other shared pool structures, you cannot independently tune those structures. Instead, you simply size the total shared pool using the **SHARED_POOL_SIZE** parameter, and Oracle automatically moves memory between the two caches as needed.

The Large Pool

The large pool is an optional part of the SGA. It is configured by setting the parameter **LARGE_POOL_SIZE**, which defaults to zero if the large pool is not required for parallel execution and the parameter **DBWR_IO_SLAVES** is not set.

The large pool is designed for operations that require large buffer sizes (on the order of a few hundred kilobytes). These include backup and restore operations, I/O server processes, and MTS session memory. By allocating these elements out of a specific pool set aside for them, the impact on the shared pool is correspondingly decreased, and the shared pool can be used for its primary purpose of caching shared SQL.

 If **MTS_DISPATCHERS** has been set, Oracle derives a default value for the **LARGE_POOL_SIZE** parameter that includes 250KB per session for MTS and a port-specific amount of memory for backup I/O buffers. The default value derived in this manner can cause performance problems and can even be too large to allocate. In this case, set **LARGE_POOL_ SIZE** low enough so that the database can start.

Background Processes

It is very important to understand the different background processes and how they interrelate with the SGA. In this section, I examine each of the processes in more detail. Although I refer to them as background processes, whether these are actually processes or not depends on your operating system. On Unix and most other operating systems, the background processes are actual processes that can be seen at the operating-system level. Windows NT and Windows 2000, however, are multithreaded architectures, and each background process is actually a thread within the Oracle process. If you look at the processes in Task Manager, you will only see oracle.exe as an executing process, not the individual threads within it.

As mentioned previously, five mandatory processes must be present at all times for Oracle to work properly: DBW*n*, LGWR, PMON, SMON, and CKPT. Other processes will be dependent upon the configurations you have running and the Oracle options you have installed.

 You must know how each of the mandatory background processes works and how they interact with other Oracle processes and the SGA. Be sure to study the following sections carefully.

Database Writer

The Database Writer (DBW*n*) processes are responsible for writing dirty or modified blocks from the data buffer cache to the datafiles. For performance reasons, DBW*n* processes use a *deferred write model*, meaning that data is not necessarily written to the datafiles during a commit operation; rather, it is written to the datafiles when the data buffer cache doesn't have enough free buffers, when a checkpoint takes place, or when DBW*n* processes hit a timeout (every three seconds).

The *n* in DBW*n* signifies that there can be more than one database writer process. Most systems need only one, but it may be necessary to have more in high-write environments. Multiple processes are needed only on systems that don't support asynchronous I/O. The number of DBW*n* processes is controlled by the initialization parameter **DB_WRITER_PROCESSES**, which is a static parameter. If you do change this parameter from its default value (which is 1), then you should also change the value of the parameter **DB_BLOCK_LRU_LATCHES** so that each DBW*n* process has the same number of latches. If you set the **DBWR_IO_SLAVES** parameter to a nonzero value, the **DB_WRITER_ PROCESSES** parameter is ignored, and you have only one DBW*n* process.

Note: Remember that DBWn processes don't read from the datafiles—server processes do that. DBWn processes write only to the datafiles.

Log Writer

The Log Writer (LGWR) process is responsible for writing information from the log buffer cache to the redo logs on commit. LGWR also writes at other times: on timeout (every three seconds), when the log buffer cache reaches one-third full, or, if necessary, when DBW*n* writes modified blocks to disk. (Oracle uses a write-ahead protocol, wherein any redo changes associated with a modified buffer must be written to the redo logs before DBW*n* can write the modified buffer to the datafiles.)

Note: Sometimes, Oracle writes redo log entries to disk before they are actually committed. This is done only if more buffer space is needed, and the entries are marked as permanent only if the transaction is later committed. Otherwise, the entries are simply ignored.

The LGWR process writes redo log entries to all the members of the currently active redo log group. If any of the files are damaged, LGWR writes an error message to both its own trace file (found in the directory specified by the initialization parameter **BACKGROUND_DUMP_DEST**) and the alert log for the database. LGWR will keep writing to the undamaged files. If, for some reason, all the files are damaged, LGWR cannot continue to function, and the database will hang.

System Monitor

The System Monitor (SMON) process has three main functions: instance recovery, coalescing free space in dictionary-managed tablespaces, and reclaiming temporary segments when they are no longer needed.

Instance recovery occurs when the database has not been shut down cleanly (such as during a power outage). When this occurs, information that has been committed and written to the redo log files but not the datafiles needs to be applied (roll forward recovery), and uncommitted transactions need to be cleaned up (rollback recovery) when the database starts up again. SMON handles the roll forward recovery and may handle the rollback recovery as well. (Rollback recovery can also be performed by a server process needing to access a block that SMON has not yet recovered.)

Dictionary-managed tablespaces may have contiguous chunks of free space that need coalescing. This is not the case for locally managed tablespaces, which is one of the main advantages of using them. For dictionary-managed tablespaces, the coalescing of these contiguous chunks of free space is performed by SMON, provided that the **PCTINCREASE** value of the **DEFAULT STORAGE** clause for the tablespace is set to a nonzero value.

The SMON process also cleans up temporary segments that are no longer needed (because the sort operation has completed). This job can be simplified if dedicated temporary tablespaces are used, because sort segments created in these do not need to be cleaned up.

The Process Monitor

The Process Monitor (PMON) is responsible for cleaning up dead transactions and restarting dead dispatcher and shared server processes if MTS is being used. The steps for cleaning up dead transactions include freeing up any SGA resources that were being used, releasing any locks, and rolling back uncommitted transactions. PMON also is responsible for registering instances and dispatchers with the listener process.

The Checkpoint Process

The Checkpoint (CKPT) process is now a mandatory process. (It was optional in earlier releases.) CKPT is responsible for waking up DBWn to flush all modified data buffers in the SGA when a checkpoint occurs. It has also taken the responsibility for writing the log sequence number in the header of all the datafiles and the control files. (LGWR performed this action in earlier releases.)

The Archiver Processes

The Archiver (ARCn) processes are responsible for copying full redo logs to the archive log destination. This can also be forced with an **ALTER SYSTEM** command before the logs are full. Multiple Archiver processes can be created either as needed by the LGWR processes, or by setting the **LOG_ARCHIVE_MAX_PROCESSES** parameter. Archiving needs to be enabled before the Archiver processes are present. The **ARCHIVE_LOG_START** parameter must be set to **TRUE** and automatic archive log mode turned on to enable the ARCn processes. The database is put into automatic archive log mode where the redo logs are automatically copied as they are filled, by using an **ALTER DATABASE** command. (The command sets a flag in the control file, and it needs to be issued only once.)

MTS Processes

When the multithreaded server (MTS) architecture is enabled, two additional sets of background processes are enabled: the Dispatcher (Dnnn) processes and the Shared Server (Snnn) processes. In an MTS configuration, users connect to dispatcher processes for the duration of their connection. Any SQL statements are passed to the dispatcher, which places the request on a single request queue in the SGA. A number of shared server processes monitor this queue and process the requests on a first-in/first-out (FIFO) basis. A shared server will take a request off the queue and provide the results on an individual response queue that is monitored by the dispatcher, which in turn returns the results to the user. Depending on load, multiple dispatchers and shared servers are created based on a number of initialization parameters, including **MTS_DISPATCHERS, MTS_MAX_DISPATCHERS, MTS_SERVERS,** and **MTS_MAX_ SERVERS.** Note that there needs to be at least one dispatcher for each network protocol being used.

Parallel Query Processes

The Parallel Query (P*nnn*) processes are used to perform parallel execution of SQL statements, including parallel queries (used for table scans, joins, **GROUP BY** and **ORDER BY** execution, and so on), parallel DML (**INSERT, UPDATE,** and **DELETE**) and parallel DDL (**CREATE TABLE AS SELECT,** index rebuilds, partition splits, and so on). One process is designated as the parallel execution coordinator. It passes the statement to be executed to multiple parallel execution servers and accumulates the results before passing them back to the user. When this functionality was first introduced way back in Oracle7, queries were the only operations that could be parallelized. Although this is no longer the case, the old terminology of *Parallel Query processes* is generally still used; however, *parallel execution* is probably more accurate.

The Recoverer Process

The Recoverer (RECO) process is only present when the initialization parameter **DISTRIBUTED_TRANSACTIONS** is set to a value other than zero. This is necessary only in a distributed environment in which network failures are a problem. The RECO process is responsible for resolving in-doubt transactions that have failed in such a distributed environment.

Snapshot Processes

The snapshot (SNP*n*) processes were originally created to execute job requests issued by the **DBMS_JOB** package, but they are now used to automatically refresh table snapshots and materialized views. With the onset of advanced queuing in Oracle8, these processes are also used to propagate queued messages from one database to another. There can be up to 36 of these processes, depending on the value of the parameter **JOB_QUEUE_PROCESSES.** Unlike most of the other background processes, an instance will not crash when a snapshot process dies. Instead, Oracle will simply restart the failed snapshot process.

Queue Monitor Processes

Up to 10 Queue Monitor (QMN*n*) processes can be started if you are using Oracle Advanced Queuing. The number of these processes is set by the

AQ_TM_PROCESSES initialization parameter. The processes are used to monitor anything that is time-based in Advanced Queuing (such as message expiration, and retry and delay). As is the case with snapshot processes, failure of a queue monitor process does not cause the instance to crash.

Other Background Processes

Other Oracle background processes include LCK*n* (used for interinstance locking in a Parallel Server environment) and LMD (the Lock Manager Daemon, used in Parallel Server). These are not covered on the exam, so I will not discuss them in any more detail.

User Processes

Although the user process is not really considered an Oracle architectural component, it makes sense to mention it briefly here. In simple terms, the user process is simply the process that issues SQL statements that are executed by server processes. The results are then returned to the user process. In most cases, the user process executes an application, which builds the SQL statements based on values keyed in by a user. For example, a user may enter selection criteria into a screen and then press the Enter Query button to return the rows that meet these selection criteria. The application builds the actual **SELECT** statement, which is then executed by the server process.

The Program Global Area

The program global area (PGA) is a memory area that contains information for a single process, either a server process or a background process. As a result, you'll sometimes see it called the *process global area*. Unlike the SGA, which is shared, the PGA is not shared with other processes.

The contents of the PGA are dependent upon the architecture being used. As noted previously, in an MTS architecture, a user's private SQL areas move from the PGA into the SGA. However, regardless of the architecture, the PGA always contains the stack space, which is used to contain a session's variables and similar information.

The PGA is fixed in size, with the size depending on your operating system as well as the values of the **OPEN_LINKS** and **DB_FILES** initialization parameters.

Commit Processing

Commit processing is an example of how the whole Oracle architecture hangs together. When a user issues a commit to complete a transaction, Oracle performs a number of steps. First, Oracle places a commit record in the log buffer cache and allocates the transaction a system change number (SCN). The LGWR process then writes the log buffer out to disk, and the user is notified that the commit has been completed successfully. Any resources held by the transaction— such as locks, rollback resources, and so on—are released, and eventually the DBW*n* process writes the modified blocks out to the datafiles.

Oracle uses two mechanisms to improve the performance of commits: *fast commits* and *group commits*. The fast commit mechanism ensures that LGWR writes redo entries to the log files as soon as a commit is issued, while deferring the actual write to the datafiles, as discussed previously. A group commit is used in heavy write environments, where LGWR hasn't had time to complete the last commit before another commit is issued. Rather than interrupting the current commit (which wouldn't make much sense anyway), LGWR completes the first commit and then writes all the redo entries for waiting transactions that haven't yet been committed in a single I/O. If the high write activity continues, each write from the log buffer could contain multiple commit records.

Practice Questions

Question 1

Which component of the SGA records changes made to the database by the current instance?

- ○ a. Log buffer cache
- ○ b. Shared pool
- ○ c. Data buffer cache
- ○ d. Dictionary cache

Answer a is correct. All four options listed are components of the SGA. The log buffer cache stores changes before they are written to the redo log files. Answer b is incorrect because the shared pool contains the library cache and data dictionary cache, not database changes. Answer c is incorrect because the data buffer cache stores the data blocks, but not changes to the data, in memory. Answer d is incorrect because the dictionary cache is in the shared pool and is used to cache the data dictionary tables.

Question 2

What is the last step of a transaction when a commit is issued?

- ○ a. The log buffer cache is written to disk by LGWR.
- ○ b. The message "Commit Complete" is sent back to the user process.
- ○ c. Dirty buffers in the database buffer cache are flushed.
- ○ d. Resource locks on the data are released.

Answer d is correct. When a commit is issued, it is processed in this order:

1. The commit record with an SCN is placed in the redo log buffer by a server process.

2. LGWR writes the redo log buffer entries with the SCN to the redo log files.

3. The user process is notified that the commit is complete.

4. The server process records that the transaction is complete and that the resource locks can be released.

Answers a and b are incorrect because these steps take place before the locks are released. Answer c is incorrect because dirty buffers in the database buffer cache are flushed independently of the commit.

Question 3

> Where is parsed code for SQL statements kept in the SGA?
>
> ○ a. Data buffer cache
>
> ○ b. Log buffer cache
>
> ○ c. Data dictionary cache
>
> ○ d. Library cache

Answer d is correct. The library cache stores the parsed code for a SQL statement. If a query is re-executed before it is aged out of the library cache, the server will use the parsed code and execution plan from the library cache instead of recompiling the statement. Answer a is incorrect because the data buffer cache stores the data blocks in memory. Answer b is incorrect because the log buffer cache stores changed data. Answer c is incorrect because the data dictionary cache is used to cache the data dictionary tables.

Question 4

> Which component interacts with, but is not defined as part of, an Oracle instance?
>
> ○ a. Background process
>
> ○ b. User process
>
> ○ c. Log buffer cache
>
> ○ d. Shared pool

Answer b is correct. When a user attempts to connect to a database, the user creates a user process. This process interacts with a server process and provides it the username and password. In a client/server environment, the user process runs on the client and communicates with the server process over a network. Answer a is incorrect because the background processes are part of an Oracle instance. Answers c and d are incorrect because the log buffer and the shared pool are part of the SGA, which in turn is part of an Oracle instance.

Question 5

> Which background process manages the data buffer cache and maintains a sufficient number of free buffers for server processes to use?
>
> ○ a. CKPT
>
> ○ b. LGWR
>
> ○ c. DBW*n*
>
> ○ d. SMON
>
> ○ e. PMON

Answer c is correct. DBW*n* writes to disk frequently enough to ensure that free blocks are available when a server process needs to store a block in the database buffer cache. To minimize I/O, DBW*n* defers writes to the datafiles until dirty buffers reach a threshold, not enough free buffers are available, or a timeout or checkpoint occurs. Answer a is incorrect because CKPT is responsible for signaling DBW*n* at checkpoints and updating all the datafiles and control files of the database to indicate the most recent checkpoint. Answer b is incorrect because LGWR writes redo log entries to disk. Answer d is incorrect because SMON performs instance recovery at instance startup. Answer e is incorrect because PMON performs process recovery when a user process fails.

Question 6

> Which background process writes dirty buffers in the database buffer cache to the datafiles?
>
> ○ a. SMON
>
> ○ b. PMON
>
> ○ c. CKPT
>
> ○ d. LGWR
>
> ○ e. DBW*n*

Answer e is correct. DBW*n* writes dirty buffers to disk to ensure that free blocks are available when a server process needs to store a block in the database buffer cache. To minimize I/O, DBW*n* defers writes to the datafiles until dirty buffers reach a threshold, not enough free buffers are available, or a timeout or checkpoint occurs. Answer a is incorrect because SMON performs instance recovery at instance startup. Answer b is incorrect because PMON performs process recovery when a user process fails. Answer c is incorrect because CKPT is responsible for signaling DBWn at checkpoints and updating all the datafiles and control files of the database to indicate the most recent checkpoint. Answer d is incorrect because LGWR writes redo log entries to disk.

Question 7

If a user abnormally terminates a database connection, which background process will release the locks held by the user?

- ○ a. PMON
- ○ b. SMON
- ○ c. LGWR
- ○ d. DBWn
- ○ e. CKPT

Answer a is correct. PMON is responsible for cleaning up after a failed user process. Answer b is incorrect because SMON coalesces tablespaces, cleans up temporary segments, and performs instance recovery at instance startup. Answer c is incorrect because LGWR writes redo log entries to disk. Answer d is incorrect because DBWn maintains the data buffer cache. Answer e is incorrect because CKPT is responsible for signaling DBWn at checkpoints and updating all the datafiles and control files of the database to indicate the most recent checkpoint.

Question 8

How does Oracle accomplish a fast commit?

- ○ a. By writing transactions immediately to the datafiles, bypassing the buffer cache
- ○ b. By breaking large transactions and writing more small transactions that are processed more quickly than larger ones
- ○ c. By writing the minimal information required to record the changes in the redo logs
- ○ d. By giving transactions requesting a commit a higher priority over other processing

Answer c is correct. Writes to the datafiles are deferred to reduce disk contention and I/O. Oracle's fast commit allows LGWR to record only the changes and SCN in the redo log files. The size of the transaction does not affect the time required to write to the redo log files. These writes are sequential and faster than writing entire blocks to the datafiles. Writes to the datafiles occur independently of the commit. The question is tricky because Oracle always uses the same method of committing, but it does allow commits to happen very quickly. The question implies that there is a special fast commit that Oracle can do; this is not the case. Answer a is incorrect because database transactions are not written directly to datafiles. Answer b is incorrect because it pertains to parallel query. Answer d is incorrect because all Oracle processes run at the same priority.

Question 9

> When transactions commit, which background process writes redo log entries to the redo log files?
>
> O a. LGWR
>
> O b. PMON
>
> O c. DBWn
>
> O d. SMON
>
> O e. CKPT

Answer a is correct. The redo log buffer stores changes to the database in memory until LGWR can write the changes to the redo log files. LGWR flushes the redo log buffer when the buffer becomes one-third full, when a timeout occurs, before DBWn writes to disk, and when a transaction commits. LGWR writes to the redo logs sequentially so that transactions can be applied in order in the event of a failure. Once a transaction is recorded in the redo log files, the changes to the data cannot be lost. LGWR writes redo log entries to disk. Answer b is incorrect because PMON performs process recovery when a user process fails. Answer c is incorrect because DBWn writes to the datafiles. Answer d is incorrect because SMON performs instance recovery at instance startup. Answer e is incorrect because CKPT is responsible for signaling DBWn at checkpoints and updating all the datafiles and control files of the database to indicate the most recent checkpoint.

Question 10

> What are free buffers in the database buffer cache?
>
> ○ a. Buffers that have changed and should be flushed to disk
>
> ○ b. Buffers that are currently in use
>
> ○ c. Buffers that are being written to disk
>
> ○ d. Buffers that can be overwritten

Answer d is correct. Only free buffers can be overwritten. Answer a is incorrect because if a buffer has not been written to disk, it can't be overwritten. Answer b is incorrect because buffers that are in use are not on the free list. Answer c is incorrect because buffers are free only after they are written to disk.

Question 11

> What files contain changed copies of the data on commit?
>
> ○ a. Datafiles
>
> ○ b. Control files
>
> ○ c. Redo log files
>
> ○ d. Initialization parameter files

Answer c is correct. Redo log entries record the changed data and are written to the redo log files on commit. Although you might think that answer a is correct, the key here is the that the question asks about where the data was at commit time. Answer a is incorrect because the datafiles may contain the changed data, but they are written to using a deferred write model, so they are written to after the commit. Answer b is incorrect because the control files record the physical structure of the database, including where the datafiles and log files are; they don't contain user data. Answer d is incorrect because the initialization parameter files are used to size memory structures, locate the control files, and control many of the performance settings for the instance; they do not contain user data.

Question 12

> What files are not considered part of the database?
>
> ○ a. Datafiles
>
> ○ b. Control files
>
> ○ c. Redo log files
>
> ○ d. Initialization parameter files

Answer d is correct. The initialization parameter files are used to size memory structures, locate the control files, and control many of the performance settings for the instance, but they are not considered part of the database. Answers a, b, and c are incorrect because these files make up an Oracle database.

Need to Know More?

Loney, Kevin, and Marlene Theriault. *Oracle8i DBA Handbook*. Oracle Press, Berkeley, CA, 1999. ISBN 0-07212-188-2. This book is a comprehensive guide and a must-have for all DBAs. Chapter 1 covers getting started with the Oracle architecture.

Scherer, Douglas, William Gaynor, Arlene Valentinsen, Sue Mavris, and Xerxes Cursetjee. *Oracle8i Tips and Techniques*. Oracle Press, Berkeley, CA, 1999. ISBN 0-07212-103-3. Provides an overview of Oracle8i architecture and administration, along with many tips, both documented and undocumented, to make the most out of Oracle8i. Chapter 1 covers the concepts of an Oracle instance, database, tablespaces, and segments. Chapter 3 covers installation and includes information on MTS.

Wong, Debbie. *Oracle8i DBA: Backup and Recovery Exam Cram*. The Coriolis Group, Scottsdale, AZ, 2001. ISBN 1-58880-045-8. Chapters 5, 6, and 11 cover RMAN in more detail, including the use of the control file as a repository.

See the Oracle documentation that is provided on CD with the Oracle RDBMS software. Pertaining to this chapter are:

Baylis, Ruth, and Joyce Fee. *Oracle8i Administrator's Guide*. Oracle Corporation, Redwood City, CA, 1999. Complete documentation of database administration tasks.

Leverenz, Lefty, Diana Rehfield, and Cathy Baird. *Oracle8i Concepts*. Oracle Corporation, Redwood City, CA, 1999. Complete documentation of Oracle concepts.

Lorentz, Diana. *Oracle8i Reference*. Oracle Corporation, Redwood City, CA, 1999. Specific details on initialization parameters, data dictionary views, and database limits.

technet.oracle.com is Oracle's technical repository of information for clients.

www.ixora.com.au is the Web site for Ixora, an Australian company run by Steve Adams. It provides excellent information in the newsletter section.

 www.revealnet.com is the site where RevealNet Corporation provides Oracle administration reference software.

Getting Started
with the Oracle Server

Terms you'll need to understand:

- ✓ Oracle Universal Installer
- ✓ Optimal Flexible Architecture (OFA)
- ✓ SQL*Plus
- ✓ Server Manager
- ✓ Operating system authentication
- ✓ Password file authentication
- ✓ **REMOTE_LOGIN_PASSWORDFILE**
- ✓ **SYSDBA**
- ✓ **SYSOPER**
- ✓ ORAPWD
- ✓ Oracle Enterprise Manager (OEM) Console
- ✓ Intelligent Agent
- ✓ Oracle Management Server (OMS)
- ✓ OEM job scheduling
- ✓ OEM repository

Techniques you'll need to master:

- ✓ Installing Oracle using the Oracle Universal Installer
- ✓ Using SQL*Plus and Server Manager to perform DBA tasks
- ✓ Setting up operating system authentication
- ✓ Setting up password file authentication
- ✓ Using OEM to monitor, administer, and tune the database

With Oracle8i, you'll use a variety of Java-based tools as well as traditional line-mode tools to install and administer the Oracle database. In this chapter, I'll explain what the Oracle Universal Installer does, and I'll examine the use of Oracle Enterprise Manager to monitor, administer, and tune the Oracle database. In addition, I'll discuss the two main methods of authenticating a user to perform administrative tasks in Oracle: operating system authentication and password file authentication.

Features of the Oracle Universal Installer

The Oracle Universal Installer (OUI) is used to install and configure the Oracle kernel. Because it's Java based, it can run on any platform that is Java enabled. You can see a list of all the Oracle products installed on a machine, as shown in Figure 3.1, simply by starting the OUI and clicking on Installed Products.

The installer prompts you for the source for the products you want to install (this is normally defaulted because you run the installer that comes on a product CD), as well as the destination Oracle Home name and its full path. See Figure 3.2.

The installer automatically determines any dependencies between products and resolves these dependencies as part of the installation. It also automatically

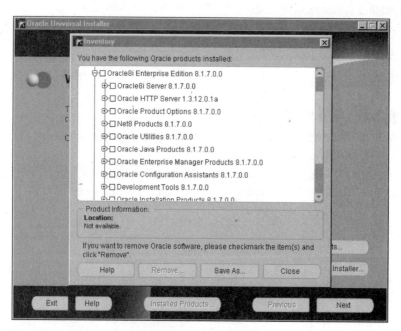

Figure 3.1 Checking which Oracle products are installed.

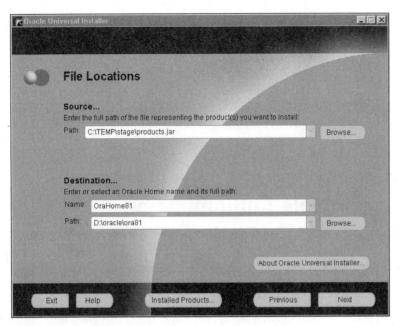

Figure 3.2   Selecting the source and destination directories.

determines the correct language for the installation, based on the language of the operating system.

If you're planning on performing multiple installations, the OUI lets you install over the Web using HTTP. All you need to do is define a staging area at a particular URL, and the installer can then be pointed to that URL to perform the installation.

You can also run the installer in silent mode. In this mode, all the responses that you would normally enter in a Java-based installation session are read from a response file. The installer is simply passed the name and location of the response file, and it reads the values it needs from the file. Sample response files are provided with the software, so you can use these as examples for building your own.

The OUI has been enhanced to support the Optimal Flexible Architecture (OFA). Cary Millsap, then with Oracle Consulting, developed the OFA several years ago to resolve a number of problems that his group had seen at customer sites. The OFA was designed to resolve these problems by providing:

➤ A proper file layout structure, to simplify administration tasks and to separate files for performance and recovery reasons

➤ Easier administration of multiple Oracle Homes, by separating files from the different Oracle Homes on different disks using a directory naming convention to identify the Oracle Home that the files belong to

➤ A more structured methodology to install Oracle databases

➤ A controlled naming and location methodology for administrative files, such as the parameter file

Although originally designed specifically for Unix, the OFA has been enhanced for NT as well. Although the OFA is the same in both environments where possible, the OFA required some modification to enable it to be used on NT, due to differences in the operating system.

Setting Up Operating System and Password File Authentication

DBA tasks, such as starting and stopping the Oracle database, require extra privileges that are not normally given to end users. This section discusses the two methods used to give these privileges to DBAs: operating system authentication and password file authentication. Which one you choose is determined by the location you'd like to use to administer the database (locally, on the same machine as the database; or remotely, via a PC client). However, to give you a little background before we look at these authentication methods, let's first examine the default DBA accounts provided in every Oracle database: SYS and SYSTEM.

The SYS and SYSTEM Accounts

When an Oracle database is created, two DBA accounts are created by default: SYS and SYSTEM.

When these accounts are created, they are given a set of roles that depend on the Oracle options you have installed. (Refer to Chapter 13 for more details.) For example, if you've installed Advanced Queuing, both SYS and SYSTEM will be automatically granted the **AQ_ADMINISTRATOR_ROLE** role. By default, both SYS and SYSTEM are granted the **DBA** role, which is a predefined role that includes all Oracle system privileges.

SYS is the owner of the data dictionary. Its default password is CHANGE_ ON_INSTALL, which is a helpful instruction that reminds you what you should do: namely, change SYS's default password.

SYS owns all the base tables in the data dictionary, so anybody who can log on as SYS can cause major havoc by deleting information from the base tables, which would cause database corruption.

SYSTEM is also a highly privileged user within the Oracle database. One notable difference from SYS is that the SYSTEM account is not by default granted the **SYSDBA** role, as SYS is. In addition, SYSTEM is granted fewer default roles when the database is created. (In my 8.1.7 database on Windows NT, SYS has 23 roles by default, whereas SYSTEM has only 10.) However, the SYSTEM account is still a highly privileged account, so you should change its password from the default of MANAGER. For some reason, SYSTEM—rather than SYS—owns some of the base data dictionary tables (notably some replication tables), providing even more reason to change its default password.

It's a good idea to create your own DBA accounts and provide them with the privileges needed to perform their jobs. For example, you might create a **JUNIORDBA** role for new DBAs and map that to the Oracle accounts you create for them. Likewise, you might create a **SENIORDBA** role for experienced DBAs and give that role more privileges than the **JUNIORDBA** role.

Authentication Methods

You can use one of two main authentication methods to connect to an Oracle database to perform administrative tasks: operating system (OS) authentication or password file authentication. As I mentioned previously, you determine which method you should use very simply. Do you want to administer the database from the same machine that the database is on? If so, then the authentication method you want to use is OS authentication. Alternatively, if you want to administer one or more databases from a single remote client, you should use password file authentication. Let's look at each in more detail now.

Operating System Authentication

OS authentication uses operating system privileges to verify your authorization to perform DBA tasks. The setup of this is different on Unix than it is on NT. On Unix, the user to be authenticated by the operating system needs to be a member of a specific group. (The default group is DBA, although this can be changed when installing the kernel via the OUI.) The group needs to be added to the /etc/group file, and the user needs to be added to that group. On an NT system, you need to create groups that can be either specific to an instance (ORA_<*SID*>_DBA and ORA_<*SID*>_OPER) or generic across all instances (ORA_DBA and ORA_OPER). The NT user is then mapped to the relevant NT group. In addition, a line needs to be added to the sqlnet.ora file (located by default under %ORACLE_HOME%/network/admin), setting the value SQLNET. AUTHENTICATION_SERVICES = (NTS).

Once these steps are performed, the remaining steps are identical for both Unix and NT. The initialization parameter REMOTE_LOGIN_PASSWORDFILE needs to be set to NONE. (The default varies with the release, but the default is

EXCLUSIVE in my 8.1.7 database.) If necessary, restart the database for the change to take effect. Then you can connect to the database as either **SYSDBA** or **SYSOPER** using the syntax:

```
CONNECT / as {SYSDBA | SYSOPER}
```

SYSDBA and **SYSOPER** are predefined privileges in the Oracle database. A user with the **SYSDBA** privilege can perform any task in the database, including point-in-time recovery and creating databases, and has all system privileges **WITH ADMIN OPTION.** (See Chapter 13 for more details on system privileges.) **SYSOPER** is slightly less powerful in that it can't be used to create databases or perform point-in-time recovery, and, although it has all system privileges, it doesn't have them **WITH ADMIN OPTION.** Note that administrators don't need to be granted **SYSDBA** or **SYSOPER** when using OS authentication. Having the OS user in the right group provides that user with the equivalent **OSDBA** or **OSOPER** operating system roles. The server simply verifies that the user has been granted these roles at the OS level.

The old methodology to connect to the database to perform administrative tasks (**CONNECT INTERNAL**) is not supported in Oracle9i. It can still be used in Oracle8i, but it's probably a good idea to get used to connecting with the **SYSDBA** syntax.

Password File Authentication

To use password file authentication, you must first create the password file. Oracle provides the password file utility ORAPWD to do this. (In earlier releases, the NT version included the version number in the file name, but with multiple Oracle Home support in 8.1 for NT, this is no longer the case.)

The syntax for ORAPWD is

```
orapwd file=<filename> password=<password> entries=<n>
```

where:

➤ *<filename>* is the name of the password file being created, including the path.

➤ *<password>* is the password for SYS and INTERNAL.

➤ *<n>* is the maximum number of distinct users to which you want to grant **SYSDBA** or **SYSOPER.**

The only optional parameter is **entries**, and there must be no spaces around the equal signs. The file that ORAPWD creates is encrypted for security reasons. Its location and file specification are specific to the operating system, so you need to examine your system's documentation to see what values are allowed by Oracle on your particular platform. Notice that **entries** should be set to the maximum number of **SYSDBA/SYSOPER** users that you ever expect to have authenticated by this password file. If you set this value too low, you can't increase it without re-creating the password file, which means you would need to grant **SYSDBA/SYSOPER** to the necessary users again.

Once the password file is set up, you need to set the value of the initialization parameter **REMOTE_LOGIN_PASSWORDFILE** to either **EXCLUSIVE** (which means the password file is used for only one database, but users other than SYS or INTERNAL can be added to it) or **SHARED** (in which case the file can be shared among multiple databases, but only SYS or INTERNAL can be added to the file).

When **REMOTE_LOGIN_PASSWORDFILE** is set to **EXCLUSIVE**, users other than SYS and INTERNAL can be granted the **SYSDBA** or **SYSOPER** privileges by SYS using the syntax:

```
GRANT SYSDBA | SYSOPER to <user>;
```

This will add *<user>* to the password file, which can also be seen in the data dictionary view **V$PWFILE_USERS**.

Using SQL*Plus and Server Manager

Oracle provides two line-mode tools to perform DBA tasks: SQL*Plus and Server Manager. Server Manager is supported only for reasons of backward compatibility, and it is not supported in Oracle9i, so you might as well get used to using SQL*Plus.

SQL*Plus has been enhanced to support most of the functionality that is available in Server Manager. (The few minor differences aren't included in the exam, so I won't cover them here.) You can now issue all the commands that you would normally use in Server Manager to administer the database from within SQL*Plus. For example, you can use the **SHUTDOWN** command to shut down an Oracle database and the **STARTUP** command to start an Oracle database. (See Chapter 4 for more details on the **STARTUP** and **SHUTDOWN** commands.)

The major reason you need to use these line-mode tools now is for scripting purposes, such as automating the startup of your Production database when the machine it resides on starts up. For most other purposes (unless you're an old-time DBA who still likes everything in command-line mode), it's easier to use one of the graphical tools that Oracle provides, such as Oracle Enterprise Manager, which I'll discuss more in the next section.

 It's important for you to understand how to use the line-mode tools, as well as Oracle Enterprise Manager. The exam includes questions on both.

Oracle Enterprise Manager

Oracle Enterprise Manager (OEM) provides a management framework to assist in managing the Oracle environment. It has a Java-based graphical user interface (GUI) that enables DBAs to perform administrative tasks without having to remember the gory details of the syntax needed to perform those tasks. It is used to provide a centralized view of the complete Oracle system, and it can manage Oracle databases, listeners, and other services. It comes complete with a free DBA Management Pack, and other additional management packs can be purchased for performance tuning, diagnostics, and change management, as well as management of Oracle Applications and SAP R/3.

OEM uses a three-tier architecture (see Figure 3.3). On the first (bottom) tier, which is the client, the OEM Console provides a single point of access into the managed nodes, and the DBA Management Pack provides a set of standard applications that can be used to manage specific parts of the Oracle environment. The middle tier is composed of the Oracle Management Server (OMS), which provides the centralized intelligence between the client side and the managed nodes. Also in the middle tier is the OEM repository, which maintains all the metadata about the system, applications, and the states of the managed nodes. Interacting with the repository and the OMS is a set of common services that help you to manage all the other nodes in the system. These common services include the Job Scheduling System, the Discovery Service, the Event Management System, and the Security Service (we'll look at these in more detail later in this chapter). The third tier consists of the managed databases, listeners, and other services being monitored by OEM. Each managed node has an Intelligent Agent that executes commands provided by the OMS and provides input and feedback back into it. The rest of this book contains information on databases. Listeners are covered in the "Oracle8i: Network Administration" exam (1Z0-026), so consult references for that exam for more on that topic. I won't cover the third tier in any more detail in this chapter, but let's look more at the first two tiers.

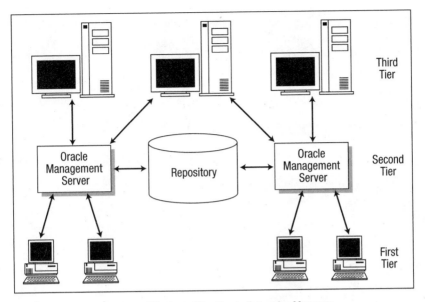

Figure 3.3   The three-tier architecture of the Oracle Enterprise Manager.

First Tier: OEM Console

The OEM Console is used to provide an overall view of the Oracle system being managed. It has both a hierarchical tree representation and a graphical representation of the objects that compose the Oracle environment. As shown in Figure 3.4, the Console has four main panes:

➤ Navigator pane

➤ Group pane

➤ Events pane

➤ Jobs pane

These panes are discussed in the following sections.

The Navigator Pane

The Navigator pane provides a hierarchical tree view of all the databases, listeners, nodes and other services in the Oracle system being managed. You can drill down from each of these to the objects they contain. For example, you can open the Databases folder to see a list of the databases, then select one database to see all the users, tablespaces, objects, and other entities defined in that database.

You can use the Navigator pane to perform a variety of administrative tasks. For example, opening a particular database folder allows you to drill into a Security

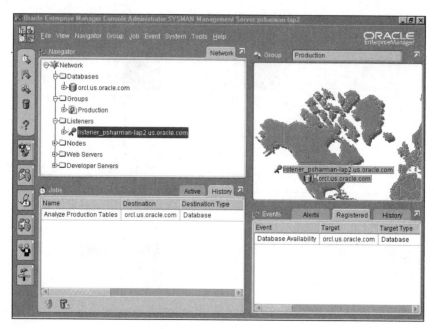

Figure 3.4   The Oracle Enterprise Manager Console, showing the four main panes.

folder, followed by a Users folder. From there, you can either click the right mouse button or choose the Navigator menu to get a list of possible operations (for example, Create User). Notice that the menus are *context sensitive*, which means that the items on the menu vary depending on which folder you are in when you select that menu item. For example, from the Users subfolder, selecting the Navigator menu produces the menu shown in Figure 3.5, whereas selecting Navigator from the Resource Consumer Groups subfolder results in the menu shown in Figure 3.6.

The Group Pane

The Group pane allows you to monitor the objects within your Oracle environment via a graphical display. You simply drag and drop objects from the Navigator pane to the Group pane to build groups of related objects that you want to monitor. (Note that, unlike in the Navigator pane, you can't perform much in the way of administrative tasks in this pane, but groups become really useful when we look at the remaining two panes: the Events pane and the Jobs pane.)

With OEM, you can create a group composed of databases, listeners, and nodes that you want to monitor. In the example shown in Figure 3.6, I have created a simple Production group to monitor all the Production objects in my environment. Even though it's composed of different objects (a database and a listener),

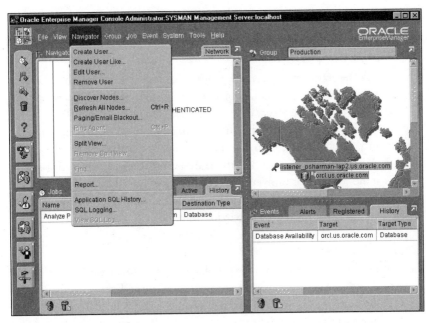

Figure 3.5 Context-sensitive menus from the Users subfolder in the Navigator pane.

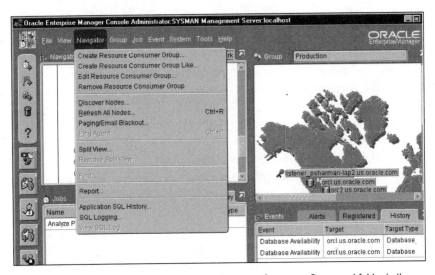

Figure 3.6 Context-sensitive menus from the Resource Consumer Groups subfolder in the Navigator pane.

I can schedule jobs against that group, and the jobs will run against only the relevant part of the group. For example, a backup job would execute against only the database, not the listener.

Monitoring the status of objects in a group or groups is very straightforward if you have registered events for the object or group (covered in the next section, "The Events Pane"). The object or group is displayed with a status flag (like the one next to the orcl database in the Group pane in Figure 3.6), provided that the Intelligent Agent is running on the machine on which the object or group is located. A green flag indicates that there are no problems; a yellow flag means there is some warning or problem condition that you need to investigate, a red flag indicates a severe error, and a circle with a slash through it means that the object is unreachable (it may be down, for example).

The Events Pane

The Events pane allows you to track and display events occurring in your Oracle system. To register an event, you need to define it in the Events pane and then tell OEM which objects or groups to register the event against. You can specify who has access to view or modify the event, as well as who should be notified when the event occurs (either through email or paging). You can even specify fix-it jobs to run automatically when the event occurs, but be careful with this. For example, it doesn't make a lot of sense to have a fix-it job attempt to restart the database when it dies without first addressing the cause of the problem.

From the Events pane, you can review events by using the event viewer, accessed through the Alerts or History tab. The Alerts tab displays events that have occurred but which have not yet been cleared by an administrator. When you clear an event from the Alerts tab, it moves to the History tab. From either the Alerts or the History tab, you can double-click on an event to bring up the event viewer, which will show you details of the event notifications. (Multiple notifications can be set for a single event when either a warning threshold or a critical threshold is reached.) You can also add comments in the Event log so other administrators can see what happened.

The Jobs Pane

The Jobs pane allows you to submit and manage jobs anywhere in the Oracle system. Jobs can be composed of either operating system or SQL commands. Jobs can be executed against a single object, or, by applying them to a group, they can run against multiple objects at once.

Jobs are composed of one or more tasks that can be configured to depend on the success or failure of earlier tasks in the job. For example, you can schedule a cold backup of the database so that it runs only if the preceding shutdown task was successful. OEM comes with a set of defined tasks, such as starting or stopping the database, running **ANALYZE** commands, loading or unloading data, and so on. The Job Scheduling System allows you to execute jobs periodically, helping to enable lights-out management of the system. As mentioned previously, the Job Scheduling System can also interact with the Event Management System, allowing fix-it jobs to be specified for events, thus automating simple problem correction. Another advantage of the Job Scheduling System is that jobs are implemented in Tool Command Language (Tcl) scripts. Tcl (pronounced Tickle) is platform independent, so you can schedule the same job to run against a Unix machine and an NT one without having to change the Tcl script.

Second Tier: OMS, Common Services, and OEM Repository

The second tier of the OEM architecture is made up of the Oracle Management Server (OMS), a set of common services, and the OEM repository.

Oracle Management Server (OMS)

The OMS provides the centralized intelligence between the Console and the managed nodes, and it processes the system management tasks, distributing them to the relevant Intelligent Agent. As the number of nodes in the Oracle system increases, you may want to consider using multiple OMSs to ensure scalability. Multiple OMSs can also be used to provide failover and load balancing.

Common Services

The common services help you to manage the nodes throughout the system. There are basically four different services: the Job Scheduling System, Event Management System, Discovery Services, and Security Services. I've covered the first two of these already in the Console discussion above. (Although not really part of the Console, they interact heavily with the Console, so it makes sense to discuss them in the context of the Jobs and Events panes, respectively.) Discovery Services are used to automatically locate the database, listeners, nodes and other services in the Oracle system. From the Console, you simply choose Discover Nodes (to discover new nodes), or Refresh All Nodes (to refresh existing services) from the Navigator menu. The actual discovery is performed by the Intelligent Agent and reported back to the OMS. The Security Service allows you to define security parameters for services, objects, and administrators. A super administrator is used to create new administrators and define the privileges they have, and can also access any other object to control its security parameters (including those owned by other administrators).

OEM Repository

All the centralized intelligence, system, and application data maintained by the OMS is stored in the OEM repository. This repository can be created in any Oracle database, but it makes sense for it to be located somewhere other than the managed nodes. (It's pretty tough reporting that a node is down to the repository if the repository database is also on that node.)

Normally, a single repository is shared. (It's accessed from multiple OMSs if OMS scalability is an issue.) This shared architecture was first introduced in OEM 2. Each administrator logs in to the Console with his or her own account, created by the super administrator. In my OEM 2.2 database on NT, the super administrator account is SYSMAN with a password of OEM_TEMP. (Regardless of your operating system, OEM warns you this is the default password when you first use it, and forces you to change the password.)

DBA Management Pack

The DBA Management Pack is a set of standard applications that are supplied with OEM, although they can also be called from DBA Studio. Figure 3.7 shows a screenshot from DBA Studio.

The tools that are available through these mechanisms are used for administering different objects:

➤ *Instance Manager*—Used for setting initialization parameters and starting or stopping an Oracle database, as well as managing sessions, in-doubt transactions, and resource plans.

➤ *Schema Manager*—Used to create, alter, or drop any schema object, such as tables, indexes, and so on.

➤ *Security Manager*—Used to create, alter, or drop users, roles, and profiles, and to grant privileges and roles to users.

➤ *Storage Manager*—Used to administer storage objects such as tablespaces, redo logs, and rollback segments.

➤ *Replication management*—Used to set up and maintain both multimaster and snapshot replication in a distributed environment.

➤ *Jserver management*—Used to manage the namespace and browse CORBA and EJB components within the namespace.

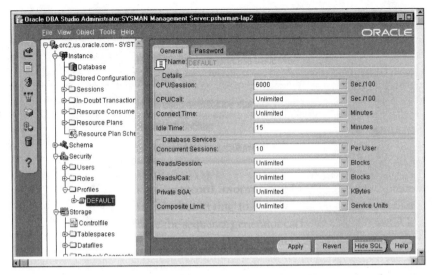

Figure 3.7 The DBA Studio tool.

Practice Questions

Question 1

> Which part of OEM would you use to schedule an OS backup of your database?
>
> ○ a. OEM Navigator pane
>
> ○ b. OEM Repository
>
> ○ c. Intelligent Agent
>
> ○ d. OEM Jobs pane

Answer d is correct. The OEM Jobs pane allows a DBA to schedule OS backups. Answer a is incorrect because the OEM Navigator pane allows the DBA to view the hierarchy of all the Oracle services on the network. Answer b is incorrect because the OEM Repository contains a set of tables that store information related to the OEM user. Answer c is incorrect because the Intelligent Agent runs on remote nodes to execute and manage the jobs and events sent out by OEM.

Question 2

> Which OEM application would you use to alter a database initialization parameter?
>
> ○ a. Security Manager
>
> ○ b. Instance Manager
>
> ○ c. Schema Manager
>
> ○ d. Storage Manager

Answer b is correct. Instance Manager is used for managing instances, sessions, startup, and shutdown, and for changing initialization parameters. Answer a is incorrect because Security Manager is used for setting up users and controlling security. Answer c is incorrect because Schema Manager is used for managing schema objects. Answer d is incorrect because Storage Manager is used for managing storage and rollback segments.

Question 3

At the operating system prompt, you enter the following command:

```
orapwd file = %ORACLE_HOME%\dbs\pwdORCL.ora
password = fred
```

Why does this command fail?

○ a. A valid value for the **entries** parameter has not been included in the command.

○ b. There is nothing wrong with the command. It will succeed.

○ c. The word "fred" is not a valid password.

○ d. There are spaces around the equal signs (=), which is not allowed.

Answer d is correct. Spaces are not allowed around the equal signs in the ORAPWD syntax. Answer a is incorrect because **entries** is the only optional parameter; it does not need to be specified. Answer b is incorrect; the command will fail because spaces are not allowed around the equal signs. Answer c is incorrect because Oracle does not place limitations on valid values for the **password** parameter. As long as "fred" is the password for SYS and INTERNAL, the value is valid. (Whether it is sensible is another issue altogether!)

Question 4

Which OEM application would you use to add a rollback segment to the rollback segment tablespace?

○ a. Instance Manager

○ b. Storage Manager

○ c. Schema Manager

○ d. Security Manager

Answer b is correct. Storage Manager is used for managing storage and rollback segments. Answer a is incorrect because Instance Manager is used for managing instances, sessions, startup, and shutdown, and for changing initialization parameters. Answer c is incorrect because Schema Manager is used for managing schema objects. Answer d is incorrect because Security Manager is used for setting up users and controlling security.

Question 5

> You set up password file authentication and set the **REMOTE_LOGIN_
> PASSWORDFILE** initialization parameter to **SHARED**. Which answers will
> be recognized by the password file? [Choose two]
>
> ❑ a. SYSDBA
>
> ❑ b. SYS
>
> ❑ c. SYSOPER
>
> ❑ d. SYSTEM
>
> ❑ e. INTERNAL

Answers b and e are correct. If you use the **SHARED** option, the password file recognizes only users SYS and INTERNAL. Answers a and c are incorrect because **SYSDBA** and **SYSOPER** are privileges, not accounts. Answer d is incorrect because SYSTEM can only be added to the password file if the REMOTE_LOGIN_PASSWORDFILE parameter is set to exclusive.

Question 6

> Why would you set the **REMOTE_LOGIN_PASSWORDFILE** initialization pa-
> rameter to **NONE**?
>
> ○ a. To use OS authentication
>
> ○ b. To use a password file for remote login
>
> ○ c. To force the Oracle server to verify a user's object privileges
>
> ○ d. To force the Oracle server to verify a user's system privileges

Answer a is correct. To allow users to connect to the database using OS authentication, set the REMOTE_LOGIN_PASSWORDFILE parameter to NONE. Answer b is incorrect because Oracle will not use a password file when REMOTE_LOGIN_PASSWORDFILE is set to NONE. Answers c and d are incorrect because the Oracle server will always verify a user's object or system privileges.

Question 7

> You have changed some database initialization parameters and added a tablespace. You now want to restart the database so the new parameters will take effect. Which OEM applications have you used to accomplish these tasks? [Choose two]
>
> ❏ a. Schema Manager
>
> ❏ b. Storage Manager
>
> ❏ c. Security Manager
>
> ❏ d. Instance Manager

Answers b and d are correct. Storage Manager is used for adding tablespaces, and Instance Manager is used for changing initialization parameters. Answer a is incorrect because Schema Manager is used for managing schema objects. Answer c is incorrect because Security Manager is used for setting up users, controlling security, and managing user privileges.

Question 8

> Which view would you use to see who has been granted the **SYSOPER** privilege?
>
> ○ a. **V$PWFILE_USERS**
>
> ○ b. **DBA_SYS_PRIVS**
>
> ○ c. **DBA_OBJ_PRIVS**
>
> ○ d. None of the above; users with the **SYSOPER** privilege are listed in the control file

Answer a is correct. **V$PWFILE_USERS** lists users who have been granted either the **SYSDBA** or **SYSOPER** privilege (or both). Answer b is incorrect because **DBA_SYS_PRIVS** displays information about system privileges (such as the **CREATE TABLE** privilege). Answer c is incorrect because **DBA_OBJ_PRIVS** lists object privileges (such as the ability to insert data into another user's table). Answer d is incorrect because users are not listed in the control file.

Need to Know More?

 Austin, David, Meghraj Thakkar, and Kurt Lysy. *Migrating to Oracle8i*. Sams Publishing, Indianapolis, IN, 1999. ISBN 0-6723-157-7. One of the most thorough treatments of migration I have ever seen, this book concentrates on the migration path rather than on the new features of the 8i release. Includes material on Enterprise Manager.

 Loney, Kevin, and Marlene Theriault. *Oracle8i DBA Handbook*. Oracle Press, Berkeley, CA, 1999. ISBN 0-07212-188-2. This book is a comprehensive guide and a must-have for all DBAs. Chapter 9 covers the use of the password file.

 Pascavage, Barbara Ann. *Oracle8i DBA: Network Administration Exam Cram*. The Coriolis Group, Scottsdale, AZ, 2001. ISBN 1-58880-046-6. See Chapter 4 for information on listeners.

 See the Oracle documentation that is provided on CD with the Oracle RDBMS software. Pertaining to this chapter specifically are the following documents:

Baylis, Ruth, and Joyce Fee. *Oracle8i Administrator's Guide*. Oracle Corporation, Redwood City, CA, 1999. This is the complete documentation of database administration tasks.

Hodge Smith, Jennifer. *Oracle Enterprise Manager Concepts Guide Release 2.1*. Oracle Corporation, Redwood City, CA, 1999. This guide is the complete documentation of OEM concepts.

Leverenz, Lefty, Diana Rehfield, and Cathy Baird. *Oracle8i Concepts*. Oracle Corporation, Redwood City, CA, 1999. This work is the complete documentation of Oracle concepts.

Lorentz, Diana. *Oracle8i Reference*. Oracle Corporation, Redwood City, CA, 1999. This document provides specific details on initialization parameters, data dictionary views, and database limits.

Oracle Corporation. *Oracle Enterprise Manager Administrator's Guide Release 2.1*. Oracle Corporation, Redwood City, CA, 1990. This guide describes the use of Enterprise Manager and its services from a DBA's perspective.

technet.oracle.com is Oracle's technical repository of information for clients.

 www.revealnet.com is the site where RevealNet Corporation provides Oracle administration reference software.

Managing an
Oracle Instance

Terms you'll need to understand:

- ✓ DB_NAME
- ✓ STARTUP
- ✓ SHUTDOWN
- ✓ Initialization parameter file
- ✓ V$SESSION
- ✓ SID and SERIAL# columns
- ✓ Alert log
- ✓ BACKGROUND_DUMP_DEST
- ✓ USER_ DUMP_DEST
- ✓ MAX_DUMP_FILE_SIZE
- ✓ SQL_TRACE

Techniques you'll need to master:

- ✓ Starting the Oracle instance and opening a database
- ✓ Closing a database and shutting down the Oracle instance
- ✓ Getting and setting parameter values
- ✓ Viewing session information and killing sessions
- ✓ Monitoring alert and trace files

The concept of an Oracle instance is often confused with that of an Oracle database. If you've been reading this book in sequence, you'll recall from Chapter 2 that an Oracle instance is composed of the system global area (SGA) and a set of background processes, some of which are mandatory and some of which are not. The database, on the other hand, is composed of the datafiles, redo log files, and control files.

All DBAs need to understand how to manage an Oracle instance. In this chapter, I'll cover the main management tasks, including creating the parameter file, setting parameter values, starting an instance and opening a database, closing a database and shutting down the instance, managing sessions, and monitoring the alert log and trace files.

Creating the Parameter File

The parameter file (sometimes referred to as init.ora, which was the file name used in earlier releases of the Oracle server) should not be considered part of an Oracle database. (Recall the strict definition of an Oracle database given previously: it's the datafiles, redo log files, and control files only.) However, it is still a very important file in the Oracle environment, because it contains the initialization parameters that are used to set up the sizes of the memory structures, the number of processes that can connect, and other important tuning information, as well as directories for trace files and the locations of the control files. Most parameters have default values, but those that you want to modify to suit your environment need to be referenced in the parameter file.

The parameter file is a text file, so you can edit it using whatever standard operating system editor you feel most comfortable with. On Unix systems, most DBAs probably use the vi editor; on NT systems, Notepad or WordPad is often used. Oracle provides you with a sample parameter file that you can use as a basis for your own file. This sample file has small, medium, and large values for the various parameters you may want to set. Unfortunately, these values are woefully inadequate because they are largely still the same settings as Oracle6, and so most DBAs recognize that they need to change these parameters.

By default, the parameter file is located in the $ORACLE_HOME/dbs directory on Unix boxes; in NT, the default location is %ORACLE_HOME%\database. The default name for the parameter file is init<*sid*>.ora on both Unix and NT, where <*sid*> is the system identifier for your database. If you have installed an Optimal Flexible Architecture (OFA)–compliant database (see Chapter 3 if you're not familiar with this), there is a directory tree under $ORACLE_BASE (%ORACLE_BASE% on NT) for administrative use, and the parameter files in the default directory may be simply pointers to the

$ORACLE_BASE/admin/<*sid*>/pfile/init.ora file. (This could be achieved using links on Unix systems or the **IFILE** parameter on NT systems.)

The parameter file is read only when the instance starts. Normally, this would mean that any changes you make to the parameter file wouldn't take effect until you bounced the instance. (*Bounce* is a colloquial term that's often used to refer to stopping and restarting the instance.) Thankfully, Oracle is making more of the parameters used to control the database and the instance dynamic. Thus, they can be changed using an **ALTER SYSTEM** command (more on this in the "Dynamic Initialization Parameters" section later in this chapter).

You can also view (and change, if you are connected as **SYSDBA**) the values of initialization parameters using Oracle Enterprise Manager (OEM). To do this, open the OEM Console, right-click on the database you want to configure, and then choose Edit Database from the context-sensitive menu. Alternatively, you can select the database to configure and then choose Edit Database from the Navigator menu. The screen shown in Figure 4.1 will appear. Click on the parameter you want to change, and then click in the Values column to enter a new value. Click on OK to save the changes.

This screen needs a bit more explanation. If you change a parameter value, you can do one of two things. You can select the Save As button to be prompted for the name of a stored configuration in the repository that the change will be loaded

Parameter Name	Value	Default	Dynamic	Category
O7_DICTIONARY_ACCESSIBILITY	TRUE	✔		Security and Auditing
active_instance_count		✔		OPS
always_anti_join	NESTED_LOO...	✔		Optimizer
always_semi_join	standard	✔		Optimizer
aq_tm_processes	0	✔	✔	Miscellaneous
audit_trail	NONE	✔		Security and Auditing
background_core_dump	partial	✔		Diagnostics and Statistics
background_dump_dest	D:\oracle\admi...		✔	Diagnostics and Statistics
backup_tape_io_slaves	FALSE	✔	✔	Backup and Restore
bitmap_merge_area_size	1048576	✔		Optimizer
blank_trimming	FALSE	✔		ANSI Compliance
buffer_pool_keep	400			Cache and I/O
buffer_pool_recycle		✔		Cache and I/O
commit_point_strength	1	✔		Distributed, Replication and Snapshot
compatible	8.1.0			Migration and Compatibility
control_file_record_keep_time	7	✔	✔	Redo log, Recovery and Control File
control_files	D:\oracle\orada...			Miscellaneous

Figure 4.1 Using OEM to change the values of initialization parameters.

in; this saves having multiple parameter files for the databases being managed by this repository. Alternatively, you can simply select the OK button. The effect now depends on whether the parameter is dynamic or not. In the Dynamic column, a checkmark indicates that the parameter is dynamic, whereas a blank indicates it is not. If the parameter is dynamic, the parameter is changed when you click on the Apply button. If the parameter is not dynamic, when you click on the Apply button, you will be prompted for the type of shutdown you want to occur so the change will take effect.

By now, you've probably noticed that there is no Apply button on this screen. You need to click on the OK button, which will return you to the Edit Database screen; that's where the Apply button is.

Table 4.1 provides some of the most commonly used parameters, a brief description of each, and their default values. (Note that these are 8.1.7 settings and that there may be minor differences from one point release to another.)

Table 4.1	Commonly used initialization parameters, their descriptions, and their default values.	
Parameter Name	**Default Value**	**Description**
ALWAYS_ANTI_JOIN	NESTED_LOOPS	Sets the algorithm that Oracle uses to evaluate anti-joins. (An anti-join returns rows that match a **NOT IN** subquery.)
ALWAYS_SEMI_JOIN	NESTED_LOOPS	Sets the algorithm that Oracle uses to evaluate semi-joins. (A semi-join returns rows that match an **EXISTS** subquery.)
AQ_TM_PROCESSES	0	Sets the number of Queue Monitor processes to monitor times in messages that specify expiration or time delay.
BACKGROUND_DUMP_DEST	Dependent upon operating system	Specifies the directory to which trace files generated by background processes are written, as well as the alert log for the database.
BUFFER_POOL_KEEP	None	Determines the size of the KEEP buffer pool, and optionally the number of least recently used (LRU) latches allocated to the KEEP buffer pool.
BUFFER_POOL_RECYCLE	None	Determines the size of the RECYCLE buffer pool, and optionally the number of LRU latches allocated to the RECYCLE buffer pool.

(continued)

Table 4.1   Commonly used initialization parameters, their descriptions, and their default values (continued).

Parameter Name	Default Value	Description
COMPATIBLE	8.0.0	Specifies the release with which the server must maintain compatibility. Features from releases since 8.0.0 cannot be used without changing this from the default.
CONTROL_FILES	Dependent upon operating system	Specifies the names and locations of the control files for the database.
DB_BLOCK_BUFFERS	48MB/ **DB_BLOCK_SIZE**	Specifies the number of database buffers in the default data buffer cache.
DB_BLOCK_SIZE	Dependent upon operating system	Specifies the size in bytes of an Oracle block for the database. It is read at database creation time and shouldn't be changed without re-creating the database (or database corruption could result).
DB_FILES	Dependent upon operating system	Specifies the number of database files that can be opened for this database. The default value is often around 30, which is usually far too low.
DB_NAME	None	Specifies a database name of up to eight characters. Checked against the same value in the control files when the database is started, and causes startup to fail if these do not match.
DB_WRITER_PROCESSES	1	Specifies the number of DBW*n* processes to start. You may need to modify this in heavy write systems that do not support asynchronous I/O.
EVENT	None	Sets a variety of events for debugging purposes. This should be used only at Worldwide Support's request.
HASH_AREA_SIZE	2 * **SORT_AREA_SIZE**	Specifies the maximum amount of memory to be used for hash joins.
HASH_JOIN_ENABLED	TRUE	Specifies whether the cost-based optimizer should consider the use of hash joins as a join method.

(continued)

Table 4.1	Commonly used initialization parameters, their descriptions, and their default values *(continued)*.	
Parameter Name	**Default Value**	**Description**
IFILE	None	Specifies an additional parameter file to read at startup. This is useful for including system-wide defaults that then need to be modified in only one location.
JAVA_POOL_SIZE	20,000KB	Specifies the size of the Java memory pool. If you aren't using Java, drop this value to 1MB or 2MB so as to not waste the memory.
JOB_QUEUE_PROCESSES	0	Specifies the number of SNP*n* processes, which are used to handle job execution, replication, and propagation in Advanced Queuing.
LARGE_POOL_SIZE	0 if parallel execution is not required and **DBWR_IO_SLAVES** is not set; otherwise, derived from a number of other parameters	Specifies the size of the large pool.
LOG_ARCHIVE_DEST_*n*	None	Specifies up to five log archive destinations. Valid only in Enterprise Edition and incompatible with the deprecated **LOG_ARCHIVE_DEST** parameter.
LOG_ARCHIVE_FORMAT	Dependent upon operating system	Specifies the default file name format when archiving is turned on. Variables can be used to pass in the thread number and the log sequence number.
LOG_ARCHIVE_START	**FALSE**	Specifies whether archiving should be automatic or manual. (**TRUE** indicates automatic.) Applicable only when the database is in **ARCHIVELOG** mode.
LOG_BUFFER	Dependent upon operating system	Specifies the size of the log buffer cache in bytes rather than Oracle blocks (in contrast to the data buffer cache).
MAX_DUMP_FILE_SIZE	**UNLIMITED**	Specifies the maximum size of trace files, not including the alert log.

(continued)

Table 4.1	Commonly used initialization parameters, their descriptions, and their default values *(continued)*.	
Parameter Name	**Default Value**	**Description**
MAX_ENABLED_ROLES	20	Specifies the maximum number of roles that a user can have enabled (including nested roles).
07_DICTIONARY_ ACCESSIBILITY	**TRUE**	Specifies that system privileges granted with the **ANY** option apply to system objects as well. For example, a user using the **INSERT ANY TABLE** command can insert rows directly into the data dictionary if this is set to **TRUE**. This is version 7 functionality, which is generally undesirable from a security perspective.
OPEN_CURSORS	50	Specifies the maximum number of open cursors a session can have at once.
OPTIMIZER_MODE	**CHOOSE**	Specifies the optimizer mode to use. **CHOOSE** indicates the use of the cost-based optimizer if there are statistics gathered on any table accessed in a SQL statement.
PROCESSES	Derived from **PARALLEL_MAX_ SERVERS**	Specifies the maximum number of operating system processes that can access the database simultaneously, including background processes.
REMOTE_LOGIN_ PASSWORDFILE	The value **NONE**	Specifies whether a password file is used for this database, and if so, how many databases can share one password file.
RESOURCE_LIMIT	**FALSE**	Specifies whether resource limits are enforced through the use of profiles.
ROLLBACK_SEGMENTS	None (public rollback segments will be used if you don't specify this)	Specifies the names of the private rollback segments to be brought online when the database is started.
SESSIONS	Derived by 1.1 * **PROCESSES** + 5	Maximum number of sessions (and therefore concurrent users) that can be created in the system.

(continued)

Table 4.1	Commonly used initialization parameters, their descriptions, and their default values *(continued)*.	
Parameter Name	**Default Value**	**Description**
SHARED_POOL_SIZE	64MB in 64-bit operating systems; 16MB in those that aren't	Specifies the size of the shared pool in bytes.
SORT_AREA_SIZE	Dependent upon operating system	Specifies the maximum amount of memory that Oracle will allocate to a sort.
SQL_TRACE	FALSE	Specifies that statistics will be gathered globally for the database to be used with SQL Trace. This is normally best done on a per session basis rather than globally for the whole database.
TIMED_STATISTICS	FALSE	Specifies whether time-related statistics are collected or not.
TRANSACTIONS	Derived by 1.1 * **SESSIONS**	Specifies the maximum number of concurrent transactions that can be executed.
USER_DUMP_DEST	Dependent upon operating system	Specifies where the server will create trace files on behalf of a user process.
UTL_FILE_DIR	None	Specifies directories that can be used for direct I/O in PL/SQL (specify multiple directories by repeating this parameter on adjacent lines).

Some syntax rules are enforced in the parameter file. If you don't meet these rules, the instance may fail to start up. The rules are:

➤ Comments are allowed. Comments are preceded by a pound sign (#), and anything from the # to the end of the line is considered a comment. This allows for inline comments as well.

➤ Parameters are not case sensitive. However, the values for some parameters may be case sensitive if the operating system is. For example, differences in case are significant in Unix for the **CONTROL_FILES** parameter, but they aren't in NT.

➤ Parameters can be listed in any order. They can even be listed multiple times, in which case the last value specified is the one that usually takes effect.

➤ Virtually all parameters are optional. Default values will be used if you don't specify a value.

➤ Parameter values that have spaces in them need double quotes.

➤ The equals sign (=) is used to separate the parameter name from its value.

➤ Parameters that can have multiple values, such as **ROLLBACK_SEGMENTS**, are generally enclosed in parentheses and delimited by commas. (The lesser-known alternative is to not use parentheses and delimit by spaces.)

➤ If a parameter listing is too long, you can use the continuation character (a backslash, "\") to continue to the next line.

Starting an Oracle Instance and Opening the Database

You can start an Oracle instance and open the database using either the OEM Console or the command line. In the OEM Console, you can right-click on the database you want to start and select Startup from the context-sensitive menu, as shown in Figure 4.2, or you can choose Edit Database from the Navigator menu.

Alternatively, you can connect as **SYSDBA** in SQL*Plus or Server Manager to start the database from the command line. (This is the approach that you would normally use to start the instance and open the database when the host machine starts, because you don't want to use an interactive tool like the Console at this time.)

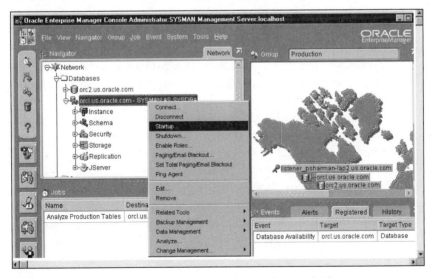

Figure 4.2   Using the OEM Console to start an instance and open a database.

Whichever option you choose, the process of starting an instance and opening a database has several stages. You can go through these separate stages one at a time, but you would normally go directly to the stage you want. The **STARTUP** command is used to start the instance and open the database. The command takes a number of options to indicate which stage you want to go to:

➤ **NOMOUNT**—This starts the instance only. The parameter file is read, the SGA allocated (based on the values for parameters for the various caches), the background processes are started, and the alert log and trace files for the various background processes are created. This stage is usually used for only two operations: creating a database or re-creating control files.

➤ **MOUNT**—In addition to the **STARTUP NOMOUNT** actions, **STARTUP MOUNT** causes the control files to be located and read to obtain the names and locations of the datafiles and redo log files that make up the database, as well as their statuses. However, no attempt is made to verify that these files are available yet. The database name is read from the control file and compared to that given in the **DB_NAME** parameter in the parameter file. If they match, the database is associated with the instance just started. It is at the **MOUNT** stage that certain specific operations need to occur: renaming files (which simply updates the control files to point to their new location), performing full database recovery, and turning on **ARCHIVELOG** mode for the database.

➤ **OPEN**—This is the default mode for the **STARTUP** command. In addition to the **STARTUP MOUNT** actions, **STARTUP OPEN** opens the database for normal users to connect to the database and perform data manipulations. It is at this stage that Oracle actually confirms that the datafiles and the redo log files are where the control files think they are. (If a file can't be located, an error is returned and the database remains in **MOUNT** mode, ready to perform file renaming operations.) Also at this stage, the log sequence number in the headers of the datafiles and the current redo log is compared to that in the control files to see if media recovery is needed. (Media recovery is normally needed because of disk failure, causing a DBA to recover lost files with old sequence numbers from backup. The logs between the old log sequence number and the current one need to be applied to bring the files into sequence with the rest of the database.) If necessary, the System Monitor (SMON) process will commence instance recovery now as well. Instance recovery is required if the instance has failed for any reason other than disk failure (such as in the event of power failure or operating system crashes). Instance recovery consists of two steps:

1. Roll forward recovery recovers any data that has been recorded in the redo log file but not in the datafiles. (This will include uncommitted data, which will be removed at the next step.) Once roll forward is complete, the database is available for normal use.

2. The uncommitted data recovered in Step 1 will be rolled back, either by the SMON process or by a normal server process that needs to access the block to be recovered before SMON gets around to recovering it.

The other options that you can specify in the **STARTUP** command are:

➤ FORCE—Performs a shutdown abort before starting the instance. This is the quickest way to shut down and restart the instance (useful, for example, when you need to quickly change a parameter in the parameter file), but it does require instance recovery on startup.

➤ PFILE=*<filename>*—Specifies a nondefault parameter file (that is, one that either uses a different naming convention or that's located in a different directory from the defaults) to be used to start the instance.

➤ RECOVER—Begins media recovery when the database starts. Most DBAs prefer to use the **RECOVER** command instead of **STARTUP RECOVER**, because it allows finer control of the recovery process.

➤ RESTRICT—Allows only users that have been granted the **RESTRICTED SESSION** privilege to connect to the database. This is useful when you want to perform administrative tasks without end users accessing the database (for example, reorganizing a tablespace).

Here's an example of the **STARTUP** command using some of these options:

```
STARTUP PFILE=/u01/oracle/admin/orc8i/pfile/initorc8i.ora RESTRICT
```

This example starts the instance, using values in the nondefault parameter file specified with **PFILE=** to size the various caches and so on; then, it mounts and opens the database, but it allows only those users with the **RESTRICTED SESSION** privilege to connect to the database.

Generally, in a production environment, you would configure the database to open automatically when the host machine starts. This is done in a Unix environment by setting the right values for entries in the oratab file (the location of this file varies from platform to platform, but it's generally either in /etc or /var/opt/oracle), and by putting the startup command into a file built in one of the directories where Unix looks for commands to execute when the machine starts. In NT, you need to go to Services (under Control Panel) and set the OracleService*<sid>* service to start automatically. You should also set the Registry value **ORA_<*sid*>_AUTOSTART** to **TRUE**.

I previously mentioned that you would normally take a database directly to the status you want. For example, you might issue the **STARTUP MOUNT** command to start the instance and mount (but not open) the database, so you could perform file renaming commands. From the **MOUNT** state, you cannot then issue a **STARTUP OPEN** command, because the instance is already started and the database mounted. Instead, you can either shut down the database (I'll discuss how this is done in the next section), or you can use the **ALTER DATABASE** command. You can either specify **ALTER DATABASE MOUNT** to move from the **NOMOUNT** stage to the **MOUNT** stage, or **ALTER DATABASE OPEN** to move from the **MOUNT** stage to the **OPEN** stage. When you open the database with this command, you can specify it in **READ WRITE** mode (the default, allowing users to change data) or **READ ONLY** mode (which restricts users from changing data).

Any database can be opened in **READ ONLY** mode, which can then be used to perform a number of useful operations, particularly offloading query processing from the production database to a standby database. (Standby databases are covered in the Oracle8i: Backup and Recovery OCP exam, so I won't go into them further here.) A database that is opened in **READ ONLY** mode can have queries executed against it, including queries that require disk sorts, provided that the user executing the query has had allocated to himself a default temporary tablespace that is a locally managed tablespace. You can also perform recovery of offline datafiles or tablespaces, and take datafiles online or offline with a **READ ONLY** database.

Closing a Database and Shutting Down an Instance

Closing an Oracle database and shutting down an instance simply reverses the process of starting an instance and opening a database. The database is closed and then dismounted, and the instance is then shut down. This can be performed in two ways: in the OEM Console, by right-clicking on the database you want to shut down and selecting Shutdown from the context-sensitive menu; or by choosing Edit Database from the Navigator menu, choosing the Shutdown radio button, and clicking on Apply to shut down the database, which results in the screen shown in Figure 4.3.

Alternatively, you can connect as **SYSDBA** in SQL*Plus or Server Manager to shut down the database from the command line. (This is the approach that you would normally use to close the database and stop the instance when the host

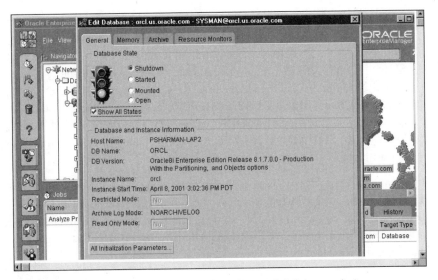

Figure 4.3 Using the OEM Console to close a database and shut down an instance.

machine shuts down, because you don't want to use an interactive tool like the Console at this time.)

Whichever option you choose, the process of closing a database and shutting down an instance also has several stages. The **SHUTDOWN** command is used to close the database and stop the instance. The command takes a number of options:

➤ **NORMAL**—This is the default option for the **SHUTDOWN** command. The **SHUTDOWN NORMAL** option prevents new connections from being made, waits for existing connections to disconnect, and—when all current sessions are closed—closes and dismounts the database and shuts down the instance. This is a clean shutdown that ensures that instance recovery is not required the next time the instance is started.

➤ **TRANSACTIONAL**—This option prevents new connections from being made, waits for existing sessions to finish their transactions, and then disconnects them. A **SHUTDOWN IMMEDIATE** (see the next option) is then performed. Again, this is a clean shutdown that ensures that instance recovery is not required the next time the instance is started.

➤ **IMMEDIATE**—This option prevents new connections from being made, but it then disconnects current sessions without waiting for them to complete. Any transactions that were being performed that have not been committed are rolled back, and the database is closed and dismounted, followed by an instance shutdown. Again, this is a clean shutdown that ensures that instance recovery is not required the next time the instance is started.

➤ **ABORT**—This option prevents new connections from being made, but it does not close or dismount the database. The instance is shut down without closing any of the files. Because uncommitted transactions are not rolled back, **SHUTDOWN ABORT** requires instance recovery when the instance is next started. Note that, in NT, if you have not set the **ORA_<sid>_SHUTDOWN%** parameters, then a **SHUTDOWN ABORT** is performed when the machine is shut down. You should set **ORA_<sid>_SHUTDOWN** to **TRUE** and **ORA_<sid>_SHUTDOWNTYPE** to **I** (immediate) to ensure that this doesn't happen.

If you want to bring the database down by stages, you can do this with the **ALTER DATABASE** command as well. You can use either the **ALTER DATABASE CLOSE** command to close an open database (but only if there are no sessions connected) or the **ALTER DATABASE DISMOUNT** command to dismount the database but leave the instance allocated.

Getting and Setting Parameter Values

You can determine what values parameters are set to in one of two main ways: by using the relevant dynamic performance view that is created when the database is created, or by using the **SHOW PARAMETER** command. The dynamic performance views (also known as fixed views) are continuously updated by Oracle, and they contain a lot of useful information for performance tuning. The views are also known as the **V$** views (the actual view names start with V_$, but Oracle creates a set of public synonyms that start with V$). These dynamic views can be thought of as windows into internal memory structures and the control files, and as such their contents are usually valid only from the last time the database was started. As a DBA, you will need to become quite familiar with them. Table 4.2 lists some of the more commonly used views and a brief description of each one.

Table 4.2 Dynamic perfomance views and their descriptions.	
View Name	**Description**
V$ACCESS	Displays objects that are currently locked and session information on the sessions accessing them.
V$ARCHIVE	Displays information on redo logs that are in need of archiving.
V$BACKUP	Displays the backup statuses of all online datafiles.
V$BGPROCESS	Displays the background processes started for the instance and their statuses.
V$BUFFER_POOL	Displays information on the buffer pools used by the instance.
V$CONTROLFILE	Provides the names, locations, and statuses of the control files.

(continued)

Table 4.2 Dynamic perfomance views and their descriptions *(continued)*.

View Name	Description
V$DATABASE	Displays database information from the control files.
V$DATAFILE	Displays information about the datafiles, including names, locations, and statuses from the control files.
V$DB_OBJECT_CACHE	Displays information about database objects that are currently cached in the library cache, including whether the object has been kept in the cache, the number of users currently locking the object, and the number of users currently pinning the object.
V$DISPATCHER	Displays information about the dispatcher processes, if they are present, including the amount of traffic through the dispatchers and their statuses.
V$FILESTAT	Displays read and write statistics for the datafiles.
V$FIXED_VIEW_DEFINITION	Contains the SQL statements that are used to define the dynamic performance views.
V$INSTANCE	Displays the state of the instance, including its status (such as **STARTED**), archiving status, and whether logins are currently allowed.
V$LATCH	Contains latch statistics.
V$LIBRARYCACHE	Displays performance statistics for the different namespaces in the library cache.
V$LOCK	Displays lock information for the database, as well as outstanding requests for locks.
V$LOG	Displays log information from the control files, including group number, sequence number, and archive status.
V$LOGFILE	Contains information about the individual redo log files, including the names and statuses of the redo log members.
V$LOG_HISTORY	Displays log history information from the control files, including log sequence number, lowest and highest system change numbers for the log files, and time of the first entry in the log files.
V$MTS	Contains information used to tune the Multithreaded Server architecture.
V$OPEN_CURSOR	Contains information on cursors that are currently open and parsed, including the username and the SQL text for the cursor.
V$OPTION	Displays the options that are installed for this database.
V$PARAMETER	Displays the initialization parameters and the values set for this instance.

(continued)

Table 4.2   Dynamic perfomance views and their descriptions (continued).

View Name	Description
V$PROCESS	Contains information about currently active processes, including the username and the program being executed.
V$PWFILE_USERS	Displays the users that have been granted either **SYSDBA** or **SYSOPER** for this database.
V$RECOVER_FILE	Contains the names of datafiles that are in need of media recovery.
V$ROLLSTAT	Contains statistics for the rollback segments, including the number of active transactions for each rollback segment, as well as the high-water mark and the number of bytes written to the rollback segment.
V$SESSION	Lists information on each session active in the database, including the session status, username, and command being issued.
V$SESSION_EVENT	Lists information on waits for an event by a session, including the name of the event, the total number of waits, and the total number of timeouts.
V$SESSION_LONGOPS	Displays information about a variety operations (including backup and recovery, statistics gathering, and query execution) that run for longer than six seconds in absolute time. This information includes the operation, the name of the target object for the operation, and statistical information.
V$SESSION_WAIT	Displays wait information for active sessions that are currently waiting, including the resource or event the session is waiting for.
V$SESSTAT	Displays statistics on an individual session basis, including statistic number and value.
V$SGA	Contains summary information for the SGA.
V$SGASTAT	Displays more detailed information for the SGA.
V$SHARED_SERVER	Contains information about the statuses and throughput for the shared server processes.
V$SQLAREA	Displays statistics for SQL statements that are in memory, parsed and ready for execution.
V$SQL	Contains the SQL statements that are in the SGA.
V$STATNAME	Lists the statistic names and numbers for the database. This can be joined to **V$SESSTAT** to provide more information on a per-session basis.
V$SYSSTAT	Lists system statistics, including the statistic name and value.
V$SYSTEM_EVENT	Contains information on total waits for an event.
V$SYSTEM_PARAMETER	Displays information about systemwide parameter settings.

(continued)

Table 4.2 Dynamic perfomance views and their descriptions *(continued)*.	
View Name	**Description**
V$TEMPFILE	Displays information about temp files, including file names and sizes.
V$TRANSACTION	Displays information about active transactions in the database, including undo block address information and transaction status.
V$WAITSTAT	Contains block contention statistics, including the class of block and a count of the number of waits. This view is updated only when **TIMED_STATISTICS** is turned on.

Note that some of these views are available when the instance is started (these are normally views that are based on memory structures), whereas others require that the database be mounted (normally these views are based on the control files).

Instead of using the relevant dynamic performance view to look at specific parameter values, you can use the **SHOW PARAMETER** command. This provides you with only the parameter values, rather than all the other information you can get from the dynamic performance views. In effect, what the command does is select from **V$PARAMETER**. You can either use the command like this

```
SQL> SHOW PARAMETER
```

without parameter names to get a list of all the parameters and their values, or you can pass the command a part of a parameter name, like this

```
SQL> SHOW PARAMETER archive
```

```
NAME                            TYPE    VALUE
------------------------------- ------  ---------------------
log_archive_dest                string
log_archive_dest_1              string
log_archive_dest_2              string
log_archive_dest_3              string
log_archive_dest_4              string
log_archive_dest_5              string
log_archive_dest_state_1        string  enable
log_archive_dest_state_2        string  enable
log_archive_dest_state_3        string  enable
log_archive_dest_state_4        string  enable
log_archive_dest_state_5        string  enable
log_archive_duplex_dest         string
log_archive_format              string  ARC%S.%T
log_archive_max_processes       integer 1
log_archive_min_succeed_dest    integer 1
```

```
log_archive_start                   boolean FALSE
log_archive_trace                   integer 0
standby_archive_dest                string  %ORACLE_HOME%\RDBMS
```

to get a list of all the parameters that have the string "archive" somewhere in their name.

Dynamic Initialization Parameters

Some of the initialization parameters can be set dynamically, rather than having to edit the initialization parameter file and restart the instance for them to take effect. This can be done in three different ways:

➤ Use the **ALTER SYSTEM** command to globally change a parameter value. The new value will be in effect either until the instance is restarted or until another **ALTER SYSTEM** command is issued to change the same parameter. Remember that the **ALTER SYSTEM** command does not write to the parameter file, so any changes you make using **ALTER SYSTEM** will be lost when you next bounce the instance. If you want the change to be permanent, you must edit the parameter file and change the relevant value there as well.

➤ Use the **ALTER SYSTEM DEFERRED** command. This command will globally reset a parameter value, but the new value effects only those sessions that connect after the command is issued.

➤ Use the **ALTER SESSION** command to change a parameter value for the current session only.

The best way to show you the effect of these commands is through an example. Let's look at some parameters before they are changed, the commands used to change them, and the effect on their values in the data dictionary. First, this query will show you the values for the parameters I am about to change:

```
SQL> SELECT name, isdefault, isses_modifiable, issys_modifiable,
  2  ismodified, isadjusted, value FROM v$parameter
  3  WHERE name IN ('timed_statistics',
  4                 'sort_area_size',
  5                 'hash_area_size');
```

NAME	ISDEFAULT	ISSES	ISSYS_MOD	ISMODIFIED	ISADJ	VALUE
timed_ statistics	TRUE	TRUE	IMMEDIATE	FALSE	FALSE	FALSE
sort_area_ size	FALSE	TRUE	DEFERRED	FALSE	FALSE	65536
hash_area_ size	TRUE	TRUE	FALSE	FALSE	FALSE	131072

Now let's change these values. The commands I use are these:

```
SQL> alter system set timed_statistics=true;
System altered.

SQL> alter system set sort_area_size=248000 deferred;
System altered.

SQL> alter session set hash_area_size=131072;
Session altered.
```

Now let's look at the values in the data dictionary again:

```
SQL> SELECT name, isdefault, isses_modifiable, issys_modifiable,
  2  ismodified, isadjusted, value FROM v$parameter
  3  WHERE name IN ('timed_statistics',
  4                 'sort_area_size',
  5                 'hash_area_size');
```

NAME	ISDEFAULT	ISSES	ISSYS_MOD	ISMODIFIED	ISADJ	VALUE
timed_statistics	TRUE	TRUE	IMMEDIATE	SYSTEM_MOD	FALSE	TRUE
sort_area_size	FALSE	TRUE	DEFERRED	FALSE	FALSE	65536
hash_area_size	TRUE	TRUE	FALSE	MODIFIED	FALSE	131072

Notice the effect here. The first command sets the value of **ISMODIFIED** to **SYSTEM_MOD** for the parameter **TIMED_STATISTICS**. The second command doesn't change the value of **ISMODIFIED** for the parameter **SORT_AREA_SIZE** at all because I have not run the select statement as a new connection. The third command sets **ISMODIFIED** to **MODIFIED** for the parameter **HASH_AREA_SIZE**. However, the column **ISDEFAULT** hasn't changed for the **TIMED_STATISTICS** and **HASH_AREA_SIZE** parameters, even though the values are now nondefault. The other two columns that are of interest here are **ISSES_MODIFIABLE** and **ISSYS_MODIFIABLE**. **ISSES_MODIFIABLE** shows whether the parameter can be changed with an **ALTER SESSION** command (**TRUE** means it can be changed, and **FALSE** means it can't). **ISSYS_MODIFIABLE** shows whether the parameter can be changed with an **ALTER SYSTEM** command (**IMMEDIATE** means it can be changed, **DEFERRED** means it can be changed but will affect only new sessions, and FALSE means it cannot be changed).

Another alternative to querying **V$PARAMETER** is to query **V$SYSTEM_ PARAMETER**. This view is made up of similar columns, but **V$PARAMETER** shows the current session value whereas **V$SYSTEM_PARAMETER** shows the current system value.

Managing Sessions

As a DBA, you sometimes need to restrict access to the database to allow you to perform database maintenance, such as reorganizing a tablespace. Although you could do this by restarting the instance in restricted mode, there is a more attractive alternative that requires you to have an understanding of how to terminate sessions. This method has three steps:

1. Put the database into restricted mode, using the **ALTER SYSTEM EN-ABLE RESTRICTED SESSION** command.

2. Terminate existing user connections. You can now perform the database maintenance.

3. Take the database out of restricted session mode, using the **ALTER SYS-TEM DISABLE RESTRICTED SESSION** command.

Let's look at these steps in more detail.

Enabling **RESTRICTED SESSION**

The ability to put a database into restricted mode to perform maintenance is more attractive than having to restart the instance in restricted mode because it means the buffer caches aren't cleared. Thus, there could be less of a performance impact, because the buffer caches are "pre-warmed." To use the **ALTER SYSTEM** command to enable or disable a restricted session, you must have the **RESTRICTED SESSION** privilege.

This privilege can be useful when you want to check if maintenance has been successful. For example, some organizations use the concept of an "owner-manager." This is the end user in charge of the application, who can be considered the real owner of the data (something a DBA never is). When you perform maintenance on an application, granting this user **RESTRICTED SESSION** means that they can log on to the application and check that the maintenance has been successful. Previously, this could be done only by granting the end user the DBA role, which is never ideal.

To place a database in restricted mode, you need to issue the **ALTER SYSTEM ENABLE RESTRICTED SESSION** command. But that's not the whole story. The effect of this command is that future connections to the database are blocked for all users that don't have the **RESTRICTED SESSION** privilege. Existing connections aren't affected, regardless of whether the users currently logged on have the **RESTRICTED SESSION** privilege. (Of course, this means you now get to perform one of the most enjoyable operations a DBA has to do—terminating user sessions. I'll cover that in more detail next.

Terminating User Sessions

To terminate a user's session, you use the **ALTER SYSTEM** command again, but now the syntax is:

```
ALTER SYSTEM KILL SESSION <sid>, <serial#>;
```

where:

➤ *<sid>* is the value of the **SID** (Session ID) column in **V$SESSION** for the user you want to remove.

➤ *<serial#>* is the value of the **SERIAL#** column in **V$SESSION** for the user you want to remove.

You need to pass the command both parameters to ensure that you remove the right user. Because the value of the **SID** column is reused, it's possible that you may find this information, but by the time you issue the command, the user you wanted to remove could have logged off and someone else could have logged on and received the same SID. The combination of **SID** and **SERIAL#** is, however, guaranteed to be unique.

To determine the values of these columns, you can simply run a select on the **V$SESSION** view, like this:

```
SQL> SELECT sid, serial# FROM v$session
  2  WHERE username = 'FRED';

       SID    SERIAL#
---------- ----------
        12         32
```

The only time you run into any problems with this is when you have multiple users connecting to the database with the same username. In this case, you need to select further columns (like **TERMINAL** or **PROGRAM**) to differentiate them.

The effect of issuing the **KILL SESSION** command is to signal PMON to clean up the killed session. PMON rolls back any uncommitted transactions, and it releases any locks and SGA resources still held by the terminated session.

The **KILL SESSION** command terminates an active session immediately, and the user receives an ORA-00028 error message that states, "Your session has been killed." If the session is not active (for example, if the user is in "think" mode), then the ORA-00028 error message is returned when the user attempts to issue the next SQL command.

Disabling **RESTRICTED SESSION**

To remove a database from restricted mode, you issue the **ALTER SYSTEM DISABLE RESTRICTED SESSION** command. Normal users can now connect to the database and perform their day-to-day work. You can check whether a database is in restricted mode by looking at the **V$INSTANCE** view. If the database is in restricted mode, the **LOGINS** column will show a value of **RESTRICTED**.

Monitoring Alert and Trace Files

The alert log and trace files provide important information about error conditions and other statuses for the database. The alert log is one of the first places where a DBA starts looking when there is an error, so you need to be familiar with it. The trace files provide more detailed information about specific errors that have occurred with the background processes. They can also be generated by server processes at the request of users.

The alert log has default naming and location conventions that vary based on your operating system. On Unix systems, for example, the alert log is called alert_<*sid*>.log and is located under $ORACLE_HOME/rdbms/log. On NT systems, the file name is <*sid*>alrt.log and is located under %ORACLE_BASE%/ADMIN/<*SID*>/BDUMP (provided you have installed an OFA-compliant database). These default locations can be overwritten by setting the initialization parameter **BACKGROUND_DUMP_DEST**. This parameter controls the location of both the alert log and the trace files for the background processes. Trace files produced by server processes are controlled by the parameters **USER_DUMP_DEST** (for the location), **MAX_DUMP_FILE_SIZE** (for the maximum file size), and **SQL_TRACE**. (Setting **SQL_TRACE** to **TRUE**, which can also be done dynamically, allows the creation of trace files by server processes.) Note that the **MAX_DUMP_FILE_SIZE** parameter does not control the size of the alert log or the size of the background process trace files.

Monitoring the alert log is an important part of a DBA's job. If you have the Enterprise Manager optional packs installed, one of the events you can ask to have monitored is information written to the alert log. (This is not available without the optional packs.) An alert status is sent if any of the following errors are written to the alert log (any other ORA errors will signal a warning status):

➤ *ORA-00060 errors*—Deadlocks

➤ *ORA-006** errors*—Internal Oracle exceptions

➤ *ORA-01578 errors*—Data block corruptions

One job you need to perform regularly is removing the alert log. Because it is a chronological file, it simply grows and grows. On a periodic basis, you should copy the file somewhere else (in case you later become aware of a problem that you need to look up in a previous alert log) and then delete the alert log. Oracle will simply create a new file when it next attempts to write to the alert log, so you don't need to shut the database down for this. You could even set this up as a job in Enterprise Manager if you want.

Practice Questions

Question 1

> If you want to rename multiple datafiles that make up the SYSTEM tablespace, which startup mode would you use to start an instance?
>
> ○ a. **OPEN**
>
> ○ b. **NOMOUNT**
>
> ○ c. **MOUNT**
>
> ○ d. **RENAME**

Answer c is correct. To rename datafiles that make up the SYSTEM tablespace, the database needs to be started in **MOUNT** mode. Answer a is incorrect because **OPEN** opens the online datafiles and redo log files and detects if instance recovery is necessary. It is the default mode for instance startup. Answer b is incorrect because **NOMOUNT** starts an instance, reads the parameter file, allocates memory for the SGA, starts the background processes, and opens the alert logs and trace files. Answers a and b are also incorrect because SYSTEM datafiles can't be renamed in the **OPEN** or **NOMOUNT** modes. Answer d is incorrect because **RENAME** is an invalid mode.

Question 2

> Which initialization parameter specifies the location of the alert file?
>
> ○ a. **BACKGROUND_DUMP_DEST**
>
> ○ b. **USER_DUMP_DEST**
>
> ○ c. **CORE_DUMP_DEST**
>
> ○ d. **LOG_ARCHIVE_DEST**

Answer a is correct. **BACKGROUND_DUMP_DEST** specifies the location of the alert file and the background trace files. Answer b is incorrect because **USER_DUMP_DEST** specifies the location of user trace files. Answer c is incorrect because **CORE_DUMP_DEST** specifies the directory where core files are dumped. Answer d is incorrect because **LOG_ARCHIVE_DEST** specifies the default location of the disk file or tape device when archiving redo log files.

Question 3

What information is written to a background process trace file?

○ a. Sequence generator cache

○ b. Initialization parameters used at instance startup

○ c. Date and time of the last full backup

○ d. Information about background process failures

Answer d is correct. Trace files record information about background process failures. These files are useful when trying to determine the cause of a failure. Answer a is incorrect because the sequence generator cache is stored in the SGA. Answer b is incorrect because initialization parameters are written in the alert file. Answer c is incorrect because backup time is not written in the trace file and can be found in different locations depending on the backup method.

Question 4

Using SQL*Plus, what methods could you use to display the current locations of the control files? [Choose four]

❏ a. Use the **SHOW SGA** command.

❏ b. Query **V$CONTROLFILE**.

❏ c. Use the **DESCRIBE** command.

❏ d. Query **V$PARAMETER**.

❏ e. Query **V$SYSTEM_PARAMETER**.

❏ f. Use the **SHOW PARAMETER** command.

Answers b, d, e, and f are correct. **V$CONTROLFILE** displays the names and locations of the control files, **V$PARAMETER** displays the current settings of any parameter, and **V$SYSTEM_ PARAMETER** displays the systemwide setting of any parameter. In Server Manager, you can view the current parameter values by using the **SHOW PARAMETER** command. Answer a is incorrect because the **SHOW SGA** command displays SGA information for the current instance. Answer c is incorrect because the **DESCRIBE** command describes tables, views, and other database objects.

Question 5

> Your database is mounted and you need to make it available for normal database operations. Which SQL*Plus command should you use?
>
> ○ a. **ALTER SYSTEM OPEN**
>
> ○ b. **ALTER SESSION OPEN**
>
> ○ c. **ALTER DATABASE NOMOUNT**
>
> ○ d. **ALTER SESSION MOUNT**
>
> ○ e. **ALTER DATABASE OPEN**

Answer e is correct. To change the state of the database from **MOUNT** to **OPEN**, use the **ALTER DATABASE OPEN** command. Answers a, b, c, and d are incorrect because **ALTER SYSTEM OPEN, ALTER SESSION OPEN, ALTER DATABASE NOMOUNT,** and **ALTER SESSION MOUNT** are all invalid commands.

Question 6

> Which shutdown mode shuts down the instance but does not dismount the database?
>
> ○ a. **IMMEDIATE**
>
> ○ b. **NORMAL**
>
> ○ c. **ABORT**
>
> ○ d. **TRANSACTIONAL**

Answer c is correct. Aborting the database stops all processes immediately. The database does not perform a checkpoint or close files. An instance recovery will be required on **STARTUP**. Answer a is incorrect because **SHUTDOWN IMMEDIATE** rolls back uncommitted transactions and dismounts the database. Answer b is incorrect because **SHUTDOWN NORMAL** waits for processes to disconnect and dismount the database. Answer d is incorrect because **SHUTDOWN TRANSACTIONAL** waits for current transactions to finish before dismounting the database.

Question 7

What is the effect of the following SQL*Plus command?

```
ALTER SYSTEM SET SORT_AREA_SIZE=327680 DEFERRED;
```

- ○ a. **SORT_AREA_SIZE** will be altered immediately.
- ○ b. **SORT_AREA_SIZE** will be set to 327680 when the next sort operation occurs.
- ○ c. **SORT_AREA_SIZE** cannot be set with an **ALTER SYSTEM** command.
- ○ d. **SORT_AREA_SIZE** will be set to 327680 for all future sessions.

Answer d is correct. The **DEFERRED** option will change the **SORT_AREA_ SIZE** for all future sessions. Answer a is incorrect because the new **SORT_ AREA_SIZE** will affect only future sessions, and an immediate change would affect current sessions. You could be tricked into answer b because, if the next sort operation is done by a new session, it would use the new value 327680; however, there's also a chance that the next sort operation will be done in the same session. Answer c is incorrect because this parameter can be changed with an **ALTER SYSTEM** command.

Question 8

Which shutdown mode waits for all current users to disconnect before shutting down the instance?

- ○ a. **NORMAL**
- ○ b. **ABORT**
- ○ c. **IMMEDIATE**
- ○ d. **TRANSACTIONAL**

Answer a is correct. **SHUTDOWN NORMAL** waits for processes to disconnect while not allowing new connections. Once all connections are disconnected, the database will shut down. **NORMAL** is the default shutdown mode. Answer b is incorrect because aborting the database stops all processes immediately; the database does not perform a checkpoint or close files. An instance recovery will be required on **STARTUP**. Answer c is incorrect because **SHUTDOWN**

IMMEDIATE rolls back uncommitted transactions and dismounts the database. Answer d is incorrect because **SHUTDOWN TRANSACTIONAL** waits for current transactions to finish before dismounting the database.

Question 9

> Which shutdown mode requires instance recovery when the instance is next started?
>
> ○ a. **IMMEDIATE**
>
> ○ b. **NORMAL**
>
> ○ c. **TRANSACTIONAL**
>
> ○ d. **ABORT**

Answer d is correct. **SHUTDOWN ABORT** closes the instance but leaves the database files untouched, so instance recovery is needed to roll back the uncommitted transactions that were left hanging in the database. Answers a, b, and c are incorrect because **SHUTDOWN IMMEDIATE, SHUTDOWN NORMAL,** and **SHUTDOWN TRANSACTIONAL** all shut down the database cleanly, so there is no need for instance recovery the next time the instance starts.

Need to Know More?

Theriault, Marlene, Rachel Carmichael, and James Viscusi. *Oracle DBA 101*. Oracle Press, Berkeley, CA, 2000. ISBN 0-07212-120-3. This book is an excellent introduction to life as an Oracle DBA. Chapters 9 and 10 and Appendix C provide information on the dynamic performance views.

Wong, Debbie. *Oracle8i DBA: Backup and Recovery Exam Cram*. The Coriolis Group, Scottsdale, AZ, 2001. ISBN 1-58880-045-8. Consult Chapter 14 for information on standby databases.

Yuhanna, Noel. *Oracle8i Database Administration*. Manning Publications Company, Greenwich Connecticut, 1999. ISBN 1-88477-788-3. This book provides a series of how-to's, including how to automatically start Oracle when the machine is restarted and how to see the values for your initialization parameters.

See the Oracle documentation that is provided on CD with the Oracle RDBMS software. Pertaining to this chapter are:

Baylis, Ruth, and Joyce Fee. *Oracle8i Administrator's Guide*. Oracle Corporation, Redwood City, CA, 1999. This is the complete documentation of database administration tasks.

Leverenz, Lefty, Diana Rehfield, and Cathy Baird. *Oracle8i Concepts*. Oracle Corporation, Redwood City, CA, 1999. This provides complete documentation of Oracle concepts.

Lorentz, Diana. *Oracle8i Reference*. Oracle Corporation, Redwood City, CA, 1999. Here you can get specific details on initialization parameters, data dictionary views, and database limits.

Oracle Corporation. *Oracle Enterprise Manager Administrator's Guide Release 2.1*. Oracle Corporation, Redwood City, CA, 1990. This document describes the use of Enterprise Manager and its services from a DBA's perspective.

technet.oracle.com is Oracle's Web site, which provides technical content for clients.

www.revealnet.com is the site of RevealNet Corporation, and it provides Oracle administration reference software.

Creating a Database

Terms you'll need to understand:

- ✓ Database Configuration Assistant (DBCA)
- ✓ **CONTROL_FILES**
- ✓ **DB_BLOCK_SIZE**
- ✓ **DB_NAME**
- ✓ **LOGFILE**
- ✓ **MAXLOGFILES**
- ✓ **MAXLOGMEMBERS**
- ✓ **MAXLOGHISTORY**
- ✓ **MAXDATAFILES**
- ✓ **ARCHIVELOG**
- ✓ **NOARCHIVELOG**
- ✓ **CHARACTER SET**
- ✓ **NATIONAL CHARACTER SET**
- ✓ **DATAFILE**

Techniques you'll need to master:

- ✓ Planning properly for creating a database
- ✓ Using the Database Configuration Assistant to create a database
- ✓ Using the **CREATE DATABASE** command to manually create a database
- ✓ Dropping a database

One of the most important tasks that a DBA performs is creating a database. The only time that certain parameters, such as the database's character set and block size, can be set is when the database is created. So you need to invest some time in the planning stages before creating the database itself.

Before You Create a Database

Depending on your installation selections, you may have already created a database when you installed the kernel. You can either modify this database for continued use or you can create a fresh one. Most DBAs tend to create a fresh database after the installation, when they have had time to think about some of the important decisions that need to be made when creating a database. As I just mentioned, certain parameter settings need to be set before the database is created. If you set these incorrectly, the only way you can change them is to either re-create the database or re-create the control file.

You also need to carefully consider the best placement of database files on disk. The placement of these files can affect the database's performance and manageability, so it needs to be done properly. Oracle recommends that—at the very least—you should have mirrored the redo log files and the control files on separate disks. If one disk should fail, you will still have a working copy of these files on another disk that you can relatively easily switch to. You should also consider the size requirements of the database, including the system objects, tables, indexes, rollback segments, temporary segments, and other objects.

Creating a Database

Once you've decided upon the file layout, file sizes, and parameter settings, you're ready to create the database. This can be done in one of two ways. Oracle provides you with the Database Configuration Assistant (DBCA), a GUI tool that prompts for the values for various settings before creating the database for you. The other option is to create the database manually, using the same SQL commands that DBCA does. The manual method is particularly useful if you want to script the database creation for later execution. Let's look at each of these separately in the following sections.

The Database Configuration Assistant (DBCA)

Using the DBCA is probably the simplest method to create a database. Indeed, if all you need is a very basic configuration, you can simply start the DBCA as part of the installation and accept the defaults as you go through the tool and end up with a working Oracle database. However, DBCA can also be used for more advanced configurations if DBAs want to have more control over the database creation.

Starting the DBCA is very straightforward. If you're creating a database on an NT system, you simply choose the Database Configuration Assistant option under Programs|Oracle_Home|Database Administration. If you're creating a database in Unix, you need to start an X session, then type in "dbca" at the operating system prompt. From then on, the screens are the same in either environment.

Figure 5.1 shows the first screen when you start the DBCA. You have three options from this screen:

➤ *Create A Database*—Choose this option to either create a typical database (that is, with minimal user input) or a custom database (that is, customizing to allow greater control over the database creation).

➤ *Change Database Configuration*—Choose this option to configure installed options that have not previously been configured for use with your database, such as Time Series, Spatial, JServer, interMedia, Visual Information Retrieval, and Advanced Replication.

➤ *Delete A Database*—Choose this option to delete all the database files for an existing database (except the parameter file).

To create a database, choose the first option. You will then be presented with a choice of proceeding with either a pretuned database or a custom configuration. The pretuned database allows you to either copy a preconfigured database from

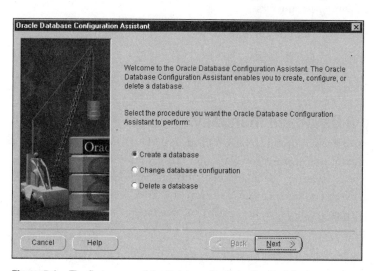

Figure 5.1 The first screen of the Database Configuration Assistant.

the Oracle installation CD or to create new database files. (Creating new database files will obviously take longer, but it's useful if you don't have access to the installation CD.)

If you choose to create new database files, you're prompted for the primary application type for the database (Online Transaction Processing, Data Warehousing, or both), the typical number of concurrent users, the global database name and system identifier (SID), and the Oracle options that you wish to install. One advantage of choosing this path is that you are then prompted to either create the database immediately or save the database creation steps to a file, which you can then run later when the system is using fewer resources. In addition, choosing to create new database files allows Oracle to customize some of the parameter settings based on the amount of memory available for your computer.

If you choose the custom configuration path rather than a pretuned database, you'll have much greater control over the process of creating a database. However, choosing the custom configuration also means that you need a correspondingly greater amount of knowledge about the database to be able to select the correct values for the settings you'll be prompted for. The settings you are prompted for include:

➤ Data, control, and redo log file settings

➤ Tablespace sizes

➤ Extent sizes

➤ Instance memory parameters

➤ Archiving formats and destinations

➤ Trace file destinations

➤ Character set values

Creating a Database Manually

Although it's extremely useful to have a GUI tool like DBCA to help create a database, you still might want to create one manually for several reasons. For example, if you're creating a database on a Unix box and don't have access to X Windows or X-emulation software, you can't run DBCA. In any case, from a theoretical perspective, it is always useful to know what operations are performed behind the scenes of a GUI tool.

The following steps guide you through the manual creation of a database:

1. Decide on an instance name, database name, and database character set.

2. Prepare the operating system environment.

3. Configure the parameter file.

4. Create a password file.

5. Start the instance.

6. Create the database.

Let's look at each of these in more detail.

Decide on an Instance Name, Database Name, and Database Character Set

The instance name and database name should be unique for the system. Naming these should be relatively straightforward, because most sites have the instance name and the database name set to the system identifier (SID) value, and they use a naming convention that's based on the environment. For example, you may have a DEV instance for Development, ACC for Acceptance Testing, and PROD for Production if you have a relatively simple environment with a single production database. If you have more than one production database, you may want to differentiate them using a simple naming convention like PRD81A, PRD81B, and so on, where *PRD* stands for *Production*, *81* tells you this is an Oracle8.1 version database, and the use of *A*, *B*, and so forth ensure that the database name is unique.

Likewise, in many cases, the database character set is easily determined. Many sites have no need for multibyte character sets or special characters to be stored in the database, so the default value of US7ASCII is often sufficient. You should consult the National Language Support (NLS) documentation if you need to use a database character set other than the default. (NLS is covered in more detail in Chapter 14.)

Prepare the Operating System Environment

The way you set up the operating system environment before creating the database depends on the particular operating system you are working with. On a Unix box, you need to set a number of environment variables, including (in order of importance):

➤ ORACLE_HOME—The location of the Oracle kernel.

➤ ORACLE_SID—The instance name (needs to be unique for this machine).

➤ ORACLE_BASE—Although not required, this is used as part of an installation that is compliant with Optimal Flexible Architecture (OFA).

➤ ORA_NLS33—This is required only when creating a database with a character set that is not US7ASCII. It points to the location of the NLS character set data.

On an NT box, Oracle uses the Registry in a similar fashion to the use of environment variables on Unix. When the installation completes, the default value of ORACLE_SID on NT is ORCL. If you want to create a new database, you must change this value with the SET command at the MS-DOS command prompt (SET ORACLE_SID=<*new_SID_name*>). If you're creating a database manually, you need to become familiar with the use of the ORADIM utility, but this is not necessary if you're using DBCA. The exam doesn't cover the ORADIM utility, which is used to create, start, stop, modify, and delete instances (but not the associated database files) at the MS-DOS command prompt, so I won't cover it any further here.

Configure the Parameter File

The initialization parameter file, which was covered in Chapter 4, contains the initialization parameters that are used to set up the sizes of the memory structures, the number of processes that can connect, and other important tuning information, as well as directories for trace files and the locations of the control files. As mentioned in Chapter 4, Oracle provides you with a sample parameter file that you can use as the basis of your own file. Keep in mind, though, that you'll need to change some settings that need to be unique for the database being created. In particular, you should set the following three parameters:

► CONTROL_FILES—This parameter is a list of the control files that Oracle will write to once the database is created. They don't actually exist yet because you haven't created the database. Oracle will create these files when creating the database.

► DB_BLOCK_SIZE—This parameter sets the size of the blocks used in the Oracle database. The main reason for setting this now is because it can't be changed after the database is created without re-creating either the database or the control file.

► DB_NAME—This parameter is the database identifier. It needs to match the database name specified in the CREATE DATABASE statement (and will also be stored in the control files). If the database name in the control files and the DB_NAME parameter don't match, Oracle will not start the database.

Create a Password File

If you're going to use password file authentication rather than OS authentication (see Chapter 3 for more details on each of these), now is the time to create the password file. Doing so will allow you to use password file authentication for the next two steps. (OS authentication can also be used.)

Start the Instance

You now need to connect as **SYSDBA** and perform a **STARTUP NOMOUNT**. This will start the instance only. (Because you don't have a database yet, it doesn't make much sense to try anything else.) If you've created a parameter file that is not in the default location, be sure to specify the **PFILE** clause to point to the correct parameter file.

Create the Database

To create a database, you need to use the **CREATE DATABASE** command. In its very simplest form, all you need to do is use the syntax:

```
SQL> create database;
Database created.
```

This will use defaults for everything. Of course, this is not an optimally tuned and configured database, so let's look at the **CREATE DATABASE** syntax in more detail. The syntax for the command is shown in Figure 5.2.

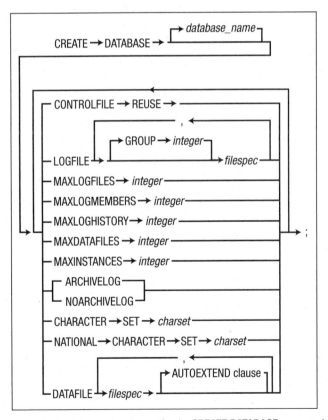

Figure 5.2 The complete syntax for the **CREATE DATABASE** command.

CREATE DATABASE is the only mandatory part of the command; *database_name* is optional. If you don't specify the database name, Oracle takes the value from the **DB_NAME** parameter in the parameter file. If you do specify the database name, it should match the value of the **DB_NAME** parameter.

You need to pay particular attention to several clauses in the **CREATE DATABASE** command:

➤ **CONTROLFILE REUSE**—You need to specify this clause only if you're re-creating a database and want to overwrite the existing control file. If you leave this clause out and any of the files given in the **CONTROL_FILES** parameter exist, Oracle will return an error.

➤ **LOGFILE** *filespec*—This clause identifies the redo log files that will be created for this database. Note that you can (and should) specify multiple redo log files in different groups with the syntax provided here.

➤ **MAX*** clauses—These clauses all set maximum numbers for different limits. The important ones to be aware of here are **MAXLOGFILES** (the maximum number of redo log file groups that can ever be created for the database), **MAXLOGMEMBERS** (the maximum number of members for a redo log group), and **MAXDATAFILES** (the maximum number of datafiles that can ever be created for the database). If you set any of these **MAX*** limits too low, the only way to change them after the database has been created is to re-create the control file. Higher limits do increase the size of the control files, but that's not generally too much of a concern.

➤ **ARCHIVELOG|NOARCHIVELOG**—Most DBAs will not specify **ARCHIVELOG** when creating a database, because doing so generates many archive logs to ensure that the database can be recovered. Because no application data is actually created with the **CREATE DATABASE** command, most DBAs will simply re-create the database at this stage if something goes wrong, rather than recover it. Once the database is completely created, you can consider turning on **ARCHIVELOG** mode. If you do create the database in **ARCHIVELOG** mode and the database creation mysteriously stops, check the archive log destination directory to make sure it's not full.

➤ **CHARACTER SET** and **NATIONAL CHARACTER SET**—These clauses are often left at the default values. **CHARACTER SET** defines the character set that the database uses to store data, and it cannot be changed without re-creating the control file. **NATIONAL CHARACTER SET** specifies the character set used to store **NCHAR**, **NCLOB**, or **NVARCHAR2** column values. See Chapter 14 for more details.

➤ DATAFILE—This clause identifies the file specification for the datafile (or datafiles) that make up the SYSTEM tablespace. As with any datafiles, you can also specify **AUTOEXTEND** for the SYSTEM tablespace. (See Chapter 8 for more details on the **AUTOEXTEND** clause.)

Here's an example of a **CREATE DATABASE** command that I used to create a database using Oracle8i version 8.1.7 on NT:

```
SQL> CREATE DATABASE orc2
  2  LOGFILE GROUP 1 ('E:\oracle\oradata\orc2\redo01a.log',
  3                   'F:\oracle\oradata\orc2\redo01b.log')
  4          SIZE 10240K,
  5          GROUP 2 ('E:\oracle\oradata\orc2\redo02a.log',
  6                   'F:\oracle\oradata\orc2\redo02b.log')
  7          SIZE 10240K,
  8          GROUP 3 ('E:\oracle\oradata\orc2\redo03a.log',
  9                   'F:\oracle\oradata\orc2\redo03b.log')
 10          SIZE 10240K
 11  MAXLOGFILES 32
 12  MAXLOGMEMBERS 5
 13  MAXLOGHISTORY 100
 14  MAXDATAFILES 254
 15  DATAFILE 'D:\oracle\oradata\orc2\system01.dbf' SIZE 264M
 16  AUTOEXTEND ON NEXT 10240K;
```

This command creates a database named ORC2, putting the SYSTEM tablespace on disk D, with three redo log groups mirrored on disks E and F for optimal recoverability, performance, and manageability. I have given the files meaningful names, and the files all follow OFA naming conventions. I've also increased the **MAX*** database limits to reasonable values for this database, based on experience of what these settings will need to be for the database being created.

Issuing the **CREATE DATABASE** command results in a database that contains the following:

➤ The SYSTEM tablespace, composed of the datafiles specified in the **DATAFILE** clause of the command

➤ One or more control files, based on the values specified in the **CONTROL_FILES** parameter

➤ Two or more redo log files, based on the values specified in the **LOGFILE** clause of the command

➤ The SYSTEM rollback segment, contained in the SYSTEM tablespace

➤ The user SYS with a password of CHANGE_ON_INSTALL

➤ The user SYSTEM with a password of MANAGER

➤ Low-level internal tables created by the SQL.BSQ script, but no data dictionary (see Chapter 6 for more details on data dictionary creation)

Dropping a Database

Although you use the **CREATE DATABASE** command to create a database in Oracle, there is no corresponding **DROP DATABASE** command to remove a database. When using DBCA, it's very easy to delete a database that you no longer want. You simply start DBCA and, on the first screen (refer back to Figure 5.1), choose Delete A Database and select Next. You will then be provided with a list of available SIDs that you can choose to delete. All database files will be deleted for the SID you choose. (Be careful you select the right one.)

If you want to drop a database manually, you will need to locate all the files that make up the database using the following command:

```
SQL> SELECT name FROM v$datafile
  2    UNION
  3    SELECT member FROM v$logfile
  4    UNION
  5    SELECT name FROM v$controlfile;
```

You will then need to use the relevant OS commands to remove all the files listed in the output from the above statement.

Practice Questions

Question 1

What is the minimum recommended control file configuration?

- ○ a. One file
- ○ b. Two files on the system disk
- ○ c. Two files on separate disks
- ○ d. Three files placed on the same disk as the SYSTEM tablespace
- ○ e. Three files placed on separate disks

Answer c is correct. Oracle recommends that you have at least two copies on separate disks, even though only one control file is required to create a database. To mirror the control file, shut down the database, alter the **CONTROL_FILES** initialization parameter, copy an existing control file to the mirror location, and restart the database. Maintaining more than two control files can be done, but the question specifically asks for the minimum. Keeping extra copies of control files on separate disks rather than having them all on one disk guards against the loss of the control file in the event of media failure.

Question 2

Why does the control file need to be re-created when the **MAXDATAFILES** parameter is changed?

- ○ a. To update it with the new datafiles
- ○ b. To reallocate the space needed for the parameter
- ○ c. To update it with the current version of the parameter file
- ○ d. To update it with any changes made to any of the initialization parameters

Answer b is correct. Oracle allocates space within the control file for **MAXDATAFILES**. The control file must be re-created, because more space must be allocated within it, when you change the following parameters:

➤ MAXLOGFILES

➤ MAXDATAFILES

➤ MAXINSTANCES

➤ MAXLOGMEMBERS

➤ MAXLOGHISTORY

Because space in the control file is preallocated, it's not necessary to re-create the file to update changes made to the database structure, as in answers a, c, and d.

Question 3

You issue a **CREATE DATABASE** command that fails because you attempted to create log files that already existed. Which answers will solve the problem so you can reissue the command? [Choose two]

❑ a. Change the **REUSE** options in the **LOGFILE** parameter of the **CREATE DATABASE** command.

❑ b. Shut down the instance and change the **SIZE** option to **REUSE** in the **LOGFILE** parameter of the **CREATE DATABASE** command.

❑ c. Issue the **DROP DATABASE** command and change the **SIZE** option to **REUSE** in the **LOGFILE** parameter of the **CREATE DATABASE** command.

❑ d. Shut down the instance, delete any datafiles created by the **CREATE DATABASE** command, and change the **SIZE** option to **REUSE** in the **LOGFILE** parameter of the **CREATE DATABASE** command.

❑ e. Shut down the instance, delete any datafiles created by the **CREATE DATABASE** command, and delete the log files that failed to create.

Answers d and e are correct. In the case of answer d, the log files already existed, so the **CREATE DATABASE** command must not have used the **REUSE** option in the **SIZE** clause. By using the **REUSE** option in the **SIZE** clause, the create error can be avoided. Alternatively, deleting the files as in answer e will also eliminate the error. After you issue a **CREATE DATABASE** command that fails, you should perform the following steps:

1. Shut down the instance.

2. Delete any files created by the failed **CREATE DATABASE** command.

3. Correct the error in the **CREATE DATABASE** command.

4. Restart the instance.

The other answers are incorrect because they do not follow this sequence. Also, **DROP DATABASE** is an invalid command. This is a tricky question because the answers are mutually exclusive, which might throw you off.

Question 4

What must be true for the following **CREATE DATABASE** command to be successful?

```
CREATE DATABASE mydb
  CONTROLFILE REUSE
  MAXLOGFILES 5
  MAXLOGMEMBERS 5
  MAXDATAFILES 75
  MAXLOGHISTORY 75
DATAFILE '/u03/oracle/mydb/system.dbf'
SIZE 10M
LOGFILE
GROUP 1 '/u01/oracle/mydb/log1a.rdo',
        '/u02/oracle/mydb/log1b.rdo' SIZE 10M,
GROUP 2 '/u01/oracle/mydb/log2a.rdo',
        '/u02/oracle/mydb/log2b.rdo' SIZE 10M;
```

- ○ a. The datafile must exist and be 10MB in size.
- ○ b. The log files must exist.
- ○ c. **/u03** must be able to hold **MAXDATAFILES**.
- ○ d. The control files specified in the parameter file must exist.
- ○ e. The user must have **SYSOPER** privileges to create the log files and datafiles.

Answer d is correct. Because the **CREATE DATABASE** command uses the **CONTROLFILE REUSE** option, the control files listed in the parameter file will be reused (and therefore must exist). Answer a is incorrect; the datafile should not exist because the **REUSE** option is not used. Answer b is incorrect because the log files do not need to exist. Answer c is incorrect because **MAX DATAFILES** is a parameter that sets a limit of datafiles for the database, but there's no requirement that the datafiles reside on any particular disk. Answer e is incorrect because a user with the **SYSOPER** role cannot create a database (the **SYSDBA** role is needed for this).

Question 5

> Which clause specifies the names of the redo log files in a **CREATE DATABASE** command?
>
> ○ a. **LOGFILE**
> ○ b. **MAXLOGFILES**
> ○ c. **MAXLOGMEMBERS**
> ○ d. **MAXLOGHISTORY**
> ○ e. **CONTROLFILE REUSE**

Answer a is correct. In the **CREATE DATABASE** command, the **LOGFILE** parameter specifies the number for the **LOGFILE** groups and the names and locations of the redo log files in each group. Answer b is incorrect because the **MAXLOGFILES** parameter determines the maximum number of groups of online redo log files per database. Answer c is incorrect because the **MAXLOGMEMBERS** parameter determines the maximum number of members per group. Answer d is incorrect because **MAXLOGHISTORY** specifies the maximum number of archived redo log files for automatic media recovery of Oracle with the Parallel Server option. Answer e is incorrect because the **CONTROLFILE REUSE** clause names a control file to overwrite and reuse.

Question 6

> What happens if the database name in the parameter file does not match the name in the control file when you issue the **STARTUP** command?
>
> ○ a. An instance would start, and the database would go into recovery mode.
> ○ b. An instance would start, but the database would not be mounted.
> ○ c. The instance would not start.
> ○ d. An instance would start and the database would be mounted, but it would not be opened.

Answer b is correct. When a database is created, the database name is specified in the **CREATE DATABASE** command, and this name must match the **DB_NAME** parameter in the parameter file. The database will not mount if the database name recorded in the control file does not match the database name in the **STARTUP** command or parameter file. Answer a is incorrect; because the instance did not attempt to mount the database, it is not necessary to go into recovery mode. Answers c and d are incorrect because the instance would start, but the database would not mount because of the mismatch between the database names.

Question 7

What should a DBA do before using the **CREATE DATABASE** command? [Choose three]

- ❑ a. Connect as **SYSDBA**.
- ❑ b. Create a control file.
- ❑ c. Start up an instance.
- ❑ d. Create a database user.
- ❑ e. Create a parameter file.
- ❑ f. Start an instance and **MOUNT** the database.

Answers a, c, and e are correct. Before using the **CREATE DATABASE** command, the DBA should have created an initialization parameter file, connected as **SYSDBA**, and started up an instance in **NOMOUNT** mode. Answers b and d are incorrect because the control file and database users are created as a result of running the **CREATE DATABASE** command. Answer f is incorrect because the database is mounted after it is created.

Need to Know More?

 Devraj, Venkat S. *Oracle 24×7 Tips and Techniques*. Oracle Press, Berkeley, CA, 2000. ISBN 0-07211-999-3. Chapter 7 takes you beyond some of the simpler steps I've covered here to set up a well-configured database.

 Loney, Kevin, and Marlene Theriault. *Oracle8i DBA Handbook*. Oracle Press, Berkeley, CA, 1999. ISBN 0-07212-188-2. This book is a comprehensive guide and a must-have for all DBAs. Chapter 1 includes information pertinent to this chapter.

 See the Oracle documentation that is provided on CD with the Oracle RDBMS software. Pertaining to this chapter are:

Baylis, Ruth, and Joyce Fee. *Oracle8i Administrator's Guide*. Oracle Corporation, Redwood City, CA, 1999. This guide is the complete documentation of database administration tasks.

Leverenz, Lefty, Diana Rehfield, and Cathy Baird. *Oracle8i Concepts*. Oracle Corporation, Redwood City, CA, 1999. This is the complete documentation of Oracle concepts.

Lorentz, Diana. *Oracle8i Reference*. Oracle Corporation, Redwood City, CA, 1999. This reference guide provides specific details on initialization parameters, data dictionary views, and database limits.

Lorentz, Diana. *Oracle8i SQL Reference*. Oracle Corporation, Redwood City, CA, 1999. This reference guide provides the complete syntax for all the SQL commands, including the **CREATE DATABASE** command.

 www.revealnet.com is the site where RevealNet Corporation provides Oracle administration reference software.

Data Dictionary Views, Standard Packages, and Trigger Types

6

. . . .

Terms you'll need to understand:

✓ Standard packages

✓ catalog.sql

✓ **USER_*** dictionary views

✓ **ALL_*** dictionary views

✓ **DBA_*** dictionary views

✓ catproc.sql

✓ Database event triggers

Techniques you'll need to master:

✓ Constructing the data dictionary views

✓ Querying the data dictionary

✓ Preparing the PL/SQL environment using administrative scripts

✓ Administering stored procedures and packages

✓ Listing database event trigger types

The data dictionary is a set of base tables that is created when the database is created. If you use the Database Configuration Assistant (DBCA) to create a database, it will automatically create the data dictionary views and standard packages that every Oracle database needs to operate correctly, but if you use the **CREATE DATABASE** command to manually create a database, you will have to create the database views and standard packages yourself.

The tables of the data dictionary are owned by the SYS account and stored in the SYSTEM tablespace. Because the data in these tables is cryptic and the interrelationships among tables are almost impossible to understand, three categories of data dictionary views are built to allow access to the underlying data dictionary base tables. These views interpret and display the information in the data dictionary for users and DBAs in a format that is much easier to understand. This chapter describes the three categories of views, how they are used, and which Oracle scripts create them.

In addition to the data dictionary views, Oracle creates a set of standard packages that both Oracle itself and database users use to perform certain actions within the Oracle database. Therefore, you need to know which Oracle scripts enable these features and which standard packages are created. You also need to understand the creation and use of database event triggers. These types of triggers execute specific actions when a particular database event occurs, such as **STARTUP** or **SHUTDOWN**.

Constructing the Data Dictionary Views

One of the most important aspects of an Oracle database is its data dictionary, which can be thought of as Oracle's metadata. In other words, it's data about data: who the users are in this database, what objects they own, who can access these objects, and so on. This data is kept in a set of base tables that composes the data dictionary. The script that is used to create the base data dictionary tables is called sql.bsq. It is located under $ORACLE_HOME/rdbms/admin on Unix boxes and %ORACLE_HOME%/rdbms/admin on NT boxes, and it's automatically executed when you issue the **CREATE DATABASE** command. Oracle specifically designed the base data dictionary tables in a way that makes it very difficult to use them directly; in fact, they are supposed to be read-only (as far as most users are concerned). Any updates to these tables are issued by the Oracle server whenever Data Definition Language (DDL) commands are executed.

 Be aware that, for the exam, you'll be expected to say that the data dictionary tables are read-only and that you cannot update them directly. As most DBAs know, however, this is not strictly true, but for the purposes of the exam, you should think of the data dictionary as read-only.

The base data dictionary tables are obfuscated to make it difficult to apply direct updates to them, but because they are the only place where Oracle keeps its metadata, it's imperative that DBAs should have a way to elucidate the information that is kept in them. For example, if I asked you what the data dictionary table **FET$** was for, you would probably be hard pressed to provide an answer. However, if I told you that the data dictionary view **DBA_FREE_SPACE** was based on the **FET$** table, you'd probably be able to guess what it was really used for. (In case you haven't guessed it, FET is an abbreviation of "free extents.")

To clarify the information in the base data dictionary tables, Oracle allows you to build a set of data dictionary views on the base data dictionary tables. These views make the data in the base tables more readable, sometimes by adding joins or other **WHERE** clauses to the base table definitions. For example, some data dictionary views can be used to view object names. In the base tables, you might see only object numbers, making it more difficult to understand which objects are being referenced.

The data dictionary views are built using the catalog.sql script, located under $ORACLE_HOME/rdbms/admin on Unix boxes and %ORACLE_HOME%/rdbms/admin on NT boxes. This script must be executed as SYS or when connected as SYSDBA (because this effectively changes your schema to SYS).

The catalog.sql script is one of the best-documented scripts I have encountered. It includes comments that document what every view is used for, and also what every column in every view is used for. If you don't have access to the Oracle documentation, catalog.sql can be the best place to learn what a particular view or column within a view is used for.

The catalog.sql script not only creates the data dictionary views, but it also creates public synonyms for these data dictionary views, and grants select access on the views to either **PUBLIC** or the **SELECT_CATALOG_ROLE** role, depending on the data dictionary view. (Roles are covered in more detail in Chapter 13.)

Querying the Data Dictionary

The data dictionary has three main uses:

> *Oracle itself uses the data dictionary to obtain information.* For example, if you attempt to insert data into a table, Oracle issues recursive SQL against the data dictionary to ensure you have the right privileges to do so, that there is sufficient storage for the data to be inserted, and so on.

➤ *Oracle updates the data dictionary whenever DDL is issued.* For example, if you create a table, information about the table is inserted into the **TAB$** and **COL$** base data dictionary tables (in addition to others).

➤ *Users of an Oracle database use the data dictionary as a reference.* You can query the data dictionary views using SQL just as you would any other table in the database (but note that some of the views are available to privileged users only, whereas others are available to any user).

The data dictionary views can be divided into three main categories, based on the level of information that is available within them:

➤ **USER_***—Contains information that pertain to the user that you're currently logged in as. For example, if you wanted to get a list of the tables that you own, you would query the **USER_TABLES** data dictionary view.

➤ **ALL_***—Contains information about objects you own, objects you have been granted access to, or objects that have **PUBLIC** access. For example, if you are logged in as user SCOTT and user FRED has granted you access to his **JOBS** table, you could query the **ALL_TABLES** data dictionary view to see this. If you queried **USER_TABLES** instead, you would see only those objects owned by SCOTT, not the **JOBS** table.

➤ **DBA_***—Contains database-wide information about objects. For example, if you are logged in as a privileged user, you could query the **DBA_TABLES** data dictionary view to see all tables created in the database. These **DBA_*** views are the views you need to become most familiar with, both in your day-to-day life as a DBA and to pass the OCP exams. (See Table 6.1 for a list of the most commonly used **DBA_*** views and their descriptions.)

All three categories have public synonyms created for each data dictionary view. However, you still need to be specifically granted access to the **DBA_*** views to be able to access them. The **DBA_*** and **ALL_*** views all have an **OWNER** column to allow you to determine the owner of the object being looked at. (Clearly, there's no need for an **OWNER** column in the **USER_*** views because they display information that's relevant only to the user you're logged on as.) Note that a few data dictionary views do not follow this sort of naming convention.

If you're ever stuck and can't remember the name of a data dictionary view, you can find this information in several places. Obviously, you can look it up in the Oracle documentation. The data dictionary views are documented in full detail in *Oracle8i Reference* (see the end of the chapter for full bibliographic details). An alternative that you always have access to in an Oracle database is to query the **DICTIONARY** and

DICT_COLUMNS data dictionary views. **DICTIONARY** (or simply **DICT**) lists all the data dictionary views, with a comment on the use of each view. **DICT_COLUMNS** lists all the data dictionary views, the column names within each view, and a comment on each column explaining the use of the column.

Table 6.1   The most commonly used DBA_* views and their descriptions.

View Name	Description
DBA_ANALYZE_OBJECTS	Lists all objects that have been analyzed, including the owner, the object name, and the object type.
DBA_BLOCKERS	Shows the session ID for sessions that are blocking other sessions by holding a lock on an object the other sessions want.
DBA_CLUSTERS	Describes all clusters in the database, including the cluster name, storage information, and cluster type.
DBA_COL_PRIVS	Lists all column level object grants in the database, including the owner of the object, object name, and privilege granted.
DBA_COLL_TYPES	Shows information on all collections (arrays, nested tables, object tables, and so on) in the database, including the collection name, collection type, and datatype information.
DBA_CONS_COLUMNS	Describes all columns in the database that are specified in the definitions of constraints, including the owner of the constraint, the table the constraint is defined on, and the columns that make up the constraint.
DBA_CONSTRAINTS	Lists all constraints for the database, including constraint name and type.
DBA_DATA_FILES	Provides information on all datafiles for the database, including the file name, tablespace name the datafile belongs to, status, and autoextensibility.
DBA_DB_LINKS	Describes links to other databases, including the link name and Net8 host string.
DBA_DDL_LOCKS	Lists all DDL locks in the database and any outstanding request for a DDL lock, including the owner and name of the lock, the mode the lock is held in, and the mode requested.
DBA_DEPENDENCIES	Provides information on dependencies between objects, such as procedures, packages, and functions, including the owner and name of the object, and the owner and name of the referenced object.
DBA_DIMENSIONS	Lists all dimensions in the database, including the dimension name and status.

(continued)

Table 6.1   The most commonly used DBA_* views and their descriptions (continued).

View Name	Description
DBA_DIRECTORIES	Provides information on all the directory objects in the database, including the directory name and operating system path for the directory.
DBA_DML_LOCKS	Lists all DML locks in the database and any outstanding request for a DML lock, including the owner and name of the lock, the mode the lock is held in, and the mode requested.
DBA_ERRORS	Provides information about errors on stored objects, such as procedures, functions and packages, including the error text and the position.
DBA_EXTENTS	Lists information on all extents for segments within the database, including the names of the segment and tablespace associated with the extent and sizing information.
DBA_FREE_SPACE	Provides information on all the chunks of free space in the database, including the name of the tablespace containing the free space and size information.
DBA_IND_COLUMNS	Details the columns that are used in indexes on tables and clusters for the database, including column names and positions, and the index and table names.
DBA_IND_PARTITIONS	Provides partition level information for each partitioned index in the database, including partition, index and tablespace names, partition bound values, and storage information.
DBA_IND_SUBPARTITIONS	Provides partition level information for each subpartitioned index in the database, including subpartition, index and tablespace names, and storage information.
DBA_INDEXES	Lists all indexes on tables and clusters in the database, including index name and type, uniqueness, and storage information.
DBA_JOBS	Describes all jobs submitted in the database, including schema information for the job submitter and job executor (these can be different), execution times, and job status.
DBA_JOBS_RUNNING	Provides information on all currently executing jobs in the database, including the job ID, a count of the number of failures for the job, and execution times.
DBA_LIBRARIES	Provides information on all libraries in the database, including library name and status, and operating system file specification associated with the library.
DBA_LOB_PARTITIONS	Displays information on partitioned LOBs (large objects) in the database, including LOB and partition names, storage information, and whether the LOB data partition is stored inline.

(continued)

Table 6.1   The most commonly used DBA_* views and their descriptions (continued).

View Name	Description
DBA_LOBS	Lists all **CLOB** (character large object) and **BLOB** (binary large object) columns defined for the database, including the LOB name, caching information, and whether the LOB is stored inline or not.
DBA_LOCKS	Lists all latches or locks held in the database, and information on outstanding requests for a latch or lock, including the lock type, mode held, mode requested, and whether the lock is blocking.
DBA_MVIEWS	Provides information on all materialized views in the database, including the materialized view name, the query that defines the materialized view, and whether the view is updatable.
DBA_OBJECT_TABLES	Describes all object tables for the database, including the table name, storage information, and whether the table is partitioned.
DBA_OBJECTS	Provides information on all objects in the database ("objects" here refers to schema objects, not just object types), including the object name, type, and status.
DBA_OUTLINES	Describes all outlines for the database, including the outline name and whether it has been used or not.
DBA_PART_HISTOGRAMS	Provides histogram data for all histograms on table partitions in the database, including the table and partition names, and histogram endpoint values.
DBA_PART_INDEXES	Provides partitioning information on all partitioned indexes in the database, including index name, partitioning or subpartitioning type, and number of partitions in the index.
DBA_PART_TABLES	Provides partitioning information on all partitioned tables in the database, including table name, partitioning or subpartitioning type, and number of partitions in the indexes.
DBA_POLICIES	Describes all security policies for the database, including the policy name and function, and security checking information.
DBA_PROFILES	Lists all profiles defined for the database and the limits set for each one, including profile name, resource name, and limit for that resource.
DBA_QUEUE_TABLES	Describes all queue tables defined in the database, including queue table name and type, and messaging sorting and recipient information.
DBA_QUEUES	Provides information on the operational characteristics of all the queues in the database, including the queue name, the queue table the queue resides in, time information, and whether the queue is enabled for messages to be added or deleted from the queue (or both).

(continued)

Table 6.1   The most commonly used DBA_* views and their descriptions (continued).

View Name	Description
DBA_REFRESH	Lists information on all the refresh groups defined in the database, including the refresh group name, information on the job that automatically refreshes the group, and the rollback segment used while refreshing the group.
DBA_REFS	Describes all the **REF** columns and **REF** attributes in object type columns for all objects in the database, including the table name and **REF** column name, and whether the **REF** column is scoped.
DBA_REPAIR_TABLE	Provides information on any corruptions found when executing the **DBMS_REPAIR.CHECK_OBJECT** procedure, including the name and tablespace of the corrupt object, corruption type, and location.
DBA_ROLES	Lists all the roles that are defined in the database, giving the role name and whether the role is password protected.
DBA_ROLE_PRIVS	Provides information on privileges granted to roles and users, including the name of the user or role receiving the grant, and whether the grant can be passed on.
DBA_ROLLBACK_SEGS	Provides information on all the rollback segments defined in the database, including the segment and tablespace name, and storage information.
DBA_RSRC_CONSUMER_GROUPS	Lists all resource consumer groups in the database, including the name and status of the resource group, as well as the CPU resource allocation method.
DBA_RSRC_PLANS	Provides information on all resource plans in the database, including the name and status of the resource plan, as well as the CPU resource allocation method.
DBA_SEGMENTS	Describes all segments in the database, including segment name and type, tablespace name, and storage information.
DBA_SEQUENCES	Lists all sequences in the database, including sequence name and owner, minimum and maximum values, number the sequence is incremented by, and cache information.
DBA_SNAPSHOTS	Provides information on all snapshots in the database, including snapshot and master table name, name of the database link to the master site, and a flag for whether the snapshot is complex.

(continued)

Table 6.1   The most commonly used DBA_* views and their descriptions (continued).

View Name	Description
DBA_SOURCE	Provides the source code for all stored objects in the database, including packages, procedures, and functions.
DBA_SYNONYMS	Describes all synonyms in the database, including the synonym name and owner, and the name and owner of the referenced object.
DBA_SYS_PRIVS	Lists all system privileges that have been granted to users or roles, including the name of the user or role receiving the privilege, the privilege name, and whether it can be granted to others.
DBA_TAB_COLUMNS	Lists columns for all tables, clusters, and views in the database, including the column name and datatype, the default value for the column (if it has one) and whether the column can be null.
DBA_TAB_HISTOGRAMS	Describes histograms on all tables in the database, including the table name and histogram endpoint values.
DBA_TAB_PARTITIONS	Provides partition level information for all partitioned tables in the database, including partition, table, and tablespace names, partition bound values, and storage information.
DBA_TAB_PRIVS	Lists grants on all objects (not just tables) for the database, including grantor and grantee, object granted access to, and type of access granted.
DBA_TAB_SUBPARTITIONS	Provides information on all subpartitions on tables in the database, including subpartition, table, and tablespace names, and storage information.
DBA_TABLES	Describes all relational tables in the database, including the table and tablespace name, and storage information.
DBA_TABLESPACES	Lists information on all tablespaces in the database, including tablespace name, storage information, extent management type, and tablespace status.
DBA_TEMP_FILES	Provides information on all tempfiles for the database, including the tempfile and tablespace name, autoextensibility, and storage information.
DBA_TRIGGERS	Describes all triggers in the database, including trigger name and type, triggering event, the type of the base object on which the trigger is defined, and the trigger status.
DBA_TS_QUOTAS	Provides information on all tablespace quotas in the database, including the tablespace name, name of the user with the quota, and the amount of space that the user can use.

(continued)

Table 6.1	The most commonly used DBA_* views and their descriptions (continued).
View Name	**Description**
DBA_TYPES	Describes all object types in the database, including the type name and the number of methods and attributes in the type.
DBA_USERS	Lists information on all users defined in the database, including username, account status, default and temporary tablespaces allocated to the user, and profile defined for the user.
DBA_VIEWS	Describes all views in the database, including the view name and text of the query that defines the view.
DBA_WAITERS	Provides information on all sessions that are waiting for a lock, including session IDs for both the waiter and the holding session, the lock type, mode held, and mode requested.

In addition to these data dictionary views, an Oracle database contains a set of dynamic performance tables or views. Oracle interchangeably uses the terms *dynamic performance tables* and *dynamic performance views* to refer to these objects. It's probably best to think of them as views, because they are not true tables. (In fact, these views can be thought of as windows into the control file and memory structures within the SGA, because that's where they actually get their information from.)

These dynamic performance views all have names that start with "V$", so you often hear them referred to as **V$** views as well. Generally, only privileged users can access them. They are owned by SYS, and as a DBA you can select from them, grant select access on them to other users, and even create your own views on top of them. You can't, however, update the data in them (even thinking about the ramifications of directly updating memory structures in the SGA is enough to send shivers down my spine), nor can you drop the views. You use the dynamic performance views to monitor and tune the database, so you will need to become very familiar with them as a DBA.

Different **V$** views can start being accessed at different stages of starting the database, depending on the underlying structure that the views are based on. For example, **V$SGA** (based on memory structures in the SGA) can be queried when the instance is started but the database is not mounted. However, **V$DATAFILE** (based on the control file) is not available until the instance is started and the database is mounted. For more information on the commonly used **V$** views that you're likely to run into on the test, refer back to Table 4.2 in Chapter 4.

Preparing the PL/SQL Environment

Much of the functionality that Oracle uses internally and that you will use as a DBA is provided through the use of PL/SQL stored program units. The definition and use of stored program units (procedures, functions, and packages) is covered in detail in the first exam in the OCP-DBA track (Exam 1Z0-001, "Introduction to Oracle: SQL and PL/SQL"), so I won't cover it in detail here. Instead, this section looks at how you need to prepare the Oracle database to be able to execute these PL/SQL program units.

To prepare an Oracle database to execute PL/SQL, you need to execute the script catproc.sql. This script is executed automatically for you when you create a database using the Database Configuration Assistant, but you'll need to execute it yourself when you create a database manually using the **CREATE DATABASE** command.

Note: You may need to run other scripts, depending on your environment and the Oracle options you have installed. These are listed in Chapter 5, "SQL Scripts," of Oracle8i Reference (see the end of the chapter for full bibliographic information).

Note that you need to execute the catproc.sql script regardless of whether you intend to use PL/SQL program units within an application. As I mentioned previously, the PL/SQL program units provide much of the Oracle's internal functionality, so if you don't execute the catproc.sql script when you create a database manually, the Oracle database won't function properly, nor will some of the tools that you use to administer it. For example, the Export and Import utilities will not execute without catproc being run first.

You may need to execute the catalog.sql and catproc.sql scripts after a patch or upgrade to the Oracle kernel. This can be done without damaging the database, so don't worry about causing unforeseen errors.

Like the catalog.sql script, catproc (and almost all the other scripts covered in this section) needs to be executed when connected as SYS. The location of these scripts is the same as that of catalog.sql ($ORACLE_HOME/rdbms/admin on a Unix box, and %ORACLE_HOME%\rdbms\admin on an NT box). The catproc.sql script simply calls many other scripts. There's not much point in remembering what all these scripts are, because they can vary from release to release. You simply need to remember that the end result is to create PL/SQL functionality and to extend RBDMS functionality in the database.

The administrative scripts that create this functionality can be broken down into four categories:

➤ *cat*.sql*—These scripts create data dictionary views. Matching catno*.sql scripts can be used to drop the data dictionary views created by the corresponding cat*.sql script. (For example, cataudit.sql creates data dictionary views dealing with database auditing; catnoaud.sql drops these views.)

➤ *dbms*.sql and dbms*.plb*—These scripts build database packages. The different file extensions simply tell you whether the script is plain text (dbms*.sql) or wrapped PL/SQL code (dbms*.plb). See Table 6.2 for more details on some of these packages.

➤ *prvt*.plb*—These scripts build package code, and in some cases they execute grant statements for the packages. Again, these are wrapped PL/SQL files.

➤ *utl*.sql*—These scripts create views and tables for some of the utilities that Oracle provides you with to monitor, tune, and configure the database.

More details on these packages are provided in *Oracle8i Supplied PL/SQL Packages Reference, Release 2 (8.1.6)*; see the "Need to Know More?" section at the end of this chapter for full bibliographic details.

Table 6.2 Some of the Oracle-provided packages.	
Package Name	**Description**
DBMS_ALERT	Provides support for asynchronous intersession communication.
DBMS_APPLICATION_INFO	Allows registering of an application for tracing purposes.
DBMS_AQ	Lets you add a message to a queue or dequeue a message.
DBMS_AQADM	Lets you perform administrative functions on a queue or queue table.
DBMS_DDL	Allows PL/SQL to execute DDL.
DBMS_DEFER, DBMS_DEFER_SYS, and **DBMS_DEFER_QUERY**	Lets you build and administer deferred remote procedure calls.
DBMS_DESCRIBE	Describes stored subprograms.
DBMS_JOB	Allows scheduling stored procedures.
DBMS_LOB	Manipulates Oracle8i large objects (LOBs).
DBMS_LOCK	Allows users to request, convert, and release locks.
DBMS_LOGMNR	Allows DBAs to initialize and run the LogMiner utility.
DBMS_OUTPUT	Provides screen output for PL/SQL programs.
DBMS_PIPE	Allows messaging between sessions.
DBMS_RANDOM	Generates a random number.

(continued)

Table 6.2 Some of the Oracle-provided packages *(continued)*.	
Package Name	Description
DBMS_REFRESH	Allows users to create groups of snapshots that can be refreshed together.
DBMS_REPCAT	Manages the advanced replication catalog and environment.
DBMS_REPCAT_ADMIN	Allows DBAs to create users with the privileges needed by the advanced replication facility.
DBMS_RESOURCE_MANAGER	Maintains plan directives, consumer groups, and plans.
DBMS_ROWID	Converts **ROWID** formats.
DBMS_SESSION	Allows alter session in PL/SQL.
DBMS_SHARED_POOL	Controls the shared pool.
DBMS_SNAPSHOT	Allows users to refresh snapshots that are not part of the same group and to purge logs.
DBMS_SPACE	Provides segment space information.
DBMS_SQL	Allows you to create dynamic SQL access to the database.
DBMS_STATS	Allows users to collect, modify, and view optimizer statistics for objects.
DBMS_TRANSACTION	Provides access to SQL transaction management commands from stored procedures.
DBMS_UTILITY	Provides additional utility procedures.
STANDARD	Declares subprograms, types, and exceptions that are available for other program units to use.
UTL_FILE	Provides file input/output (I/O).
UTL_HTTP	Enables HTTP callouts from SQL and PL/SQL.

Administering Stored Procedures and Packages

From an administrative perspective, administering the Oracle-supplied packages is exactly the same as administering any other stored procedure or package. The program units themselves are stored in the data dictionary (hence the term *stored program units*). You can see the source code for a program unit (provided it has not been wrapped by the Oracle Wrap utility, which encodes the PL/SQL so it can't be read) by querying the *_SOURCE data dictionary views. USER_SOURCE shows you the source code for program units you own, ALL_SOURCE shows you source code for program units you own or have been granted access to, and DBA_SOURCE shows the source code for all program units in the database.

The status of a program unit can be obtained by querying the relevant *_OB-JECTS view. (These also share a similar breakdown: into **USER_OBJECTS**, **ALL_OBJECTS**, and **DBA_OBJECTS**.) You can query these views like this:

```
SQL> SELECT owner, object_name, object_type, status
  2> FROM dba_objects
  3> WHERE status = 'INVALID';
```

Any program units that are returned from this query (which can also return other object types, such as views) can be recompiled manually using one of the following commands, depending on the object type (Oracle will also try to recompile invalid program units automatically the next time they are executed):

```
ALTER PACKAGE <package_name> COMPILE;
ALTER PACKAGE <package_name> COMPILE BODY;
ALTER PROCEDURE <procedure_name> COMPILE:
ALTER FUNCTION <function_name> COMPILE;
```

The difference between the first two statements is that the first compiles the entire package (both the header and the body), whereas the second compiles only the package body.

Although these commands can be used on Oracle-supplied packages, it's often better to simply rerun catproc.sql if you have problems with these packages. The reason is that many of the supplied packages have dependencies on each other, so recompiling one package can invalidate many others. Rather than tracking the dependency tree (which can be done using the utldtree script provided by Oracle), it may just be simpler to re-execute catproc.

To use the **ALTER** commands given above, you either need to own the program unit or be granted the **ALTER ANY PROCEDURE** privilege. The **GRANT** and **REVOKE** commands (covered in more detail in Chapter 13) are used to control access to stored program units. The **EXECUTE** privilege is the only one that you need to grant to—or revoke from—a user to execute a stored program unit.

Probably the only other command you need to know about from an administrative viewpoint with packages is the **DESCRIBE** command. This is particularly useful when you want to use one of the procedures in an Oracle-supplied package and you can't remember the number or types of the arguments that are passed to it. Here is an example using the **DBMS_SPACE** package in my 8.1.7 for NT database:

```
SQL> DESC dbms_space.unused_space
PROCEDURE dbms_space.unused_space

Argument Name                Type                 In/Out Default?
---------------------------  -------------------  ------ --------
SEGMENT_OWNER                VARCHAR2             IN
SEGMENT_NAME                 VARCHAR2             IN
SEGMENT_TYPE                 VARCHAR2             IN
TOTAL_BLOCKS                 NUMBER               OUT
TOTAL_BYTES                  NUMBER               OUT
UNUSED_BLOCKS                NUMBER               OUT
UNUSED_BYTES                 NUMBER               OUT
LAST_USED_EXTENT_FILE_ID     NUMBER               OUT
LAST_USED_EXTENT_BLOCK_ID    NUMBER               OUT
LAST_USED_BLOCK              NUMBER               OUT
PARTITION_NAME               VARCHAR2             IN     DEFAULT
```

The four columns show you the parameters that need to be passed in (Argument Name); their datatypes (Type); whether they are in, out, or in/out parameters (In/Out); and whether they have default values or not (Default?).

Listing Database Event Trigger Types

Triggers are stored PL/SQL program units that are executed implicitly (the term *fired* is synonymous with *executed implicitly*) by the Oracle server, whenever the triggering event occurs. They can be fired by a table modification (that is, an **INSERT, UPDATE,** or **DELETE** operation) when an object is created or a specific database or user action occurs (for example, database startup or user logon). The trigger firing is independent of the tool or application being used, or the user that is connected at the time. In earlier releases of Oracle, triggers were fired by DML only. In Oracle8i, you have the capability of defining database event triggers that can be separated into two different types:

➤ *Schema triggers*—These triggers are created in the current user's schema and fire only for that user. An example of a schema trigger would be a trigger that logs **DROP** statements by a particular user.

➤ *Database triggers*—These triggers, which are independent of the user, fire whenever a particular database event occurs. Database events include **LOGON, LOGOFF, STARTUP, SHUTDOWN** and **SERVERERROR.**

Like any other operation in an Oracle database, creating a trigger requires privileges. (Privileges are covered in more detail in Chapter 13.) You need the **CREATE TRIGGER** privilege to create a trigger on a table in your schema or a schema trigger on your schema. To create a trigger on a table in someone else's schema or on another user's schema requires the **CREATE ANY TRIGGER** privilege. To create a database trigger requires the **ADMINISTER DATABASE TRIGGER** privilege in addition to the privileges mentioned earlier.

Here's an example of a database trigger that may make this clearer:

```
CREATE TRIGGER log_errors AFTER SERVERERROR ON DATABASE
   BEGIN
      IF (IS_SERVERERROR (1034)) THEN
         <code that we want to execute when database is not
         available>
      ELSE
         <code that we want to execute for other SERVERERROR
         numbers>
      END IF;
   END;
```

Database event triggers are stored in the data dictionary like any other trigger. You can query the **USER_TRIGGERS**, **ALL_TRIGGERS**, or **DBA_ TRIGGERS** view to see information on these triggers. If you specifically want to see information on database event triggers, issue a query like this:

```
SQL> SELECT owner, trigger_name, trigger_type, triggering_event
  2  FROM dba_triggers
  3  WHERE base_object_type LIKE 'DATABASE%';
```

Note: You would replace the word **DATABASE** *with the word* **SCHEMA** *to get information on schema triggers. The reason I've used the % sign is that, for some reason in my 8.1.7 database, the value* **DATABASE** *is right-padded with eight blanks. This may be a version-specific problem, but in any case, this query will avoid any possible problems like that.*

Practice Questions

Question 1

> Which table or view contains information on only the data dictionary views and the dynamic performance views?
>
> ○ a. **DB_NAME**
>
> ○ b. **DBA_VIEWS**
>
> ○ c. **DICTIONARY**
>
> ○ d. **DBA_DATA_FILES**

Answer c is correct. The **DICTIONARY** view contains the name of each data dictionary view and a comment field describing the purpose of that view. Answer a is incorrect because **DB_NAME** is the name assigned to the database. Answer b is incorrect because the **DBA_VIEWS** view contains the text of all views in the database, not just data dictionary views. Answer d is incorrect because **DBA_DATA_FILES** contains information about database files.

Question 2

> Which category of scripts contains database package specifications and is usually run during the execution of catproc.sql?
>
> ○ a. prvt*.plb
>
> ○ b. utl*.sql
>
> ○ c. cat*.sql
>
> ○ d. dbms*.sql

Answer d is correct. The dbms*.sql scripts define the database package header specification. Answer a is incorrect because the prvt*.plb script provides wrapped package code. Answer b is incorrect because the utl*.sql script creates views and tables for database utilities. Answer c is incorrect because the cat*.sql script provides catalog and data dictionary information.

Question 3

> Which data dictionary category would a privileged user query to find the owner of the **PRODUCT1** table?
>
> ○ a. **ALL_**
>
> ○ b. **DBA_**
>
> ○ c. **USER_**

Answer b is correct. **DBA_**, which is accessible to the DBA or anyone with the **SELECT ANY TABLE** privilege, provides information on all the objects in the database. It has an owner column. Because **ALL_** has an owner column, you might choose answer a incorrectly, but remember that **ALL_** does not show all the tables in the database; it shows only the ones accessible by the user doing the query, making answer a incorrect. Answer c is incorrect because **USER_** provides information on objects owned by the user.

Question 4

> Which data dictionary view should you update when you drop a table?
>
> ○ a. **USER_DATA**
>
> ○ b. **DBA_OBJECTS**
>
> ○ c. **DBA_SEGMENTS**
>
> ○ d. **USER_SEGMENTS**
>
> ○ e. None

Answer e is correct. You should never attempt to update the data dictionary directly. This is done automatically by Oracle. Answer a is incorrect because **USER_DATA** is not a valid view. Answers b, c, and d are incorrect because, although **DBA_OBJECTS, DBA_SEGMENTS,** and **USER_SEGMENTS** are valid data dictionary views, you should never attempt to update or modify them.

Question 5

During database creation, which script creates the base data dictionary tables?

○ a. sql.bsq

○ b. catexp.sql

○ c. cataudit.sql

○ d. catproc.sql

○ e. utlxplan.sql

Answer a is correct. The sql.bsq script creates the base data dictionary tables. Because most of the information in these tables is encoded, most database users do not directly access these tables. Answer b is incorrect because the catexp.sql script is executed from the catalog.sql script and creates the export views. Answer c is incorrect because the cataudit.sql script creates the audit views. Answer d is incorrect because the catproc.sql script runs all the SQL scripts for the procedural features. Answer e is incorrect because the utlxplan.sql script creates the execution plan table.

Question 6

Which data dictionary view would you query to see information about database event triggers?

○ a. **DBA_DB_EVENTS**

○ b. **DATABASE_EVENTS**

○ c. **DBA_TRIGGERS**

○ d. **DBA_EVENT_TRIGGERS**

Answer c is correct. **DBA_TRIGGERS** shows information about database event triggers. If you want to select information specific to database event triggers, you need to restrict the query based on values of the **BASE_OBJECT_TYPE** column. Answers a, b, and d are incorrect because **DBA_DB_EVENTS**, **DATABASE_EVENTS**, and **DBA_EVENT_TRIGGERS** are all invalid view names.

Question 7

> Which script is used to create the data dictionary views?
>
> ○ a. sql.bsq
>
> ○ b. catproc.sql
>
> ○ c. dbmsutil.sql
>
> ○ d. catalog.sql

Answer d is correct. The catalog.sql script creates the data dictionary views to decode and summarize the data in the base tables. The script creates synonyms on the views to allow users easy access to the views. User SYS owns the data dictionary views. Answer a is incorrect because the sql.bsq script creates the base data dictionary tables. Answer b is incorrect because the catproc.sql script runs all the SQL scripts for the procedural features. Answer c is incorrect because the dbmsutil.sql script creates a variety of utility packages.

Question 8

> Which would be the best way to recompile the **STANDARD** package if it becomes invalid?
>
> ○ a. Use the **ALTER PACKAGE standard COMPILE;** command.
>
> ○ b. Use the **ALTER PACKAGE standard COMPILE BODY;** command.
>
> ○ c. Use the **ALTER PACKAGE standard RECOMPILE;** command.
>
> ○ d. Run catproc.sql.

Answer d is correct. This question needs careful reading. The important words in the question are "best way". The best way to recompile the **STANDARD** package is to run catproc.sql, which would ensure that all dependent packages are also rebuilt. Answer a is incorrect because, although the command would probably work, it would invalidate many other packages that are dependent on **STANDARD**. Answer b is incorrect because we want to recompile the whole package, not just the package body. Answer c is incorrect because there is no **RECOMPILE** clause in the **ALTER PACKAGE** command.

Need to Know More?

 Ault, Michael R. *Oracle8i DBA: SQL and PL/SQL Exam Cram*. The Coriolis Group, Scottsdale, AZ, 2001. ISBN 1-58880-037-7. This book provides an introduction to Oracle concepts, including stored program units such as procedures, functions, and packages.

 Feuerstein, Steven. *Oracle PL/SQL Programming: Guide to Oracle8i Features*. O'Reilly and Associates, Sebastopol, CA, 1999. ISBN 1-56592-675-7. Chapter 6 covers database event triggers.

 Feuerstein, Steven, Charles Dye, and John Beresniewicz. *Oracle Built-In Packages*. O'Reilly and Associates, Sebastopol, CA, 1998. ISBN 1-56592-238-7. This book covers all the built-in packages provided with the database.

 Sarin, Sumit. *Oracle DBA Tips and Techniques*. Oracle Press, Berkeley, CA, 2000. ISBN 0-07212-245-5. This book includes chapters on the dynamic performance views and using Oracle-supplied packages.

 See the Oracle documentation that is provided on CD-ROM with the Oracle RDBMS software. The following documents specifically pertain to this chapter:

Baylis, Ruth, and Joyce Fee. *Oracle8i Administrator's Guide*. Oracle Corporation, Redwood City, CA, 1999. This is the complete documentation of database administration tasks.

Cyran, Michele, and Mark Bauer. *Oracle8i Supplied PL/SQL Packages Reference, Release 2 (8.1.6)*. Berkeley, CA, 1999. This document describes the PL/SQL packages that are shipped with Oracle.

Leverenz, Lefty, Diana Rehfield, and Cathy Baird. *Oracle8i Concepts*. Oracle Corporation, Redwood City, CA, 1999. This work is the complete documentation of Oracle concepts.

Lorentz, Diana. *Oracle8i Reference*. Oracle Corporation, Redwood City, CA, 1999. This document provides detailed descriptions for the data dictionary views and the SQL scripts that might need to be executed to completely build a database.

technet.oracle.com is Oracle's technical repository of information for clients.

 www.revealnet.com is the site where RevealNet Corporation provides Oracle administration reference software.

Managing Control Files and Redo Log Files

Terms you'll need to understand:

- ✓ Control file
- ✓ V$CONTROLFILE
- ✓ V$CONTROLFILE_RECORD_ SECTION
- ✓ V$PARAMETER
- ✓ Redo log
- ✓ Checkpoint
- ✓ LOG_CHECKPOINT_INTERVAL
- ✓ LOG_CHECKPOINT_TIMEOUT
- ✓ FAST_START_IO_TARGET
- ✓ Log switch
- ✓ V$LOG
- ✓ V$LOGFILE
- ✓ V$THREAD

Techniques you'll need to master:

- ✓ Explaining the uses of the control file
- ✓ Describing the contents of the control file
- ✓ Multiplexing the control file
- ✓ Obtaining control file information
- ✓ Explaining the use of the online redo log files
- ✓ Obtaining log and archive information
- ✓ Controlling log switches and checkpoints
- ✓ Multiplexing and maintaining online redo log files
- ✓ Planning online redo log files
- ✓ Troubleshooting common redo log file problems
- ✓ Analyzing online and archived redo logs

Because control files and redo log files are created when the **CREATE DATA-BASE** command is executed and are automatically maintained by Oracle, many DBAs tend to forget about them after they create a database. However, it's crucial that DBAs understand how to manage these files. Making a mistake while making changes to control files or redo log files can render the database unusable and make recovery efforts necessary. And, if proper backups aren't performed, you could even find yourself with a database that can't be recovered. Therefore, you must know what these files are used for, how to re-create or move them, and which configuration Oracle recommends.

The Uses of the Control File

The control file is a binary file that contains the physical structure of the database. Each control file is used by a single Oracle database on database mount to find the locations of all the files that make up the database. The Oracle server also writes to the control file throughout normal use of the database. As you can imagine, the control file is very important in an Oracle database. In fact, the database cannot start without a control file, and if during normal database usage errors occur while writing to a control file, the database will suffer a fatal error and no longer function properly. Either of these situations means that you'll need to perform recovery before the affected database can be reopened for normal use.

The Contents of the Control File

The control file has two main sections. The first part, called the reusable section, is used to store information, such as backup datafile names and log file names, for Recovery Manager (Oracle's backup and recovery tool, which is covered in detail in the third OCP exam—Exam 1Z0-025, "Oracle8i: Backup and Recovery"—so I won't cover it further here). The second part is the nonreusable section, and it's this part that you need to be most familiar with for the "Oracle8i: Architecture and Administration" exam. The size of this part of the control file is determined by settings you give in either the **CREATE DATABASE** or **CREATE CONTROLFILE** commands for the **MAXLOGFILES**, **MAXLOGMEMBERS**, **MAXLOGHISTORY**, and **MAXDATAFILES** keywords. If you want to change the amount of space allocated in the control file for these keywords, you need to re-create the control file.

The contents of the nonreusable section of the control file, in addition to the database creation date, are:

> ➤ *The database name and identifier*—The database name can come either from the **DB_NAME** initialization parameter or the database name given in the **CREATE DATABASE** statement.

➤ *The names and locations of all datafiles and redo logs for the database*—This information is updated whenever a file-management operation occurs. File management operations include creating, renaming, or removing datafiles or redo log files. Information is also kept about operations that take datafiles offline. Because this information is updated whenever one of these operations occurs, it's vitally important that you back up the control file after any of these changes to ensure database recoverability.

➤ *Tablespace names*—Tablespace names are recorded whenever a tablespace is added to or removed from the database.

➤ *Log history*—Log history information is recorded in the control file (up to the **MAXLOGHISTORY** setting) when log switches take place.

➤ *Current log sequence number*—The current log sequence number is written into the control file and the headers of all the datafiles for the database. Oracle uses this information on database startup to ensure that all the datafiles are at the same log sequence number as the control file. If any files have an earlier log sequence number, Oracle signals the need for database recovery. (This normally happens only when a DBA loads a backup copy of one or more datafiles in preparation for recovery.)

➤ *Checkpoint information*—When a checkpoint occurs, the Checkpoint (CKPT) process updates all the datafiles and the control files for the database with the most recent checkpoint information.

Multiplexing the Control File

The control file is clearly a very important file in the Oracle database, so Oracle allows you to multiplex (mirror) the control file on separate disks. You can have up to eight control-file mirrors.

 Oracle strongly recommends that you have at least two copies of the control file located on different devices. Be sure to remember that Oracle considers this a "best practice."

Unlike the redo log files, which can be multiplexed at either the operating system or database levels (or both, if you're really paranoid), the control files are mirrored only at the operating system level. The steps involved with mirroring a control file are very simple, but they do require database shutdown. For this reason (as well as the obvious availability and recoverability issues mentioned previously in the section on uses of the control file), I strongly recommend that you mirror the control files as soon as the database is created. The steps you need to perform are as follows:

1. If the database is open, shut down the database, preferably using a **SHUT-DOWN NORMAL** command.

2. Copy the existing control file (created when the database is created) to another device using whatever operating system utility you're most comfortable with.

3. Edit the initialization parameter file in one of two ways so that the **CONTROL_FILES** parameter points to both the old and the new control files. The first option is to enclose the file names in one set of parentheses and separate them with a comma, like this:

```
CONTROL_FILES = (/u01/oradata/prd1/control01.ctl, \
                 /u02/oradata/prd1/control02.ctl)
```

The second option is to enclose each of the file names in double quotes and separate with a space, like this:

```
CONTROL_FILES = "/u01/oradata/prd1/control01.ctl" \
                "/u02/oradata/prd1/control02.ctl"
```

Note that the backslash continuation character (\) is included here for ease of readability.

4. Start the database again.

You can also specify multiple control files when you create the database, rather than add them after database creation. This can be done fairly easily when using the Database Configuration Assistant (DBCA), because it prompts you for multiple locations. If you create the database manually, you'll need to have the **CONTROL_FILES** parameter set to multiple locations before the **CREATE DATABASE** command is issued. Oracle then automatically mirrors the control file in the locations specified in the **CONTROL_FILES** parameter.

Obtaining Control File Information

Control file information is kept in a number of dynamic performance views:

➤ **V$CONTROLFILE**—Contains the names and locations of the control files. You can issue the following query to display this information:

```
SQL> SELECT name FROM v$controlfile;
NAME
---------------------------------------------------------
/u01/oradata/prd1/control01.ctl
/u02/oradata/prd1/control02.ctl
```

➤ **V$CONTROLFILE_RECORD_SECTION**—Displays information about the different sections of the control file. You can issue the following query to display this information:

```
SQL> SELECT type, record_size, records_total, records_used
  2  FROM v$controlfile_record_section
  3  ORDER BY type;
```

TYPE	RECORD_SIZE	RECORDS_TOTAL	RECORDS_USED
ARCHIVED LOG	584	1608	0
BACKUP CORRUPTION	44	185	0
BACKUP DATAFILE	116	70	0
BACKUP PIECE	736	66	0
BACKUP REDOLOG	76	107	0
BACKUP SET	40	204	0
CKPT PROGRESS	4084	16	0
COPY CORRUPTION	40	204	0
DATABASE	192	1	1
DATAFILE	180	32	8
DATAFILE COPY	660	74	0
DELETED OBJECT	20	1633	0
FILENAME	524	97	11
LOG HISTORY	36	1815	125
OFFLINE RANGE	56	145	0
PROXY COPY	852	134	0
REDO LOG	72	32	3
REDO THREAD	104	16	1
RESERVED1	56	32	0
RESERVED2	1	1	0
RESERVED4	1	8168	0
TABLESPACE	68	32	8

```
22 rows selected.
```

➤ **V$PARAMETER**—You can query this either directly using a **SELECT** statement or indirectly using the **SHOW PARAMETER** command to display the control file names. You need the following query (the output has been edited to fit the page width of this book):

```
SQL> SELECT name, value
  2  FROM v$parameter
  3  WHERE name = 'control_files';
```

```
NAME                    VALUE
----------------        --------------------------------------------
control_files           /u01/oradata/prd1/control01.ctl,
                        /u02/oradata/prd1/control02.ctl
```

The far simpler **SHOW PARAMETER** syntax is:

```
SQL> SHOW PARAMETER control_files

NAME                    TYPE    VALUE
-------------------     ------  ----------------------------
control_files           string  /u01/oradata/prd1/control01.ct
                                1, /u02/oradata/prd1/control02
                                .ctl
```

In addition to these views that you can query to obtain control file information, the control file itself is used to obtain the information displayed in a number of other dynamic performance views. These include (but are not limited to):

➤ **V$ARCHIVE**—Contains information on redo logs that need archiving.

➤ **V$BACKUP**—Displays the backup status of all online datafiles.

➤ **V$DATABASE**—Contains database information such as the database name, creation date, archive log mode, and checkpoint information.

➤ **V$DATAFILE**—Includes datafile information such as the file name, size, and status.

➤ **V$LOG**—Contains log information, including archive status, log status, log sequence number, and group and thread numbers.

➤ **V$LOGFILE**—Displays information about the individual redo log files, including name and status.

➤ **V$LOG_HISTORY**—Contains information about archived logs, including log sequence number and SCN details.

➤ **V$TEMPFILE**—Includes tempfile information such as the file name, size, and status.

Oracle Enterprise Manager (OEM) can be used to display information about the control files as well. In the Navigator pane, choose Databases, and then choose the database you want to look at. After that, click on Storage, right-click on Controlfile, and choose Edit from the context-sensitive menu. Figure 7.1 shows

Figure 7.1 The Edit Controlfile screen, displaying information about the database and control files.

the Edit Controlfile screen that results, which displays the names and locations of the control files, as well as other information derived from the control files.

By clicking on the Record Section tab, you can display information about each of the control file record sections. If you click on the Show Description button, you can access more information on a particular record section type. In Figure 7.2, you can see that I'm accessing information about the Datafile record section type. (You can click on the Hide Description button to hide this information.)

The Uses of the Online Redo Log Files

Oracle uses the online redo log files to minimize the loss of data. Online redo log files contain the redo entries that represent changed data values due to inserts, updates, or deletes (unless an operation is done in **NOLOGGING** mode). The files are read from only when there is a need for database recovery, such as after an instance failure due to a power outage. Committed data that has not yet been written to the datafiles by the Database Writer process(es) is recovered from the online redo log files during the recovery process.

The initial redo log files are created when the database is created. The DBCA prompts you for the information that's necessary to create multiple groups and members, but you'll need to do this yourself if you're creating a database manually. Remember that you need to specify some settings when you create a

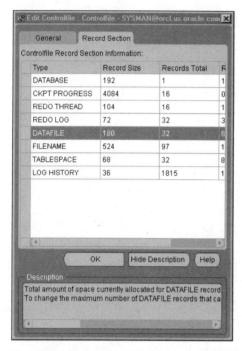

Figure 7.2 Displaying control file record section information in OEM.

database; these settings are recorded in the control files, and they cannot be changed without re-creating the control files. The settings that are related to log files are:

➤ **MAXLOGFILES**—The maximum number of redo log file groups that can ever be created for the database

➤ **MAXLOGMEMBERS**—The maximum number of members for a redo log group

The maximum and default values for these parameters are dependent on your operating system.

*Note: The **LOG_FILES** parameter that used to be important for specifying the maximum number of redo log files has been made obsolete in version 8.1.*

Redo log entries are written from the redo log buffer to the redo log files by the Log Writer (LGWR) process. LGWR writes to the current redo log group. (Remember that all log members in a redo log group contain the same information and are written to concurrently.) A number of events can cause LGWR to write to the redo log files:

➤ A transaction is committed.

➤ A timeout occurs. (LGWR timeouts occur every three seconds.)

➤ More than 1MB of entries has been written to the log buffer cache.

➤ The log buffer becomes more than one-third full.

➤ DBWn needs to write modified data blocks to disk. (LGWR will be signaled to write before this occurs.)

The LGWR process writes information from the log buffer cache to the current redo log group until the group fills up. When the current redo log group fills, Oracle performs a log switch and starts writing to the next redo log group. Once all the redo log groups have been filled, LGWR starts writing to the first online redo log group again. It is also possible for DBAs to force a log switch if they want to use the **ALTER SYSTEM SWITCH LOGFILE** command.

Regardless of what causes the log switch, any log switch also forces a checkpoint to occur. During a checkpoint, the following two events happen:

➤ The Checkpoint (CKPT) process writes the new log sequence number to the headers of all the datafiles and the control files for the database.

➤ Dirty buffers are written from the data buffer cache to the datafiles by the DBWn process(es). The number of dirty buffers written is set by the **FAST_START_IO_TARGET** parameter, if it is specified. (This is a new parameter in version 8.1, and it's available only in Oracle's Enterprise Edition.) The **FAST_START_IO_TARGET** parameter defaults to the size of the data buffer cache, and it can be used to attempt to limit the amount of time needed for instance recovery.

Checkpoints normally occur for all datafiles, but some operations (such as taking a datafile offline) cause a checkpoint only for specific datafiles. Although log switches cause a checkpoint, the following events can also cause a checkpoint:

➤ An instance shutdown can cause a checkpoint, provided the shutdown is not a **SHUTDOWN ABORT**. (In other words, only **NORMAL, IMMEDIATE**, or **TRANSACTIONAL** shutdowns cause checkpoints.)

➤ The settings for three initialization parameters also control checkpointing: **LOG_CHECKPOINT_TIMEOUT** (the number of seconds since the last write to the redo log files), **LOG_CHECKPOINT_INTERVAL** (the number of operating system blocks since the last write to the redo log files), and **FAST_START_IO_TARGET** (defined previously). I'll cover these in more detail in the "Controlling Log Switches and Checkpoints" section later in this chapter.

➤ You can also use an **ALTER SYSTEM CHECKPOINT** command to manually force a checkpoint.

Archiving Redo Log Files

One of the most important decisions a DBA needs to make is whether to turn on archiving for the database. If archiving is turned on, log switches cause the Archiver (ARC*n*) process(es) to wake up and physically copy to an archive directory the redo log that has just been switched from. This operation has to complete before the redo log file can be used again.

Fortunately, making this decision is fairly straightforward. The database needs to be running in **ARCHIVELOG** mode for you to perform hot backups (backups performed while the database is up and running) or if you believe that you ever will need to perform a point-in-time recovery. Hot backups and point-in-time recoveries are both included in Exam 1Z0-025, "Oracle8i: Backup and Recovery," so I won't cover them in more detail here. Suffice it to say that almost all production environments run with archiving turned on, to protect from both media recovery and user error.

To enable automatic archiving for the database, you need to set the initialization parameter **LOG_ARCHIVE_START** to **TRUE** and set a flag in the control file by using the **ALTER DATABASE ARCHIVELOG** command. This command enables automatic archiving.

 The **ALTER DATABASE ARCHIVELOG** command must be performed after a clean shutdown, and when the database is mounted but not open. If you attempt to use this command after a **SHUTDOWN ABORT**, you will get the error message "ORA-00265: instance recovery required, cannot set **ARCHIVELOG** mode."

Manual archiving can also be performed by direct DBA intervention, but this is almost never used exclusively for production systems. (It may be used to force archiving of a particular log, however.) Many other parameters are used to control where the archive logs are copied to, but these topics are covered in Exam 1Z0-025, "Oracle8i: Backup and Recovery," so I won't discuss them further here.

Obtaining Log and Archive Information

Information about both the online redo log files and the archive redo log files is kept in the data dictionary. It can be queried directly using the dynamic performance views. The views that are related to the log files are:

➤ **V$ARCHIVE**—Contains information about redo log files that need archiving.

➤ **V$DATABASE**—Can be used to determine whether the database is in **ARCHIVELOG** mode by issuing the query:

```
SQL> SELECT name, log_mode
  2  FROM v$database;

NAME      LOG_MODE
--------  -----------
ORCL      ARCHIVELOG
```

➤ **V$INSTANCE**—Can be used to query the archiver status by issuing the query:

```
SQL> SELECT archiver
  2  FROM v$instance;

ARCHIVE
-------
STOPPED
```

Notice that the archiver is stopped in this example. The reason is that I haven't yet set the initialization parameter **LOG_ARCHIVE_START** in the parameter file. When you first turn archiving on, it can be easy to forget that this is a two-step process, so you should get into the habit of either issuing these two queries or the command **ARCHIVE LOG LIST** to see output like this:

```
SQL> archive log list
Database log mode              Archive Mode
Automatic archival             Enabled
Archive destination            D:\oracle\ora81\RDBMS
Oldest online log sequence     135
Next log sequence to archive   137
Current log sequence           137
```

 The important things to look at in this output for determining whether you've set up archiving properly are the values for "Database log mode" (Archive Mode) and "Automatic archival" (Enabled).

➤ **V$LOG**—Displays information from the control files about the log groups, including the number of members in the group, archive status (that is, whether the group has been archived), and the log status. The **STATUS** column can have the following values:

➤ UNUSED—The log has never been written to.

➤ CURRENT—This is the current redo log.

➤ ACTIVE—The log group is active, possibly because it's in use for crash or block recovery, but it's not the current log.

➤ CLEARING—The log is being cleared by an **ALTER DATABASE CLEAR LOGFILE** command. (When it is completely cleared, the status will become **UNUSED**.)

➤ CLEARING_CURRENT—This value should be seen only if there is an I/O error while clearing the log.

➤ INACTIVE—The log group is no longer needed for instance recovery.

➤ V$LOGFILE—Contains information about the individual log files, including the log member name and status. The **STATUS** column can have the following values:

➤ INVALID—The file is inaccessible or Oracle has never attempted to access it. (This will be the case immediately after a log file is added to the database.)

➤ STALE—The file was switched from before it was completely filled, for example by an **ALTER SYSTEM SWITCH LOGFILE** command.

➤ DELETED—The file is no longer used.

➤ *Blank*—The file is currently in use.

➤ V$LOG_HISTORY—Contains information about archived redo log files, including information about the log sequence number and system change number.

➤ V$THREAD—Can be used in a single instance configuration to see the number of online redo log groups, the current log group, and log sequence information (but it is primarily of use in a Parallel Server environment).

You can also see information about the redo logs in OEM. To display the redo log groups, individual members, and their locations, choose Databases in the Navigator pane, choose the database you want to examine, click on Storage, and then click on Redo Log Groups. This opens a list of the redo log groups. Right-clicking on an individual group and selecting the Edit option opens the Edit Redo Log Group screen, as shown in Figure 7.3. The name of this screen is a bit of a misnomer in my opinion, because its main use is to see the name and location of the redo log members that compose that group. All you can really edit on this screen is the file specification (either the name or directory the file is located in).

By following the same path but choosing Archive Logs instead of Redo Log Groups, you can display a list of the archive logs for the database. You can then right-click on an individual archive log and choose the Edit option to see more information on this particular file, as shown in Figure 7.4.

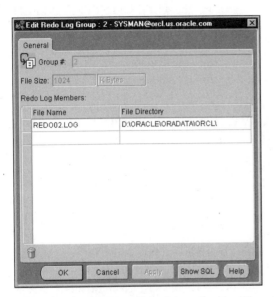

Figure 7.3 Using OEM to display information about the redo log files.

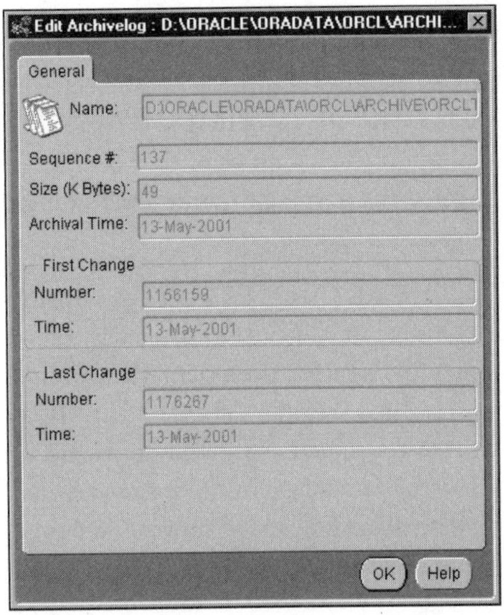

Figure 7.4 Using OEM to display information about the archive logs.

Controlling Log Switches and Checkpoints

I mentioned earlier that it's possible to manually force log switches and checkpoints, as well as to control them with greater granularity by setting initialization parameters. In this section, we'll look at this capability in more detail.

Manual log switches can be performed using the **ALTER SYSTEM SWITCH LOGFILE** command, and manual checkpoints can be forced with the **ALTER SYSTEM CHECKPOINT** command. Normally, this is necessary only if the system you're administering has particularly large redo logs and an operation has occurred that you specifically want to ensure is archived or flushed to disk.

You can also set the granularity of log switches and checkpoints using the **LOG_CHECKPOINT_INTERVAL, LOG_CHECKPOINT_TIMEOUT,** and **FAST_START_IO_TARGET** initialization parameters.

LOG_CHECKPOINT_INTERVAL has changed its meaning in version 8.1. For releases prior to version 8.1, a checkpoint was initiated whenever LGWR had written the number of operating system blocks specified by **LOG_CHECKPOINT_INTERVAL**. In version 8.1, however, **LOG_CHECKPOINT_INTERVAL** specifies that the target for the checkpoint position must be closer than a specified number of operating system blocks to the end of the redo log file. This parameter tries to control the amount of redo that needs to be applied in case of instance recovery. If the value of this parameter is greater than the size of the redo log file, checkpoints will occur only when log switches occur. (Regardless of the setting of this parameter, checkpoints always occur on log switch.)

LOG_CHECKPOINT_TIMEOUT has also changed its meaning in version 8.1. For releases prior to version 8.1, it set the number of seconds between checkpoints. In version 8.1, however, **LOG_CHECKPOINT_TIMEOUT** specifies that the target for the checkpoint position must be closer than this number of seconds to the end of the redo log file. Again, this is trying to control the amount of redo that needs applying in case of instance recovery.

Although release 8.1 introduced the **FAST_START_IO_TARGET** parameter, it's available only in Enterprise Edition. This parameter can be changed dynamically with the **ALTER SYSTEM** command. (Oracle's documentation erroneously states that this parameter can be changed with an **ALTER SESSION** command, but that obviously doesn't make too much sense and is incorrect.) This parameter controls the amount of I/O needed during instance recovery, and the DBW*n* processes use this setting to determine how much to write to ensure that recovery will need to perform only this amount of I/O. A smaller value for this parameter improves the performance of an instance recovery, because fewer I/O operations need to be performed for the recovery, but it also forces more frequent writes to disk, which can adversely affect your online performance.

Multiplexing and Maintaining Online Redo Log Files

Redo log files can be multiplexed or mirrored, renamed or relocated, dropped from the database, or cleared. In this section, we'll examine each of these operations.

Adding Redo Log Files and Groups

Obviously, the redo log files fulfill a vital role in an Oracle database. As a result, although all that Oracle needs to create a database is two redo logs, more are usually involved. To protect against a loss of the redo log itself, Oracle allows you to multiplex (mirror) the redo log files on different disks. The database can be created with multiplexed redo logs, or you can add the redo log mirrors after the database is created using the **ALTER DATABASE** command. Here's an example of the command to add log groups to the database:

```
SQL> ALTER DATABASE
  2    ADD LOGFILE GROUP 4
  3                ('/u03/oradata/prd1/log4a.rdo',
  4                 '/u04/oradata/prd1/log4b.rdo') SIZE 20M,
  5            GROUP 5
  6            ('/u03/oradata/prd1/log5a.rdo',
  7             '/u04/oradata/prd1/log5b.rdo') SIZE 20M;
```

You could also add individual log members to an existing log group using another variety of the **ALTER DATABASE** command:

```
SQL> ALTER DATABASE
  2    ADD LOGFILE MEMBER
  3                ('/u05/oradata/prd1/log4c.rdo') TO GROUP 4;
```

Notice in this case that you don't specify the size because you're adding a file to an existing group. To create the new log file member, Oracle automatically uses the same file size as the other members of the group. If the file already exists, you need to specify the keyword **REUSE**, or Oracle will return an error.

Alternatively, you can use OEM to add log groups or log members. Use the same path as I mentioned previously when getting to the screen displayed in Figure 7.3. However, if you want to add another log group, right-click on Redo Log

Groups in the Navigator pane and choose the Create option to see the screen displayed in Figure 7.5. Alternatively, choose one of the existing groups and then choose either Create Redo Log Group or Create Redo Log Group Like from the Navigator menu. If you choose Create Redo Log Group, a screen that lists all the objects that can be created appears. The Redo Log Group option will be highlighted. You then need to click on the Create button. However, you can avoid these extra steps by choosing Create Redo Log Group Like. Whichever path you choose, you'll see the screen displayed in Figure 7.5.

Notice that Oracle has automatically filled in the group number, file size, file name, and file directory values, but you can override all of these if you want. Oracle has provided information for only one member of the redo log group, but you can simply click in the next row on the display and enter values for the extra members. When you've changed these values as you wish, simply click on the Create button to add the new group.

If you wanted to add extra log members to a particular group, either right-click on the group and select the Edit option, or choose Edit Redo Log Group from the Navigator menu to display the screen shown in Figure 7.6.

Click on the empty row below the existing log member information and enter values for the new log member name and location, and then click on OK to create the new log file member.

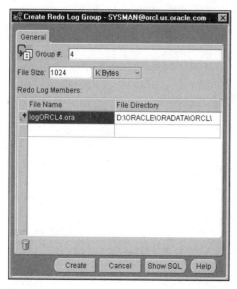

Figure 7.5 Using OEM to create redo log groups.

Figure 7.6 Using OEM to add log members to an existing group.

Renaming and Relocating Redo Log Files

You can also rename or relocate a redo log file, but only if the log file is not a member of the current group (that is, the group being written to). If the file is part of the current group, then simply execute an **ALTER SYSTEM SWITCH LOGFILE** command to switch to the next group, and then perform the file maintenance. Renaming or relocating a log file is a two-step operation: You need to copy the old file to the new file name or location, and then change the name in your control file by using the **ALTER DATABASE RENAME FILE** command. For example, if I wanted to change the name of my redo log files on my 8.1.7 database on NT (let's say I realized I hadn't mirrored them and now wanted to rename REDO1.LOG to be REDO1A.LOG before I added the second member as REDO1B.LOG), I could issue the following commands:

```
SQL> host copy d:\oracle\oradata\orcl\redo01.log -
>            d:\oracle\oradata\orcl\redo01a.log

SQL> ALTER DATABASE
  2  RENAME FILE 'd:\oracle\oradata\orcl\redo01.log'
  3  TO 'd:\oracle\oradata\orcl\redo01a.log';
```

In this case, I have simply renamed the file, but, by changing the directory path, I could just as easily relocate the log file as well. Alternatively, I could use OEM to rename or relocate the file. To do so, copy the file to its new name or location using a similar command to the first one above. Then, using the same path to get to the Edit Redo Log Group screen as I did to reach the screen shown in Figure 7.6, all you need to do to rename or relocate the file is to click on the file name and/or file directory, change one or both of them appropriately, and click on the OK button.

Dropping Redo Log Files

You can drop individual redo log file members or an entire redo log group. Normally, the only reason you want to drop an entire group is because the group needs to be resized. An individual log file member may need to be dropped because it has been corrupted at the operating system level.

You need to meet the following conditions before you can drop log files:

➤ You cannot drop an active or current redo log group or members of it. However, you can switch the redo log group to another group and then drop the first one.

➤ You cannot drop a redo log group or member that has not been archived, if you are running in **ARCHIVELOG** mode.

➤ You must leave at least two redo log groups of at least one member each in the database.

The drop operation does not delete the operating system files. It simply removes the entries for those files from the control file, so Oracle no longer attempts to access them. You need to delete the files yourself after the drop operation completes.

The **ALTER DATABASE** command is used to drop redo log file members and entire groups. You can drop a redo log group simply by referring to its number, as in:

```
SQL> ALTER DATABASE DROP LOGFILE GROUP 4;
```

If you want to drop an individual log file member, you need to provide the file specification to the command, like this:

```
SQL> ALTER DATABASE
  2  DROP LOGFILE MEMBER '/u01/oradata/prd1/redo1a.log';
```

Multiple members can be dropped in a single operation simply by providing a comma-separated list of file specifications, like this:

```
SQL> ALTER DATABASE
  2  DROP LOGFILE MEMBER '/u01/oradata/prd1/redo1a.log',
  3                      '/u02/oradata/prd1/redo1b.log';
```

You can also use OEM to drop redo log groups and individual members. In the Navigator pane, select the database you want to maintain, choose Storage, and then click on Redo Log Groups. To drop an entire group, right-click on the group you want to delete and select the Remove option, or highlight the group you want to delete and select Remove Redo Log Group from the Navigator menu. Then select Yes when you're prompted with a dialog box asking if you're sure that you want to drop this group.

If you want to drop an individual member from a group, use the same path as mentioned previously to get to the Edit Redo Log Group screen, highlight the file you want to drop (you can use either the file name, as I've done in Figure 7.7, or the file directory), and then click on the trash can icon in the bottom-left corner of the screen (or right-click on the square to the left of the file name and select Remove from the context-sensitive menu).

Clearing Redo Log Files

Clearing a redo log file is like dropping the file and then adding it again. The only real difference is that it can be performed when you have only two log groups consisting of one member each. (Dropping a log file member is not possible in this case.) Although a redo log file can be cleared at the entire group level or at an individual log file member level, it's probably more likely to be done at the log file member level. The reason is that the operation is normally needed only when a file has become corrupted, and it's unusual for more than one log member of a

Figure 7.7 Using OEM to drop an individual redo log file member.

group to become corrupted at once. (After all, this is why we have multiple log members in a group—to ensure that corruption in one member does not affect the normal operation of the database.)

In any case, Oracle has provided you with the capability to do both with the **ALTER DATABASE CLEAR [UNARCHIVED] LOGFILE** command. The **UNARCHIVED** keyword is optional, and is needed only if you're trying to issue the command when the database is in **ARCHIVELOG** mode and the log file to be cleared has not yet been archived. Use of the **UNARCHIVED** keyword means that any recovery situation that needs to access this archive file will fail, so make sure that you take a clean backup after this operation is performed. Here's an example of using the command to clear an entire group:

```
SQL> ALTER DATABASE CLEAR LOGFILE GROUP 4;
```

Alternatively, here's an example of using the command to clear an individual log file member (multiple members can also be cleared in one operation by providing a comma-separated list of file specifications):

```
SQL> ALTER DATABASE CLEAR LOGFILE '/u01/oradata/prd1/redo1a.log';
```

Interestingly enough, there doesn't seem to be an equivalent way of performing this operation in OEM, so you have to use the SQL command.

Planning Online Redo Log Files

Determining the appropriate number of redo log files for a database can be a fairly daunting task for a new DBA. Generally, it's best to test a number of different configurations to see what works best. Two redo log groups may be sufficient if the database is fairly small or if it doesn't have much write activity. (However, in my experience of more than 14 years as a DBA, the only time two redo log groups has been enough has been in nonproduction environments, such as development, acceptance test, or training.) In most situations, a database needs more than two redo log groups to ensure that LGWR can write without interruption. Keep an eye on the alert log or the trace files for the LGWR process, and see if there are times when LGWR is waiting for a group to become available because either archiving or checkpointing has not been completed. If this occurs too often, you may need to add more log groups.

Determining the correct size for the redo log files can also be difficult. Although you can have members of different sizes in different groups (members of a specific group must always be the same size), there is little value in this. Normally, the only time that this is seen is when you are partway through resizing the log files—that is, one group has been resized but another group has not. The minimum size of a log file is 50KB, and the maximum size depends upon the operating system. The actual sizing is dependent on a variety of things, including the number and size of individual redo entries being produced, the number of log switches and checkpoints, and the desired archiving frequency.

Once you have determined the appropriate number and size of redo log files, you also need to plan the locations for them. Clearly, multiplexing redo log files on separate disks is required for maximum recoverability and manageability of the database, but you should take into account some other considerations as well. For reasons of performance and recoverability, it's best to have redo log files separated from data files and also from archived redo log files. This separation ensures that the DBWn, LGWR, and ARCn processes don't have disk contention issues with each other. However, all these considerations need to be balanced with the fact that disks are getting larger. For example, if all you have is a disk farm of 9GB disks (a not uncommon disk size nowadays), you'll waste a lot of space by keeping a whole 9GB disk to store three 20MB redo logs. Also, the number of disks that you have places limitations on your ability to spread files across multiple disks.

Troubleshooting Common Redo Log File Problems

The most common redo log file problems that you'll encounter as a DBA are:

➤ A redo log file member is not available.

➤ The current redo log group becomes unavailable.

➤ The next redo log group to be switched to becomes unavailable.

If a redo log file member becomes unavailable, the database can keep running, provided that at least one member of the group is still available. The LGWR process will keep writing to the available group members, and it will flag an error in the alert file and the LGWR trace file. If the log file that becomes unavailable isn't the current one, then the member can simply be dropped and re-created using the commands listed earlier. If the log file that becomes unavailable is part of the current log group, you'll need to perform an **ALTER SYSTEM SWITCH LOGFILE** command before dropping and re-creating the unavailable member.

If all members of the current redo log group become unavailable, the instance will shut down. This should be a very unusual situation, because a multiple disk crash is normally needed for multiple members to become unavailable at once. If, however, you're ever unlucky enough to find yourself in this situation, you will probably need to perform media recovery on the database to make it available again. Normally, this process results in data loss.

Likewise, it's unusual for all members of the next redo log group to become unavailable at the same time. If it does happen, the instance will again shut down. However, media recovery is not normally needed in this case unless the group that becomes unavailable is still active. If the group is no longer active, then dropping the group and adding a new one will resolve the problem.

Analyzing Online and Archived Redo Logs

One of the really useful tools that Oracle made available with the 8.1 release was the LogMiner utility. Prior to version 8.1, no supported tool was available to translate the contents of the redo log files (which are in binary format) into readable SQL. Prior to the 8.1 release, various third-party tools were available to perform this translation, but none of them were supported by Oracle. Because Oracle keeps the format of the redo logs confidential and proprietary (and can change the format from point release to point release), I was never particularly confident using these tools because I was never sure that the tools kept up with all the changes.

The LogMiner utility removes these issues. LogMiner is a tool developed by Oracle, so it does understand the format of the redo log files and is kept in sync with any format changes from release to release. It can be used to track database changes, even at the individual table or user level, and most importantly, it allows you to undo changes that have been made to the database. On a technical note, LogMiner was released with version 8.1 of the database, but it can be used against 8.0 redo logs as well. (Unfortunately, the changes in the redo log format from release 7.3 to 8.0 were so significant that LogMiner cannot be used against 7.3 databases.)

Using LogMiner

Using LogMiner involves this series of steps:

1. Set the value of the initialization parameter **UTL_FILE_DIR**, if it isn't already set. This sets the value for a directory in which PL/SQL I/O can occur.

2. Create a dictionary file. LogMiner is normally used with a dictionary file. (Although using it without a dictionary file is possible, if you do so, the SQL statements generated with LogMiner use internal object identifiers instead of the object name and hex values for the column data.) The dictionary file is used to analyze the log files, and it contains dictionary information from the database whose logs you want to analyze. You create the dictionary file by using the **DBMS_LOGMNR_D.BUILD** procedure, which takes two

parameters. The first is the name of the external file you want to create for the dictionary, and the second is the directory you want to create the file in (which is the same directory that's specified by the **UTL_FILE_DIR** parameter). The dictionary file allows you to mine redo logs from one database in another database and get object resolution. This allows you to offload the load of the mining process (and subsequent work) to other systems.

3. Add log files to the list of files to be analyzed during this LogMiner session using the **DBMS_LOGMNR.ADD_LOGFILE** procedure. The first file you add needs to have the **DBMS.LOGMNR.NEW** constant specified to initiate the list. Any other files you add need to have the **DBMS_ LOGMNR.ADDFILE** constant specified. LogMiner can analyze both online and archived redo log files, so either can be added using this procedure.

4. Start the LogMiner analysis session using the **DBMS_LOGMNR. START_LOGMNR** procedure. This procedure takes the dictionary file created in Step 2 as a parameter, as well as other parameters that can be used to specify the search window, such as **StartTime** and **EndTime**.

5. Query the output from the analysis by looking at the **V$LOGMNR_CONTENTS** dynamic performance view. Note that the contents of this view are available only to the session performing the analysis, so if you want to share this information with other sessions, you'll need to copy the information to another table. Doing so is also useful if you want to keep the information after the LogMiner session is disconnected (normally, the view is emptied at this point).

6. Finish the analysis session using the **DBMS_LOGMNR.END_LOGMNR** procedure.

This all seems reasonably simple, doesn't it? Let's have a look at some code that shows this procedure working:

```
SQL> SHOW PARAMETER utl_file_dir

NAME                                 TYPE    VALUE
------------------------------------ ------  --------------------
utl_file_dir                         string  c:\temp

SQL> EXEC dbms_logmnr_d.build('v817dict.ora', 'c:\temp');

PL/SQL procedure successfully completed.

SQL> EXEC dbms_logmnr.add_logfile( -
>        'd:\oracle\oradata\orcl\archive\orclt001s00137.arc', -
>        DBMS_LOGMNR.NEW);
```

```
PL/SQL procedure successfully completed.

SQL> EXEC dbms_logmnr.add_logfile( -
>           'd:\oracle\oradata\orcl\archive\orclt001s00138.arc', -
>           DBMS_LOGMNR.ADDFILE);

PL/SQL procedure successfully completed.

SQL> EXEC dbms_logmnr.add_logfile( -
>           'd:\oracle\oradata\orcl\archive\orclt001s00139.arc', -
>           DBMS_LOGMNR.ADDFILE);

PL/SQL procedure successfully completed.

SQL> EXEC dbms_logmnr.add_logfile( -
>           'd:\oracle\oradata\orcl\archive\orclt001s00140.arc', -
>           DBMS_LOGMNR.ADDFILE);

PL/SQL procedure successfully completed.

SQL> EXEC dbms_logmnr.start_logmnr( -
>           dictfilename => 'c:\temp\v817dict.ora');

PL/SQL procedure successfully completed.

SQL> SELECT timestamp, username, sql_redo
  2  FROM v$logmnr_contents
  3  WHERE seg_name = 'EMP';

TIMESTAMP   USER   SQL_REDO
----------  ----   ---------------------------
11-MAY-01   FRED   UPDATE scott.emp SET sal =...
11-MAY-01   FRED   UPDATE scott.emp SET sal =...

SQL> EXEC dbms_logmnr.end_logmnr;

PL/SQL procedure successfully completed.
```

Note that I've changed the format of the output slightly to conform to this book's page width. Besides querying the **V$LOGMNR_CONTENTS** view, as I've done in this code, you can also find information about the LogMiner session by querying the views **V$LOGMNR_DICTIONARY** (to see the dictionary file currently in use) and **V$LOGMNR_PARAMETERS** (to see the current settings for LogMiner parameters).

Practice Questions

Question 1

> What is the maximum number of control files that you can specify in the
> **CONTROL_FILES** parameter?
>
> ○ a. 2
>
> ○ b. 4
>
> ○ c. 8
>
> ○ d. 12
>
> ○ e. 16
>
> ○ f. Unlimited

Answer c is correct. You can specify a maximum of eight control files for a database. Oracle recommends a minimum of two control files.

Question 2

> If you rename the control file for your database without updating the parameter file, what happens when you attempt to start up an instance for the database?
>
> ○ a. The database opens after creating a new control file with the
>   default name.
>
> ○ b. The database opens and prompts you for the new control file
>   location.
>
> ○ c. The database is mounted but does not open.
>
> ○ d. The database is not mounted.

Answer d is correct. When the control file name or location is changed, the **CONTROL_FILES** initialization parameter must be altered to specify the current control file name and location. Answer a is incorrect because the default name is used only if the control file is not specified in the **CREATE DATABASE** command. Answer b is incorrect because the database does not prompt you for the new control file location. Answer c is incorrect; the database cannot mount, because doing so requires reading the control file.

Question 3

You notice in review of a client's database that it has only one control file. What are the proper steps to multiplex a control file for an existing database?

○ a. Shut down the database, copy the existing control file using OS commands, edit the **CONTROL_FILES** initialization parameter, and restart the instance.

○ b. Use the **ALTER DATABASE COPY CONTROLFILE** command to copy the existing control file and update the parameter file.

○ c. Use the **ALTER SYSTEM COPY CONTROLFILE** command to copy the existing control file and update the parameter file.

○ d. Shut down the database, copy the existing control file using OS commands, restart the instance, and update the **V$PARAMETER** view.

Answer a is correct. Following the process in answer a allows you to have up to eight copies of the control file as needed. Answers b and c are incorrect because the commands **ALTER DATABASE COPY CONTROLFILE** and **ALTER SYSTEM COPY CONTROLFILE** are invalid. Answer d is incorrect because V$PARAMETER allows you to view, but not update, parameters.

Question 4

When you start an instance and open a database, at what stage is the control file read?

○ a. **NOMOUNT**

○ b. **MOUNT**

○ c. **OPEN**

○ d. **RESTRICT**

Answer b is correct. Because the control file records the database structure, the control file is read when a database is mounted by an instance. Answer a is incorrect because the **NOMOUNT** state is used for re-creating control files and recovery operations, and the control file hasn't been read yet. Answer c is incorrect because the instance must have already read the control file when the database was opened. Answer d is incorrect because **RESTRICT** examines only the privilege level that users need to have to access the database; it has no impact on whether the control file has been read.

Question 5

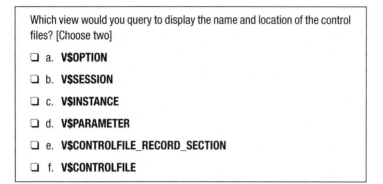

Which view would you query to display the name and location of the control files? [Choose two]

❑ a. **V$OPTION**

❑ b. **V$SESSION**

❑ c. **V$INSTANCE**

❑ d. **V$PARAMETER**

❑ e. **V$CONTROLFILE_RECORD_SECTION**

❑ f. **V$CONTROLFILE**

Answers d and f are correct. **V$PARAMETER** displays the information about the initialization parameters (including the **CONTROL_FILES** parameter), and **V$CONTROLFILE** displays the name and location of each control file. Answer a is incorrect because the **V$OPTION** view lists options that are installed with the Oracle server. Answer b is incorrect because the **V$SESSION** view lists session information for each current session. Answer c is incorrect because the **V$INSTANCE** view displays the state of the current instance. Answer e is incorrect because the **V$CONTROLFILE_RECORD_SECTION** view displays information about the records contained in the control file.

Question 6

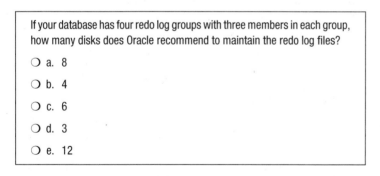

If your database has four redo log groups with three members in each group, how many disks does Oracle recommend to maintain the redo log files?

○ a. 8

○ b. 4

○ c. 6

○ d. 3

○ e. 12

Answer d is correct. Oracle recommends that each member should be placed on a different disk, so three members require three disks, four members would require four disks, and so forth.

Question 7

> You are tuning the database and need to know the sequence number of the current redo log group. Which view would you query to display the sequence number of online redo log groups?
>
> ○ a. **V$DATABASE**
>
> ○ b. **V$LOG_HISTORY**
>
> ○ c. **V$THREAD**
>
> ○ d. **V$INSTANCE**

Answer c is correct. **V$THREAD** displays the current redo log group, the number of online redo log groups, and the current sequence number. Answer a is incorrect because **V$DATABASE** contains database information from the control file, but it does not show redo log information. Answer b is incorrect because **V$LOG_HISTORY** shows information on archived redo log files rather than online redo logs. Answer d is incorrect because **V$INSTANCE** shows the state of the current instance and does not list the current redo log group.

Question 8

> Which of the following files are read from only during recovery operations?
>
> ○ a. Data
>
> ○ b. Trace
>
> ○ c. Control
>
> ○ d. Redo log
>
> ○ e. Parameter

Answer d is correct. In the event of an instance failure, the redo log files are used to recover committed data that hasn't yet been written to the datafiles. Answer a is incorrect because datafiles are used to store user data, not for recovery. Answer b is incorrect because trace files are used to troubleshoot database or user process problems, not for recovery. Answer c is incorrect because control files are used in recovery operations, but the control file is also read by the instance when it mounts a database. Answer e is incorrect because parameter files are read during startup.

Question 9

Assuming the instance is shut down, how would you move an online redo log file to a new location?

○ a. Use OS commands to copy the file, mount the database, and issue the **ALTER DATABASE RENAME FILE** command.

○ b. Mount the database and issue the **ALTER DATABASE MOVE FILE** command to move the file and update the control file.

○ c. Open the database, use OS commands to copy the file, and issue the **ALTER DATBASE RENAME FILE** command.

○ d. Copy the existing control file using OS commands, restart the instance, and use the **ALTER SYSTEM** command to update the parameter file.

Answer a is correct. Use OS commands to copy the file, mount the database, and issue the **ALTER DATABASE RENAME FILE** command to update the control file. Answer b is incorrect because **ALTER DATABASE MOVE FILE** is an invalid command. Answer c is incorrect because the database can't be opened when the instance is shut down. Answer d is incorrect because copying the control file does not move the redo log file.

Question 10

What would you do if your database has two redo log groups and the second group becomes corrupted?

○ a. Drop the second group and add a new group.

○ b. Drop all the groups and issue the **ALTER DATABASE ADD LOGFILE** command.

○ c. Reinitialize the log files in the second group with the **ALTER DATABASE CLEAR LOGFILE** command.

○ d. Clear the second group by issuing the **ALTER DATABASE CLEAR LOGFILE** command, drop the group, and create a new group.

Answer c is correct. You can clear a group if all its members become corrupt by issuing the **ALTER DATABASE CLEAR LOGFILE** command. Answers a, b, and d are incorrect because you must have at least two log groups at all times.

Need to Know More?

 Devraj, Venkat. *Oracle 24×7 Tips and Techniques*. Oracle Press, Berkeley, CA, 2000. ISBN 0-07-211999-3. Chapter 7 covers some of the parameters I mentioned here in more detail, as well as providing more information on mirroring redo log groups and log file placement. Chapter 14 includes information on repairing damaged redo log files.

 Wong, Debbie. *Oracle8i DBA: Backup and Recovery Exam Cram*. The Coriolis Group, Scottsdale, AZ, 2001. ISBN 1-58880-045-8. Consult this book for more information on Recovery Manager, hot backups, and point-in-time recovery.

See the Oracle documentation that is provided on CD with the Oracle RDBMS software. Pertaining to this chapter are:

Baylis, Ruth, and Joyce Fee. *Oracle8i Administrator's Guide*. Oracle Corporation, Redwood City, CA, 1999. See Chapter 5 for details on managing control files, and consult Chapters 6 and 7 for information on managing the online redo log and managing archived redo logs, respectively.

Lorentz, Diana. *Oracle8i Reference Manual*. Oracle Corporation, Redwood City, CA, 1999. See Chapter 3 for more information on the contents of dynamic performance views.

 technet.oracle.com is Oracle's technical repository of information for clients.

 www.revealnet.com is the site where RevealNet Corporation provides Oracle administration reference software.

8

Managing Tablespaces and Datafiles

Terms you'll need to understand:

✓ Tablespaces

✓ Datafiles

✓ **MINIMUM EXTENT**

✓ **AUTOEXTEND**

✓ Online tablespaces

✓ Offline tablespaces

✓ Temporary tablespaces

✓ **COALESCE**

✓ Read-only tablespaces

✓ Online datafiles

✓ Offline datafiles

Techniques you'll need to master:

✓ Creating tablespaces

✓ Changing the size of tablespaces

✓ Allocating space for temporary segments

✓ Changing the status of tablespaces

✓ Changing the storage settings of tablespaces

✓ Relocating tablespaces

As discussed in Chapter 2, a tablespace is a logical structure for either permanent storage of data segments or temporary storage to facilitate sorting, grouping, and summarizing data. Tablespaces are composed of datafiles that are located on disk. In this chapter, you'll learn how to create and manage tablespaces and their underlying datafiles. Such management skills are critical so that you can keep the data intact and available for your users.

Creating Tablespaces

To create a tablespace, you'll use the **CREATE TABLESPACE** command. Figure 8.1 shows the full syntax of the command.

First I'll explain the syntax, and then I'll give an example. There are several different keywords and clauses associated with the **CREATE TABLESPACE** command; let's look at those that you need to really understand for the exam:

➤ *tablespace*—The name of the tablespace you are creating.

➤ *filespec*—The name of the datafile (or datafiles) that make up the tablespace.

➤ AUTOEXTEND *clause*—Specifies whether **AUTOEXTEND** is on or off for this tablespace. See the "Changing the Size of Tablespaces" section later in this chapter for more details on **AUTOEXTEND**.

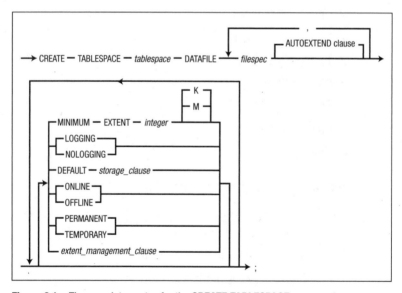

Figure 8.1 The complete syntax for the **CREATE TABLESPACE** command.

➤ **MINIMUM EXTENT**—Controls free space fragmentation in the tablespace. Every extent created in the tablespace will be at least as large as—or a multiple of—the size specified in **MINIMUM EXTENT**. You can specify a size in bytes, kilobytes (K in the syntax diagram), or megabytes (M in the diagram). This clause has no meaning for dictionary-managed temporary tablespaces (which are covered later in this chapter).

➤ **LOGGING/NOLOGGING**—Specifies whether certain operations are logged for objects created in this tablespace. (**LOGGING** is the default.) Not all operations support **NOLOGGING**. The operations that do support **NOLOGGING** are direct load insert statements, direct path SQL*Loader, **CREATE TABLE ... AS SELECT, ALTER TABLE ... SPLIT PARTITION, ALTER TABLE ... MOVE PARTITION, CREATE INDEX, ALTER INDEX ... REBUILD, ALTER INDEX ... REBUILD PARTITION,** and **ALTER INDEX ... SPLIT PARTITION**. When an operation occurs in **NOLOGGING** mode, only minimal information is written to the redo log files (mainly to record data dictionary changes). Because so little information is written to the redo logs, **NOLOGGING** operations cannot be recovered during media recovery. If you can't afford to lose the object referred to by a **NOLOGGING** operation, you should perform a backup as soon as the operation is completed.

➤ **DEFAULT** *storage_clause*—Provides the storage parameters for all objects created in the database that do not have specific storage given in the **CREATE** statement. For dictionary-managed temporary tablespaces, **NEXT** is the only parameter that Oracle uses from this clause; the rest are ignored. Storage parameters are covered in more detail in Chapters 9 and 11.

➤ **ONLINE/OFFLINE**—Controls whether the tablespace will be created as **ONLINE** (and therefore immediately available for use) or **OFFLINE** (and therefore immediately unavailable for use). **ONLINE** is the default.

➤ **PERMANENT/TEMPORARY**—Specifies whether this tablespace can be used for permanent and temporary objects (the default) or temporary objects only (such as segments created for disk sorts). You can't specify **TEMPORARY** if you specify **EXTENT MANAGEMENT LOCAL**. (See the next item.)

➤ *extent_management_clause*—Controls whether extents of the tablespace are managed in data dictionary tables (the default behavior) or by a bitmap in the header of the datafiles for the tablespace. The syntax for dictionary-managed tablespaces is **EXTENT MANAGEMENT DICTIONARY** (this is the default). The syntax for locally managed tablespaces is **EXTENT MANAGEMENT LOCAL**. If you specify **EXTENT MANAGEMENT**

LOCAL, you can also specify **AUTOALLOCATE** or **UNIFORM**. **AUTOALLOCATE**, which is the default, means that you can specify the size of the initial extent and then Oracle will determine the optimal size of additional extents, with a minimum extent size of 64KB. **LOCAL** allows you to either use the default size of 1MB for extents or to specify a **UNIFORM SIZE** in bytes, kilobytes, or megabytes. Currently, the SYSTEM tablespace cannot be created using the **EXTENT MANAGEMENT LOCAL** clause.

Now that I've explained the syntax, let's look at an example that should clarify its use. Here's a **CREATE TABLESPACE** command I used to create a tablespace on my 8.1.7 NT database:

```
SQL> CREATE TABLESPACE user_data
  2   DATAFILE 'd:\oracle\oradata\orcl\user_data_01.dbf' SIZE 500M
  3   EXTENT MANAGEMENT LOCAL UNIFORM SIZE 5M;

Tablespace created.
```

This statement creates a tablespace called USER_DATA, which is composed of one 500MB datafile. I've specified that I want the extents of the tablespace to be managed in a bitmap in the header of the datafile (**EXTENT MANAGEMENT LOCAL**), with each extent a **UNIFORM SIZE** of 5MB. In this case, I haven't specified a **DEFAULT STORAGE** clause, so any objects created in this tablespace will either use the database-wide defaults or override those defaults in the **CREATE** statement for the object. The tablespace will be online and can contain both permanent and temporary objects. Because these are the defaults, they will be used, even though I haven't specifically listed them in the **CREATE TABLESPACE** command.

You can also use Oracle Enterprise Manager (OEM) to create a tablespace. To do this, go to the Navigator pane, click on the database you want, click on the Storage folder, then right-click on the Tablespaces folder and choose Create from the context-sensitive menu. Alternatively, you can click on the Tablespaces folder, choose Create from the Navigator menu, and then pick Tablespace from the list of objects to create. In either case, you'll see the screen shown in Figure 8.2.

Oracle has filled in default values for the location and size of the datafile, and it will complete the datafile name based on the value that you enter for the tablespace name. You can override any of these values simply by selecting the value and entering your own setting. You can choose whether the tablespace is online or offline, and permanent or temporary, simply by selecting the correct value using the radio buttons. Oracle has also provided a couple of useful extra tricks in this screen. If you click on the pencil symbol located under the list of datafiles that compose the tablespace, the screen shown in Figure 8.3 appears.

Figure 8.2 Creating a tablespace using OEM.

Figure 8.3 Editing datafile properties using OEM.

From here, you can edit the datafile name, location, and size, as well as reuse an existing datafile (if there is one). By clicking on the Storage tab, you can set the autoextend functionality for the datafile (this functionality is covered in the "Automatic Datafile Resizing" section later in this chapter).

The other neat feature in the Create Tablespace screen is the Show SQL button. Clicking on this allows you to see the SQL that Oracle has built for you based on the values you've entered.

The Storage tab on the Create Tablespace screen is used to provide extent management information and logging configuration. Notice that the default settings for this (shown in Figure 8.4) are **EXTENT MANAGEMENT LOCAL** (**AUTOALLOCATE** is the default, so you can't see it even in the SQL that Oracle generates for you) and **LOGGING** (for some reason, this does appear, even though it's the default).

If I chose to have the tablespace configured as dictionary-managed instead, the default storage options would appear where the **EXTENT MANAGEMENT LOCAL** options of Automatic Allocation and Uniform Allocation are currently located.

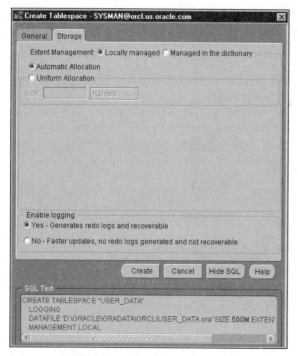

Figure 8.4 Setting extent management and logging configuration using OEM.

When you have finished specifying all the options for the **CREATE TABLESPACE** command in these screens, simply click on the Create button to have Oracle create the tablespace for you.

As you might have guessed from the default screen settings in OEM that I've just covered, Oracle recommends using tablespaces that are locally managed rather than using those that are dictionary managed. Locally managed tablespaces are preferable for a number of reasons:

➤ Locally managed tablespaces automatically track adjacent free space, thus eliminating the need for free space coalescence.

➤ Extent sizing can be performed automatically by Oracle; alternatively, you can specify uniform extent sizes for all segments in a locally managed tablespace.

➤ Locally managed tablespaces avoid recursive space management, which can occur in dictionary-managed tablespaces when extent allocation or deallocation results in recursive operations that allocate or deallocate space in rollback segments or data dictionary tables.

➤ Locally managed tablespaces reduce contention on the data dictionary tables that are used to track free space. The reason is that the tracking is done in the bitmaps in the headers of datafiles for locally managed tablespaces, rather than the data dictionary tables used for dictionary-managed tablespaces. (Note that you can still have contention on other data dictionary tables; only contention for the tables that track free space is removed.)

➤ Changes to the bitmaps in the headers of the datafiles for locally managed tablespaces generally don't require rollback information to be written to the rollback segments because they don't update data dictionary tables (except in special cases such as tablespace quota information).

Changing the Size of Tablespaces

You can change the size of a tablespace in one of two ways: You can change the size of an existing datafile (either automatically or manually), or you can add an additional datafile to an existing tablespace.

Automatic Datafile Resizing

To enable or disable automatic datafile resizing, you need to use the **AUTOEXTEND** clause. This clause can be used in the **CREATE DATABASE**, **CREATE TABLESPACE**, and **ALTER TABLESPACE ... ADD DATAFILE** commands for new datafiles, and in the **ALTER DATABASE ... DATAFILE** command for existing datafiles. You add the **AUTOEXTEND** clause to the *filespec* clause for new datafiles, and after the *filename* clause for existing datafiles. Here are some examples:

```
SQL> ALTER TABLESPACE user_data
  2   ADD DATAFILE '/u01/oradata/prd1/user01.dbf' SIZE 500M
  3   AUTOEXTEND ON NEXT 50M MAXSIZE UNLIMITED;

Tablespace altered.

SQL> ALTER DATABASE
  2   DATAFILE '/u01/oradata/prd1/user01.dbf'
  3   AUTOEXTEND OFF;

Database altered.
```

The first command adds a new datafile to the USER_DATA tablespace, and turns **AUTOEXTEND** on for the datafile. When the datafile becomes full, it will grow in increments of 50MB with no maximum size. The second command turns **AUTOEXTEND** off for the same datafile.

You can also use OEM to automatically extend data files. To do this for existing datafiles, go to the Navigator pane, click on the database you want, click on the Storage folder, then right-click on the Tablespaces folder and choose Edit from the context-sensitive menu. Alternatively, you can click on the Tablespaces folder, choose the tablespace you want to alter, and then choose Edit Tablespace from the Navigator menu. In either case, choose the datafile you want to enable **AUTOEXTEND** for, then click on the pencil symbol under the list of datafiles that compose the tablespace. Click on the Storage tab and set the values you want for the **AUTOEXTEND** clause. Notice that clicking on the OK button here doesn't actually issue the command; rather, it returns you to the Edit Tablespace screen where you can click on OK again (or on Apply if you want to remain in the Edit Tablespace screen) to actually issue the SQL command.

If you want to add a new datafile to an existing tablespace with **AUTOEXTEND** turned on, you need to click the empty row below the existing datafiles, then click on the pencil symbol to bring up the Create Datafile screen. Enter the relevant values on the Storage tab for the **AUTOEXTEND** clause. Again, clicking on the OK button here doesn't actually issue the command; rather, it returns you to the Edit Tablespace screen where you can click on OK again (or on Apply if you want to remain in the Edit Tablespace screen) to actually issue the SQL command.

Manually Resizing Datafiles

Instead of allowing Oracle to automatically extend datafiles, you can manually increase or decrease the size of a datafile by using the **ALTER DATABASE ... DATAFILE ... RESIZE** command. If any objects are stored above the specified size, you'll receive an error ("ORA-03297: the file contains used data beyond requested RESIZE value").

 The Oracle Education courseware is in error on this point. It states that the **RESIZE** command will succeed, but that the file size will decrease only to the last block used by the last object in the datafile. This error may be corrected in subsequent printings, but if it isn't, you should expect the exam to make the same mistake.

Here's an example of using the **ALTER DATABASE** command to resize a datafile:

```
SQL> ALTER DATABASE
  2  DATAFILE '/u01/oradata/prd1/user01.dbf' RESIZE 750M;
```

You can also use OEM to resize datafiles. From the Edit Tablespace screen referred to previously, double-click on the row containing the datafile you want to resize, edit the file size as required, and click on OK. Notice that the row now shows the new size. This can be misleading, because the change does not take effect until you click on the OK button on the Edit Tablespace screen.

Adding Datafiles to an Existing Tablespace

The commands shown in the previous two sections allow you to increase the size of an existing datafile. However, you can also add more datafiles to an existing tablespace to provide more space for it. In earlier versions, this was the only way to add more space to a tablespace. Now, it is less useful, unless you want to *stripe* a tablespace across multiple disks by spreading the datafiles across different devices. However, the operation can still be performed, and you'll need to know how to do this for the exam.

The command used to add a new datafile to an existing tablespace is **ALTER TABLESPACE ... ADD DATAFILE**. This is done in the same way as adding a datafile to a tablespace with **AUTOEXTEND** turned on (as described previously), so refer back to that section for the details.

Allocating Space for Temporary Segments

As I mentioned in the "Creating Tablespaces" section earlier in this chapter, you can specify that a tablespace can contain only temporary objects when you create it (that is, you can't create permanent objects), by using the **CREATE TABLESPACE ... TEMPORARY** command. The only problem with this is that you can't use the **TEMPORARY** clause when you're creating a locally managed tablespace. As you learned previously, there are a number of advantages to using locally managed tablespaces, so it would be useful to create a locally managed temporary tablespace. Oracle does allow you to do this, but you need to specify a slightly different command. Instead of using the **CREATE TABLESPACE ... TEMPORARY** command, you need to use the **CREATE TEMPORARY TABLESPACE** command (confusing, isn't it?) to create a locally managed temporary tablespace. The **CREATE TEMPORARY TABLESPACE** command has very similar clauses to the **CREATE TABLESPACE** command, except you need to specify **TEMPFILE** instead of **DATAFILE**. Here's an example of a command that creates a temporary tablespace:

```
SQL> CREATE TEMPORARY TABLESPACE temp
  2  TEMPFILE '/u01/oradata/prd1/temp_data.dbf' SIZE 500M
  3  EXTENT MANAGEMENT LOCAL UNIFORM SIZE 10M;
```

This command creates a locally managed temporary tablespace called temp, using the tempfile specified of size 500MB. If you specify a **UNIFORM SIZE** clause, the value for **UNIFORM SIZE** should be a multiple of **SORT_AREA_SIZE** for best performance.

Notice the use of the **TEMPFILE** keyword on line 2 of the command just given. Tempfiles are similar to ordinary datafiles, except for the following differences:

➤ Tempfiles are always created in **NOLOGGING** mode.

➤ You cannot rename a tempfile.

➤ You cannot create a tempfile with the **ALTER DATABASE** command.

➤ Tempfiles cannot be read-only.

➤ Media recovery cannot be used to recover tempfiles.

➤ The **ALTER DATABASE BACKUP CONTROLFILE** command creates a backup control file that contains no information about tempfiles.

➤ The **CREATE CONTROLFILE** command does not allow you to specify tempfiles.

You can create a temporary tablespace in OEM in the same way that you create normal tablespaces, but there's a trick to it. You need to click on the Temporary radio button on the General tab (refer back to Figure 8.2), then go to the Storage tab. If you click on Show SQL now, you'll see that the syntax uses the **CREATE TABLESPACE ... TEMPORARY** command. If you click on the Managed In The Dictionary radio button, and then switch back to the Extent Management Local radio button, the syntax will change to **CREATE TEMPORARY TABLESPACE**.

Changing the Status of Tablespaces

Tablespaces are normally online. However, you'll need to take a tablespace offline for some operations. These include:

➤ Recovering a tablespace or datafile while the database is open

➤ Moving a tablespace or datafile while the database is open

➤ Taking an offline backup of a tablespace (although this is possible, it's an option that is rarely used because tablespaces can be backed up while they are open)

➤ Making part of the database unavailable while the rest remains open for normal use

When a tablespace is offline, it is unavailable for normal use. Users attempting to access the tablespace will receive an error that indicates that the tablespace is offline. Taking a tablespace offline is recorded in the control file, and Oracle won't attempt to access a tablespace that is marked as offline when the database is started.

In some situations, Oracle takes a tablespace offline automatically (usually when a number of attempts to write to the tablespace have failed), but generally you have to take a tablespace offline manually. All tablespaces can be taken offline, except the SYSTEM tablespace (which contains the data dictionary, which must remain available, of course) or any tablespace that contains an active rollback segment. The datafiles that make up the tablespace are also taken offline by the operation of taking a tablespace offline.

To take a tablespace offline, you use the **ALTER TABLESPACE** command. The syntax for the relevant part of the command is **ALTER TABLESPACE** *tablespace_name* **ONLINE | OFFLINE NORMAL | TEMPORARY | IMMEDIATE | FOR RECOVER**. The default for an **ALTER TABLESPACE OFFLINE** command is **NORMAL**. The parameters are as follows:

➤ **NORMAL**—Forces a checkpoint before the **OFFLINE** command is processed. This ensures that media recovery is not needed when the tablespace is brought back online again.

➤ **TEMPORARY**—Forces a checkpoint on any online datafiles that make up the tablespace, but any offline tablespaces may need recovery when they are brought back online.

➤ **IMMEDIATE**—Does not perform a checkpoint before the tablespace is brought offline. Any datafiles in this tablespace will need to undergo media recovery when they are brought back online.

➤ **FOR RECOVER**—Indicates that the tablespace is being taken offline for tablespace point-in-time recovery. Note that tablespace point-in-time recovery should be undertaken only with the help of Worldwide Support.

Tablespaces can also be taken offline using OEM. To do this, go to the Navigator pane, click on the database you want, click on the Storage folder, then right-click on the Tablespaces folder and choose Edit from the context-sensitive menu. Alternatively, you can click on the Tablespaces folder, choose the tablespace you want to alter, and then choose Edit Tablespace from the Navigator menu. Click on the Offline radio button and then choose the mode (Normal, Temporary, Immediate, or For Recover) and click on the OK button.

You can also use the **ALTER TABLESPACE** command to toggle a tablespace from read-write to read-only (or vice versa). Making a tablespace read-only prevents any further writes from occurring to the tablespace. A tablespace that has been marked as read-only can be moved to read-only media, such as a CD-ROM or WORM (Write Once, Read Many) device. You need to do this as three steps:

1. Make the tablespace read-only.

2. Copy the datafiles to the read-only media using the relevant OS command.

3. Issue the **ALTER TABLESPACE ... RENAME DATAFILE** command to tell Oracle that the datafile is in the new location.

Making a tablespace read-only also allows you to back up the tablespace once and then largely ignore it from your backup routines.

The reason I say *largely* ignore it is that most DBAs realize that you can't totally ignore a read-only tablespace from your backup routine. For example, you make a tablespace read-only, back it up to tape once, and then remove it from your backup routine. A year later, the disk that contains the tablespace fails, and you need to recover it. Can you imagine going back through a year of backups to try and locate the tablespace? However, for purposes of the exam, be prepared to say that read-only tablespaces can be ignored from your backup routine.

The command to toggle the status of a tablespace from read-only to read-write is **ALTER TABLESPACE** *tablespace_name* **READ ONLY.** You can toggle the status back again using the command **ALTER TABLESPACE** *tablespace_name* **READ WRITE.**

You can also use OEM to toggle the status of a tablespace from read-only to read-write and back again. Using the same path that I mentioned previously to edit a tablespace's status from online to offline, click on the Read Only radio button and select OK to make a tablespace read-only, or deselect the Read Only radio button and select OK to make a tablespace read-write.

When you make a tablespace read-only, Oracle places the tablespace in a transitional read-only mode. No new write operations are allowed for the tablespace, but those that are already taking place are allowed to either commit or rollback. This wasn't the case in earlier releases, in which no active transactions could be occurring in the tablespace when the **ALTER TABLESPACE** command was issued. However, the Oracle8i command still has a couple of restrictions: The tablespace cannot contain active rollback segments, nor can it be currently involved in an online backup when the **ALTER TABLESPACE** command occurs.

Note: Making a tablespace read-only does not prevent objects from being dropped from the tablespace. This can be confusing; after all, if a tablespace is read-only, how can you drop objects from it? The answer is relatively simple: all the object removal does is update the data dictionary, not the tablespace itself. Because the data dictionary is not read-only, dropping an object in a read-only tablespace is not a problem.

Changing the Storage Settings of Tablespaces

You can change the storage settings of a tablespace using the **ALTER TABLESPACE** command. Using this command, you can change the values of **MINIMUM EXTENT** and the **DEFAULT STORAGE** clauses. (You can use the **ALTER TABLESPACE** command for much more than this, but these parts of the command are the ones that are relevant to this section of the chapter.) Here are some examples of using this command:

```
SQL> ALTER TABLESPACE user_data
  2   MINIMUM EXTENT 5M;

Tablespace altered.

SQL> ALTER TABLESPACE user_data
```

```
2  DEFAULT STORAGE (INITIAL 5M
3                   NEXT 5M
4                   MAXEXTENTS 500
5                   PCTINCREASE 0);
```

The first example changes (or sets, if it wasn't set before) the **MINIMUM EXTENT** size for the tablespace so that it is a multiple of 5MB. The second example changes (or sets, if it wasn't set before) the **DEFAULT STORAGE** clause for the tablespace. (The parameters for the **DEFAULT STORAGE** clause are covered in more detail in Chapter 11.)

You can also change the storage settings for a tablespace in OEM. In the Navigator pane, select the database that contains the tablespace you want to alter, choose the Storage folder, then the Tablespaces folder, right-click on the tablespace you want to alter, and choose Edit from the context-sensitive menu. Alternatively, click on the tablespace you want to alter and choose Edit Tablespace from the Navigate menu. In either case, the Edit Tablespace screen shown in Figure 8.5 appears.

From the General tab, you can change a tablespace status from online to offline or from permanent to temporary. Click on the Storage tab to change the default storage if the tablespace is dictionary-managed. Although you won't be able to change the settings if the tablespace is locally managed, you can still see what they are.

Figure 8.5   Altering a tablespace using the Edit Tablespace screen in OEM.

Relocating Tablespaces

You can relocate or move the datafiles for a tablespace with either of two commands: the **ALTER TABLESPACE** command or the **ALTER DATABASE** command. (Remember that what you're really doing here is relocating the datafiles rather than the tablespaces themselves.)

The **ALTER TABLESPACE** command can be used to relocate datafiles for a tablespace that does not contain an active rollback segment. This includes the SYSTEM tablespace, which can't be relocated in this manner anyway because we need access to the data dictionary for other users. The steps involved are:

1. Take the tablespace offline.

2. Copy the datafiles that you want to move to their new location using the relevant OS command (the files must exist in the new location before the **ALTER TABLESPACE** command will succeed).

3. Issue the **ALTER TABLESPACE ... RENAME DATAFILE** command to update the control file with the new datafile locations.

4. Bring the tablespace back online.

5. Delete the original copies of the datafiles, if necessary.

Here's an example of the command:

```
SQL> ALTER TABLESPACE user_data
  2   RENAME DATAFILE '/u01/oradata/prd1/user01.dbf'
  3   TO '/u02/oradata/prd1/user01.dbf';

Tablespace altered.
```

You can rename multiple datafiles in a single operation by providing a comma-delimited list of old and new file names. Oracle will rename the first old file to the first new file, the second old file to the second new file, and so on.

The **ALTER DATABASE** command can be used to rename any datafile, whether or not it contains the data dictionary or an active rollback segment. However, because the database has to be mounted but not open to use this command, you normally see it used only to rename those datafiles that cannot be renamed using the **ALTER TABLESPACE** command. Because the command can be used to rename log files as well as datafiles, the syntax is slightly different. Here's an example:

```
SQL> ALTER DATABASE
  2   RENAME FILE '/u01/oradata/prd1/system.dbf'
```

```
    3  TO '/u02/oradata/prd1/system.dbf';

Database altered.
```

You can also use OEM to rename or relocate datafiles. From the Edit Tablespace screen, double-click on the datafile to be renamed or relocated, edit the File Name or File Directory values appropriately, and click on OK. Before applying the changes, click on the Show SQL button. You'll notice that OEM uses only the **ALTER DATABASE** version of the command. Click on OK again to apply the changes. If you attempt to use OEM to rename a file that can be renamed only when the database is mounted, you'll receive an error that the file is in use and cannot be renamed. You'll then need to take the database to the mounted stage first, and then perform the rename operation.

Dropping Tablespaces

To remove a tablespace from the database, you use the **DROP TABLESPACE** command. Dropping a tablespace is not allowed if the tablespace still contains objects, unless you specify the **INCLUDING CONTENTS** option. Likewise, a tablespace cannot be dropped if it contains objects that contain primary or unique keys that are referenced as foreign key constraints in objects that exist outside the tablespace, unless the **CASCADE CONSTRAINTS** option is included. (See Chapter 12 for more details on constraints.) Here's an example of a **DROP TABLESPACE** command:

```
SQL> DROP TABLESPACE user_data
    2  INCLUDING CONTENTS CASCADE CONSTRAINTS;

Tablespace altered.
```

This command drops the USER_DATA tablespace, including any objects that it contains, and also removes any foreign keys from other tables that reference objects located in the USER_DATA tablespace.

Dropping a tablespace that contains a lot of objects may generate a lot of rollback. If this is a concern, you should drop the objects first and then drop the tablespace. The **DROP TABLESPACE** command affects only Oracle's knowledge of the tablespace. The data dictionary is updated to reflect that the tablespace no longer exists, but the OS files are not removed; you'll need to do this manually.

Oracle9i allows you to issue the **DROP TABLESPACE** *tablespace_name* **INCLUDING CONTENTS AND DATAFILES** command to remove the datafiles from the OS level as well as the database level.

As usual, you can also use OEM to drop a tablespace. In the Navigator pane, select the database you want to issue the command against, then select the Storage folder and the Tablespaces folder, then right-click on the tablespace name you want to drop and choose the Remove option from the context-sensitive menu. Click on OK when you are prompted "Are you sure you want to remove tablespace *tablespace_name?*", and the tablespace will be dropped. Again, the datafiles are not removed with this operation until Oracle9i.

Obtaining Tablespace Information

Information about tablespaces is kept in a variety of data dictionary views. The most important ones are:

➤ **DBA_DATA_FILES**—Provides information on datafiles in the database, including file names, the names of the tablespaces that the datafiles are in, and the size, status, and autoextensibility settings.

➤ **DBA_TABLESPACES**—Describes all the tablespaces in the database, including their names, storage information, logging configuration, extent management, and statuses.

➤ **DBA_TEMP_FILES**—Contains information about the tempfiles in the database, including file names, names of the tablespaces that the tempfiles are in, and the size, status, and autoextensibility settings.

➤ **V$DATAFILE**—Displays datafile information from the control file, including file names, sizes, checkpoint information, and statuses.

➤ **V$TABLESPACE**—Lists the tablespace numbers and tablespace names from the control file. This is mainly used in joins with **V$DATAFILE** and **V$TEMPFILE** to display tablespace information for those views.

➤ **V$TEMPFILE**—Displays tempfile information from the control file, including file names, sizes, and statuses.

Practice Questions

Question 1

> When moving datafiles, what do the **ALTER DATABASE RENAME FILE** and **ALTER TABLESPACE RENAME DATAFILE** commands do?
>
> ○ a. Move datafiles.
>
> ○ b. Rename datafiles.
>
> ○ c. Copy datafiles.
>
> ○ d. Reset internal file pointers in the control file.

Answer d is correct. **ALTER DATABASE RENAME FILE** and **ALTER TABLESPACE RENAME DATAFILE** update only the control file. Answers a, b, and c are incorrect because you must use OS commands when moving, renaming, or copying a datafile.

Question 2

> When moving datafiles, when would you use the **ALTER DATABASE** command rather than the **ALTER TABLESPACE** command?
>
> ○ a. When the tablespace is offline
>
> ○ b. When the tablespace is the SYSTEM tablespace
>
> ○ c. When the tablespace does not contain active data segments
>
> ○ d. When the tablespace does not contain active temporary segments

Answer b is correct. The **ALTER DATABASE** command must be used when datafiles for the SYSTEM tablespace are being renamed or moved. Answer a is incorrect because the **ALTER TABLESPACE** command can be used on an offline tablespace. Answers c and d are incorrect because data and temporary segments have no bearing on which command you would use to move datafiles.

Question 3

> Which condition will prevent the DATA01 tablespace from being dropped in
> the following command?
>
> ```
> DROP TABLESPACE data01;
> ```
>
> ○ a. It is online.
> ○ b. It is offline.
> ○ c. It is read-only.
> ○ d. It contains objects.

Answer d is correct. To drop a tablespace with objects, you must use the **IN-CLUDING CONTENTS** option in the **DROP TABLESPACE** command. Answers a and b are incorrect because, although it is a better practice to put tablespaces offline before dropping them, no requirement exists to do so. Answer c is incorrect because read-only tablespaces can be dropped like any other type of tablespace.

Question 4

> What happens when a tablespace is taken offline normally?
>
> ○ a. A checkpoint occurs.
> ○ b. Recovery is needed before the tablespace can be brought online.
> ○ c. Users can query objects in the tablespace, but they cannot alter
>   the objects.
> ○ d. Users can create new objects in the tablespace, but they cannot
>   query any objects.

Answer a is correct. Before the datafiles associated with the tablespace are taken offline, a checkpoint occurs. Answer b is incorrect because recovery is not needed when a tablespace is taken offline normally. Answer c is incorrect because a tablespace cannot be queried when it is taken offline. Answer d is incorrect because new objects cannot be created in an offline tablespace.

Question 5

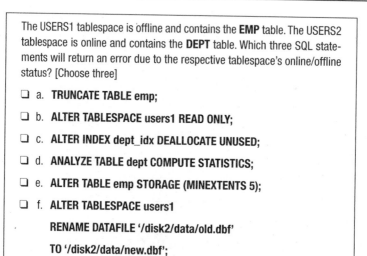

The USERS1 tablespace is offline and contains the **EMP** table. The USERS2 tablespace is online and contains the **DEPT** table. Which three SQL statements will return an error due to the respective tablespace's online/offline status? [Choose three]

❑ a. **TRUNCATE TABLE emp;**

❑ b. **ALTER TABLESPACE users1 READ ONLY;**

❑ c. **ALTER INDEX dept_idx DEALLOCATE UNUSED;**

❑ d. **ANALYZE TABLE dept COMPUTE STATISTICS;**

❑ e. **ALTER TABLE emp STORAGE (MINEXTENTS 5);**

❑ f. **ALTER TABLESPACE users1**

   RENAME DATAFILE '/disk2/data/old.dbf'

   TO '/disk2/data/new.dbf';

Answers a, b, and e are correct. When a tablespace is offline, SQL statements cannot be issued against any of the tablespace objects. Answers c and d will succeed because they are being executed against an online tablespace. Answer f will succeed based on the online/offline status. This question is tricky because you must assume that the datafile has already been copied using OS commands.

Question 6

Which command would you use to change the size of the minimum extent allocated to the USERS tablespace from 2MB to 3MB?

○ a. **ALTER SYSTEM**

○ b. **ALTER DATABASE DATAFILE**

○ c. **ALTER TABLESPACE MINIMUM EXTENT**

○ d. **ALTER TABLESPACE DEFAULT STORAGE**

Answer c is correct. Use the **ALTER TABLESPACE** command to change the **MINIMUM EXTENT** value for a tablespace. Answer a is incorrect because the **ALTER SYSTEM** command does not affect tablespace storage parameters. Answer b is incorrect because the **ALTER DATABASE DATAFILE** command is used to rename or relocate datafiles. Answer d is incorrect because the **DEFAULT STORAGE** clause changes the storage parameters for objects created in a tablespace, but it cannot change **MINIMUM EXTENT**.

Question 7

> Why will the following statement fail?
>
> ```
> CREATE TABLESPACE user_data
>     DATAFILE '/disk2/us_data01.dbf' SIZE 10M
>     MINIMUM EXTENT 500K
>     DEFAULT STORAGE
>         (INITIAL 100K NEXT 100K
>          MAXEXTENTS 500 PCTINCREASE 0);
> ```
>
> ○ a. **MAXEXTENTS** is set too high.
>
> ○ b. **MINIMUM EXTENT** cannot be set at the tablespace level.
>
> ○ c. **INITIAL** and **NEXT** should be a multiple of **MINIMUM EXTENT**.
>
> ○ d. The datafile is too large for the default storage parameters.

Answer c is correct. When **MINIMUM EXTENT** is specified, every extent allocated in the tablespace should be a multiple of **MINIMUM EXTENT**. Answer a is incorrect because **MAXEXTENTS** is not too high; in fact, it could be set to unlimited because Oracle8i has no limit to extents. Answer b is incorrect because **MINIMUM EXTENT** is a valid tablespace parameter. Answer d is incorrect because the default storage parameters affect the objects that are created in a tablespace without a storage clause of their own. A datafile can be too small for the default storage parameters, but not too large.

Question 8

Which is the correct sequence of steps to move datafiles in the USERS tablespace?

- ○ a. Take the tablespace offline, issue the **ALTER TABLESPACE** command, move the files using OS commands, and bring the tablespace back online.

- ○ b. Issue the **ALTER TABLESPACE** command, take the tablespace offline, move the files using OS commands, and bring the tablespace back online.

- ○ c. Take the tablespace offline, move the files using OS commands, bring the tablespace back online, and issue the **ALTER TABLESPACE** command.

- ○ d. Take the tablespace offline, move the files using OS commands, issue the **ALTER TABLESPACE** command, and bring the tablespace back online.

Answer d is correct. The correct sequence of steps to move a datafile that is not in the SYSTEM tablespace is as follows: Take the tablespace offline, move the files using OS commands, issue the **ALTER TABLESPACE** command, and bring the tablespace back online. Answers a and b are incorrect because the files must exist before the **ALTER TABLESPACE** command is used. Answer c is incorrect because you must execute the **ALTER TABLESPACE** command before the files are brought back online.

Need to Know More?

Devraj, Venkat S. *Oracle 24×7 Tips and Techniques*. Oracle Press, Berkeley, CA, 2000. ISBN 0-07211-999-3. Chapter 4 covers locally managed tablespaces.

Loney, Kevin, and Marlene Theriault. *Oracle8i DBA Handbook*. Oracle Press, Berkeley, CA, 1999. ISBN 0-07212-188-2. This book is a comprehensive guide and a must-have for all DBAs. Chapter 4 discusses physical database layout and goes into more detail on moving and resizing datafiles.

See the Oracle documentation that is provided on CD with the Oracle RDBMS software. Pertaining to this chapter are:

Baylis, Ruth, and Joyce Fee. *Oracle8i Administrator's Guide*. Oracle Corporation, Redwood City, CA, 1999. This guide provides complete documentation of database administration tasks. Chapter 9 looks at managing tablespaces.

Leverenz, Lefty, Diana Rehfield, and Cathy Baird. *Oracle8i Concepts*. Oracle Corporation, Redwood City, CA, 1999. This is the complete documentation of Oracle concepts. Chapter 3 covers tablespaces and datafiles.

Lorentz, Diana. *Oracle8i Reference*. Oracle Corporation, Redwood City, CA, 1999. Here you'll find specific details on initialization parameters, data dictionary views, and database limits.

technet.oracle.com is Oracle's technical repository of information for clients.

www.revealnet.com is the site where RevealNet Corporation provides Oracle administration reference software.

Storage Structure and Relationships

Terms you'll need to understand:

✓ Segment
✓ Index segment
✓ Rollback segment
✓ Temporary segment
✓ Data block
✓ Data segment
✓ **PCTUSED**
✓ **PCTFREE**
✓ Free list
✓ Extent

Techniques you'll need to master:

✓ Listing the segment types and their uses
✓ Knowing the keywords that control block space usage
✓ Obtaining information about storage structures from the data dictionary
✓ Understanding the criteria for separating segments

In this chapter, I'll drill down to the basic storage structures of Oracle—or, more specifically, data blocks, extents, and segments—that make up the tablespaces I covered in the last chapter. Understanding these elements and how they are allocated is important to many database designs and tuning concepts, and misunderstanding these concepts can cause incorrect usage, resulting in poor performance and misallocation of database space.

Segment Types and Their Uses

Chapter 2 provided a brief introduction to the different types of segments. Now let's look at the different segment types in more detail.

Tables

Tables are the most common method of storing data in Oracle. A table segment is created implicitly whenever a table is created that is neither a nested table nor a partitioned table. (Partitioned table segments and nested table segments are explained further in the next two sections.) Data is kept in rows and columns within a table, and generally without any particular order. This randomness can be overridden temporarily by loading a table with sorted data, but the data stays sorted only while it is static. Any new data inserted into the table will not be inserted in sorted order. The data within a table segment resides in only one tablespace.

Partitioned Tables

Oracle8 introduced partitioned tables to ease the performance, availability, and manageability problems that are common to very large tables. Tables can be partitioned either by a range of values (for example, all data for January in one partition, all data for February in another partition, and so on) or by a hashing algorithm. Each partition within a partitioned table is stored in a different segment, so the table can be stored in multiple tablespaces across multiple devices. It is this ability to spread the partitions that resolves the problems of performance, availability, and manageability. Partitioned tables can also be subpartitioned for further improvements in these areas. For example, you could partition a table by a range of values to make manageability easier, and then by a hashing algorithm to increase performance. To make partitions of either type, you must use the partitioning option (available at additional cost) in the Enterprise Edition of Oracle.

Nested Tables

A nested table is created when a column within a table is defined as a user-defined table. An obvious example is the commonly seen **ORDERS** and **ITEMS** objects. These could be kept as separate tables with a master detail relationship (multiple rows in the **ITEMS** table are the children of only one parent order in the **ORDERS** table), but it may be more beneficial to create a type (for instance, **CREATE TYPE orderitem_table AS TABLE OF order_item**) that then can be referred to as the datatype for a column within the **ORDERS** table definition. The values for the nested table are kept out of line from the **ORDERS** table.

LOB Segments

You also may create a column or columns to store large objects (LOBs), such as Word documents, WAV_files, or images. Generally, these LOBs can be quite large (up to 4GB in Oracle8.1), so Oracle keeps them in separate LOB segments in different tablespaces from the rest of the table. The actual division point is 4KB; objects larger than this are not stored inline with the rest of the values for that row.

Index Clusters

Clusters are a different way of storing data (rather than normal tables). In a cluster, one or more tables are clustered together because they share common columns and are often used together, with the rows sharing the same blocks. In an index cluster, rows are stored together because they have the same cluster key value. The cluster key is the column or columns that the tables share in common. For example, the **EMP** and **DEPT** tables share the **DEPTNO** column. If **EMP** and **DEPT** were clustered together in an index cluster, the **DEPTNO** column would be used to store rows with the same **DEPTNO** together. The value of the cluster key (that is, the values of **DEPTNO**) is stored only once for all rows that share the cluster key value. A cluster index is built upon the cluster key, and the cluster index must be created before rows can be inserted into the index cluster. Because the rows are stored together, index clusters are useful for reducing disk I/O for joins of clustered tables as well as for improving access times.

Hash Clusters

Hash clusters are very similar to index clusters, but the rows are stored together and retrieved based on a hashing algorithm. To store or locate a row in the cluster, Oracle applies the hashing algorithm, which can be user specified, to the cluster key values. As is true of index cluster values, the cluster key values can be from one or more columns. If the cluster key values are not well distributed (which is necessary for best performance of the hashing algorithm), a user-defined function may better distribute the cluster rows. Hash clusters have improved performance benefits in some cases because it's possible to retrieve rows in a hash cluster in a single I/O. (In comparison, an index cluster lookup will cause at least two I/Os: one to read the index and the other to retrieve the data from the cluster.)

Indexes

Indexes are optional structures that are created on one or more columns of a table or cluster to improve performance when accessing the rows in the underlying table or cluster. A composite index is one that is created across multiple columns (up to 32 for normal B-tree indexes, or up to 30 for bitmap indexes). Indexes can also be unique (in which case every value in the column or columns being indexed can occur only once) or nonunique (in which duplicate values are allowed in the index). Although Oracle has a number of different types of indexes, the exam expects you to know about only the three main types: B-tree, reverse key, and bitmap.

B-Tree Indexes

In a B-tree index (the most common type of index), the B-tree structure is balanced to ensure roughly similar access times to every row. The leaf blocks at the end of the B-tree contain the data values for the columns that are indexed and the **ROWID** that points directly to the remainder of the row on disk.

Reverse Key Indexes

Reverse key indexes use exactly the same structure as B-tree indexes, but the order of the bytes in the index columns is reversed (except for the **ROWID**). Reverse key indexes are most useful in Parallel Server configurations, but they can also be used to improve the performance of indexes on a monotonically increasing column (where the values are increasing by one). Because of the nature of the byte reversal, reverse key indexes can't be used in range scans; however, they are still useful for index key lookups and full index scans.

Bitmap Indexes

A bitmap index stores a bitmap for each key value, instead of the **ROWID** that's used in normal indexes. Each bit in the bitmap is set when the row with the corresponding **ROWID** contains the key value. This is particularly useful in data warehousing environments with low cardinality columns (columns that have a low number of distinct values relative to the total number of rows in the table). Online Transaction Processing (OLTP) applications are not well suited to bitmap indexes because updates to a bitmap index lock at the bitmap level (that is, multiple rows can be affected by the lock). Bitmap indexes are available only in the Enterprise Edition.

Partitioned Indexes

Partitioned indexes are used for many of the same reasons that partitioned tables are, and they have similar rules to those of partitioned tables (including rules that indexes on clusters can't be partitioned, partitioned tables can have partitioned or nonpartitioned indexes, nonpartitioned tables can have partitioned or nonpartitioned indexes, and bitmap indexes can't be partitioned if they are built on nonpartitioned tables). However, partitioned indexes have an added layer of complexity because Oracle supports three different types of partitioned indexes: local prefixed, local nonprefixed, and global prefixed. (Oracle doesn't support the global nonprefixed type, but these indexes aren't very useful in real applications anyway.)

Local partitioned indexes (both prefixed and nonprefixed) have a one-to-one mapping with the partitioning of the underlying table. In other words, a local index is equipartitioned with the table. It is partitioned on the same columns and with the same bounds as the underlying table. If the index refers to the same leading columns as the underlying table partitioning, then it is a local prefixed index. If the index doesn't refer to the same leading columns, it's a local nonprefixed index. For example, if a **SALES** table is partitioned by **QUARTER** and **MONTH**, an index on **QUARTER** would be considered a local prefixed index. An index on **MONTH** would be considered a local nonprefixed index because the leading column **QUARTER** is not included. In a global prefixed index, the values in a particular index partition can point to rows in more than one underlying table partition. For this reason, global partitions are not normally equipartitioned. As a result, they also are harder to manage because many partition management operations (such as **SPLIT** or **DROP**) cause a global index to be marked unusable, and it needs to be rebuilt before it can be used.

LOB Indexes

In earlier releases of Oracle8, you could specify a LOB index clause when you created a table containing LOBs. This is deprecated in Oracle8i. Although it's still possible to use the LOB index clause in the **CREATE TABLE** statement, Oracle strongly recommends that you don't. As of Oracle8i, LOB index segments are created automatically for every LOB column, but Oracle names and manages the LOB indexes internally.

Index-Organized Tables

An index-organized table (IOT) is a table that contains all its data in a B-tree index. Rather than having an index key that contains the key value and the **ROWID** for the rest of the row, the index key in an IOT contains the primary key value followed by the nonprimary key values, all within the structure of a B-tree. An IOT is useful for queries that look up the primary key, or the leading columns of the primary key. Because the data values are stored with the primary key in an IOT, IOTs are useful for queries that use an exact match or a range search of the IOT. The storage requirements are less than that of a normal (also known as *heap-organized* or just *heap*) table because an IOT doesn't require storage for both a table and an index. Unlike a normal index, in which the index entry is usually quite small because it simply contains the key values and a **ROWID**, entries in an IOT can be quite large because they store the primary key values and the nonprimary key values in the index entry. You can end up with a leaf node only containing one row, or even one row piece, if the rows are too large.

Oracle resolves this by allowing you to specify an **OVERFLOW** clause. The **OVERFLOW** clause can include the tablespace name for the overflow, as well as a threshold value (**PCTTHRESHOLD**) that tells Oracle what percentage of the block should be filled before storing the remaining column values in the overflow tablespace. Oracle also allows you to create secondary indexes on IOTs. These are indexes on nonkey columns that you create for performance reasons. The only difference between these indexes and normal indexes is that secondary indexes use a logical **ROWID** based on the primary key rather than on a physical one. The logical **ROWID** can include a physical guess of where the row in the IOT is located. Because rows in an IOT don't have permanent physical locations, these guesses can become stale as rows migrate to new blocks.

Rollback Segments

Rollback segments store the old values of data changed in a transaction and are used for three main purposes:

➤ The old data is needed if a transaction rolls back the changes. This could be because the user decided not to enter the data, and they issued a **ROLLBACK** command, or it could be because the user session was disconnected abnormally. In this case, the Process Monitor (PMON) rolls back the uncommitted data as part of the cleanup for the disconnected session.

➤ Rollback segments are used for read-consistency. Users cannot see data that has been changed by another user but has not yet been committed. (To allow other users to see uncommitted data is called a *dirty read*.) When a user wants to access data that another user has changed but not yet committed, Oracle retrieves the old value of the data from the rollback segments. (For more on read-consistency, see Chapter 10.)

➤ Rollback segments are used for the rollback phase of recovery. When an instance crashes, crash recovery needs to take place—that is, data that has been changed but not yet committed needs to be rolled back, and the rollback segments are used in this process.

Temporary Segments

Temporary segments are used for certain operations that are too large to occur in memory. These operations can include sorts, **GROUP BY**s, and index builds.

Oracle will try to perform these operations in memory, but if the **SORT_AREA_SIZE** parameter that controls the amount of memory for this is too small, Oracle will need to write temporarily to disk. Temporary segments are used to temporarily store the data on disk in the temporary tablespace that's defined for the user performing the operation.

Bootstrap Segment

The bootstrap segment, also known as the *cache segment*, is used to initialize the data dictionary cache when the instance is started. The SQL.BSQ script creates it when a database is created. The segment name in **DBA_SEGMENTS** is 1.173 for my 8.1.7 on NT database. (This odd name reflects its offset in the SYSTEM datafile: block 173, file 1.) It is a very small segment (only one block), and you can't do anything to it. It cannot be dropped, updated, or queried, and you don't need to manage it in any way.

 For the exam, all you need to know about the bootstrap segment is that it exists.

Controlling Block Space Usage

As mentioned in Chapter 2, an Oracle data block is the smallest unit of I/O that can be performed by the database. Every data block in an Oracle database has the same format (refer back to Figure 2.1). The common and variable header contains general block information, such as the segment and the block address. The table directory is a list of tables that contain data in this block. (This is usually relevant only for clusters.) The row directory contains information about rows in the block, including pointers to where the rows are. The remaining part of the block is made up of free space and the actual row data. Depending on the size of the rows, a single row may span one or more data blocks.

Space usage within an Oracle block for data and indexes is controlled by two sets of parameters. (I'm referring here to parameters for the storage clause, not initialization parameters.) The level of user concurrency allowed for the block (that is, the number of users who are allowed to access the block at any one time) is controlled by the parameters **INITRANS** and **MAXTRANS**. The **INITRANS** parameter specifies the initial number of transaction slots that are created in the block. When a user needs to make changes to the block, they must take out one of these transaction slots. (Only one transaction slot is needed, regardless of the number of rows being changed by the transaction.) **INITRANS** defaults to 1 for table segments and 2 for index segments and cluster segments. If more than this number of users wants to change the data in a block, additional transaction slots can be allocated from the free space in the block. The **MAXTRANS** parameter specifies the maximum number of transaction slots that are created in the block. The default depends on the block size for the database. The maximum value is 255, and the minimum value is 1.

 Although you can increase **INITRANS** from the default to a maximum of 255 to minimize the performance hit of allocating extra transaction slots, I've never found this to be particularly useful. (One problematic aspect is that you have to guess how many users are concurrently accessing a block because Oracle provides you with no statistics at this level for you to examine.) Likewise, you can change **MAXTRANS** to a value lower than 255, but this also is rarely useful.

The other two block space usage parameters are **PCTUSED** and **PCTFREE**. The **PCTUSED** parameter, which sets how much of a block is to be used for inserts, defaults to 40 percent. Once the amount of space left in a block drops below **PCTUSED**, the block is placed on the free list for the segment. The free list is a list of blocks that previously have been used for the segment that are now available for data to be inserted into again. By default, a segment is created with a single free list, but you can increase the number of free lists by using the **FREELISTS** parameter in the storage clause. Free lists are covered more in the "Oracle8i: Performance and Tuning" exam (1Z0-024), so I won't cover them more here. The **PCTFREE** parameter for a data segment, which sets how much of a block is to be left free for updates that increase the size of rows that are already stored in the block, defaults to 10 percent. **PCTFREE** works differently for an index segment because index entries are not updated. (They are logically deleted and reinserted instead.) For an index segment, **PCTFREE** is used to reserve space for index entries that may need to be inserted into the block during index creation only.

The settings for **PCTUSED** and **PCTFREE** do not include the header space for a block (that is, they are set based on the amount of free space left after the header space is subtracted from the total block size). The sum of **PCTUSED** and **PCTFREE** must be equal to or less than 100 percent. To see how **PCTUSED** and **PCTFREE** work together, let's look at an example of a data block for which **PCTUSED** has been set to 60 percent and **PCTFREE** has been set to 30 percent. Rows can be inserted into the block until the remaining free space (PCTFREE) is 30 percent or less.

You might wonder how a block can be inserted into until it hits **PCTFREE**, when **PCTUSED** is the parameter that sets the amount of space available for inserts. Let's say in our example block that 57 percent of the block is used. Can a new row be inserted into the block? Yes, because **PCTUSED** is set to 60 percent, which we haven't reached yet. However, Oracle knows nothing about the size of the new row. It could be large enough to take the amount of space used from 57 percent to 70 percent (100 minus **PCTFREE**) or even higher. That's why the last sentence of the preceding paragraph ends by saying "30 percent or less."

So, now this remaining amount of free space—30 percent or less—is available for updates to rows that are already in the block and that increase the size of the row (updates that don't increase the size of the row occur without row movement in the block). If rows are deleted from the block, or row updates occur that decrease the size of the row, the block may now drop below 70 percent utilization (that is, the amount of free space may increase to more than our **PCTFREE** setting), but new rows cannot be inserted into the block until the block utilization drops to 60 percent (our **PCTUSED** setting). Once this point is reached, rows can be inserted into the block again, and the whole cycle starts over from the beginning.

Obtaining Information about Storage Structures from the Data Dictionary

The relationships among the different storage structures in an Oracle database can be determined by querying the data dictionary. The following views are of particular relevance for storage structures:

➤ **DBA_DATA_FILES**—This view describes all the datafiles in the database, including the file name, tablespace name, size information, status, and an autoextensible indicator.

➤ **DBA_EXTENTS**—This view provides information for all used extents in the database, including the name of the owner of the segment that contains the extent, the segment name and type, the tablespace name, and size information for the extent.

➤ **DBA_FREE_SPACE**—This view lists all free extents of space in the database, including the name of the tablespace containing the free space, the file ID for the datafile containing the free space, and the size of the free space.

➤ **DBA_SEGMENTS**—This view describes all segments in the database, including the owner of the segment, the segment name and type, the tablespace name the segment is in, size and storage information for the segment, and the default buffer pool used by the segment.

➤ **DBA_TABLESPACES**—This view lists all tablespaces in the database, including the tablespace name, default storage values, minimum extent size, tablespace status, and extent management information.

It's very important that you understand the relationship among these data dictionary views. Every administration exam I have taken over the course of the certification program since its inception with Oracle7 release 7.3 has included questions that test this understanding.

To aid you in understanding the relationships among these views, here are a number of **SELECT** statements that illustrate the contents of the views and the relationships among them. (I've edited the output so that it fits the page width of this book.) First, let's look at the big picture with a **SELECT** statement that joins **DBA_TABLESPACES** and **DBA_DATA_FILES**:

```
SQL> SELECT ts.tablespace_name, df.file_name, ts.min_extlen,
  2    ts.extent_management, ts.allocation_type, df.autoextensible
  3    FROM dba_data_files df, dba_tablespaces ts
  4    WHERE ts.tablespace_name = df.tablespace_name
  5    ORDER BY ts.tablespace_name;
```

TABLESP	FILE_NAME	MIN_EXTLEN	EXTENT_MAN	ALLOCATIO	AUT
DRSYS	D:\...\ORCL\DR01.DBF	65536	DICTIONARY	USER	YES
INDX	D:\...\ORCL\INDX01.DBF	131072	DICTIONARY	USER	YES
OEM_REP	D:\...\ORCL\OEM_REP.DBF	65536	LOCAL	SYSTEM	YES
RBS	D:\...\ORCL\RBS01.DBF	524288	DICTIONARY	USER	NO
SYSTEM	D:\...\ORCL\SYSTEM01.DBF	65536	DICTIONARY	USER	YES
TEMP	D:\...\ORCL\TEMP01.DBF	65536	DICTIONARY	USER	YES
TOOLS	D:\...\ORCL\TOOLS01.DBF	32768	DICTIONARY	USER	YES
USERS	D:\...\ORCL\USERS01.DBF	131072	DICTIONARY	USER	YES

```
8 rows selected.
```

Next, here's an example of a **SELECT** against **DBA_SEGMENTS**:

```
SQL> SELECT segment_name, segment_type, tablespace_name,
  2           extents, blocks
  3    FROM dba_segments
  4    WHERE owner = 'SCOTT'
  5    ORDER BY segment_name;
```

SEGMENT_NAME	SEGMENT_TYPE	TABLESPACE	EXTENTS	BLOCKS
ACCOUNT	TABLE	USERS01	1	8
BONUS	TABLE	USERS01	1	8
DEPT	TABLE	USERS01	1	8
EMP	TABLE	USERS01	1	8
PK_DEPT	INDEX	USERS01	1	8
PK_EMP	INDEX	USERS01	1	8

```
RECEIPT          TABLE           USERS01            1         8
SALGRADE         TABLE           USERS01            1         8

8 rows selected.
```

Now, let's look at a **SELECT** from **DBA_EXTENTS**:

```
SQL> SELECT extent_id, file_id, block_id, blocks
  2  FROM dba_extents
  3  WHERE segment_name = 'RBS1';

EXTENT_ID    FILE_ID    BLOCK_ID     BLOCKS
---------- ---------- ---------- ----------
        0          2         514         64
        1          2         578         64
        2          2         642         64
        3          2         706         64
        4          2         770         64
        5          2        3586         64
        6          2         898         64
        7          2         962         64

8 rows selected.
```

Although all of this information may be of interest, it's more important for a
DBA to know when there's not going to be any space for an object to grow. To
find this information, you usually need to join together some of these data dictionary views. Here's an example:

```
SQL> SELECT s.owner, s.segment_name, s.tablespace_name
  2  FROM dba_segments s, dba_tables t
  3  WHERE s.segment_type = 'TABLE'
  4  AND s.segment_name = t.table_name
  5  AND s.owner = t.owner
  6  AND NOT EXISTS (SELECT tablespace_name
  7                  FROM dba_free_space fs
  8                  WHERE fs.tablespace_name = t.tablespace_name
  9                  AND fs.bytes >= t.next_extent);

OWNER      SEGMENT_NAME                            TABLESPACE_NAME
---------- ------------------------------- -------------------
SYSMAN     EPC_CLI_COLLECTION                      OEM_REPOSITORY
SYSMAN     EPC_CLI_COLLECT_BY_EVENTID              OEM_REPOSITORY
SYSMAN     EPC_CLI_COLLECT_BY_USERID               OEM_REPOSITORY
SYSMAN     EPC_CLI_ENVIRONMENT                     OEM_REPOSITORY
```

This statement queries **DBA_SEGMENTS**, **DBA_TABLES**, and **DBA_FREE_SPACE** to find any tables that cannot allocate the next extent if needed because the tablespace to which they belong is too full. Normally, of course, this is the sort of query that you hope comes back with a "no rows selected" message. (I've artificially downsized my OEM repository to produce output for this example). You can write your own statements to perform the same operation for other database objects.

Criteria for Separating Segments

You might use a number of criteria for separating segments, based on concerns for performance, manageability, and recoverability. The main criterion you need to know about for the "Oracle8i: Architecture and Administration" exam is separation based on segment fragmentation propensity (that is, how likely a segment is to suffer from any type of fragmentation problems). Different types of segments have different levels of fragmentation propensity, as you can see from Table 9.1.

Table 9.1	Fragmentation propensity for different segment types.	
Fragmentation Propensity	**Segment Type**	**Description**
Zero	Data dictionary segments	Other than the audit trail, data dictionary segments are almost never dropped or truncated, so they have zero fragmentation propensity.
Very low	Repository segments	Repository segments are those used for storing repository data for tools such as Oracle Designer and Oracle Enterprise Manager. Although these are normal table segments, the data in them is normally only deallocated when reorganizing the segments, so they have a very low fragmentation propensity.
Low	Application data and index segments	User applications have more frequent need for data reorganization than repository data, and as a result generally have higher fragmentation propensity.
High	Rollback segments	By their very nature, rollback segments expand and shrink. In high-update systems, this can mean that rollback segments have high fragmentation propensity.
Very high	Temporary segments	Temporary segments in permanent tablespaces will allocate and deallocate space fairly frequently. As a result, they have very high fragmentation propensity. This is not the case for temporary segments built in temporary tablespaces built on tempfiles.

In addition to fragmentation propensity, the other criteria that may cause you to separate segments include:

➤ Distributing tablespaces across multiple devices for optimal I/O spread and availability

➤ Controlling space allocation by setting different quotas for different users

➤ Locating read-only tablespaces on read-only devices

➤ Taking tablespaces online or offline to control availability

➤ Performing partial backup and recovery operations

Practice Questions

Question 1

Which view would you use to find the size of the first extent allocated to a table?

○ a. **DBA_EXTENTS**

○ b. **DBA_SEGMENTS**

○ c. **DBA_DATA_FILES**

○ d. **DBA_TABLESPACES**

Answer b is correct. **DBA_SEGMENTS** displays the size and storage settings for all the segments in the database. Answer a is incorrect because, although **DBA_EXTENTS** lists the extents that make up all segments in the database, it does not show the size of the storage settings for segments. Answer c is incorrect because **DBA_DATA_FILES** shows information on the datafiles that make up tablespaces, not segments. Answer d is incorrect because **DBA_TABLESPACES** lists information about tablespaces, not data segments.

Question 2

Typically, which type of segment consumes the largest amount of space in a database?

○ a. Data

○ b. Index

○ c. Library

○ d. Rollback

○ e. Temporary

Answer a is correct. Data segments are the most common segment in a database. Answer b is incorrect because, in most databases, less space is used for indexing than for data. Answer c is incorrect because library is not a valid segment type. Answer d is incorrect because rollback segments shrink back to an optimal size and represent a very small portion of overall data space. Answer e is incorrect because temporary segments are used for sort operations that can't be completed in memory, and it is highly unlikely that sort operations will be larger than total data volumes.

Question 3

Which parameter specifies the percentage of space in each data block reserved for updates?

- ○ a. **MAXTRANS**
- ○ b. **PCTUSED**
- ○ c. **INITRANS**
- ○ d. **PCTFREE**

Answer d is correct. **PCTFREE** determines the percentage of space in each block that will be reserved for updates. Answer a is incorrect because **MAXTRANS** is the limit of concurrent transactions allowed in a data block. Answer b is incorrect because **PCTUSED** is the amount of space available for insert that the Oracle server maintains in each data block. Answer c is incorrect because **INITRANS** is the initial number of transaction blocks in a data block.

Question 4

What is the result of extents being frequently deallocated from a segment?

- ○ a. Fragmented blocks
- ○ b. Truncated segments
- ○ c. Fragmented tablespace
- ○ d. Nonincremental extents

Answer c is correct. Fragmentation in a tablespace is caused by frequent allocation and deallocation of extents to objects in the tablespace. Answer a is incorrect because fragmented blocks are caused by frequent insert, update, and delete activities. Answer b is incorrect because truncated segments are the result of the **TRUNCATE** command, not frequent deallocation of extents. Answer d, nonincremental extents, is incorrect because there is no such concept in an Oracle database.

Question 5

Which type of segment speeds data retrieval?

○ a. Table

○ b. Rollback

○ c. Temporary

○ d. Index

Answer d is correct. An index segment can decrease the amount of time required for queries. Answer a is incorrect because a table is searched via a full scan of the data unless an index is available. Answer b is incorrect because rollback segments are used for rollback, read-consistency, and recovery. Answer c is incorrect because temporary segments are used for sorting.

Question 6

What happens when a segment needs more space?

○ a. The segment is truncated.

○ b. Extents are allocated to the segment.

○ c. Extents are deallocated within the segment.

○ d. Extents are compressed within the segment.

Answer b is correct. As a segment grows and requires more space, extents are added to the segment. Answer a is incorrect because Oracle does not truncate segments automatically. Answer c is incorrect because extents are deallocated when segments are dropped. Answer d is incorrect because extents are not compressed within a segment.

Question 7

Which type of segment is used to store a read-consistent state as of a certain point in time?

○ a. Data

○ b. Index

○ c. Rollback

○ d. Temporary

Answer c is correct. Rollback segments are used for read-consistency. Answer a is incorrect because data segments store table data. Answer b is incorrect because index segments are used to store pointers to table data to improve performance. Answer d is incorrect because temporary segments are used for sort operations.

Question 8

> What is the minimum number of extents for a segment?
>
> ○ a. 0
> ○ b. 1
> ○ c. 2
> ○ d. 5
> ○ e. 15

Answer b is correct. When a segment is created, it is allocated at least one extent as specified by the initial extent parameter at the segment or the tablespace level. This question is a bit tricky because rollback segments must have a minimum of two extents. If you read the question quickly, you might choose answer c instead.

Question 9

> Which data dictionary view would you query to find out information about free extents in the database?
>
> ○ a. **DBA_FREE_SPACE**
> ○ b. **DBA_SEGMENTS**
> ○ c. **DBA_FREE_EXTENTS**
> ○ d. **DBA_EXTENTS**

Answer a is correct. **DBA_FREE_SPACE** contains information about all the free extents in the database. Answer b is incorrect because **DBA_SEGMENTS** displays information about all the segments in the database. Answer c is incorrect because **DBA_FREE_EXTENTS** is not a valid data dictionary view name. Answer d is incorrect because **DBA_EXTENTS** shows information about all the used extents in the database.

Need to Know More?

 Devraj, Venkat S. *Oracle 24×7 Tips and Techniques*. Oracle Press, Berkeley, CA, 2000. ISBN 0-07211-999-3. Chapter 12, which discusses space and growth management, is relevant to the areas covered here.

 Habeeb, Zulfiqer. *Oracle8i DBA: Performance and Tuning Exam Cram*. The Coriolis Group, Scottsdale, AZ, 2001. ISBN 1-58880-047-4. Consult this book for more information on free lists.

 Loney, Kevin, and Marlene Theriault. *Oracle8i DBA Handbook*. Oracle Press, Berkeley, CA, 1999. ISBN 0-07212-188-2. This book is a comprehensive guide and a must-have for all DBAs. Chapter 4 discusses physical database layout and includes a section on database space usage and the different types of segments.

 See the Oracle documentation that is provided on CD with the Oracle RDBMS software. Specifically pertaining to this chapter are:

Baylis, Ruth, and Joyce Fee. *Oracle8i Administrator's Guide*. Oracle Corporation, Redwood City, CA, 1999. This guide is the complete documentation of database administration tasks. Chapter 12 covers **PCTFREE, PCTUSED, INITRANS**, and **MAXTRANS**, and Chapter 19 looks at some of the data dictionary views covered above.

Leverenz, Lefty, Diana Rehfield, and Cathy Baird. *Oracle8i Concepts*. Oracle Corporation, Redwood City, CA, 1999. This is the complete documentation of Oracle concepts. Chapter 4 covers data blocks, extents, and segments.

Lorentz, Diana. *Oracle8i Reference*. Oracle Corporation, Redwood City, CA, 1999. Specific details on data dictionary views can be found in this reference.

 technet.oracle.com is Oracle's technical repository of information for clients.

 www.revealnet.com is the site where RevealNet Corporation provides Oracle administration reference software.

Managing Rollback
Segments

Terms you'll need to understand:

✓ Rollback segment

✓ **OPTIMAL**

✓ Shrink

✓ Offline

✓ Online

✓ Transaction

✓ "Snapshot too old" error

Techniques you'll need to master:

✓ Creating rollback segments using appropriate storage settings

✓ Maintaining rollback segments

✓ Planning the number and size of rollback segments

✓ Obtaining rollback segment information from the data dictionary

✓ Troubleshooting common rollback segment problems

Every Oracle database contains one or more rollback segments, which provide transaction rollback, read-consistency, and instance recovery. The rollback segment records changes for multiple transactions. Each transaction is assigned to a single rollback segment extent. In terms of the storage space used by rollback segments, the most costly statement is the **UPDATE** statement because it must capture both the before and the after image. The least expensive statement is a delete because the rollback captures the deleted **ROWID**s only.

Overview of Rollback Segments

Although I briefly mentioned in Chapter 9 each of the uses of a rollback segment—transaction rollback, read-consistency, and instance recovery—you need to know more about read-consistency than I could cover there.

Read-Consistency

Data that another user has changed but hasn't yet committed cannot be seen by other users. (Remember from Chapter 9 that allowing other users to see uncommitted data is called a *dirty read.*) When a user wants to access data that another user has changed but hasn't yet committed, Oracle retrieves the old value of the data from the rollback segments. Oracle guarantees that a statement sees data as it was at the point in time that the statement started, even if other transactions have modified the data since. To do this, Oracle determines the system change number (SCN) at the time the statement started. Any changes that have been committed after this will have different SCNs. When Oracle is retrieving data (say for a long-running **SELECT**) and reaches a block that has been changed since the **SELECT** started, it will go to the rollback segments and retrieve the block that was changed from there, ensuring that the old values of the data are retrieved. This gives a read-consistent image of the data for the select statement.

Read-consistency is provided for a statement by default. You can expand this read-consistency to the transaction level by one of two commands, discussed next. (A transaction in Oracle terms starts at login or the end of the previous transaction, and ends when a **COMMIT** or **ROLLBACK** statement is issued.)

The SET TRANSACTION READ ONLY Command

This command makes an entire transaction read-only. It must be the first statement in a transaction, and inserts, updates, and deletes are not allowed for the remainder of the transaction (thus ensuring that the whole transaction is read-only). This command provides read-consistency for the duration of the read-only transaction. Like any transaction, you end a read-only transaction by issuing a **COMMIT** or **ROLLBACK** command. (Note that because the command is read-only, you aren't actually committing or rolling back any data changes, just ending the transaction.)

The SET TRANSACTION SERIALIZABLE Command

This command ensures read-consistency for a transaction that includes Data Manipulation Language (DML), which is used to refer to inserts, updates, and deletes. Again, the command must be the first statement in the transaction, and you end the transaction by issuing a **COMMIT** or **ROLLBACK** command. One notable difference between the two commands is that the **SET TRANS-ACTION SERIALIZABLE** command can have a noticeable effect on performance, so you should use it only when necessary.

Types of Rollback Segments

An Oracle database has three main kinds of rollback segments:

➤ *SYSTEM*—The SYSTEM rollback segment is created when the database is created. It's located in the SYSTEM tablespace, and it's used only for changes to the data dictionary.

➤ *Non-SYSTEM*—Non-SYSTEM rollback segments are needed in any database where you want to insert or update data in non-SYSTEM tablespaces. (In other words, just about every Oracle database uses them.) They can be either private rollback segments (created with the **CREATE ROLLBACK SEGMENT** command) or public rollback segments (created with the **CRE-ATE PUBLIC ROLLBACK SEGMENT** command). Public rollback segments were initially designed for Oracle Parallel Server, but even there they're not used much anymore. Other than knowing they exist, you don't need to know about them for the "Oracle8i: Architecture and Administration" exam, so I won't cover them further here. Private rollback segments need to be brought online when the database is started. This is normally performed automatically by listing them in the **ROLLBACK_SEGMENTS** initialization parameter, or you can bring them online manually using the **ALTER ROLLBACK SEGMENT** command.

➤ *Deferred*—Deferred rollback segments are automatically created by Oracle when a tablespace goes offline while transactions are still active against it. Normally, this happens as a result of a disk crash, so it's something you hope not to see. The transactions that were still active will need to be rolled back when the tablespace is brought online again, and deferred rollback segments are used to store this rollback information. Deferred rollback segments are dropped automatically when they are no longer needed. Because Oracle creates, manages, and drops these segments, you don't need to perform any maintenance or administration on them.

Using Rollback Segments with Transactions

The Oracle server automatically allocates a rollback segment to a transaction that performs DML. Oracle chooses the rollback segment with the least existing transactions to ensure load balancing across the rollback segments that are online. You can override this default mechanism of allocating a rollback segment by using the command **SET TRANSACTION USE ROLLBACK SEGMENT** *rollback_segment_name*. This command is generally used when you are about to start a long-running transaction and you want to ensure a large rollback segment is allocated to the transaction.

Rollback segment extents are used in a circular, sequential manner. A transaction will write to an extent until it is full, and then it will move to the next extent. (This is called a *wrap*.) Note that multiple transactions can use a single extent in a rollback segment; however, only one transaction will write to an individual block within the rollback segment. A single transaction will write all of its undo information to a single rollback segment (that is, it cannot span rollback segments). The header information for the rollback segment uses a transaction table to keep track of the transactions that are currently using the rollback segment.

Growth of Rollback Segments

As I mentioned earlier, rollback segments are used in a circular, sequential manner. The head of a rollback segment will move to a new extent when the previous extent is filled. This can occur only when the new extent has no active transactions. If the new extent has any transactions that are active, the head cannot skip to it, so it allocates a new extent. This operation is called an *extend*. The rollback segment will continue to grow until it reaches the maximum number of extents for the rollback segment, as specified by the **MAXEXTENTS** storage parameter.

Shrinkage of Rollback Segments

In earlier releases of the Oracle database (Oracle7), a rollback segment grew until it reached **MAXEXTENTS** and an error was returned. In Oracle8 version 8.0, a new parameter was introduced called **OPTIMAL**, which allows you to set the optimal size for the rollback segment. Extents are actually deallocated if the current rollback segment size is greater than the **OPTIMAL** setting and the rollback segment contains adjacent inactive extents. When the head of a rollback segment reaches an extent boundary and needs to allocate a new extent, it will first attempt to shrink the rollback segment back to the size specified by the **OPTIMAL** storage parameter. (This parameter is used only for rollback segments.) The rollback segment may not actually be able to shrink back to the **OPTIMAL** setting for two reasons. First, active transactions may be blocking shrinkage back to **OPTIMAL**. Second, the **OPTIMAL** setting may be badly defined. If an incorrect value is set for **OPTIMAL** (that is, it isn't set to a value divisible by the **INITIAL** storage parameter), then Oracle won't be able to shrink back to the value set by **OPTIMAL**. One of the jobs you need to perform as a DBA is to ensure a valid setting of **OPTIMAL**, based on transaction rates and the settings for **INITIAL** and **MINEXTENTS**.

Creating Rollback Segments Using Appropriate Storage Settings

To create a rollback segment, you use the **CREATE [PUBLIC] ROLLBACK SEGMENT** command. (PUBLIC is an optional keyword, and as I mentioned earlier, it isn't used very much.) Here's an example of the command:

```
SQL> CREATE ROLLBACK SEGMENT rbs04
  2  TABLESPACE rbs
  3  STORAGE (INITIAL 200K
  4           NEXT 200K
  5           MINEXTENTS 20
  6           MAXEXTENTS 500
  7           OPTIMAL 4000K);

Rollback segment created.
```

Notice that I've specified a tablespace name and a **STORAGE** clause for the command. Although these are optional clauses for the command, you really shouldn't think of them that way. If you don't specify the tablespace, the rollback segment will be created in the SYSTEM tablespace and be owned by SYS. Note that this is a deviation from the usual default; normally, an object created without a tablespace being specified will be created in the default tablespace for the user and will be owned by the user. Also, the **STORAGE** clause is very important for rollback segments. Here are a few guidelines for the **STORAGE** clause for rollback segments:

➤ The value of **MINEXTENTS** must be at least 2.

➤ **PCTINCREASE** is not a valid storage parameter and cannot be specified.

➤ If **OPTIMAL** is set (and it always should be), then it must be at least equal to **INITIAL * MINEXTENTS**.

➤ Don't set **MAXEXTENTS** to **UNLIMITED**. Doing so leaves the database open to rogue processes filling the rollback segment tablespace.

➤ For recoverability reasons, you must ensure that rollback segments are created in a separate, dedicated tablespace.

➤ To minimize fragmentation, **INITIAL** and **NEXT** should always be the same for rollback segments.

Once you've created a rollback segment using the **CREATE ROLLBACK SEGMENT** command, you need to bring it online. (By default, rollback segments are left offline when they are created by this command.) To bring a rollback segment online, you need to either list its name in the **ROLLBACK_SEGMENTS** initialization parameter and bounce the database, or use the **ALTER ROLLBACK SEGMENT** command. The **ROLLBACK_SEGMENTS** initialization parameter provides a list of rollback segments that will be brought online automatically when the database is started. The format of the parameter is a list of rollback segment names, generally enclosed in parentheses and delimited by commas. (The lesser-known alternative is to not use parentheses and delimit by spaces.) Here is an example of the **ALTER ROLLBACK SEGMENT** command in use:

```
SQL> ALTER ROLLBACK SEGMENT rbs01 ONLINE;
```

A rollback segment that is brought online in this fashion remains online only until the database is restarted. If you want this rollback segment to be online automatically when the database is started, you also need to edit the **ROLLBACK_SEGMENTS** parameter in the parameter file to include the rollback segment name. The maximum number of rollback segments that you can bring online at once is determined by the **MAX_ROLLBACK_SEGMENTS** parameter. This is a static parameter, so you need to restart the database if you set it too low. The default setting is either 30 or the value of **TRANSACTIONS** divided by **TRANSACTIONS_PER_ROLLBACK_SEGMENT**, whichever is greater.

You also can use Oracle Enterprise Manager (OEM) to create rollback segments. To do this, start the OEM Console, click on the Databases folder, choose the database you want to add the rollback segment to, and click on the Storage folder. Then, either right-click on the Rollback Segments folder and choose Create from the context-sensitive menu, or click on the Rollback Segments folder, choose Create from the Navigator menu, and then choose the Create button. In either case, if you select the Show SQL button, the screen shown in Figure 10.1 appears.

In the figure, you can see that I've chosen sensible settings for the **STORAGE** clause and specified the tablespace. Also, I've made sure the SQL code is showing (by having previously clicked on the Show SQL button) to illustrate a particular point. When you use OEM to create rollback segments, the default is to

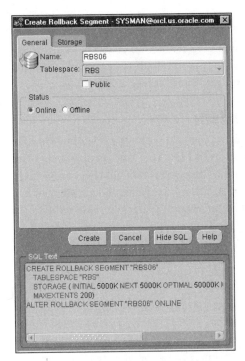

Figure 10.1   Creating a rollback segment using OEM.

have the online radio button selected. What this does is seen in the SQL text part of the window. OEM creates the rollback segment and then issues the relevant statement to bring the rollback segment online. This is generally a more user-friendly way to create a rollback segment than to do it manually.

I mentioned previously that the **ROLLBACK_SEGMENTS** parameter is used to determine what rollback segments are brought online when the database is started. If you have public rollback segments in the same database as private rollback segments, an extra step is necessary. If this is the case, the private rollback segments listed in the **ROLLBACK_SEGMENTS** parameter will be brought online as usual. The formula of **TRANSACTIONS** divided by **TRANSACTIONS_PER_ROLLBACK_SEGMENT** is then evaluated. If the formula returns a value greater than the number of private rollback segments listed in the **ROLLBACK_SEGMENTS** parameter, Oracle will attempt to acquire public rollback segments until the difference is made up. If there are no public rollback segments or they are insufficient in number, no errors are returned and the database opens normally.

Maintaining Rollback Segments

The maintenance operations that can be performed on rollback segments are changing the storage parameters, deallocating unused space within a rollback segment, taking a rollback segment offline, and dropping a rollback segment.

Changing Storage Parameters

The only storage parameters that can be changed without re-creating the rollback segment are **MAXEXTENTS** and **OPTIMAL**. (You can also change the value of **NEXT**, but remember that rollback segments should always have **INITIAL** and **NEXT** set to the same value. Therefore, if the rollback segment has been created correctly, there should be no reason to alter the value of **NEXT**.) The **ALTER ROLLBACK SEGMENT** command is used to perform these changes. Here's an example of an **ALTER ROLLBACK SEGMENT** command where I'm altering both **OPTIMAL** and **MAXEXTENTS** in one statement:

```
SQL> ALTER ROLLBACK SEGMENT rbs04
  2  STORAGE (OPTIMAL 6000K MAXEXTENTS 250);
```

You can also perform this change in OEM. Using the same path as I mentioned previously to bring a rollback segment online, choose the Storage tab on the Edit Rollback Segment screen, enter the new values, and click on OK. Note that, although OEM does not provide a warning when you set the value of **NEXT** to something other than **INITIAL**, it's still not a good idea to do this.

Deallocating Unused Space

You may want to free up unused space in a rollback segment for immediate use. This could be because **OPTIMAL** has not been set (and therefore automatic shrinkage will not occur) or because you don't want to wait for the automatic shrinking to take place. Here's an example of how to shrink a rollback segment:

```
SQL> ALTER ROLLBACK SEGMENT rbs05
  2  SHRINK TO 4M;
```

Note that the **TO 4M** part of the statement is optional. If you don't specify it, Oracle will attempt to shrink the rollback segment to the value of **OPTIMAL** or, if **OPTIMAL** is not set, to **MINEXTENTS** (you cannot shrink a rollback segment so it will have less than **MINEXTENTS**). Regardless of whether you specify the **TO 4M** part of the clause or not, the shrinkage does not change the value of **OPTIMAL**. So, once the rollback segment grows again, automatic shrinkage will shrink the rollback segment to only the value of **OPTIMAL**. The rollback segment will not shrink to less than two extents. (Remember that this is the minimum number of extents for a rollback segment.) In any case, it may not actually be possible to shrink to the specified size because of active transactions. To determine how much a rollback segment has shrunk, query **DBA_SEGMENTS**, looking at the **EXTENTS** column and either the **BYTES** or **BLOCKS** column.

You can also shrink a rollback segment using OEM. Use the same path to get to the rollback segment as I mentioned previously to bring a rollback segment online, only in this case you must right-click on the rollback segment that you want to shrink and select Shrink from the context-sensitive menu. (The Navigator menu has no Shrink option.) The small dialog box shown in Figure 10.2 will appear. You can either choose the Optimal radio button to shrink the segment back to the **OPTIMAL** setting or specify a size in kilobytes or megabytes.

Taking a Rollback Segment Offline

To take a rollback segment offline, you need to either remove its name from the **ROLLBACK_SEGMENTS** initialization parameter and bounce the database, or use the **ALTER ROLLBACK SEGMENT** command. An example using the **ALTER ROLLBACK SEGMENT** command is shown here:

```
SQL> ALTER ROLLBACK SEGMENT rbs01 OFFLINE;
```

If a rollback segment is brought online, you can take it back offline with OEM. To do this, follow the same path that I mentioned previously. Once you've clicked on the Rollback Segments folder, you can either right-click on the rollback segment that you want to take offline and choose Edit from the context-sensitive menu, or you can simply click on the rollback segment and choose Edit Rollback Segment from the Navigator menu. The Edit Rollback Segment screen will appear, as shown in Figure 10.3.

Toggle the Online/Offline radio button so that Offline is highlighted, and select OK to take the rollback segment offline. Offline rollback segments are very easy to recognize in OEM: The little icon to the left of the name of the offline segment in the Navigator pane will have a red X through the power cord, as shown in Figure 10.4.

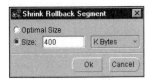

Figure 10.2   Shrinking a rollback segment using OEM.

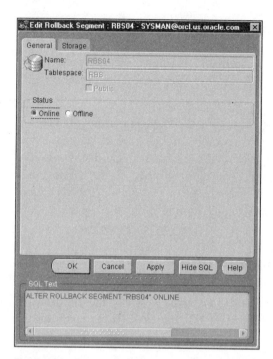

Figure 10.3 Bringing a rollback segment online using OEM.

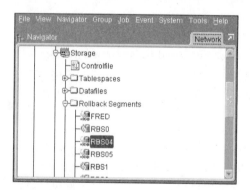

Figure 10.4 Recognizing offline rollback segments in OEM.

Taking a rollback segment offline completely succeeds only when no active transactions are using the rollback segment. If active transactions are using the rollback segments, the rollback segment will be made unavailable for any new transactions, and it will be taken completely offline when the active transactions either rollback or commit. The SYSTEM rollback segment cannot be taken offline at any time, except by shutting down the database.

Dropping a Rollback Segment

To completely remove a rollback segment from the database, or to change the values of **INITIAL** or **MINEXTENTS**, you need to use the **DROP ROLL-BACK SEGMENT** command. Here's an example of its use:

```
SQL> DROP ROLLBACK SEGMENT rbs02;
```

A rollback segment must be offline before it can be dropped. (This ensures that no active transactions need to use the rollback segment.)

You can drop a rollback segment through OEM as well. To do this, start the OEM Console, click on the Databases folder, and choose the database that you want to remove the rollback segment from. Click on the Storage folder, and then either right-click on the Rollback Segments folder and choose Remove from the context-sensitive menu, or click on the Rollback Segments folder, choose the rollback segment that you want to drop, and choose Remove Rollback Segment from the Navigator. In either case, select Yes when you're prompted "Are you sure you want to drop the rollback segment <*rollback segment name*>?", and the rollback segment will be dropped.

You would think that if you attempt to drop a rollback segment that is online, it should either stop you from attempting it at all (by disabling the Remove functionality) or give you a meaningful error message when you click on the Yes button. Unfortunately, the Remove functionality is disabled only from the context-sensitive menu that appears from a right mouse click. The Remove Rollback Segment menu option is still available on the Navigator menu.

Even worse, if you try to drop an online rollback segment using the Remove Rollback Segment menu option, clicking on the Yes button returns the error message "ORA-01545: rollback segment <*rollback segment name*> specified not available". Now, anyone in their right mind would expect that a rollback segment would have to be unavailable before it could be dropped. However, in Oracle, a rollback segment that is online is said to be "IN USE" (its status in the data dictionary view **V$ROLLSTAT**, discussed later in this chapter), and a rollback segment that is offline has a status of "AVAILABLE".

Planning the Number and Size of Rollback Segments

The number and size of the rollback segments in your database is really dependent upon the type of transaction mix you have. If you have an Online Transaction Processing (OLTP) environment with many active small transactions, the transaction tables in the headers of the rollback segments can be points of contention. The reason is that the transaction tables need to be updated frequently because the states of the transactions using the rollback segments change. To reduce this contention issue, many small rollback segments are recommended in an OLTP environment. Oracle's recommendation for such an environment is to allow, when possible, four concurrent transactions per rollback segment.

If you have an environment that is largely batch-oriented in its work, you normally find that fewer jobs are executing against the database, but that these jobs tend to update large amounts of information. In this case, it is better to have fewer but larger rollback segments, and to allocate each job its own rollback segment so that you have only one transaction per rollback segment. This is where you may find the **SET TRANSACTION USE ROLLBACK SEGMENT** command valuable.

Planning the number of extents per rollback segment is again fairly straightforward. For best performance, create rollback segments with **MINEXTENTS** set to 10 for small databases and 20 for larger databases. Doing so reduces the amount of dynamic extension that needs to take place as rollback segments grow.

 The values I've given you here (10 for small databases and 20 for large ones) come directly from a paper by Cary Millsap. As touched on in Chapter 3, Cary was in charge of the Systems Performance Group in Oracle Consulting for many years and was responsible for the development of the Optimal Flexible Architecture (OFA). Cary's paper is fairly mathematical in nature (which is one of the reasons I've only stated the findings here rather than trying to prove them to you). However, Oracle Education discusses only the larger number in its courseware, and therefore the exam expects you to assume that the number 20 is best for **MINEXTENTS**. Just be aware it's not that simple. It really does depend on the size of your database.

Planning the size of rollback segments is not so straightforward. Here you need to determine the mix of inserts, updates, and deletes in your environment. Inserts store only the **ROWID** in the rollback segments. Updates store the **ROWID** and the old values of the columns that have been changed. Deletes store the

ROWID as well as the entire row that has been deleted. In general, it's easier to run a test to see how much rollback segment space is needed than it is to try to figure it out from the numbers and sizes of the different DML operations.

Obtaining Rollback Segment Information from the Data Dictionary

The data dictionary has five main data dictionary views that contain information about rollback segments:

➤ **DBA_ROLLBACK_SEGS**—Contains information about all rollback segments in the database (regardless of whether they are online), including the segment name, status, tablespace name, and owner. The owner column can contain two values: **SYS** means that it's a private rollback segment, and **PUBLIC** means that it's a public rollback segment. The remaining views listed here contain information about only online rollback segments.

➤ **V$ROLLNAME**—Has only two columns: **USN** (the undo segment number, which is basically a unique number for the rollback segment) and the segment name. The main use of this view is to join it with **V$ROLLSTAT** to display the name of the rollback segment in the resulting output.

➤ **V$ROLLSTAT**—Contains statistics for currently online rollback segments, including the number of extents in the rollback segment, its current size in bytes, the number of active transactions, header gets and waits, optimal size, the high-water mark size, and status and information about the number of shrinks and extends for the rollback segment. This view does not contain the rollback segment name, but it can be joined to **V$ROLLNAME** using the **USN** column in each view to retrieve this information.

➤ **V$SESSION**—Provides information in conjunction with the **V$TRANSACTION** view (described next) about rollback segment use by currently active transactions. Session information comes from this view, including the username and session status. The **SADDR** column of this view is used to perform the join with **V$TRANSACTION**.

➤ **V$TRANSACTION**—Provides information in conjunction with the **V$SESSION** view about rollback segment use by currently active transactions. Transaction information comes from this view, including the undo segment number, transaction status, the location being written to in the rollback segment, and start undo block address information. The **SES_ADDR** column of this view is used to perform the join with **V$SESSION**.

Troubleshooting Common Rollback Segment Problems

Rollback segments are susceptible to four main problems that you'll need to be able to troubleshoot as a DBA. These problems are insufficient space for transactions, read-consistency errors, blocking session problems, and errors taking a tablespace offline.

Insufficient Space for Transactions

A transaction uses a single rollback segment for the duration of the transaction, so it's possible for a transaction to run out of space if the rollback segment cannot grow any more. This problem has two causes. First, it might result from the tablespace where the rollback segment is located being full. The resolution here depends on why the tablespace has filled up. If **OPTIMAL** has not been set (or has been set badly), automatic shrinking may not be taking place. Setting **OPTIMAL** correctly—or issuing a manual shrink command—will fix this problem. If the problem isn't because of an incorrect **OPTIMAL** setting, you may need to increase the size of the tablespace. You can do this by resizing the tablespace, turning **AUTOEXTEND** on, or adding another datafile to the tablespace.

The second cause for insufficient space is when **MAXEXTENTS** has been reached for the rollback segment. The easiest solution to this is to increase **MAXEXTENTS** (remembering our guideline of not setting it to **UNLIMITED**). The alternative response is to drop and re-create the rollback segment with larger **INITIAL** and **NEXT** values to stop the problem from recurring.

Read-Consistency Errors

As I mentioned earlier, Oracle guarantees that a user will see only that data that has been committed at the time that the user's **SELECT** statement executes. It does this by ensuring that blocks with an SCN later than that of the **SELECT** statement are not queried, but rather that the old values of those blocks (stored in the rollback segments) are queried to retrieve the values from the correct time. Because rollback segments are circular in nature and fixed in size, it's possible for a long-running transaction to require access to information that has been flushed from the rollback segments. This situation can occur because the information was committed by the transaction that made the change, and either the transaction slot in the rollback segment header has been reused or the old values of the data have been overwritten.

In these scenarios, the long-running transaction will receive the dreaded ORA-01555 "Snapshot too old" error message. It may not be possible to completely eradicate this error. (After all, a very rare job may need information for a very long time, and we did not take this job into account when building the rollback segment.) However, the "Snapshot too old" error can be minimized by ensuring that rollback segments have a high enough **MINEXTENTS** value, a high enough **OPTIMAL** size, and larger extents sizes. It's a common misconception that increasing **MAXEXTENTS** will fix this problem—it won't.

Blocking Session Problems

I mentioned previously that a transaction will write to an extent of a rollback segment until it is full. When the extent boundary is reached, Oracle checks if an active transaction is using the next extent. If one is, then the transaction that filled the previous extent won't be able to write to the next extent, but will instead allocate another extent.

In the blocking session scenario, a transaction that has been idle for a long time and that made only a few changes can block other transactions from writing to the extent it is in. If this continues long enough, the rollback segment can waste a lot of space as new extents are being allocated. If this occurs, you may need to step in as the DBA and identify the blocking session. Here's the SQL to do that:

```
SQL> SELECT s.username, s.sid, s.serial#, t.start_time, t.xidusn
  2  FROM v$session s, v$transaction t, v$rollstat r
  3  WHERE s.saddr = t.ses_addr
  4  AND t.xidusn = r.usn
  5  AND ((r.curext = t.start_uext-1) OR
  6     ((r.curext = r.extents-1) AND t.start_uext=0));
```

Once you've identified the blocking session, you'll need to contact the user responsible to see if that user can release the resources that he or she is taking up. Alternatively, you can kill the session with an **ALTER SYSTEM** command.

Taking a Tablespace Offline

You cannot take a tablespace offline if it contains an active rollback segment. If you attempt to do so, you will receive an ORA-01546 "Tablespace contains active rollback segment *<rollback segment name>*" error. To resolve this, you need to perform a number of steps:

1. Determine what rollback segments are in the tablespace by querying **DBA_ROLLBACK_SEGS**.

2. Take all these rollback segments offline. (Remember, this will ensure that no further transactions can use the rollback segment, and the rollback segment will be brought offline when all active transactions have been committed or rolled back.)

3. Identify the transactions that are actively using the rollback segments by querying **V$TRANSACTION**.

4. Identify the sessions that are actively using the rollback segments by querying **V$SESSION** with the **SES_ADDR** values that you identified in the previous step.

5. Have the users responsible for those sessions end the transactions or, alternatively, kill the sessions using the **ALTER SYSTEM** command.

6. Once all users have finished the transactions, wait for the rollback segments to complete being taken offline (query **V$ROLLNAME** until they no longer appear), and then take the tablespace offline.

Practice Questions

Question 1

> If you run the following code, in which tablespace will the R01 rollback
> segment be created?
>
> ```
> CREATE ROLLBACK SEGMENT R01
>   STORAGE (INITIAL 200K NEXT 200K OPTIMAL 2M
>         MINEXTENTS 20 MAXEXTENTS 100);
> ```
>
> ○ a. RBS
>
> ○ b. TEMP
>
> ○ c. DATA
>
> ○ d. INDEX
>
> ○ e. SYSTEM

Answer e is correct. In a **CREATE ROLLBACK SEGMENT** command, the
tablespace clause is optional. If it is not included, the rollback segment will be
created in the SYSTEM tablespace. This question can be tricky because all other
objects would be created in the user's default tablespace.

Question 2

> How would you find out if a rollback segment is online?
>
> ○ a. Query the **DBA_OBJECTS** data dictionary view.
>
> ○ b. Query the **DBA_SEGMENTS** data dictionary view.
>
> ○ c. Query the **DBA_TABLESPACES** data dictionary view.
>
> ○ d. Query the **DBA_ROLLBACK_SEGS** data dictionary view.

Answer d is correct. The **DBA_ROLLBACK_SEGS** view shows the status of
all rollback segments for an instance. Answer a is incorrect because the
DBA_OBJECTS view lists information about database objects, but it does not
contain any information on rollback segments. Answer b is incorrect because,

although the **DBA_SEGMENTS** view shows storage information on all segments including rollback segments, it doesn't include status information. Answer c is incorrect because the **DBA_TABLESPACES** view contains the status of tablespaces, not the status of rollback segments.

Question 3

> If an instance fails, which type of segment is used to recover uncommitted transactions?
>
> ○ a. Table
>
> ○ b. Index
>
> ○ c. Rollback
>
> ○ d. Temporary

Answer c is correct. Transaction recovery occurs after an instance failure. All uncommitted transactions are rolled back using the redo log files and the before images that are stored in rollback segments. Answer a is incorrect because a table is a data segment and is not used in recovery. Answer b is incorrect because an index segment is used for performance reasons or to ensure uniqueness, and is not used in recovery either. Answer d is incorrect because temporary segments are used for sorting, not for recovery.

Question 4

> During a long-running transaction, you receive an error message stating that insufficient space exists in the R04 rollback segment. The error leads you to believe that the storage parameters for the rollback segment should be changed. Which storage parameter would you increase to solve this problem?
>
> ○ a. **NEXT**
>
> ○ b. **INITIAL**
>
> ○ c. **OPTIMAL**
>
> ○ d. **MAXENTENTS**
>
> ○ e. **MINEXTENTS**

Answer d is correct. Increase the **MAXEXTENTS** value. The long-running trans-action has reached the **MAXEXTENTS** value for the rollback segment, and increasing this value will allow the rollback segment to acquire more extents. Answer a is incorrect because the **NEXT** parameter controls the size of extents only after the initial extent. Answer b is incorrect because **INITIAL** is the first extent for a database object; if the rollback segment has already been created, then **INITIAL** is clearly not the problem. Answer c is incorrect because **OPTI-MAL** is the size that rollback segments shrink to, and if set correctly, it will help to minimize this problem rather than causing it. Answer e is incorrect because **MINEXTENTS** specifies the minimum number of extents that will be created with the database object; increasing this would only exacerbate the problem if it were the cause.

Question 5

Which dynamic performance views would you join to display the current size of the RO3 rollback segment? [Choose two]

❑ a. **V$SESSION**

❑ b. **V$ROLLNAME**

❑ c. **V$ROLLSTAT**

❑ d. **V$PARAMETER**

❑ e. **V$DATAFILE**

❑ f. **V$TRANSACTION**

❑ g. **V$DATAFILE_HEADER**

Answers b and c are correct. **V$ROLLNAME** displays the name and USN of each rollback segment. **V$ROLLSTAT** displays the USN, status, optimal size, current size, and the current and active extent of each rollback segment. Answer a is incorrect because **V$SESSION** provides session information for current ses-sions. Answer d is incorrect because **V$PARAMETER** lists information about initialization parameters. Answer e is incorrect because **V$DATAFILE** shows datafile information from the control file. Answer f is incorrect because **V$TRANSACTION** describes transactions that are currently active against the database. Answer g is incorrect because **V$DATAFILE_HEADER** lists datafile information from the datafile headers.

Question 6

> You are executing a long-running transaction, and it stops with an ORA-01555 "Snapshot too old" error message. Which storage parameters might you increase to address this problem? [Choose two]
>
> ❑ a. **MINEXTENTS**
>
> ❑ b. **MAXEXTENTS**
>
> ❑ c. **PCTINCREASE**
>
> ❑ d. **OPTIMAL**
>
> ❑ e. **MINIMUM EXTENT**

Answers a and d are correct. The "Snapshot too old" error message can be minimized in frequency by increasing **MINEXTENTS** and **OPTIMAL,** as well as setting a larger value for **INITIAL** and **NEXT.** Answer b is incorrect because increasing **MAXEXTENTS** has no impact on the frequency of the "Snapshot too old" error. Answer c is incorrect because **PCTINCREASE** is not a valid storage parameter for rollback segments. Answer e is incorrect because **MINIMUM EXTENT** is a parameter to the **CREATE TABLESPACE** statement and has no affect on rollback segments.

Question 7

> Which command would you use to shrink the RBS04 rollback segment to 10MB?
>
> ○ a. **ALTER ROLLBACK SEGMENT rbs04 DEALLOCATE 10M;**
>
> ○ b. **ALTER ROLLBACK SEGMENT rbs04 SHRINK TO 10M;**
>
> ○ c. **ALTER ROLLBACK SEGMENT rbs04 SIZE 10M;**
>
> ○ d. None of the above. You cannot manually shrink a rollback segment.

Answer b is correct. The **ALTER ROLLBACK SEGMENT rbs04 SHRINK TO 10M** command will shrink the RBS04 rollback segment to 10MB. Answers a and c are incorrect because **DEALLOCATE** and **SIZE** are not valid parameters for the **ALTER ROLLBACK SEGMENT** command. Answer d is incorrect because it is possible to manually shrink a rollback segment using the **ALTER ROLLBACK SEGMENT** command.

Question 8

> What type of rollback segment does Oracle automatically create when a tablespace with active transactions goes offline?
>
> ○ a. Offline
>
> ○ b. SYSTEM
>
> ○ c. Private
>
> ○ d. Deferred

Answer d is correct. Deferred rollback segments are automatically created to store the rollback information that the active transactions will need to have applied when the tablespace is brought back online. Answer a is incorrect because an offline rollback segment is not automatically created; it is simply a rollback segment that has not been brought online. Answer b is incorrect because the SYSTEM rollback segment is created when the database is created and is used only for updates to the data dictionary. This segment is kept in the SYSTEM tablespace, which cannot go offline without crashing the database. Answer c is incorrect because private rollback segments are created with the **CREATE ROLLBACK SEGMENT** command, not automatically.

Need to Know More?

 Lewis, Jonathan. *Practical Oracle8i: Building Efficient Databases.* Addison-Wesley, Boston, MA, 2001. ISBN 0-20171-584-8. The author brings a wealth of experience to this book, including sections on undo data and rollback tablespaces.

 Loney, Kevin, and Marlene Theriault. *Oracle8i DBA Handbook.* Oracle Press, Berkeley, CA, 1999. ISBN 0-07212-188-2. This book is a comprehensive guide and a must-have for all DBAs. See Chapter 7, which addresses managing rollback segments.

 See the Oracle documentation that is provided on CD with the Oracle RDBMS software. Specifically pertaining to this chapter are:

Baylis, Ruth, and Joyce Fee. *Oracle8i Administrator's Guide.* Oracle Corporation, Redwood City, CA, 1999. This guide is the complete documentation of database administration tasks. Chapter 11 covers managing rollback segments.

Leverenz, Lefty, Diana Rehfield, and Cathy Baird. *Oracle8i Concepts.* Oracle Corporation, Redwood City, CA, 1999. This is the complete documentation of Oracle concepts. Chapter 16 covers transaction management, and Chapter 24 covers Oracle's read-consistency model.

Lorentz, Diana. *Oracle8i Reference.* Oracle Corporation, Redwood City, CA, 1999. Here you'll find specific details on initialization parameters, data dictionary views, and database limits.

 technet.oracle.com is Oracle's technical repository of information for clients.

 www.revealnet.com is the site where RevealNet Corporation provides Oracle administration reference software.

Managing Tables, Indexes, and Integrity Constraints

. . . .

Terms you'll need to understand:

✓ **ROWID**

✓ **INITIAL**

✓ **NEXT**

✓ **MINEXTENTS**

✓ **MAXEXTENTS**

✓ **PCTINCREASE**

✓ Row migration and row chaining

✓ High-water mark

✓ Composite (concatenated) index

✓ B-tree and bitmap indexes

✓ Function-based index

✓ Reverse key index

✓ Foreign, primary, and unique keys

✓ **ENABLE NOVALIDATE**

✓ **ENABLE VALIDATE**

Techniques you'll need to master:

✓ Creating tables using appropriate storage settings

✓ Controlling the space used by tables

✓ Analyzing tables to check integrity and migration

✓ Retrieving information about tables from the data dictionary

✓ Converting between different formats of **ROWID**

✓ Listing the different types of indexes and their uses

✓ Creating B-tree and bitmap indexes

✓ Reorganizing indexes

✓ Dropping indexes

✓ Getting index information from the data dictionary

✓ Implementing data integrity constraints

✓ Maintaining integrity constraints

✓ Obtaining constraint information from the data dictionary

Some Information Systems departments separate the database tasks into system DBA tasks and application DBA tasks. Managing tables and indexes falls under the domain of the application DBA, whereas installation, database creation, and backup and recovery fall within the domain of the system DBA. However, even system DBAs install tools that create tables and indexes that need management, so every DBA needs to know and understand how to manage tables and indexes.

 There is substantial overlap between the material covered in the "Oracle8i: Architecture and Administration" exam (1Z0-023) and the material covered in the "Introduction to Oracle: SQL and PL/SQL" exam (1Z0-001) on the topic of managing tables, indexes, and integrity constraints. In this chapter, I'll assume you have an understanding of the basic information on these topics and I'll concentrate on the material that's most relevant in these areas from the perspective of a DBA.

Creating Tables Using Appropriate Storage Settings

User data can be stored in a variety of objects, including normal tables, index-organized tables, clustered tables, and partitioned tables. Because the "Oracle8i: Architecture and Administration" exam covers only normal tables (the others are covered in other exams), that's what I'm going to concentrate on here. When you see the term *table* mentioned in this chapter, I'm referring to normal tables unless I specify otherwise.

Tables contain rows stored in random order. As I mentioned in Chapter 9, you can temporarily dictate the order of the rows by inserting data into a table in sorted order, but Oracle doesn't maintain the table that way. Rows are inserted in random order by default, depending only on the time of the insert activity.

Structure of a Row

Before we discuss tables any further, it's important for you to understand exactly how a row is structured in an Oracle table. This brief section will help you understand the storage settings that you need to define for a table.

A row is stored in variable length format. (The only time a row is fixed in length is if all the columns are fixed in length.) Columns in the row are stored in the order in which the columns are listed in the **CREATE TABLE** statement, with any columns added after table creation being added to the end of the row. A row starts with row header information, which tells Oracle about the number of columns in the row (this can vary because trailing **NULL** columns aren't stored), the lock state of the row, and row chaining. After the header, the data for each column is stored, with each column being preceded by a length indicator to tell Oracle how long the column data is. This length indicator takes up 1 byte if the column data is less than or equal to 250 bytes. Longer columns require a 3-byte length indicator. The next row starts immediately after the preceding row.

Because a row is stored in this variable length format with no space kept between it and the next row, it's not a good idea from a performance perspective to add a mandatory column to a table after it's been created using the **ALTER TABLE** command. Doing so almost ensures that row migration (covered later in this chapter) will take place, because there's no space for the extra column to be added to existing rows. If you want to add a mandatory column, the best way to do this (again, from the perspective of performance) is to re-create the table with the mandatory column included.

Oracle ROWIDs

Oracle provides you with a set of built-in datatypes that cover scalar data, collections, and relationships. Alternatively, you can create your own user-defined datatypes, which are covered in detail in the "Introduction to Oracle: SQL and PL/SQL" exam, so all I want to cover here is the concept of a **ROWID**.

ROWID is a unique identifier in an Oracle database. It is a pseudo-column that is associated with every row in the database, but it isn't explicitly stored with the row unless you create a column of **ROWID** datatype and specifically keep the **ROWID** pseudo-column with the row. (This is not something that Oracle recommends, because the **ROWID** can change if a table is reorganized.) The **ROWID** is the fastest way to access a row in an object. It is also used in indexes to directly locate the row in a table if you need access to columns that are not indexed.

The **ROWID** has different formats: restricted **ROWID**, extended **ROWID**, and **UROWID**. In releases prior to Oracle8, Oracle used what it now calls a *restricted* **ROWID** format. A restricted **ROWID** takes up less room than either a **ROWID** or **UROWID** (it's stored as six bytes internally), because it doesn't include a data object number (which is explained in more detail in the next paragraph). The format of a restricted **ROWID** is BBBBBB.RRRR.FFFF, where BBBBBB refers to the block number within the file, RRRR refers to the row number within the block, and FFFF refers to the file number within the database. The restricted **ROWID** format is still used in Oracle8 databases for nonpartitioned tables and indexes, in which each object is a segment. (Contrast this with partitioned objects, in which each partition is a segment.)

The restricted **ROWID** format was restricted to allow only 1,022 datafiles per database because it does not allow tablespace-relative file numbers. This restriction has been removed in Oracle8 by the introduction of the extended **ROWID** format (now simply called the **ROWID** format). The format of the **ROWID** pseudo-column is OOOOOO.FFF.BBBBBB.RRR, where OOOOOO is the data object number (a unique identifier for any object in the database), FFF is the relative file number (this is unique to each file in a tablespace—that is, files in different tablespaces can have the same tablespace-relative file number), BBBBBB is the block number within the file, and RRR provides the row number within the block. The **ROWID** takes up 10 bytes of storage: 32 bits for the data object number, 10 bits for the relative file number, 22 bits for the block number, and 16 bits for the row number, for a total of 80 bits (which is 10 bytes). The **ROWID** uses a base 64 encoding scheme, which uses six characters for the data object number, three characters for the relative file number, six characters for the block number, and three characters for the row number. Here's a query that displays some **ROWID**s in this format:

```
SQL> SELECT empno, rowid FROM emp;

    EMPNO ROWID
---------- ------------------
     7369 AAAGDxAABAAAH9EAAA
     7499 AAAGDxAABAAAH9EAAB
     7521 AAAGDxAABAAAH9EAAC
     7566 AAAGDxAABAAAH9EAAD
     7654 AAAGDxAABAAAH9EAAE
     7698 AAAGDxAABAAAH9EAAF
     7782 AAAGDxAABAAAH9EAAG
     7788 AAAGDxAABAAAH9EAAH
     7839 AAAGDxAABAAAH9EAAI
     7844 AAAGDxAABAAAH9EAAJ
     7876 AAAGDxAABAAAH9EAAK
     7900 AAAGDxAABAAAH9EAAL
     7902 AAAGDxAABAAAH9EAAM
     7934 AAAGDxAABAAAH9EAAN

14 rows selected.
```

In this example, AAAGDx is the data object number, AAB is the relative file number, AAAH9E is the block number, and AAA through AAN are the row numbers. As you can see, it's not exactly easy to identify what each of these parts actually means in recognizable format. Oracle provides the **DBMS_ROWID** package to allow you to translate these base 64 encoding values to something more understandable. The more commonly used functions in this package are:

➤ **ROWID_OBJECT**—Returns the deciphered data object number from a **ROWID**.

➤ **ROWID_TO_ABSOLUTE_FNO**—Returns the deciphered absolute file number for a **ROWID**.

➤ **ROWID_BLOCK_NUMBER**—Returns the deciphered block number from a **ROWID**.

➤ **ROWID_ROW_NUMBER**—Returns the deciphered row number from a **ROWID**.

➤ **ROWID_TO_RESTRICTED**—Converts a **ROWID** from extended format to restricted format.

➤ **ROWID_TO_EXTENDED**—Converts a **ROWID** from restricted format to extended format.

The following query illustrates the use of some of these functions:

```
SQL> SELECT empno, ROWID,
  2  DBMS_ROWID.ROWID_OBJECT(ROWID)"DAO",
  3  DBMS_ROWID.ROWID_TO_ABSOLUTE_FNO(ROWID,'SCOTT',
  4                    'EMP') "FILE",
  5  DBMS_ROWID.ROWID_BLOCK_NUMBER(ROWID)"BLOCK",
  6  DBMS_ROWID.ROWID_ROW_NUMBER(ROWID)"ROW"
  7  FROM emp;
```

EMPNO	ROWID	DAO	FILE	BLOCK	ROW
7369	AAAGDxAABAAAH9EAAA	24817	1	32580	0
7499	AAAGDxAABAAAH9EAAB	24817	1	32580	1
7521	AAAGDxAABAAAH9EAAC	24817	1	32580	2
7566	AAAGDxAABAAAH9EAAD	24817	1	32580	3
7654	AAAGDxAABAAAH9EAAE	24817	1	32580	4
7698	AAAGDxAABAAAH9EAAF	24817	1	32580	5
7782	AAAGDxAABAAAH9EAAG	24817	1	32580	6
7788	AAAGDxAABAAAH9EAAH	24817	1	32580	7
7839	AAAGDxAABAAAH9EAAI	24817	1	32580	8
7844	AAAGDxAABAAAH9EAAJ	24817	1	32580	9
7876	AAAGDxAABAAAH9EAAK	24817	1	32580	10
7900	AAAGDxAABAAAH9EAAL	24817	1	32580	11
7902	AAAGDxAABAAAH9EAAM	24817	1	32580	12
7934	AAAGDxAABAAAH9EAAN	24817	1	32580	13

14 rows selected.

In Oracle8 version 8.1, Oracle introduced a new universal **ROWID**, or **UROWID**. This can be used to store any **ROWID** format, and it can also be used to support **ROWID**s of non-Oracle tables. The **COMPATIBLE** parameter needs to be set to 8.1 or higher to use **UROWID**.

Creating a Table

You use the **CREATE TABLE** command to create a table. Here's an example that you're probably familiar with: the syntax used to create the **EMP** table:

```
SQL> CREATE TABLE EMP
  2          (EMPNO NUMBER(4) NOT NULL,
  3           ENAME VARCHAR2(10),
  4           JOB VARCHAR2(9),
  5           MGR NUMBER(4),
  6           HIREDATE DATE,
  7           SAL NUMBER(7, 2),
  8           COMM NUMBER(7, 2),
  9           DEPTNO NUMBER(2));
```

Although this code successfully creates the **EMP** table, it is somewhat lacking from the DBA's perspective because it omits two important clauses: the **STORAGE** clause and the **TABLESPACE** clause. Without these two clauses, the table is created for the default tablespace for the user who created it, using the default storage for that tablespace. (The **DEFAULT STORAGE** clause for the tablespace allows you to set defaults for all the **STORAGE** clause keywords at the tablespace level, which can then be overridden at the object level.) Let's look at these two clauses in more detail.

The STORAGE and TABLESPACE Clauses

For DBAs, the **STORAGE** and **TABLESPACE** clauses are the most important clauses in the **CREATE TABLE** command, because they affect both the performance and the disk usage for the table. Here's the relevant syntax for the two clauses that I haven't covered in previous chapters:

```
STORAGE (
         INITIAL n
         NEXT n
         MINEXTENTS n
         MAXEXTENTS n
         PCTINCREASE n)
TABLESPACE tablespace_name
```

The keywords are defined as follows:

➤ INITIAL—Specifies the amount of space taken up by the first extent when the object is created. This can be specified in bytes, kilobytes, or megabytes. The default value is five data blocks. If you specify a size larger than this, Oracle rounds the size to the next multiple of five.

➤ NEXT—Specifies the amount of space taken up by the next extent for an object. Again, this can be specified in bytes, kilobytes, or megabytes. The default value is five blocks, and if you specify a size larger than this, Oracle allocates a size that is dependent on the extent management for the tablespace (that is, locally managed or dictionary managed). Note that **INITIAL** and **NEXT** values will be rounded up to the next highest multiple of the size set by **MINIMUM_EXTENT** at the tablespace level.

➤ MINEXTENTS—Sets the minimum number of extents to be allocated when an object is created. The default value is 1 for objects other than rollback segments (where the default value is 2). Note that if **MINEXTENTS** is set to greater than 1 and the tablespace that the table will be created in has more than one datafile, the extents will be allocated from the different datafiles for the tablespace.

➤ MAXEXTENTS—Sets the maximum number of extents to be allocated during the lifetime of an object. The default value depends on your block size for the database. You can specify **UNLIMITED** for this if desired.

Oracle's documentation recommends that the **MAXEXTENTS** value should not be set for rollback segments due to the possibility of uncontrolled transactions filling disks. If you are managing a database on a day-to-day basis, I extend this recommendation to all objects. In my opinion, the only time that this value should be set is when you aren't available to monitor the database regularly and you want to reduce the number of out-of-space errors.

➤ PCTINCREASE—Specifies the percentage size by which third and subsequent extent sizes will grow. The default is 50 percent, which is generally a pretty awful default because of the fragmentation it can cause. This should be set to 0 at the object level to minimize fragmentation issues.

Setting **PCTINCREASE** to 0 at the tablespace level disables System Monitor (SMON) coalescence of free space for that tablespace. This may be an issue if you have different objects in the same tablespace using multiple extent sizes. If this is a problem, I would recommend that you either set **PCTINCREASE** to 0 at the tablespace level and then use Oracle Enterprise Manager (OEM) to schedule a regular job that issues the **ALTER TABLESPACE COALESCE** command, or that you not include the **PCTINCREASE** keyword at the tablespace level and ensure that all objects in the tablespace have **PCTINCREASE** set to 0.

➤ TABLESPACE—Tells Oracle what tablespace the table is to be created in. It must be one for which the user creating the table has been granted a quota. Tables (except for temporary tables) cannot be created in temporary tablespaces. (Although the **TABLESPACE** keyword isn't strictly part of the **STORAGE** clause, many people tend to think of it as such because the **STORAGE** clause and the **TABLESPACE** clause are used together so frequently.)

Creating Temporary Tables

Oracle also allows you to create, in addition to permanent tables, temporary tables to hold data for the duration of either a session or a transaction. The **CREATE GLOBAL TEMPORARY TABLE** command is used for this purpose. The data that is created in a temporary table is visible only to the user who is creating the temporary table, but all users can see the table's definition. The data in temporary tables can be kept for either the duration of a session (by using the **ON COMMIT PRESERVE ROWS** clause) or for the duration of a transaction (by using the **ON COMMIT DELETE ROWS** clause). Temporary tables do not generate redo entries, nor are locks acquired on data in temporary tables. You can, however, build indexes, constraints, views, and triggers on temporary tables just as you would normal tables. You can even use the Export and Import utilities to export and import the definitions of temporary tables, although you can't export and import the data within them.

Guidelines for Creating Tables

You need to be aware of a few important guidelines for creating tables. The main ones you need to remember for the exam are:

➤ Use locally managed tablespaces to avoid fragmentation. Uniform extent sizing ensures that all extents are of the same size, so extents can be easily reused when they are empty.

➤ If you are not using locally managed tablespaces, use a few standard extent sizes that are a multiple of 5 * **DB_BLOCK_SIZE**. This will minimize fragmentation in dictionary-managed tablespaces.

➤ Create extents that are a multiple of **DB_FILE_MULTIBLOCK_READ_ COUNT**, an initialization parameter that defines how many blocks are read in a single I/O. This will improve the performance of full table scans.

➤ Ensure that small, frequently used tables are cached, using either the **CACHE** clause (remember this is deprecated now) or the KEEP buffer pool.

➤ For maximum availability, recoverability, and performance, locate tables in tablespaces that do not contain rollback segments, temporary segments, or indexes.

> The exam will expect you to say that tables and indexes should be located in separate tablespaces on different devices for performance reasons, even though current conventional wisdom from Oracle is that this is not necessary for performance reasons. (However, I believe it is still important for availability and manageability reasons.)

Setting **PCTFREE** and **PCTUSED**

PCTFREE and PCTUSED are two of the least understood keywords when creating a table. You might recall from Chapter 9 that **PCTUSED** sets how much of a block is to be used for inserts and defaults to 40 percent, whereas **PCTFREE** for a data segment sets how much of a block is to be left free for updates that increase the size of rows that are already stored in the block. (It defaults to 10 percent.) You can determine the necessary values for these two keywords by using the following two formulas (provided by Oracle):

PCTFREE = ((Average row size – Initial row size) * 100) / Average row size

PCTUSED = 100 – PCTFREE – (Average row size * 100 / Available
          data space)

The average row size can be determined by using the **ANALYZE** command.

You need to set the **PCTFREE** value higher in two instances: for tables in which columns are initially created with null values and later populated, and for tables in which row updates can increase the size of a row. The formula just given for **PCTFREE** allows for this row growth. Remember that setting **PCTFREE** higher will result in fewer rows per block and therefore greater storage requirements.

You need to set **PCTUSED** so that a block is returned to the free list (recall that the free list is the list of blocks that are available for inserts into this table) only when there is enough room for an average-sized row. When Oracle looks for a block on the free list, it will scan each block until it finds one that contains enough space for the row that needs to be inserted. Using the preceding formula ensures that Oracle will find a block with the right amount of space, thus reducing the time spent scanning the free list.

Row Migration

One of the ramifications of setting **PCTFREE** and **PCTUSED** incorrectly is the potential for row migration, which occurs when an update to a row increases the size of the row to a point where the row no longer fits in the block. Recall that rows in an Oracle block are stored adjacent to one another, so when a row increases in size, Oracle attempts to move the row within the block. However, if enough free space cannot be found, the row needs to migrate to another block. A pointer is left in the old row location to point to the new row location, so any access to the row now requires two I/Os: one to read the pointer and one to access the new row location.

Row Chaining

Row chaining is sometimes confused with row migration (even in some areas of the Oracle documentation). Row chaining is the result of a row being bigger than a single block. The row has to span multiple blocks that are chained together (hence, the term *row chaining*). Because modern databases can store all kinds of data in addition to text (such as images, sound, and video), row chaining can be inevitable. Although the DBA can do little to affect this, it's something to be aware of.

Controlling the Space Used by Tables

Once a table exists, the space it utilizes can be controlled through the **ALTER TABLE** command. Some of the storage parameters and all of the block utilization parameters can be changed. The effect of changing these parameters can vary from parameter to parameter. Here's a list of parameters that describes what these changes are:

➤ INITIAL—The value of **INITIAL** cannot be changed with an **ALTER TABLE** command. To change this value, you need to re-create the table.

➤ NEXT—When you change the value of **NEXT**, the new value is used by Oracle the next time an extent needs to be allocated. Subsequent extent allocations also take into account the set **PCTINCREASE** value. The actual value that **NEXT** is changed to is rounded up to the next multiple of the database block size.

➤ MINEXTENTS—This parameter can be changed only to a value that's equal to or less than the current number of extents in a table. Consequently, changing **MINEXTENTS** really has little impact until the table is truncated.

➤ MAXEXTENTS— This parameter can be changed to any value equal to or greater than the current number of extents in a table.

➤ PCTINCREASE—Changes to this parameter take effect only when a new extent is allocated. For example, if a table currently has two extents, **NEXT** is set to 20KB, and **PCTINCREASE** is changed to 100 percent, the next extent that is allocated will be 20KB (because this is the third extent), the next extent will be 40KB, and so on.

➤ PCTFREE—Changes to this parameter affect only future inserts. Blocks that are not on the free list currently will not be affected until they are returned to the free list.

➤ PCTUSED—Changes to this parameter affect all blocks for the table. When a row is updated or deleted, the block will be checked to see if the used space is less than the new **PCTUSED** value. It will be used only if it is lower.

➤ INITRANS—Changes to this parameter affect only new blocks.

➤ MAXTRANS—Changes to this parameter affect all blocks.

You can change all these parameters using the **ALTER TABLE** command. Here's an example of its use:

```
SQL> ALTER TABLE emp
  2   STORAGE (NEXT 50K
  3            MINEXTENTS 1
  4            MAXEXTENTS 500
  5            PCTINCREASE 0)
  6   PCTFREE 30
  7   PCTUSED 50
  8   INITRANS 5
  9   MAXTRANS 200;

Table altered.
```

You can also alter a table using OEM. To do this, start the OEM Console, select the database that contains the table you want to alter, choose the Schema folder, then the Tables folder, and then the user that owns the table. Next, right-click on the table to be altered, choose Edit from the context-sensitive menu, and click on the Storage tab. By default, the screen shown in Figure 11.1 appears.

Notice that the values shown for each of the parameters are what I set them to in the previous example of an **ALTER TABLE** statement. (The value of **NEXT**, 56K, is the next highest multiple of the database block size above the 50K value I specified.) OEM has queried the data dictionary to populate these fields with their current values.

If I choose the Auto Calculation radio button and then click on Show SQL, the screen shown in Figure 11.2 appears.

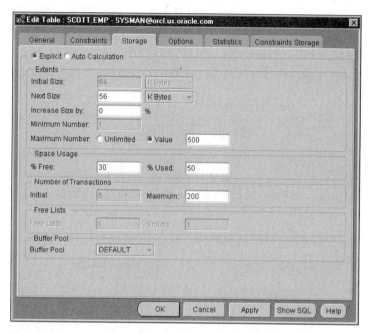

Figure 11.1 Using OEM to edit explicit storage parameters for a table.

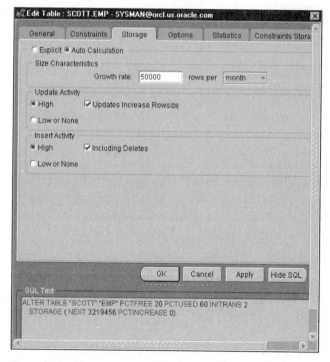

Figure 11.2 Allowing OEM to automatically calculate storage parameters for a table.

This screen prompts you for activity types (to work out values of **PCTFREE** and **PCTUSED**) and the number of rows to be inserted to determine the optimal storage settings for the table. In the figure, I've clicked on the Show SQL button so you can see the results of adding 50,000 rows per month to the **EMP** table.

Manually Allocating Extents

You may want to manually allocate extents to a table for one of two reasons:

➤ You are about to load a large amount of data into the table and you want to avoid dynamic space allocation.

➤ You want to stripe a table manually across datafiles within a tablespace.

You can accomplish either with the **ALTER TABLE ALLOCATE EXTENT** command. You can specify a size for the extent (the value of **NEXT** is used if you don't) and a datafile for the extent to be allocated in. (Oracle uses a round-robin algorithm to determine the datafile if you don't specify it.) We need to note a couple of points about this. First, manually allocating an extent does not result in immediate I/O redistribution. The extent needs to be loaded with data before there is any affect on the I/O spread. Second, specifying a size has no affect on the value of **NEXT** in the data dictionary. The next extent to be allocated after the manual extent allocation will use the value of **NEXT** that is in the data dictionary, not the size specified in the manual extent allocation command. Third, if you specify a datafile, it must belong to the tablespace in which the table exists; otherwise, an error is returned. Here's an example of using the command:

```
SQL> ALTER TABLE emp
  2   ALLOCATE EXTENT (SIZE 20M
  3   DATAFILE '/u03/oradata/prd/data01.dbf');

Table altered.
```

Relocating a Table

Oracle8i provides you with the functionality to relocate or reorganize a table without using the Export and Import utilities. You may want to use this functionality to eliminate row migration, or simply to move a table to another tablespace. The **ALTER TABLE** command is used for this. Here's an example:

```
SQL> ALTER TABLE emp
  2   MOVE TABLESPACE users;

Table altered.
```

When you move a table with this command, the indexes, constraints, privileges, and so on are preserved. However, any index will be marked unusable because the index now contains invalid **ROWID**s, so you'll need to rebuild the indexes using a command such as this:

```
SQL> ALTER INDEX pk_emp REBUILD;

Index altered.
```

The High-Water Mark

One of the things you need to understand about Oracle and the way it stores data is the concept of the high-water mark. The high-water mark, stored in the segment header for the table, indicates the position of the last block that was used for a table. As data is inserted into a table and extra blocks are allocated to it, the high-water mark gradually moves. It is not reset when data is deleted (except with a **TRUNCATE** command, which we'll cover later in this chapter).

When Oracle performs a full table scan, it scans up to the high-water mark, regardless of the number of empty blocks below the high-water mark. This can have an obvious performance impact, so you need to be able to determine where the high-water mark is. To do this, Oracle provides the **DBMS_SPACE. UNUSED_SPACE** procedure. Using this procedure, you can find the number of blocks above the high-water mark that haven't been used. Remember that Oracle adds space as whole extents, whereas the high-water mark is at the block level, so it's highly probable that there is unused space above the high-water mark in the last extent allocated to a table. Here's some PL/SQL code that allows you to determine how many blocks are unused in this way:

```
SQL> DECLARE
  2    v_owner VARCHAR2(30) := 'SCOTT' ;
  3    v_segment_name VARCHAR2(30) := 'EMP';
  4    v_segment_type VARCHAR2(30) := 'TABLE';
  5    v_total_blocks NUMBER;
  6    v_total_bytes NUMBER;
  7    v_unused_blocks NUMBER;
  8    v_unused_bytes NUMBER;
  9    v_last_used_extent_file_id NUMBER;
 10    v_last_used_extent_block_id NUMBER;
 11    v_last_used_block NUMBER;
 12  BEGIN
 13    DBMS_SPACE.UNUSED_SPACE(v_owner,
 14                            v_segment_name,
 15                            v_segment_type,
 16                            v_total_blocks,
```

```
17                           v_total_bytes,
18                           v_unused_blocks,
19                           v_unused_bytes,
20                           v_last_used_extent_file_id,
21                           v_last_used_extent_block_id,
22                           v_last_used_block
23  );
24  DBMS_OUTPUT.PUT_LINE('Segment name: '||v_segment_name);
25  DBMS_OUTPUT.PUT_LINE('Segment type: '||v_segment_type);
26  DBMS_OUTPUT.PUT_LINE('Total Blocks:'
27     ||TO_CHAR(v_total_blocks));
28  DBMS_OUTPUT.PUT_LINE('Total Bytes:'
29     ||TO_CHAR(v_total_bytes));
30  DBMS_OUTPUT.PUT_LINE('Blocks above HWM:'
31     ||TO_CHAR(v_unused_blocks));
32  DBMS_OUTPUT.PUT_LINE('Bytes above HWM:'
33     ||TO_CHAR(v_unused_bytes));
34  DBMS_OUTPUT.PUT_LINE('File ID:'
35     ||TO_CHAR(v_last_used_extent_file_id));
36  DBMS_OUTPUT.PUT_LINE('Block ID:'
37     ||TO_CHAR(v_last_used_extent_block_id));
38  DBMS_OUTPUT.PUT_LINE('Last Used Block:'
39     ||TO_CHAR(v_last_used_block));
40  END;
41  /
Segment name: EMP
Segment type: TABLE
Total Blocks: 16
Total Bytes: 131072
Blocks above HWM: 14
Bytes above HWM: 114688
File ID: 3
Block ID: 2
Last Used Block: 2

PL/SQL procedure successfully completed.
```

If the script I've just listed shows a lot of unused space above the high-water mark (HWM in the example), you can deallocate the unused space with a command such as this:

```
SQL> ALTER TABLE scott.emp
  2  DEALLOCATE UNUSED KEEP 500;

Table altered.
```

If I now reexecute the PL/SQL script, I get the following result:

```
Segment name: EMP
Segment type: TABLE
Total Blocks: 3
Total Bytes: 24576
Blocks above HWM: 1
Bytes above HWM: 8192
File ID: 3
Block ID: 2
Last Used Block: 2

PL/SQL procedure successfully completed.
```

I could have left out the **KEEP** clause in the **ALTER TABLE** statement, in which case Oracle will deallocate all the space above the high-water mark. (The value I used is in bytes because **EMP** is such a small table, but you would normally specify K or M after the integer value for kilobytes or megabytes.) If the high-water mark is currently in an extent that is less than the value indicated by **MINEXTENTS**, then only space above **MINEXTENTS** will be released.

Truncating a Table

The **TRUNCATE** command allows you to delete all the rows from a table and to reset the high-water mark. It is a very fast operation because it generates no rollback information. The command is a DDL command, so it performs an implicit commit before and after the operation. Any indexes on the table are truncated as well. You can use either the **DROP STORAGE** clause (this is the default) to completely free up space and return it to the tablespace, or the **REUSE STORAGE** clause to keep the extents truncated by the command available for only this table to reinsert data into it. Each option cascades to any indexes for the table. Here's an example of the command:

```
SQL> TRUNCATE TABLE emp REUSE STORAGE;

Table truncated.
```

You should be aware of a couple points regarding the **TRUNCATE** command. First, you cannot truncate a table that is referenced by a foreign key. (Dropping the foreign key first will avoid this problem.) Second, delete triggers are not fired when the command is issued. Third, if you truncate a table without specifying **REUSE STORAGE**, the value of **NEXT** will be reset to the value of the last allocated extent.

Dropping Columns from a Table

When a table is no longer required in an Oracle database, you can use the **DROP TABLE** command to remove it completely. In Oracle8i, you also have the ability to drop individual columns from a table. This is far simpler than the manual methodology you had to use to drop columns before Oracle8i. Dropping a column can take quite some time, because you are deleting all of the information for that column from the table. It can also generate a lot of rollback information, so you can tell Oracle to issue a checkpoint after a certain number of rows are deleted to minimize the use of rollback segment space. The table is marked as invalid until the **ALTER TABLE** command completes. Here is an example of the command. First I describe the table, then I alter it to drop a foreign key column, and then I describe it again to show that the column has in fact gone:

```
SQL> desc emp
 Name                                      Null?    Type
 ---------------------------------------- -------- --------------

 EMPNO                                              NUMBER(4)
 ENAME                                              VARCHAR2(10)
 JOB                                                VARCHAR2(9)
 MGR                                                NUMBER(4)
 HIREDATE                                           DATE
 SAL                                                NUMBER(7,2)
 COMM                                               NUMBER(7,2)
 DEPTNO                                             NUMBER(2)

SQL> ALTER TABLE emp
  2  DROP COLUMN deptno CASCADE CONSTRAINTS
  3  CHECKPOINT 500;

Table altered.

SQL> desc emp
 Name                                      Null?    Type
 ---------------------------------------- -------- --------------

 EMPNO                                              NUMBER(4)
 ENAME                                              VARCHAR2(10)
 JOB                                                VARCHAR2(9)
 MGR                                                NUMBER(4)
 HIREDATE                                           DATE
 SAL                                                NUMBER(7,2)
 COMM                                               NUMBER(7,2)
```

If the instance had failed in the middle of the **DROP COLUMN** operation, I could restart the instance and then restart the column drop by using the **ALTER TABLE emp DROP COLUMNS CONTINUE** command.

If you didn't want to take the time to perform a drop column operation, you could simply mark the column as unused and then physically delete it later. Marking a column as unused is much quicker than dropping it because doing so only updates the data dictionary rather than removing the data from the file. To drop a column like this, you need to use two commands:

```
SQL> ALTER TABLE emp
  2   SET UNUSED COLUMN comm
  3   CASCADE CONSTRAINTS;

Table altered.

SQL> ALTER TABLE emp
  2   DROP UNUSED COLUMNS CHECKPOINT 500;

Table altered.
```

Again, I could continue the last command if the instance fails, using the **ALTER TABLE emp DROP COLUMNS CONTINUE** syntax.

Dropping a column has a number of restrictions. You can't do any of the following in Oracle8i:

➤ Drop all the columns in a table.

➤ Drop a column from an object type table or a nested table.

➤ Drop a column that is a partition key.

➤ Drop columns from any table owned by SYS.

➤ Drop a column from an index-organized table (IOT) if the column to be dropped is the primary key for the IOT.

➤ Drop a parent key column.

➤ Mark a column as unused and then change your mind.

Retrieving Table Information from the Data Dictionary

Although a large number of views in the data dictionary contain table information, I'm going to concentrate in this section on the few that are the most applicable to the material we've covered so far in this chapter:

➤ **DBA_OBJECTS**—Describes all objects in the database, not just the tables. It includes information on the object owner, object name, the last DDL time, and the status for the object.

➤ **DBA_SEGMENTS**—Describes the storage allocated for all segments in the database, not just tables. It includes the segment name and owner, segment type, tablespace name, and storage information.

➤ **DBA_TABLES**—Describes all tables in the database and includes the table name, tablespace name, storage information, and statistics that have been gathered for the table using the **ANALYZE** command.

➤ **DBA_UNUSED_COL_TABS**—Describes all tables in the database that have unused columns. The three columns in this view are the owner, table name, and a count of the number of unused rows.

Let's look at some **SELECT** statements that use these tables:

```
SQL> REM First let's join some of these tables so we can
SQL> REM see the results
SQL> SELECT t.table_name, o.data_object_id,
  2         s.header_file, s.header_block
  3  FROM dba_objects o, dba_segments s, dba_tables t
  4  WHERE t.owner=o.owner
  5  AND t.owner=s.owner
  6  AND t.table_name=o.object_name
  7  AND t.table_name=s.segment_name
  8  AND t.owner='SCOTT';

TABLE_NAME DATA_OBJECT_ID HEADER_FILE HEADER_BLOCK
---------- -------------- ----------- ------------
DEPT            12536          4           12
EMP             12548          4           15
2 rows selected.

SQL> REM Now let's look at how many extents and blocks one of
SQL> REM these tables is in
SQL> SELECT file_id, COUNT(*) AS Extents, SUM(blocks) AS Blocks
  2  FROM dba_extents
  3  WHERE owner = 'SCOTT'
  4  AND segment_name='EMP'
  5  GROUP BY file_id;

FILE_ID EXTENTS BLOCKS
------- ------- ------
      4       1      1

1 row selected.
```

Listing Index Types and Their Uses

Indexes can be classified in one of two ways: logically or physically.

Logical Classifications

Logically, indexes are broken down into single-column or concatenated indexes, unique or nonunique indexes, and function-based indexes. Let's take a look at each of these:

➤ *Single-column indexes*—Indexes that have only one column in the index key. An example is the **PK_EMP** index created on the **EMP** table in Oracle's demonstration tables. It is a single-column index on the **EMPNO** column.

➤ *Concatenated indexes (also known as composite indexes)*—Indexes that have more than one column in the index key. A composite index can have up to 32 columns in the index key (except for bitmap indexes, which can have only 30 columns in the index key). However, an additional limitation prevents a single index entry from exceeding roughly one-third of a block in size.

➤ *Unique indexes*—Indexes that guarantee that a single index key value occurs only once in the index. No duplicates are allowed in the column that the index is created on. An index that's created to enforce a primary key (see later in this chapter) is by definition unique. Non-unique indexes allow duplicate index key values in the index.

➤ *Function-based indexes*—Indexes that can be created only as B-tree or bitmap indexes. They store the precomputed results of an expression on one or more columns in the index. For example, I could create an index on **UPPER(ENAME)** for the **EMP** table. The index would store the uppercase values of the employee name, regardless of the case in which the employee name is entered into **ENAME**. Queries that reference **UPPER(ENAME)** could then use the index to satisfy the query, rather than having to retrieve the information from the table.

Physical Classifications

Physically, indexes can be broken down into partitioned or nonpartitioned indexes, reverse key indexes, B-tree indexes, and bitmap indexes. The "Oracle8i: Architecture and Administration" exam covers only B-tree indexes and bitmap indexes in any detail from the physical classification side, so I'll briefly cover the other index types in the physical classification here, and then cover B-tree and bitmap indexes in more detail in the next main section. The physical classifications not covered in much detail on the exam are:

➤ *Partitioned indexes*—Indexes that are used to break indexes for large tables into smaller pieces. Each partition in a partitioned index is a segment in its own right. The partitions can be spread across tablespaces and placed on different devices for optimal I/O performance, recoverability, availability, and manageability. Partitioned indexes can be created on nonpartitioned or partitioned tables. Nonpartitioned indexes are not broken up in this way.

➤ *Reverse key indexes*—Indexes that reverse the order of the bytes in the index key value (except for the **ROWID**), but still keep the column order intact for composite reverse key indexes. This is done to reduce I/O bottlenecks that can sometimes occur with inserts because the inserts are all performed at the same place in the index structure. This issue is normally seen with indexes that are populated by a sequence. Range scans are not possible with a reverse index because logically adjacent rows are no longer stored next to each other in the index. They can be used, however, for queries with an equality predicate (that is, queries in which the reverse key index entry equals a certain value).

Creating B-Tree and Bitmap Indexes

Both B-tree and bitmap indexes use the same underlying structure (a B-tree). However, the way the data is stored in the B-tree is slightly different in each. Let's look at each of these in more detail.

B-Tree Indexes

The term *B-tree index* usually refers to an index that stores the column values being indexed along with the **ROWID**. Figure 11.3 shows this structure.

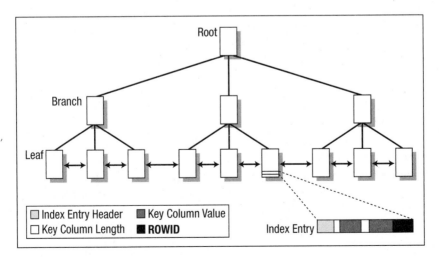

Figure 11.3   The structure of a B-tree index.

The tree structure is obvious in this figure. Each level points to blocks of the next level, with the final leaf blocks containing the actual key values. The leaf blocks are linked in the form of a doubly linked list—that is, the index can be scanned in both ascending and descending order. (Previous releases of Oracle had this linked list format, but descending index scans were not supported.) The index leaf entries contain a header (which includes the number of columns in the entry and locking information), a set of column length/value pairs, and the restricted **ROWID** that points to the location on disk of the row in the table. If all the columns that make up the index are null for a particular row, that row has no entry in the index.

Although the effect of Data Manipulation Language (DML) operations varies depending on the type of DML, the Oracle server automatically updates an index in all cases. An **INSERT** results in the addition of the index key values and the **ROWID** in the appropriate block. A **DELETE** results only in a logical deletion of the index value. (The free space resulting from the delete is not available until the entire block is empty, unless the same key value is used again.) An **UPDATE** performs a logical delete followed by an insert into the index. **PCTFREE** has no effect on an index except when the index is created, which means that a new index entry can be created in a block even when the block has less than **PCTFREE** space available to it.

Bitmap Indexes

A bitmap index also uses a B-tree structure, but it stores a bitmap instead of **ROWID**s. The structure of the index entry is also somewhat different. An index entry contains header information (including the number of columns in the entry and locking information), a set of column length/value pairs, a start and end **ROWID**, and a bitmap segment. The start and end **ROWID** points are the **ROWID**s of the first and last rows that the bitmap segment points to. Each bit in the bitmap corresponds to a **ROWID**. If the bit is set, then the row with the corresponding **ROWID** contains the key value. By their very nature, bitmap indexes cannot be unique.

Let's look at an example that might make this clearer. Let's say we had a **GENDER** column in the database that stores two values: male and female. The first **ROWID** that contains the value female is in file 4, block 6, row 7. The last **ROWID** that contains this value is in file 4, block 9, row 5. If the first five rows in this sequence store the values female, male, female, female, male, the index entry for female will appear as shown in Table 11.1. (Note that, in the Bitmap column, the number of values will be the same as the number of rows—that is, there is a bitmap entry for every row.)

Table 11.1 Structure of a bitmap index entry.			
Key	Start ROWID	End ROWID	Bitmap
Female	4.6.7	4.9.5	10110 ...

When an update is made to a bitmap index, the bitmap must be locked. Because the bitmap stores information from multiple rows, this means that more than one row can be locked when an update is made to a bitmap index. For this reason, bitmap indexes are most useful in read-only or low-update situations, such as data warehousing. They are also best used on columns that have low cardinality (that is, columns that have few distinct values). This is a relative determinant because tables that have millions of rows may benefit from a bitmap index on a column even if there are a few thousand distinct values in the column, whereas smaller tables would benefit with correspondingly fewer distinct values. The other scenario in which bitmap indexes can be advantageous is for queries with large **WHERE** clauses that include multiple **OR** statements. Bitmap indexing can merge indexes in this scenario very efficiently, resulting in better performance and reduced I/O.

Comparing Bitmap and B-Tree Indexes

As mentioned previously, bitmap indexes can be very useful in data warehousing environments. They are suitable for columns with low cardinality and efficient for queries with large **WHERE** clauses that include multiple **OR** statements. They can take advantage of bitmap compression algorithms, so they can have relatively frugal storage requirements. Updates to index keys can be quite expensive because locking is done at the bitmap level.

B-tree indexes, on the other hand, are more efficient in Online Transaction Processing (OLTP) environments with dynamic tables. They are more suited for columns with high cardinality and are not very efficient for queries with large **WHERE** clauses that include multiple **OR** statements. They also require more storage than bitmap indexes. Locking is done at the row level, so updates to index keys are inexpensive.

Guidelines for Creating Indexes

You need to remember a few guidelines when creating indexes:

➤ Don't create an index unless you know it's going to be useful. You need to balance the needs of query performance and slower DML operations.

➤ For performance, availability, recoverability, and manageability considerations, separate indexes from rollback segments, temporary segments, and tables.

➤ Consider using **NOLOGGING** and **PARALLEL** when creating a large index. The performance gains may be significant.

➤ Minimize fragmentation by using a few standard extent sizes that are a multiple of five database blocks.

➤ Set a low **PCTFREE** value for indexes on sequence values or other monotonically increasing column values. Index entries for sequence values are appended to existing index entries, so there is no need to insert a new index entry between two existing entries.

➤ Set a higher **PCTFREE** value for indexes on columns in which new values can occur between existing values.

➤ Set the initialization parameter **CREATE_BITMAP_AREA_SIZE** higher when creating bitmap indexes on columns with higher cardinality. This parameter controls the amount of memory that's available for creating bitmap indexes, and higher-cardinality columns will require more memory.

Reorganizing Indexes

Once an index exists, you can control the space it uses with the **ALTER INDEX** command. Some of the storage parameters and the block utilization parameters can be changed, and because the effect of changing these parameters is the same as it is with the **ALTER TABLE** command, you should refer back to the "Controlling the Space Used by Tables" section for details.

Allocating and Deallocating Index Space

You may want to manually allocate extents to an index for one of two reasons:

➤ You are about to load a large amount of data into the underlying table, and you want to avoid dynamic space allocation.

➤ You want to stripe an index manually across datafiles within a tablespace.

Either reason can be accomplished with the **ALTER INDEX ALLOCATE EXTENT** command. You can specify a size for the extent (the value of **NEXT** is used if you don't) and a datafile for the extent to be allocated in. (Oracle uses a round-robin algorithm to determine the datafile if you don't specify it.) You need to be aware of a few related points:

➤ Manually allocating an extent does not result in immediate I/O redistribution. The extent needs to be loaded with data before there is any impact on the I/O spread.

➤ Specifying a size has no impact on the value of **NEXT** in the data dictionary. The next extent to be allocated after the manual extent allocation will use the value of **NEXT** that is in the data dictionary, not the size specified in the manual extent allocation command.

➤ If you specify a datafile, it must belong to the tablespace in which the index exists; otherwise, an error is returned.

You can also deallocate space above the high-water mark from an index using the **ALTER INDEX DEALLOCATE EXTENT** command. The functionality and syntax here is the same as they are for the **ALTER TABLE DEALLOCATE EXTENT** command, so refer back to the "Controlling the Space Used by Tables" section for more details.

Rebuilding Indexes

In the form of the **ALTER INDEX** command, Oracle8i provides you with the functionality to rebuild an index without using the Export and Import utilities. You may want to use this functionality to improve space usage by removing deleted entries, to swap a reverse key index to nonreverse (or vice versa), or simply to move an index to another tablespace. Here's an example of how to use the **ALTER INDEX** command to move an index:

```
SQL> ALTER INDEX pk_emp
  2  REBUILD TABLESPACE users;

Index altered.
```

Notice that the command here is slightly different than the command used to move a table. You use the **MOVE** keyword to move a table, whereas you use the **REBUILD** keyword to move an index.

While you are moving an index, you need to have sufficient storage for both the old index and the new one. Because the new index is created from the old one, with deleted entries being removed, there is no need to access the table during the move. Queries can continue to use the old index while the new one is being built. You can use the **ONLINE** keyword with the **ALTER INDEX REBUILD** statement to allow DML access to the table while the index is being rebuilt. However, this is not recommended for large DML operations for performance reasons, and it has the following restrictions:

➤ You cannot deallocate unused space and rebuild an index online in the same operation.

➤ You cannot rebuild indexes for temporary tables online.

➤ If the index is partitioned, you can rebuild only the individual partitions online, rather than the whole index.

➤ Because DML locks are still taken out during the rebuild, other DDL operations are not allowed at the same time.

Oracle allows you not only to rebuild indexes, but to coalesce index blocks with free space. Here's an example of the command:

```
SQL> ALTER INDEX pk_emp COALESCE;

Index altered.
```

Getting Index Information from the Data Dictionary

You can access several views to get index information. The main data dictionary views dealing with indexes are:

➤ **DBA_IND_COLUMNS**—Describes the columns used in indexes in the database, including the index name, table name, column name, each column's position in the index, and the column length.

➤ **DBA_INDEXES**—Describes all indexes in the database, including the index name, table name, index type, uniqueness, storage information, and statistical information.

Here are some examples of **SELECT** statements using these two views:

```
SQL> REM show me all the indexes owned by scott.
SQL> REM this query would not return any reverse key indexes
SQL> REM (you need to query the base data dictionary tables
SQL> REM for this, which is beyond the scope of this book)
SQL> SELECT index_name, table_name, index_type, status
  2  FROM dba_indexes
  3  WHERE owner = 'SCOTT';

INDEX_NAME TABLE_NAME INDEX_TYPE STATUS
---------- ---------- ---------- --------
PK_DEPT    DEPT       NORMAL     VALID
PK_EMP     EMP        NORMAL     VALID

SQL> REM show me all the columns in these indexes
SQL> REM and their positions
```

```
SQL> REM these are single column indexes, but the query works on
SQL> REM composite ones as well
SQL> SELECT index_name,table_name,column_name,
  2          column_position AS POS
  3  FROM dba_ind_columns
  4  WHERE index_owner ='SCOTT'
  5  ORDER BY index_name, column_position;


INDEX_NAME  TABLE_NAME  COLUMN_NAME        POS
----------  ----------  ---------------    -----------
PK_DEPT     DEPT        DEPTNO               1
PK_EMP      EMP         EMPNO                1
```

Implementing Data Integrity Constraints

You can maintain data integrity through application code, database triggers, or declared integrity constraints. Unless you can guarantee that all interactions with your data will happen through applications, it is a good idea to keep data integrity checking at the database level. Although database triggers allow you to define and enforce integrity rules, a database trigger is not the same as an integrity constraint. You can define a database trigger to enforce an integrity rule, but it cannot check data that's already loaded into a table. Therefore, you should use database triggers only when the integrity rule cannot be enforced by integrity constraints.

An Oracle database has five types of declarative integrity constraints: primary key, unique key, foreign key, not null, and check constraints. Creating and maintaining these constraints is covered in the first OCP exam, "Introduction to Oracle: SQL and PL/SQL," so I'm going to concentrate here on constraint states and enforcement modes. For more information on creating and maintaining constraints, refer to Mike Ault's excellent *Oracle8i DBA: SQL and PL/SQL Exam Cram*. (See the "Need to Know More?" section at the end of this chapter for full bibliographic details.)

Constraint States

Constraints can be defined in one of four states, which are used as keywords in the constraint definition:

➤ **DISABLE NOVALIDATE**—Constraints in this state are not checked. The constraint definition is stored in the data dictionary, but existing data is not checked against the constraint, nor is any new data that is entered checked after the constraint is created.

In some versions of the Oracle Education courseware, it states that **DISABLE NOVALIDATE** is the normal state of operation for OLTP systems. This is completely wrong; it's the normal state of operations for data warehouse systems. This error has not been a part of any questions for the exams I've seen—so I can't tell you if the exam makes the same mistake—but, if the exam does follow the courseware, you'll be expected to give an answer that you know is incorrect.

➤ **DISABLE VALIDATE**—Modifications to constraint columns are not allowed if constraints are in this state. Any indexes created implicitly for the constraint are dropped. This constraint is really useful only for exchanging nonpartitioned tables with partitions, which is not covered in this exam.

➤ **ENABLE NOVALIDATE**—Constraints in this state are enforced for new data only. Existing data is not checked when the constraint is enabled. This is generally used as an intermediary stage, before existing data is cleaned up, to ensure that no new data is entered that could violate the constraint.

➤ **ENABLE VALIDATE**—This is the default state for a constraint. Constraints in this state guarantee that all data in the table meets the constraint criteria. In addition, any new data must also satisfy the constraint before it can be entered. This is really the normal state for constraints in OLTP systems.

When a data load is performed, it's advisable to move a constraint from **DISABLE NOVALIDATE** to **ENABLE NOVALIDATE** and then **ENABLE VALIDATE**. A move directly between the first and last states (that is, from **DISABLE NOVALIDATE** to **ENABLE VALIDATE**) causes the table to be locked so existing rows can be checked, which may take a while.

Constraint Enforcement Modes

Constraints can either be enforced immediately (that is, for every row inserted into a table) or at the end of a transaction (a process called *deferred constraint checking*). If a DML statement attempts to violate an immediate constraint, the DML statement is immediately rolled back. For example, if you attempt to enter a row into the **EMP** table with a **DEPTNO** value that is not listed in the corresponding **DEPTNO** column for the **DEPT** table, you are attempting to violate the primary key. The **INSERT** statement will fail immediately. However, if you're executing a series of inserts in a single transaction, a later insert into the **DEPT** table may resolve this problem. To allow a row to temporarily violate a constraint like this, the constraint must be defined as a deferred constraint. In this way, the constraint checking is deferred until the end of the transaction.

The default behavior for constraints is immediate enforcement. If you want to configure a constraint as deferred, you can do this only when the constraint is created. Use the **INITIALLY IMMEDIATE** keywords for the constraint definition to create a constraint that is enforced immediately, or the **INITIALLY DEFERRED** keywords to create a deferred constraint. A constraint that was created as an immediate constraint cannot be modified with an **ALTER TABLE** command to become a deferred constraint. However, you can change the behavior of a constraint in an application, either by using the **ALTER SESSION SET CONSTRAINT IMMEDIATE | DEFERRED** command or the **SET CONSTRAINT IMMEDIATE | DEFERRED** command.

Defining a primary or unique key constraint as deferred also changes the default index behavior for the implicit index created to support the constraint. The default behaviors are to create an index only if the constraint is enabled and to use a unique index to enforce the constraint. (An existing index will be used if one is defined on the constraint columns in the correct order.) If either type of constraint is defined as deferred, the index that is used to enforce the constraint is defined as nonunique, rather than unique.

Maintaining Integrity Constraints

Integrity constraints can swap from enabled to disabled and vice versa. Disabling constraints is covered in the "Introduction to Oracle: SQL and PL/SQL" exam, so I won't cover it further here. To enable a constraint, you use the **ALTER TABLE** command. Here's an example:

```
SQL> ALTER TABLE emp
  2   ENABLE NOVALIDATE CONSTRAINT pk_emp;

Table altered.
```

VALIDATE is the default behavior, so you don't need to specify that if you want to swap a constraint to the **ENABLE VALIDATE** state. If you swap a constraint to the **ENABLE VALIDATE** state, existing data in the table is checked and an error is returned. Here's an example:

```
SQL> REM First, insert new row with DEPTNO=60 (this doesn't
SQL> REM exist in DEPT)
SQL> REM The foreign key FK_DEPTNO exists but is in
SQL> REM DISABLE NOVALIDATE state
SQL> INSERT INTO emp
  2   VALUES (1234, 'Sharman', 'Author', 5678,
  3          to_char('14-FEB-01'), 10000, 0, 60);
```

```
1 row created.

SQL> REM Commit the data
SQL> commit;

Commit complete.

SQL> REM Swap the foreign key to ENABLE NOVALIDATE state
SQL> REM - no errors
SQL> ALTER TABLE emp
  2   ENABLE NOVALIDATE CONSTRAINT fk_deptno;

Table altered.

SQL> REM Now try to swap to ENABLE VALIDATE state
SQL> ALTER TABLE emp
  2   ENABLE VALIDATE CONSTRAINT fk_deptno;
ENABLE VALIDATE CONSTRAINT fk_deptno
                  *
ERROR at line 2:
ORA-02298: cannot validate (SCOTT.FK_DEPTNO) - parent keys not
found
```

You can avoid these errors by using the **EXCEPTIONS** clause, which identifies those rows that are going to fail validation. (When rows fail validation, the constraint is left in the **NOVALIDATE** state.) To use this clause, you need to follow these steps:

1. Create the **EXCEPTIONS** table. To do this, you need to run the utlexcpt.sql script (located under $ORACLE_HOME/rdbms/admin on Unix boxes, and %ORACLE_HOME%\rdbms\admin on NT boxes). This can be done by a user other than the one performing the validation, in which case the table name needs to be qualified with the schema name while performing the validation.

2. Try to enable the constraint, but this time use the **EXCEPTIONS** clause, as in the following example. (The same error is returned, but we'll fix that in the remaining steps.)

```
SQL> ALTER TABLE emp
  2   ENABLE VALIDATE CONSTRAINT fk_deptno
  3   EXCEPTIONS INTO exceptions;
ENABLE VALIDATE CONSTRAINT fk_deptno
                  *
```

```
ERROR at line 2:
ORA-02298: cannot validate (SCOTT.FK_DEPTNO) - parent keys not
found
```

3. Identify the invalid data in the **EMP** table:

```
SQL> SELECT rowid, empno, ename
  2  FROM EMP
  3  WHERE rowid in (SELECT row_id FROM exceptions);

ROWID                    EMPNO ENAME          DEPTNO
------------------ ---------- ---------- ----------
AAAGMpAADAAAAAEAAB        1234 Sharman            60
```

 Notice that the **ROW_ID** column in the **EXCEPTIONS** table has an underscore in its name. If you omit the underscore, you'll get an "ORA-01410: invalid ROWID" error, which can be rather confusing.

4. You can now correct the error and enable the constraint properly:

```
SQL> UPDATE emp SET deptno = 40
  2  WHERE rowid IN (SELECT row_id FROM EXCEPTIONS);

1 row updated.

SQL> commit;

Commit complete.

SQL> ALTER TABLE emp
  2  ENABLE VALIDATE CONSTRAINT fk_deptno;

Table altered.
```

5. Now truncate the **EXCEPTIONS** table to ensure that old data doesn't confuse later use of the **EXCEPTIONS INTO** clause:

```
SQL> TRUNCATE TABLE exceptions;

Table truncated.
```

Obtaining Constraint Information from the Data Dictionary

Two data dictionary views contain information on constraints:

➤ **DBA_CONS_COLUMNS**—Lists all columns used in constraints in the database, including the constraint name, table name, column name, and column position.

➤ **DBA_CONSTRAINTS**—Describes all constraints in the database, including the constraint and table names, constraint type, state and enforcement mode information, and information about other objects referenced if the constraint is a foreign key constraint. The constraint type can be C (check constraint), O (with read-only, on a view), P (primary key), R (referential integrity—that is, a foreign key), U (unique key), or V (with check option, on a view). Not null constraints are created as check constraints (**CHECK <column_name> IS NOT NULL**), so they appear as type C.

Here are some queries on these views:

```
SQL> REM Show me all the constraints owned by scott
SQL> SELECT table_name, constraint_name,
  2  constraint_type, deferred, status
  3  FROM dba_constraints
  4  WHERE owner ='SCOTT'
  5  ORDER BY table_name, constraint_name;

TABLE_NAME CONSTRAINT_NAME C DEFERRED   STATUS
---------- --------------- - --------   --------

DEPT       PK_DEPT         P IMMEDIATE  ENABLED
EMP        FK_DEPTNO       R IMMEDIATE  ENABLED
EMP        PK_EMP          P IMMEDIATE  ENABLED

SQL> REM Now show me the column information for these constraints
SQL> SELECT table_name, constraint_name, column_name, position
  2  FROM all_cons_columns
  3  WHERE owner = 'SCOTT'
  4  ORDER BY table_name, constraint_name;

TABLE_NAME CONSTRAINT_NAME COLUMN_NAME      POSITION
---------- --------------- ---------------  ----------

DEPT       PK_DEPT         DEPTNO                   1
EMP        FK_DEPTNO       DEPTNO                   1
EMP        PK_EMP          EMPNO                    1
```

Practice Questions

Question 1

What is the format of the restricted **ROWID** in Oracle8i tables? (In the answers, FFFF is the file number, BBBBBB is the block number, and RRRR is the row number.)

○ a. FFFF.RRRR.BBBBBB

○ b. RRRR.BBBBBB.FFFF

○ c. BBBBBB.RRRR.FFFF

○ d. Restricted **ROWID**s are not allowed in Oracle8i tables.

Answer c is correct. The format of a restricted **ROWID** is block number first, then row number, then file number. Answers a and b are incorrect because they do not match the format of a restricted **ROWID**. Answer d is incorrect because Oracle8i tables support restricted **ROWID**s.

Question 2

Which keyword indicates the rate of growth for each subsequent extent allocated to a table?

○ a. **MINEXTENTS**

○ b. **PCTINCREASE**

○ c. **MAXEXTENTS**

○ d. **INITIAL**

Answer b is correct. **PCTINCREASE** is the percentage by which the next extent will increase. Answer a is incorrect because **MINEXTENTS** sets the minimum number of extents to be created when the table is created. Answer c is incorrect because **MAXEXTENTS** is the maximum number of extents that can be allocated to the table. Answer d is incorrect because **INITIAL** is the size of the first extent allocated to the table.

Question 3

> Which data dictionary view would you query to find out if an index is valid?
>
> ○ a. **DBA_TABLES**
> ○ b. **DBA_IND_COLUMNS**
> ○ c. **DBA_SEGMENTS**
> ○ d. **DBA_INDEXES**

Answer d is correct. **DBA_INDEXES** displays the status of each index. Answer a is incorrect because **DBA_TABLES** provides information on tables, not indexes. Answer b is incorrect because **DBA_IND_COLUMNS** shows the columns of an index, not the status of an index. Answer c is incorrect because **DBA_SEGMENTS** contains information about storage allocated for all database segments.

Question 4

> Which statement is true about bitmap indexes?
>
> ○ a. They should be used only for very small tables.
> ○ b. They are slower than all other indexing techniques.
> ○ c. They can use substantially less space compared to other indexing techniques.
> ○ d. A unique bitmap index will outperform a unique B-tree index.

Answer c is correct. Bitmap indexes generally require less space than other kinds of indexes do. Answer a is incorrect because bitmap indexes can be very useful for large tables, depending on the cardinality of the column being indexed. Answer b is incorrect because bitmap indexes can outperform other indexing techniques when the data is of a low cardinality. Answer d is incorrect because bitmap indexes cannot be unique.

Question 5

When a table is truncated with the **DROP STORAGE** clause specified, what happens to the index?

○ a. The index is truncated, and the index space is deallocated.

○ b. Truncating a table does not affect the table indexes.

○ c. The index is truncated, but the index space remains allocated.

○ d. The index is not truncated, but the index space is deallocated.

Answer a is correct. The **TRUNCATE** command cascades to indexes, deleting all the rows in the corresponding indexes and deallocating space if the **DROP STORAGE** clause is used on the **TRUNCATE** command. Answers b and d are incorrect because all indexes associated with the table will get truncated. Answer c is incorrect because the **DROP STORAGE** clause cascades. If the **REUSE STORAGE** clause is used, the space remains allocated for both the table and the index.

Question 6

What is the maximum number of columns allowed in a concatenated index?

○ a. 1

○ b. 5

○ c. 16

○ d. 32

○ e. Unlimited

Answer d is correct. The maximum number of columns in a concatenated index is 32.

Question 7

> Which command would you use to disable a constraint?
>
> ○ a. **ALTER TABLE**
> ○ b. **DROP CONSTRAINT**
> ○ c. **ALTER SESSION**
> ○ d. **DELETE CONSTRAINT**

Answer a is correct. The **ALTER TABLE** command is used to disable a constraint. Answer b is incorrect because **DROP CONSTRAINT** is a clause of the **ALTER TABLE** command that completely removes a constraint rather than disabling it. Answer c is incorrect because **ALTER SESSION** cannot be used to disable a constraint; it only changes its validation behavior from immediate to deferred or deferred to immediate. Answer d is incorrect because **DELETE CONSTRAINT** is not a valid command.

Question 8

> Which keywords are used to allow existing data in a table to violate a constraint while enforcing the constraint for new data?
>
> ○ a. **ENABLE VALIDATE**
> ○ b. **DISABLE NOVALIDATE**
> ○ c. **ENABLE NOVALIDATE**
> ○ d. **DISABLE VALIDATE**

Answer c is correct. The **ENABLE NOVALIDATE** keywords allow existing data to violate a constraint while still enforcing it for new data. Answer a is incorrect because existing data must meet the constraint criteria if **ENABLE VALIDATE** is specified. Answer b is incorrect because constraints are not enforced for existing or new data when **DISABLE NOVALIDATE** is specified. Answer d is incorrect because the constraint is disabled and no new data is allowed to be entered when a constraint is in the **DISABLE VALIDATE** state.

Question 9

When will data be checked against a deferred constraint?
○ a. At the end of every DML statement
○ b. When a trigger fires
○ c. At regular time intervals
○ d. When a transaction commits

Answer d is correct. A deferred constraint is checked when a transaction commits. Answer a is incorrect because constraints are checked at the end of every DML statement when checking is set to immediate. Answer b is incorrect because triggers do not fire when constraints are checked. Answer c is incorrect because constraints are not checked at regular time intervals.

Need to Know More?

 Ault, Michael R. *Oracle8i DBA: SQL and PL/SQL Exam Cram.* The Coriolis Group, Scottsdale, AZ, 2001. ISBN 1-58880-037-7. This book provides an introduction to Oracle concepts, including creating and dropping tables, indexes, and constraints.

 Lewis, Jonathan. *Practical Oracle8i: Building Efficient Databases.* Addison-Wesley, Boston, MA, 2001. ISBN 0-20171-584-8. The author brings a wealth of experience to this book. Particularly relevant to this chapter are Chapters 6 and 7, on basic indexing and enhanced indexing, respectively, and Chapter 18, which discusses data integrity.

 See the Oracle documentation that is provided on CD with the Oracle RDBMS software. The following documents pertain to this chapter:

Baylis, Ruth, and Joyce Fee. *Oracle8i Administrator's Guide.* Oracle Corporation, Redwood City, CA, 1999. Here you'll find the complete documentation of database administration tasks. Of particular importance are Chapters 13 and 14, which cover managing tables and indexes, respectively, and Chapter 19, which covers general management of schema objects, including integrity constraints.

Leverenz, Lefty, Diana Rehfield, and Cathy Baird. *Oracle8i Concepts.* Oracle Corporation, Redwood City, CA, 1999. This is the complete documentation of Oracle concepts. Chapter 10 covers tables and indexes, and Chapter 25 addresses data integrity.

Lorentz, Diana. *Oracle8i Reference.* Oracle Corporation, Redwood City, CA, 1999. This document provides specific details on initialization parameters, data dictionary views, and database limits.

 technet.oracle.com is Oracle's technical repository of information for clients.

 www.revealnet.com is the site where RevealNet Corporation provides Oracle administration reference software.

Loading and Reorganizing Data

Terms you'll need to understand:

✓ SQL*Loader
✓ Direct path load
✓ Conventional path load
✓ Control file
✓ Bad file
✓ Discard file
✓ Table mode export
✓ User mode export
✓ Full database mode import/export
✓ Table mode import
✓ User mode import
✓ Direct-load insert

Techniques you'll need to master:

✓ Loading data using direct-load insert
✓ Loading data into Oracle tables using the SQL*Loader conventional path or direct path
✓ Reorganizing data using the Export and Import utilities
✓ Moving data using transportable tablespaces

This chapter discusses how and when to use the primary tools for loading and reorganizing data: direct-load insert, SQL*Loader, the Import and Export database utilities, and transportable tablespaces. With the proliferation of data warehousing, it's become even more important to understand how to effectively use these tools. Unlike online transaction-processing systems, data warehouses receive bulk loads of new data on a regular basis; thus, they can grow very quickly.

Loading Data Using Direct-Load Insert

You can use direct-load inserts to copy data from one table to another within the same database. Because direct-load inserts bypass the buffer cache completely and write directly into the datafiles, the speed of the insert operation is considerably increased. To perform a direct-load insert, you need to use the **APPEND** hint in the **INSERT** statement. Here's an example of how to do this:

```
SQL> INSERT /*+APPEND */ INTO my_large_table
  2  NOLOGGING
  3  SELECT * FROM scott.my_large_table;
```

Notice that I've also specified the **NOLOGGING** clause. Although doing so wasn't strictly necessary, it will improve the performance of the **INSERT** statement even more than just using direct-load inserts. **LOGGING** is the default configuration, so you will need to specify **NOLOGGING** if you don't want Oracle to generate redo entries for the rows inserted with the direct-load insert. (Even with **NOLOGGING**, you may get some redo entries, but these are for data dictionary updates such as space allocation rather than the insert operation itself.)

Direct-load inserts have the following restrictions:

➤ Direct-load inserts are available only when you issue an **INSERT** statement with a subquery.

➤ **INSERT** statements that use the **VALUES** clause cannot use direct-load inserts.

➤ Direct-load inserts can be performed for partitioned or nonpartitioned tables.

All constraints and indexes are maintained during the insert operation, and users can continue to access other rows in the table concurrently with the direct-load insert.

When executing direct-load inserts, you may need to consider that the rows are inserted above the high-water mark for the table. The high-water mark is then reset above the rows inserted with the direct-load insert after the operation completes. If you have many empty blocks below the high-water mark because of

DELETE statements, you may end up with a lot of wasted space as a result. One unwanted effect of this is that full table scans will be slower, because full table scans always scan to the high-water mark, regardless of the number of empty blocks below the high-water mark.

Direct-load inserts can also be performed in parallel if the table to be inserted into has a degree of parallelism defined for it (either with the **CREATE TABLE** or **ALTER TABLE** commands). Alternatively, you can specify a **PARALLEL** hint, like this:

```
SQL> INSERT /*+PARALLEL(my_large_table, 5) */ INTO my_large_table
  2  NOLOGGING
  3  SELECT * FROM scott.my_large_table;
```

This statement will start five parallel query slaves to perform the direct-load insert in parallel. Each of the slaves will create a temporary segment to load the data into, and these segments will be merged with the original table when the transaction is committed. To perform parallel DML, you need to begin the transaction with the **ALTER SESSION ENABLE PARALLEL DML** statement. Once the **INSERT** statement completes, issue a **COMMIT** to complete the transaction. The table that was inserted into with the parallel direct-load insert operation cannot be queried or modified again in the same transaction, so you need to end the transaction and start a new one before you can use the table again.

Loading Data Using SQL*Loader

In contrast to direct-load inserts (which copy data from one table to another table), the SQL*Loader utility takes data from external files and loads it into Oracle tables. Some of the main features of SQL*Loader are:

➤ Data can be loaded from multiple input files.

➤ Data being loaded can be appended to existing data, or it can replace the existing data.

➤ Multiple physical records (that is, lines in the external file) can be combined into a single logical record as the data is being inserted.

➤ Input data can be of any format (character, binary, date, and so on).

➤ Fields in the input data can be fixed or variable in length.

➤ Data can be loaded from disk, tape, or named pipes.

➤ Some SQL functions can be applied to the data as it is being inserted.

➤ Column values can be generated through such mechanisms as sequences.

➤ Data can be loaded into more than one table in a single run.

➤ Data can be loaded directly into the table without populating the data buffer cache.

The following files are used when loading data with SQL*Loader: control file, data files, log file, bad file, discard file, and parameter file. Don't confuse the file names of SQL*Loader with the database file names. Both have control files and data files (although *datafile* is usually one word when referring to the database datafiles), and each also has a parameter file, but they are used for completely different things. The SQL*Loader files have the following uses:

➤ *Control file*—Tells SQL*Loader all about the load. It provides the names of the tables into which the data is going to be loaded, the format of the input data, and optional conditions that might be used to reject records that are in the wrong format or that don't meet selected criteria (specified in a **WHEN** clause).

➤ *Data files*—Provide the input data for SQL*Loader to load into the database. These are optional files because the data can be kept in the control file as well, but you'll normally see data kept in data files instead.

➤ *Log file*—Is created by SQL*Loader and provides a record of the log, including statistics for CPU usage, errors that have occurred, and so on.

➤ *Bad file*—Contains records that have been rejected either by SQL*Loader during data validation of the input data or by the server (for example, because a mandatory field was missing). The records in the bad file are in the same format as they are in the data file, so once the errors that caused the rejections have been fixed, the load can be run again using the bad file as the new data file.

➤ *Discard file*—Contains records that have been rejected because they did not meet the criteria specified in the control file. Again, the discard file records are in the same format as the data file records.

➤ *Parameter file*—Is an optional file where you can specify inputs that are otherwise provided as command-line parameters during the load.

Conventional and Direct Path Loads

SQL*Loader can be executed in conventional path or direct path. Conventional path loads build an array of **INSERT** statements from the data that is being loaded and the table information provided in the control file. The **INSERT** statements are then processed like any other inserts: the statements are parsed and executed, and the data is loaded into the table unless it is rejected because of field validation errors or discarded because it doesn't meet the selection criteria. Data can be loaded into either clustered or unclustered tables using conventional path. Redo entry generation is determined by the **LOGGING** characteristic of the table being loaded.

Direct path loads completely bypass the data buffer cache. Data blocks are built in memory and then written directly into extents for the tables being loaded. The system global area (SGA) is accessed only for extent management and to adjust the high-water mark at the end of the load. Redo entries are not generated if the database is in **NOARCHIVELOG** mode, or if the database is in **ARCHIVELOG** mode and **NOLOGGING** is specified. (This can be done either at the table level or by using the **UNRECOVERABLE** clause in the control file.) Because of the bypassing of the data buffer cache and the lack of redo generation, direct path can be faster than conventional path. However, it can't be used in some situations:

➤ Direct path load is not supported for clustered tables.

➤ Direct path load locks the table being loaded, and other transactions cannot make changes to the table being loaded. (The exception to this—parallel direct path load—is covered in the next section.) If you need to allow other transactions to make changes concurrently with the data load, you need to use conventional path.

➤ **INSERT** triggers are automatically disabled before direct path loads and re-enabled afterwards. If you require the **INSERT** triggers to be fired as part of the load, you must use conventional path loads.

➤ Foreign key and **CHECK** constraints (covered in Chapter 11) are automatically disabled before a direct path load and re-enabled afterwards. Foreign key constraints are disabled because they reference other rows or tables, and **CHECK** constraints are disabled because they may use SQL functions. If you want to enforce these constraint types during a data load, you must use conventional path.

The other main difference between conventional and direct path loads is the way in which they save the data to the database. Conventional path uses normal commit processing, as any other **INSERT** statements do. When the array of inserts is built and executed, a commit is issued, so a single data load may be composed of multiple transactions.

Direct path loads, on the other hand, use data saves to write blocks to datafiles. Some of the differences between data saves and commits are:

➤ Data saves write only complete blocks to the datafiles. With commits, changed records are written to the database.

➤ Data saves write blocks above the high-water mark and then move the high-water mark. Commits usually write below the high-water mark.

➤ A data save does not complete a transaction, whereas a commit does. Because the transaction is not completed, internal resources such as locks are not released.

➤ Indexes are not updated during a data save, but they are updated during a conventional path load.

Parallel Direct Loads

To improve the performance of direct-load operations, you can run several concurrent sessions to load data into a table in parallel. To do this, each session runs a direct load, specifying the keyword **PARALLEL** (keywords are covered later in this chapter), and uses its own data file. Each session creates its own temporary segments to load the data into. You can specify as part of the data load the storage for the temporary segment and the database datafile in which the segment will be created. (By default, the storage attributes are the same as those for the table being loaded.) When each session completes, the last extent in each temporary segment is trimmed of unused space. The individual temporary segments are then merged and the resultant single temporary segment is added to the table.

Parallel direct loads have a number of restrictions, mainly related to the difficulty of coordinating the multiple sessions executing the load. The restrictions include:

➤ You have to manually disable insert triggers, referential integrity constraints, and check constraints before the load, and re-enable them after the load.

➤ Indexes are not updated as part of the load. You will need to drop the indexes before the load and re-create them afterwards.

➤ Parallel direct loads can only append data to a table. If you need to replace the data in the table, truncate the table before the load operations.

Ways to Execute SQL*Loader

You can execute SQL*Loader from the command line or from Oracle Enterprise Manager (OEM). Let's look at each of these methods in more detail.

Executing SQL*Loader from the Command Line

The command to execute SQL*Loader is the same on both Unix and NT. (Earlier releases on NT systems included the database version number in the file name, but this is no longer the case in Oracle8.1.) SQL*Loader is executed from the command line—that is, it is not executed from a SQL*Plus session. Here's an example of the syntax:

```
C:\> sqlldr scott/tiger my_control.ctl log=my_load.log direct=true
```

Notice that I've used two different mechanisms for specifying the parameters. The first is positional (**scott/tiger**)—that is, just using the value rather than *keyword=value*. The second uses a *keyword=value* syntax (**direct=true**). You can use positional notation only if you know the correct order of the parameters, whereas you can use the *keyword=value* syntax if you don't know their correct order.

 Most of the time I use positional notation for the username and password (that's always the first parameter), and then use keyword notation for the rest. It saves me from having to remember the order of the parameters.

If you don't have the documentation handy when executing SQL*Loader, you can simply type "sqlldr" at the command prompt to view a list of all the parameters. You'll need to be familiar with these parameters for the exam, so examine their meanings carefully. Here's the output of that command from my 8.1.7 database running on NT (edited to fit the page format for this book). Notice that the usage line is incorrect (an old bug that hasn't been fixed yet). The correct usage is (note that the output has been reformatted to meet the page width requirements of this book):

```
SQLLDR keyword=value [,keyword=value,...]

C:\>sqlldr
SQL*Loader: Release 8.1.7.0.0 - Production on Sat Jun 9 21:41:48
2001 (c) Copyright 2000 Oracle Corporation. All rights reserved.

Usage: SQLLOAD keyword=value [,keyword=value,...]

Valid Keywords:

    userid -- ORACLE username/password
   control -- Control file name
       log -- Log file name
       bad -- Bad file name
      data -- Data file name
   discard -- Discard file name
```

```
       discardmax -- Number of discards to allow          (Default all)
             skip -- Number of logical records to skip    (Default 0)
             load -- Number of logical records to load    (Default all)
           errors -- Number of errors to allow            (Default 50)
             rows -- Number of rows in conventional path bind array or
                     between direct path data saves
                     (Default: Conventional path 64, Direct path all)
         bindsize -- Size of conventional path bind array in bytes
                     (Default 65536)
           silent -- Suppress messages during run (header, feedback,
                     errors, discards, partitions)
           direct -- use direct path                      (Default FALSE)
          parfile -- parameter file: name of file that contains
                     parameter specifications
         parallel -- do parallel load                     (Default FALSE)
             file -- File to allocate extents from
skip_unusable_indexes -- disallow/allow unusable indexes or index
                         partitions  (Default FALSE)
skip_index_maintenance -- do not maintain indexes, mark affected
                          indexes as unusable   (Default FALSE)
commit_discontinued -- commit loaded rows when load is
                       discontinued             (Default FALSE)
         readsize -- Size of Read buffer         (Default 1048576)
```

PLEASE NOTE: Command-line parameters may be specified either by
position or by keywords. An example of the former case is
'sqlload scott/tiger foo'; an example of the latter is 'sqlload
control=foo userid=scott/tiger'. One may specify parameters by
position before but not after parameters specified by keywords.
For example, 'sqlload scott/tiger control=foo logfile=log' is
allowed, but 'sqlload scott/tiger control=foo log' is not, even
though the position of the parameter 'log' is correct.

Executing SQL*Loader from OEM

You can also use OEM to execute SQL*Loader. To do this, start the OEM Console, right-click on the database you want to load data into, and choose Data Management and then Load from the context-sensitive menu.

OEM has a small quirk here. Even though you've chosen Load by right-clicking on the database you want to load data into, this works only if you have set preferred credentials for the node you are working on. To do this, choose Preferences from the System menu, then click on the Preferred Credentials tab, choose the node you are working on, and enter the values for username and password.

Once you've chosen Load from the context-sensitive menu, the Load Wizard will begin guiding you through the process of loading data into the database. After the Introduction window displays, you will be prompted for the control file name, the data file location, and the load method (conventional, direct, or parallel direct). Click on the Advanced button on this screen to display the screen shown in Figure 12.1.

In this screen, you can use the General tab to control the number of rows in the data file to be skipped before starting the load, the maximum number of errors to accept, whether to skip index maintenance and allow unusable indexes, and whether to fail on errors or warnings. The Tuning tab allows you to set the bind array size, the commit frequency, and the size of the read buffer. The Optional Files tab allows you to specify locations for the bad file, discard file, log file, and the data file to be used for temporary segments in parallel direct loads. (The data file option will be ghosted if you are not performing this type of load.)

Once you have completed entering information on the Advanced Options screen, you'll be asked for scheduling information (the load will be scheduled as a job in OEM) and for the job name. You'll also be asked if you want to run the job now, have it submitted to the job library, or both. A summary screen will appear, and if you select OK, the job will either be executed immediately or scheduled for later execution, depending on the options you chose in the last two screens.

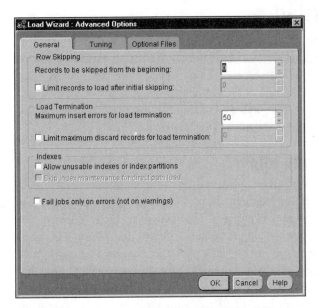

Figure 12.1   The Advanced Options screen in the Load Wizard.

SQL*Loader Usage Guidelines

You can reduce the number of errors and improve performance for SQL*Loader by following a number of simple usage guidelines:

➤ Use a parameter file if you are going to regularly execute a load. The parameter file will contain those parameters that remain the same from load to load. You can specify those parameters that change on the command line. The smaller the number of parameters specified on the command line, the less error-prone the operation will be.

➤ Likewise, keeping the data in the data files rather than the control file allows the control file to be reused for future loads.

➤ Preallocate space for the data to be loaded. This reduces dynamic space allocation and improves performance.

➤ Sort the data before the load is executed to improve sort space usage for index generation.

➤ Use a different database file for each session to store the temporary segments created by parallel direct loads to improve performance.

Reorganizing Data Using the Export and Import Utilities

The Export and Import utilities provided by Oracle allow you to move data from one Oracle database to another, or to reorganize data within a database for better performance and more efficient storage. The Export utility creates a binary dump file that contains object definitions for the objects being exported and the data they contain. The Import utility takes the dump file produced by an export and loads the object definitions and data into the database.

Uses of Export and Import

Although the Export and Import utilities have a number of uses, they're most frequently used to reorganize fragmented data and to perform a logical backup of the database. (The logical backup provides more flexibility in your recovery capabilities, but it cannot be used in conjunction with archive logs to restore the database to a point in time in the past.) Data reorganizations could be required for several reasons: because a table was configured with the wrong storage and now has many migrated rows, because an object needs to be moved to another tablespace, or because a table has had a large number of deletes that leave many underutilized blocks or empty blocks below the high-water mark. However, apart from these main uses, the Export and Import utilities can also be used for the following reasons:

➤ *To migrate from one version of the Oracle kernel to another version*—Other methods can be used to perform this migration, but because migrating to a new version of the kernel normally involves downtime, many DBAs take advantage of this downtime to reorganize the data using Export and Import as well.

➤ *To migrate from one operating system to another*—The dump file produced by the Export utility is independent of the operating system—that is, it can be read by the Import utility on any other operating system. Because the files that physically make up the database (datafiles, redo log files, and control files) are not operating system independent, Export and Import are often the easiest tools to use to migrate to a new operating system.

➤ *To move data between databases*—It can be easier to set up lookup tables in one environment (for example, a development environment) and then simply use the Export and Import utilities to move those tables to another environment, such as production, than to manually re-enter the data. Alternatively, you may want to use Export and Import to move data from your main Online Transaction Processing (OLTP) system to a data warehouse environment (although it can be easier to do this with transportable tablespaces, which I cover later in this chapter, than exporting at the table level).

➤ *To move data from one user to another user in the same database*—You may want to change the ownership of some data, particularly if the current owner is being removed from the database. (If the current owner isn't being removed, it would be better to use synonyms for this, though, rather than duplicating data.) This could also be performed by a parallel **CREATE TABLE AS SELECT** statement.

The "Oracle8i: Architecture and Administration" exam covers only the data reorganization and data move between users functions of the Export and Import utilities. Using these utilities for backup is covered in the "Oracle8i: Backup and Recovery" exam.

Export Modes

The Export utility can be run in one of three modes:

➤ *Database mode export*—Allows you to export the entire database except objects owned by SYS but including objects that aren't owned by specific users, such as user, tablespace, profile, and role definitions. To perform a full database export, you need to have the **EXP_FULL_DATABASE** role. (See Chapter 13 for more information on roles.)

➤ *User mode export*—Allows you to export all or a subset of the objects owned by a particular user. If you are a privileged user (that is, a user with the **EXP_FULL_DATABASE** role), you can perform exports of any user in the database. The objects that can be exported are all objects that are owned by the user being exported except for triggers or indexes that the user has created on another user's tables, as well as any triggers or indexes that another user has created on the exported user's tables. If you are not a privileged user, then you can export only those objects that you own. In this case, any triggers or indexes created by other users on your tables will not be exported.

➤ *Table mode export*—Allows you to export all or a subset of the tables owned by a particular user. If you are a privileged user, you can export another user's tables. If you aren't a privileged user, then you can export only your own tables. Table mode exports include the table definition, the data within the table, constraints and grants on the table, all indexes for the table if you are a privileged user (if not, only the indexes you created are exported), all triggers for the table if you are a privileged user (if not, only the triggers you created are exported), and the **ANALYZE** method to be used on import.

Conventional and Direct Path Exports

Like SQL*Loader, Export can be used in both conventional path and direct path. Conventional path exports use the **SELECT** statement to extract data from tables. The data is read into the data buffer cache like any normal **SELECT** statement, and rows are passed to the session performing the export to be loaded into the dump file.

Direct path exports can be much faster than conventional path exports, because the SQL command-processing layer is completely bypassed. Rows are loaded directly into the data buffer cache and then passed to the export file. The Import utility can read dump files produced in either manner. (The use of conventional or direct path export doesn't have a significant impact on performance of the Import utility.)

Using the Export Utility

The Export utility can be invoked in one of three modes: interactive, command line, and graphical interface. The interactive mode is still available only for the purpose of backward compatibility; it doesn't allow all options to be used with Export. Oracle now recommends that you don't use it, so it won't be covered in the exam and I won't cover it further here.

The command-line interface is executed from the operating system prompt and looks much the same as the SQL*Loader command-line interface. Instead of the

sqlldr command, you use the **exp** command, and then pass in parameters either positionally or using the *keyword=value* syntax.

I remember only one keyword/value pair: **help=y**. It provides you with a list of all the parameters that can be used, their meanings, and default values. Here's an example (again, the output has been reformatted because of this book's page width requirements):

```
C:\>exp help=y
Export: Release 8.1.7.0.0 - Production on Sun Jun 10 11:17:59
2001 (c) Copyright 2000 Oracle Corporation. All rights reserved.

You can let Export prompt you for parameters by entering the EXP
command followed by your username/password:

      Example: EXP SCOTT/TIGER

Or, you can control how Export runs by entering the EXP command
followed by various arguments. To specify parameters, you use
keywords:

      Format:  EXP KEYWORD=value or KEYWORD=(value1,value2,....,
               valueN)
      Example: EXP SCOTT/TIGER GRANTS=Y TABLES=(EMP,DEPT,MGR)
               or TABLES=(T1:P1,T1:P2), if T1 is partitioned
               table

USERID must be the first parameter on the command line.
```

Keyword	Description (Default)	Keyword	Description (Default)
USERID	username/password	FULL	export entire file (N)
BUFFER	size of data buffer	OWNER	list of owner usernames
FILE	output files (EXPDAT.DMP)	TABLES	list of table names
COMPRESS	import into one extent (Y)	RECORDLENGTH	length of IO record
GRANTS	export grants (Y)	INCTYPE	incremental export type
INDEXES	export indexes (Y)	RECORD	track incr. export (Y)
ROWS	export data rows (Y)	PARFILE	parameter filename

```
CONSTRAINTS export constraints (Y)    CONSISTENT    cross-table
                                                     consistency
LOG       log file of screen output   STATISTICS    analyze objects
                                                     (ESTIMATE)
DIRECT    direct path (N)             TRIGGERS      export triggers
                                                     (Y)
FEEDBACK display progress every x rows (0)
FILESIZE maximum size of each dump file
QUERY    select clause used to export a subset of a table

The following keywords only apply to transportable tablespaces
TRANSPORT_TABLESPACE export transportable tablespace metadata (N)
TABLESPACES list of tablespaces to transport

Export terminated successfully without warnings.
```

You can also use OEM to export data. To do this, start the OEM Console, right-click on the database from which you want to export data, and choose Data Management and then Export from the context-sensitive menu. The Export Wizard Introduction screen appears, and you are then guided through a series of screens to perform the export. The first screen (Figure 12.2) allows you to specify one or more export files.

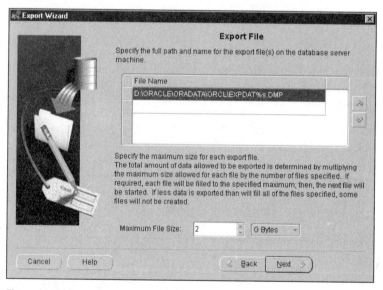

Figure 12.2 The Export File screen of the Export Wizard.

If you specify more than one file, or use the %s string as I've done in Figure 12.2, you can specify a maximum file size for the files as well. The %s string tells Oracle that you want multiple files with a sequence number in the name (for example, in the case of the string in the figure, expdat1.dmp, expdat2.dmp, and so on). You are then prompted for the export type. (This is the export mode we discussed earlier—database, user, or table—but for some reason the Export Wizard uses the term *export type* here.) Depending on which mode you choose here, the next screen will differ. For example, if you choose database mode, you are prompted for a list of associated objects that you want to export. If you choose user or table mode, you are prompted with a screen of users or tables that you can export, before you reach the associated objects screen. The screens appear much the same (as you can see in Figures 12.3 and 12.4), but notice the icons next to the usernames. In Figure 12.3 (user mode), you can choose from a list of users.

In Figure 12.4 (table mode), the usernames can be expanded by clicking on the plus sign to display a list of tables to choose from. Alternatively, you can simply click on the username and then the right-arrow button to see all the tables for that user that will be moved to the list of tables to be exported.

After selecting the information you need from the associated objects screen, you will be prompted for scheduling information (do you want to run the job now or execute it later?), a name for the job, and whether you want to run it only once or have it added to the job library as well.

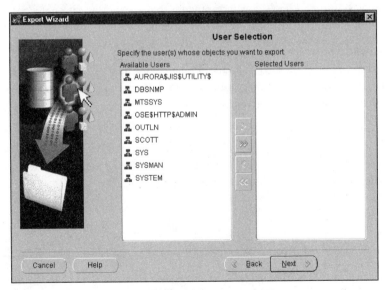

Figure 12.3   The User Selection screen of the Export Wizard.

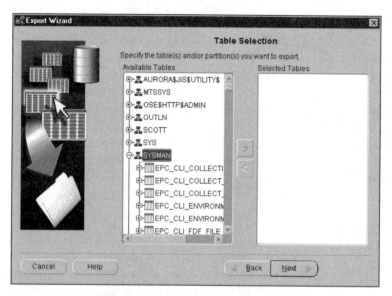

Figure 12.4 The Table Selection screen of the Export Wizard.

Using the Import Utility

Like the Export utility, the Import utility can be invoked in one of three modes: interactive, command line, and graphical interface. Again, the interactive mode is really available only for backward compatibility, and it doesn't allow all options to be used with Import. Oracle now recommends that you don't use it, so it won't be covered in the exam and I won't cover it further here.

The command-line interface is executed from the operating system prompt and looks much the same as the SQL*Loader command-line interface. Instead of the **sqlldr** command, you use the **imp** command, and then pass in parameters either positionally or using the *keyword=value* syntax.

The tip I included earlier in this chapter for the Export utility applies here as well: I remember only one keyword/value pair: **help=y**. It provides you with a list of all the parameters that can be used, their meanings, and default values. Here's an example (again, the output has been reformatted):

```
C:\>imp help=y
Import: Release 8.1.7.0.0 - Production on Sun Jun 10 11:52:37
2001 (c) Copyright 2000 Oracle Corporation. All rights reserved.

You can let Import prompt you for parameters by entering the IMP
command followed by your username/password:

    Example: IMP SCOTT/TIGER
```

Or, you can control how Import runs by entering the IMP command followed by various arguments. To specify parameters, you use keywords:

```
Format:   IMP KEYWORD=value or KEYWORD=(value1,value2,...,
          valueN)
Example:  IMP SCOTT/TIGER IGNORE=Y TABLES=(EMP,DEPT) FULL=N
          or TABLES=(T1:P1,T1:P2), if T1 is partitioned
          table
```

USERID must be the first parameter on the command line.

Keyword	Description (Default)	Keyword	Description (Default)
USERID	username/password	FULL	import entire file (N)
BUFFER	size of data buffer	FROMUSER	list of owner usernames
FILE	input files (EXPDAT.DMP)	TOUSER	list of usernames
SHOW	just list file contents (N)	TABLES	list of table names
IGNORE	ignore create errors (N)	RECORDLENGTH	length of IO record
GRANTS	import grants (Y)	INCTYPE	incremental import type
INDEXES	import indexes (Y)	COMMIT	commit array insert (N)
ROWS	import data rows (Y)	PARFILE	parameter filename
LOG	log file of screen output	CONSTRAINTS	import constraints (Y)

```
DESTROY   overwrite tablespace data file (N)
INDEXFILE write table/index info to specified file
SKIP_UNUSABLE_INDEXES  skip maintenance of unusable indexes (N)
ANALYZE   execute ANALYZE statements in dump file (Y)
FEEDBACK display progress every x rows(0)
TOID_NOVALIDATE  skip validation of specified type ids
FILESIZE maximum size of each dump file
RECALCULATE_STATISTICS recalculate statistics (N)
```

The following keywords only apply to transportable tablespaces
```
TRANSPORT_TABLESPACE import transportable tablespace metadata (N)
TABLESPACES tablespaces to be transported into database
DATAFILES datafiles to be transported into database
```

```
TTS_OWNERS users that own data in the transportable tablespace
set
```

```
Import terminated successfully without warnings.
```

I want to specifically mention one keyword here because it can be so dangerous to use: **DESTROY**. This defaults to no, but if you set it to yes, the entire tablespace for the objects being imported is overwritten. All objects currently in the tablespace will no longer be available.

You can also use OEM to import data. To do this, start the OEM Console, right-click on the database you want to export data from, and choose Data Management and then Import from the context-sensitive menu. The Import Wizard Introduction screen appears, and you are then guided through a series of screens to perform the import. The screens are all fairly similar to the ones I previously described for the Export Wizard, so I won't cover them in any detail here.

When you import data with the Import utility, it reads through the dump file in the same order as it's produced by the Export utility. The order in which objects are imported is as follows:

1. Type definitions

2. Table definitions

3. Row data

4. B-tree indexes

5. Constraints, views, procedures, and triggers

6. Bitmap, function-based, and domain indexes

This order is important because it ensures that objects that are dependent upon the existence of other objects (such as views) are not imported until after the other objects are created. It also ensures that triggers are not fired twice (once when the data was originally inserted and again when the import occurs). It's possible for some objects to be invalidated, however. To check this, simply query **DBA_OBJECTS** for objects with a **STATUS** of **INVALID** and recompile any objects that you find to be invalid.

When you import data into tables that already contain rows, you can still get errors from failing referential integrity constraints. To avoid this problem, disable the referential integrity constraints before the import and re-enable them afterwards.

Normally, objects are imported into the same tablespaces as they were exported from. This rule, however, has two restrictions:

➤ If the tablespace no longer exists or the user's quota has been exceeded, the Import utility will attempt to create the object in the user's default tablespace. If that fails, then the object is not imported, and an error is returned.

➤ A LOB segment must be imported into the same tablespace it was exported from. If this operation fails, the table containing the LOB cannot be imported.

Export and Import Guidelines

You can reduce the number of errors and improve performance for SQL*Loader by following a number of simple usage guidelines:

➤ Only use **CONSISTENT=Y** where there is no heavy concurrent update activity. Using this keyword can produce "Snapshot too old" error messages in these situations. You can sometimes avoid this by creating a single large rollback segment and taking all others offline, but this is generally not an optimal configuration in which to run an OLTP system.

➤ Use a parameter file to store commonly used keywords and their values. This will reduce the amount of human error due to typing mistakes.

➤ If you have deleted many rows from a table, do not use **COMPRESS=Y**. The effect of this keyword setting is for the Export utility to specify a single extent that is the sum of all the existing extents in size. When Import creates the table, a lot of wasted space will result.

➤ To improve performance, allocate as large a buffer as you can afford, and run the export in direct path mode.

Moving Data Using Transportable Tablespaces

One of the useful new features in Oracle8.1 is the ability to move data using transportable tablespaces. These provide a way for you to plug a tablespace from one database into another database, which is a very quick way of moving data in an Oracle environment. This is particularly useful when moving data to a staging area for a data warehouse, but it can also be used to release data on read-only media to branch offices.

Transportable Tablespace Process

The following steps are necessary to move data using transportable tablespaces:

1. Make the source tablespace read-only by using the **ALTER TABLESPACE** *tablespace_name* **READ ONLY** command. This ensures that no changes are made while the tablespace is being moved.

2. Use the Export utility to capture metadata about the source tablespace from the data dictionary. The **TRANSPORT_TABLESPACE** keyword and the **TABLESPACES** keyword are used to capture this metadata. You can also specify the new keyword **TRIGGERS**, along with **GRANTS** and **CON-STRAINTS**, to specify that these associated objects are exported as well.

3. Move the tablespace to the target machine, ensuring that the copy is done in binary format. It's probably easiest to do this using FTP.

4. Move the dump file produced in Step 2 to the target machine, again ensuring that the copy is done in binary format.

5. Use the Import utility to load the metadata captured in Step 2 into the target database. The **TRANSPORT_TABLESPACE** keyword is also used with the Import utility to load the metadata exported in Step 2, but you also need to specify the **DATAFILES** keyword to tell Oracle what datafiles the data is being loaded into. These file names can be different from those used in the source database.

6. If necessary, make the tablespaces in the source and/or target databases read-write, using the **ALTER TABLESPACE** *tablespace_name* **READ WRITE** command.

Because this is a new functionality in Oracle8.1, you may not be overly familiar with it, so here's an example of how the code works. I'm moving the DEMO tablespace, currently located on D:\ORADATA\ORA81\PROD, to another machine, with the target location of E:\ORADATA\ORA81\DW. This code is executed on the source machine:

```
SQL> ALTER TABLESPACE demo READ ONLY;
C:\> exp system/manager FILE=demo.dmp TRANSPORT TABLESPACE=y \
TABLESPACE=demo TRIGGERS=n CONSTRAINTS=n
```

Now I copy the DEMO tablespace data files to the target machine and change the file names on the way. I also now copy the export file to the target machine. Then, on the target machine, I import the tablespace metadata into the target database, using the file names from the target machine:

```
E:\> imp system/manager FILE=demo.dmp TRANSPORT_TABLESPACE=y \
DATAFILES=(\oradata\ora81\dw\demo01.dbf, \
\oradata\ora81\dw\demo02.dbf)
```

Now the data in the DEMO tablespace is available in read-only mode on both systems. I can now swap the tablespace read-write mode on either or both machines:

```
SQL> ALTER TABLESPACE demo READ WRITE;
```

Transportable Tablespace Restrictions

You need to be aware of a few restrictions when using the transportable tablespace functionality:

➤ The source and target machines need to be binary compatible. In effect, what this means is that the machines need to be on the same operating system release.

➤ The set of tablespaces being transported must be self-contained. This means that the objects in the tablespaces being transported cannot reference objects in other tablespaces that are not being transported. Oracle provides you with the **DBMS_TTS.TRANSPORT_SET_CHECK** procedure and **DBMS_TTS.ISSELFCONTAINED** function to check if a set of tablespaces is self-contained.

➤ Tablespaces with bitmap indexes and tables with **VARRAY**s or nested tables cannot be transported.

➤ Tablespaces that contain objects that reference **BFILE**s can be transported, but it is up to you to move the associated operating system files for the **BFILE** columns.

➤ It's also up to you to resolve any dependencies between objects in the tablespaces being transported and objects in the target database.

Practice Questions

Question 1

> Which SQL*Loader file specifies the database tables to be loaded?
>
> ○ a. Log
> ○ b. Loader
> ○ c. Control
> ○ d. Bad

Answer c is correct. The control file specifies the table to be loaded. Answer a is incorrect because the log file generated by SQL*Loader stores information about the load. Answer b is incorrect because loader is not a valid SQL*Loader file. Answer d is incorrect because the bad file contains records that have been rejected, not table names for the load.

Question 2

> In which sequence is the import file loaded?
>
> ○ a. Type definitions, table data, integrity constraints, triggers, bitmap indexes, indexes on the table, and table definitions
>
> ○ b. Table definitions, type definitions, table data, indexes on the table, integrity constraints, triggers, and bitmap indexes
>
> ○ c. Type definitions, indexes on the table, integrity constraints, triggers, bitmap indexes, table definitions, and table data
>
> ○ d. Type definitions, table definitions, table data, B-tree indexes, constraints, views, procedures and triggers, and bitmap, function-based, and domain indexes
>
> ○ e. Table definitions, table data, integrity constraints, type definitions triggers, bitmap indexes, and indexes on the table
>
> ○ f. Table definitions, integrity constraints, triggers, bitmap indexes, indexes on the table, and table data

Answer d is correct. The correct order of import is type definitions, table definitions, table data, B-tree indexes, constraints, views, procedures and triggers, and bitmap, function-based, and domain indexes.

Question 3

Which SQL*Loader parameter specifies the number of logical records to load?

- ○ a. **LOG**
- ○ b. **ROWS**
- ○ c. **LOAD**
- ○ d. **BINDSIZE**

Answer c is correct. The **LOAD** parameter in the SQL*Loader command specifies the number of records to load. Answer a is incorrect because **LOG** specifies the log file name. Answer b is incorrect because **ROWS** specifies the number of rows in the conventional path bind array or between saves in direct path. Answer d is incorrect because **BINDSIZE** is the size, in bytes, of the conventional path bind array.

Question 4

Which export parameter ensures that, when the data is imported, the initial extent will be equal to the current size of the table?

- ○ a. **FULL**
- ○ b. **DIRECT**
- ○ c. **GRANTS**
- ○ d. **COMPRESS**
- ○ e. **CONSTRAINTS**

Answer d is correct. Setting the **COMPRESS** export parameter to **YES** creates an initial extent the size of the current segment when the data is imported. Answer a is incorrect because the **FULL** option does a full database export. Answer b is incorrect because the **DIRECT** option exports the data directly from the datafiles without going through the SQL layer. Answer c is incorrect because the **GRANTS** option determines if **GRANTS** are exported. Answer e is incorrect because the **CONSTRAINTS** option determines if **CONSTRAINTS** are exported.

Question 5

> Which SQL*Loader file holds detailed information about the results of the load?
>
> O a. Bad
> O b. Log
> O c. Discard
> O d. Control

Answer b is correct. The log file generated by SQL*Loader stores information about the load. Answer a is incorrect because the bad file is used to hold records that are rejected by Oracle. Answer c is incorrect because the discard file is used to hold records that SQL*Loader discards because they do not match the record selection criteria of the control file. Answer d is incorrect because the control file contains the SQL*Loader Data Definition Language (DDL) definitions that show the format of the data and the Oracle table that they will be loaded to.

Question 6

> What utility would you use to duplicate a test database from your production database?
>
> O a. Direct-load insert
> O b. SQL*Loader direct path
> O c. Export/import utilities
> O d. SQL*Loader conventional path

Answer c is correct. Use a full database export/import to move the whole database to a new system for testing. Answer a is incorrect because direct-load insert only moves data from one table to another; it does not build all schema objects. Answers b and d are incorrect because SQL*Loader can't unload data and move it to another database.

Question 7

Which SQL*Loader file holds rejected records?

- O a. Bad
- O b. Log
- O c. Discard
- O d. Control
- O e. Data file

Answer a is correct. The bad file holds the rejected records. Answer b is incorrect because the log file generated by SQL*Loader stores information about the load. Answer c is incorrect because the discard file is used to hold records that SQL*Loader discards because they do not match the record selection criteria of the control file. Answer d is incorrect because the control file contains the SQL*Loader DDL definitions that show the format of the data and the Oracle table that they will be loaded to. Answer e is incorrect because the data file is an optional file that contains the data records to be loaded into the database.

Question 8

For which two reasons would you use direct-load inserts when loading data into a table? [Choose two]

- ❑ a. Redo is generated in case of failure.
- ❑ b. Indexes are dropped to speed the data load.
- ❑ c. Direct-load inserts load data below the high-water mark to reclaim disk space.
- ❑ d. Other users can concurrently modify other rows in the same table.
- ❑ e. Data can be quickly copied from one table into another within the same database because it bypasses the buffer cache.

Answers d and e are correct. During a direct-load insert, users can concurrently modify existing data in the table. In addition, the buffer cache is bypassed to speed the insert. Answer a is incorrect because redo information would slow down the load. Answer b is incorrect because direct-load insert does not drop indexes. Answer c is incorrect because data is loaded above the high-water mark.

Question 9

> Which export utility keyword exports triggers?
>
> ○ a. **ROWS**
>
> ○ b. **DIRECT**
>
> ○ c. **TABLES**
>
> ○ d. **CONSISTENT**

Answer c, **TABLES,** is correct. When a table is exported in table mode, it includes the table definition, data, indexes, triggers, constraints, and grants on the table. This can be a tricky question because no trigger keyword exists for export. Triggers just follow the table they are associated with. Answer a is incorrect because the **ROWS** parameter determines whether rows of data or only the object definitions are exported. Answer b is incorrect because setting **DIRECT=YES** causes export to read data directly without using the public buffer cache or the SQL command-processing layer. Answer d is incorrect because if **CONSISTENT** is set to **YES,** export makes the export consistent to a single point in time.

Question 10

> What keywords do you need to specify for the Export utility when you want to transport a tablespace? [Choose two]
>
> ❑ a. **TRANSPORT_TABLESPACE**
>
> ❑ b. **DATAFILES**
>
> ❑ c. **TABLESPACES**
>
> ❑ d. **FILE**
>
> ❑ e. **ISSELFCONTAINED**

Answers a and c are correct. **TRANSPORT_TABLESPACE=y** tells the Export utility to transport tablespace metadata, and **TABLESPACES** provides the tablespace names to be transported. Answer b is incorrect because **DATAFILES** is an Import keyword that provides the target datafile names for the transported tablespaces. Answer d is incorrect because **FILE** provides the names of the output files for Export and the input files for Import. They are not specific to transportable tablespaces. Answer e is incorrect because **ISSELFCONTAINED** is a function in the **DBMS_TTS** package that is used to determine if the tablespace set to be transported is self-contained.

Need to Know More?

 Loney, Kevin, and Marlene Theriault. *Oracle8i DBA Handbook*. Oracle Press, Berkeley, CA, 1999. ISBN 0-07212-188-2. This book is a comprehensive guide and a must-have for all DBAs. See Chapter 8 for more information on tuning bulk data inserts, Chapter 10 for details on the Export and Import utilities, and Chapter 12 for more information on loading data.

 Scherer, Douglas, William Gaynor, Arlene Valentinsen, Sue Mavris, and Xerxes Cursetjee. *Oracle8i Tips and Techniques*. Oracle Press, Berkeley, CA, 1999. ISBN 0-07212-103-3. This book provides an overview of Oracle8i architecture and administration, along with many tips, both documented and undocumented, to make the most out of Oracle8i. See Chapter 6 for more details on transportable tablespaces.

 See the Oracle documentation that is provided on CD with the Oracle RDBMS software. The following documents specifically pertain to this chapter:

Baylis, Ruth, and Joyce Fee. *Oracle8i Administrator's Guide*. Oracle Corporation, Redwood City, CA, 1999. This is the complete documentation of database administration tasks. Chapter 9 includes information on transportable tablespaces.

Leverenz, Lefty, Diana Rehfield, and Cathy Baird. *Oracle8i Concepts*. Oracle Corporation, Redwood City, CA, 1999. This is the complete documentation of Oracle concepts. Chapter 22 covers direct-load inserts.

Rich, Kathy. *Oracle8i Utilities*. Oracle Corporation, Redwood City, CA, 1999. This document covers SQL*Loader and the Export and Import utilities in detail.

 technet.oracle.com is Oracle's technical repository of information for clients.

 www.revealnet.com is the site where RevealNet Corporation provides Oracle administration reference software.

Managing Security

Terms you'll need to understand:

✓ Users

✓ Profiles

✓ Resource limits

✓ Account locking

✓ Password history

✓ **PASSWORD_VERIFY** function

✓ Grants

✓ System privileges

✓ Object privileges

✓ Roles

Techniques you'll need to master:

✓ Creating, altering, and dropping users

✓ Monitoring information about users

✓ Identifying system and object privileges

✓ Granting and revoking privileges

✓ Identifying auditing capabilities

✓ Creating, altering, and dropping roles

✓ Controlling availability of roles

✓ Using predefined roles

✓ Displaying role information from the data dictionary

✓ Administering profiles

✓ Managing passwords using profiles

✓ Controlling resource usage with profiles

✓ Obtaining information about profiles, password management, and resources

Database access begins with the creation of users, who are then assigned specific rights to perform actions either directly or through roles. These rights to perform actions are called *system privileges* and *object privileges*. System privileges are rights to perform actions in a database, and object privileges are rights to access an object (such as a table, index, synonym, procedure, and so on) within a database, including the columns within tables.

This chapter explains how Oracle uses object and system privileges, along with profiles and roles, to manage users and objects.

Creating, Altering, and Dropping Users

As a DBA, it's your role to define the security domain under which users access the database. The security domain can be divided into the following areas:

➤ *Default tablespace*—The tablespace where objects are created if the **CREATE** statement does not explicitly specify a tablespace.

➤ *Temporary tablespace*—The tablespace used for most sort operations that the user needs to perform.

➤ *Tablespace quotas*—The amount of space in each tablespace that the user can insert data into. (There is no need for a quota for the user's temporary tablespace.)

➤ *Resource limits*—The amount of resources, such as CPU and I/O, that a user is allowed to consume. (Resource limits are covered further in Exam 1Z0-024, "Oracle8i: Performance and Tuning," so I won't cover them further here.)

➤ *Privileges*—The rights to perform certain actions in the database, both at the system level (for example, the **CREATE USER** privilege) and the object level (for example, the privilege to select data from another user's table).

➤ *Authentication mechanism*—The way a user is authenticated for access to the database. This can be done by the database, the operating system, or the network. (Network authentication is discussed more in Exam 1Z0-026, "Oracle8i: Network Administration," so I won't cover it further here.)

In this chapter, I'll cover in greater detail the areas that are applicable to Exam 1Z0-023, "Oracle8i: Architecture and Administration." Let's start off by looking at how a user is created.

Creating a User

As I mentioned previously, it's part of your role as a DBA to create users. Before you do that, you need to make a number of decisions:

➤ What authentication mechanism and username will you use?

➤ What default and temporary tablespaces will you allocate to the user?

➤ What tablespaces will the user need access to, and what quota will you allocate for each tablespace?

➤ What privileges will the user need to perform daily work, and how will these privileges be grouped?

Once you've made these decisions, you can create the user with the **CREATE USER** command. Here's an example:

```
SQL> CREATE USER jim IDENTIFIED BY smith
  2   DEFAULT TABLESPACE users
  3   TEMPORARY TABLESPACE temp
  4   QUOTA UNLIMITED ON users
  5   QUOTA 5M ON indx
  6   PASSWORD EXPIRE;

User created.
```

This statement creates a user named jim with a password of smith. Jim has been given unlimited write access to the USERS tablespace, but only 5MB of storage in the INDX tablespace. His password has been forced to expire, which means that he'll be prompted to enter a new one the first time he logs on.

You can also use Oracle Enterprise Manager (OEM) to create a new user. To do this, start the OEM Console, click on the Databases folder, click on the database you want to add the user to, and then click on the Security folder. Then, you can either right-click on the Users folder and choose Create from the pop-up menu, or click on the Users folder, choose Create User from the context-sensitive Navigator menu, and then click on the Create button. Either method displays the Create User screen, shown in Figure 13.1.

Choosing the General tab, you can fill in most of the information I just provided in the **CREATE USER** example. (You can also lock accounts and set up profiles from this tab; see the "Altering a User" and "Administering Profiles" sections later in this chapter.) You need to click on the Quota tab to create the user quota on the different tablespaces, as shown in Figure 13.2.

Figure 13.1   Creating a user with OEM.

Figure 13.2   Giving a user tablespace quota with OEM.

The examples I've provided thus far create a user that is identified by the database. If you want to create a user that is identified by the operating system, the syntax is slightly different. To do this, you must use the **IDENTIFIED EXTERNALLY** clause in your **CREATE USER** statement. Here's an example:

```
SQL> CREATE USER joan IDENTIFIED EXTERNALLY
  2  DEFAULT TABLESPACE users
  3  TEMPORARY TABLESPACE temp;

User created.
```

In this case, you can't automatically expire the password, so I've left that clause out. Also, joan has no need to store objects in the database, so she haven't been given a quota on any tablespaces. This is often the case when you have application objects owned by one user. Other users are granted access to the application owner's tables, but they do not need their own quotas on the tablespace. Instead, the applications owner's quota is used.

The **IDENTIFIED EXTERNALLY** clause is normally used for users who are directly logging on to the machine on which the database is located. The format of the user's name in the database depends on the value of the **OS_AUTHENT_PREFIX** initialization parameter. The default value for this is set to **OPS$** (for backward compatibility to earlier releases), so I could use the following **CREATE USER** statement to map the operating system user joan to the database user **OPS$JOAN**:

```
SQL> CREATE USER ops$joan IDENTIFIED EXTERNALLY
  2  DEFAULT TABLESPACE users
  3  TEMPORARY TABLESPACE temp;

User created.
```

If you don't want to use any prefix, you can change the value of the initialization parameter to a null string (that is, **OS_AUTHENT_PREFIX** = ").

Some versions of the Oracle Education courseware don't mention the fact that the default installation can override the default value for this parameter on some operating systems. For example, the default 8.1.7 for NT parameter file has **OS_AUTHENT_PREFIX** set to ''.

The username behavior is also different from that stated in the courseware (and therefore, from that tested in the exam as a corollary). The **CREATE USER ops$joan** example I just showed does not create a

> database user "ops$joan" in my 8.1.7 for NT database. Instead, it creates a user named joan. However, for the exam, you would be expected to say that the example I just showed creates a database user "ops$joan".

Altering a User

You use the **ALTER USER** command for the following operations:

➤ *To change a user's password*—Any user can change his or her own password in the database.

➤ *To change a user's default or temporary tablespace*—These both default to SYSTEM. The SYSTEM tablespace should be used for only data dictionary objects, so if you forget to change these keywords from their default values, you need to use the **ALTER USER** command to change them back again.

➤ *To change the user's quota for a tablespace*—If there is unanticipated growth in an application, or if application modifications require additional objects, you may need to increase the amount of quota you have given the user. Alternatively, if you don't want to allow any new extents to be allocated to existing objects for a user in a particular tablespace, you could modify their quota for that tablespace to zero. (Note that this action takes effect only when the user next tries to allocate an extent. Existing extents can still be inserted into.)

➤ *To lock a user's account*—This disables the account being used.

To be able to change another user's password requires the **ALTER USER** privilege. (We'll cover privileges later in this chapter—see the "Identifying System and Object Privileges" section.)

The syntax for the **ALTER USER** command is reasonably straightforward. Here's an example:

```
SQL> ALTER USER joan IDENTIFIED BY jones
  2   QUOTA 2M ON indx
  3   QUOTA 0 ON users
  4   DEFAULT TABLESPACE users
  5   TEMPORARY TABLESPACE temp;

User altered.
```

Any keywords that aren't specified in the **ALTER USER** command remain unchanged.

If you are in an environment in which you want to create your own DBA accounts, you may find it useful to disable the default privileged accounts for SYS and SYSTEM. (They can always be enabled again later, if necessary.) Here's how to do this. If you issue the command **ALTER USER sys IDENTIFIED by values 'x'**, you are setting the encrypted value of the password for the user SYS to be **'x'**. To connect as the user SYS after this command is issued, you will need to be able to determine what value encrypts to the value **'x'**. Because Oracle doesn't publish its encryption algorithm, this will be very difficult (if not downright impossible!) to perform.

You can also alter a user with OEM. Use the same path as I mentioned previously to get to the Users folder, then either right-click on the user you want to alter and choose Edit from the pop-up menu, or simply click on the user and select Edit User from the context-sensitive Navigator menu. In either case, the screen shown in Figure 13.3 appears.

As you can see, this screen is fairly similar to the Create User screen in Figure 13.1, but now the fields for the relevant keywords are automatically populated with their existing values from the data dictionary instead of having to be entered manually. Change the options you want to on the General and Quota tabs, and then click on OK.

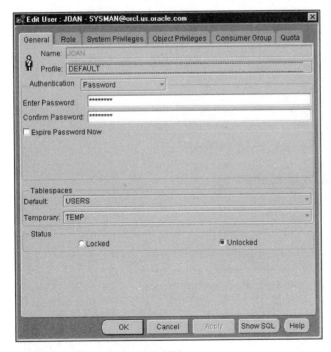

Figure 13.3 Altering users with OEM.

Dropping a User

To drop a user, use the **DROP USER** command. However, this command cannot be used if the user is currently connected to the database. If you want to drop a user who owns objects, you have to either first drop all his or her objects or use the **CASCADE** option for the command.

 It's always a good idea to do an export of a user's objects before dropping them, just in case you need to retrieve the data later. A simple export will save you from having to restore the database to a point in time before the user was dropped.

Here's an example of the command:

```
SQL> DROP USER jim CASCADE;

User dropped.
```

You can also drop a user with OEM. (Again, the user cannot be connected to the database at the time.) Using the same path as I used to alter a user, choose Remove instead of Edit, or Remove User instead of Edit User. You'll be presented with either of the two message boxes shown in Figures 13.4 and 13.5, depending on whether the user you're removing owns objects.

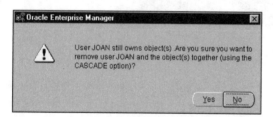

Figure 13.4   Using OEM to drop a user who owns objects.

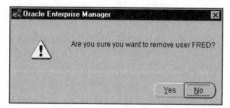

Figure 13.5   Using OEM to drop a user who doesn't own objects.

Note that, once you choose Yes in either screen, there is no going back. The user is dropped immediately. If you attempt to drop a connected user with OEM, an error message is returned.

Monitoring Information about Users

Two main data dictionary views contain information about users:

➤ **DBA_TS_QUOTAS**—Displays quotas for each tablespace that a user has been granted a quota on. (Tablespaces that a user has no access to are not listed.) The columns **MAX_BYTES** and **MAX_BLOCKS** show the maximum amount of space that can be taken up by the user (in bytes and Oracle blocks, respectively). If a quota of **UNLIMITED** has been set, these columns will contain a value of -1.

➤ **DBA_USERS**—Displays information about all users defined in the database, including the username, the default and temporary tablespaces, the account status (a value of **OPEN** means the account is not locked), and the lock information (if the account is locked).

The following queries show you the information in these views:

```
SQL> SELECT tablespace_name, bytes, max_bytes
  2  FROM dba_ts_quotas
  3  WHERE username = 'JOAN';

TABLESPACE_NAME                      BYTES  MAX_BYTES
------------------------------ ---------- ----------
USERS                               131072         -1

SQL> SELECT username, default_tablespace, temporary_tablespace,
  2          account_status
  3  FROM dba_users
  4  WHERE username = 'JOAN';

USERNAME   DEFAULT_TABLESPACE TEMPORARY_TABLESPACE ACCOUNT_STATUS
---------- ------------------ -------------------- --------------
JOAN       USERS              TEMP                 OPEN
```

Identifying System and Object Privileges

As previously mentioned, an Oracle database has two types of privileges: system privileges and object privileges. System privileges allow a user to perform a certain operation, or class of operations, in the database. For example, you need system privileges to create, alter, or drop tables, users, tablespaces, rollback segments, and so on. Object privileges allow a user to perform actions for a specific object, such as inserting, updating, or deleting data in tables. You also need object privileges to execute packages, procedures, or functions. Let's look at each of these types of privileges in more detail.

System Privileges

More than 120 different system privileges are available, and the number seems to grow with each release. System privileges can be divided into three main groups:

➤ *The ability to perform an action that is systemwide*—Examples of this include the **CREATE TABLESPACE** and **CREATE USER** privileges.

➤ *The ability to perform an action in your own schema*—Examples of this include the **CREATE TABLE** and **CREATE PROCEDURE** privileges.

➤ *The ability to perform an action in any schema*—Examples of this include the **CREATE ANY TABLE** and **CREATE ANY PROCEDURE** privileges.

Note: The ability to perform an action in any schema is further impacted by the O7_DICTIONARY_ACCESSIBILITY initialization parameter. This defaults to TRUE in Oracle8i. If you set it to FALSE, users who have been granted the ability to perform an action in any schema will be able to perform those actions in any schema except SYS. For example, a user with the SELECT ANY TABLE privilege could not select data from data dictionary tables. Setting this parameter to FALSE restricts access to dictionary objects to users with the SYSDBA or SYSOPER privileges.

Granting System Privileges

The **GRANT** command is used to grant a system privilege. Here's an example:

```
SQL> GRANT create session TO joan WITH ADMIN OPTION;

Grant succeeded.
```

This statement grants the **CREATE SESSION** privilege to the user joan. The **WITH ADMIN OPTION** clause allows the user joan to pass this grant on to other users in the database. This ability should not be granted lightly for security reasons. Also, if you pass on system privileges with the **WITH ADMIN OPTION** clause, the user you grant the privilege to can later remove the privilege from any user, including the user who granted it in the first place. (See the next section, "Revoking System Privileges," for details on how to remove system privileges from a user.)

If I wanted to provide a privilege to any user who exists (or will exist) in the database, I would use the keyword **PUBLIC** instead of the username joan. Likewise, I can use a role name (roles are discussed later in this chapter) rather than the username if I want to grant privileges through roles rather than directly to each user. For reasons I discuss in the "Creating, Altering, and Dropping Roles" section later in this chapter, this is generally the preferred way of granting both system and object privileges.

You can also grant system privileges through OEM. To do this, you need to go through the same steps as I mentioned before to get to the Edit User screen, but now click on the System Privileges tab to see the screen shown in Figure 13.6.

Select the privileges you want to grant from the list of available privileges at the top of the screen (you can use the Shift and Control keys to select multiple privileges in one statement if you like) and click on the down arrow button to move the privileges to the list of granted privileges. (Note that you have not actually granted the privileges yet.) If you want any of the privileges to be granted **WITH ADMIN OPTION**, click on the cross in the Admin Option column and it will turn into a checkmark. Now simply click on the Apply or OK button to grant the privileges (the Apply button leaves you in this screen, ready to grant more privileges).

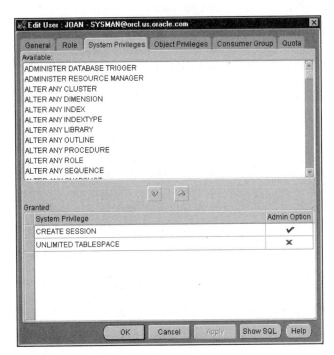

Figure 13.6   Granting system privileges with OEM.

Revoking System Privileges

Revoking system privileges is done using the **REVOKE** command. Here's an example:

```
SQL> REVOKE unlimited tablespace FROM joan;

Revoke succeeded.
```

Note that you don't need any additional syntax to remove the **WITH ADMIN OPTION** clause; revoking the privilege also revokes the **WITH ADMIN OP-TION** clause. If you need to remove the ability to pass on grants from a user, you need to revoke the privilege completely and then re-grant it without the **WITH ADMIN OPTION** clause. Also, the **REVOKE** command does not cascade. If user1 (who has been granted the ability to pass on system privileges) grants user2 a system privilege, and then user1's privilege is removed, user2 retains the system privilege.

Revoking system privileges may have an impact on dependent objects. For example, if a user has been granted the **SELECT ANY TABLE** privilege and uses that to create views or procedures that access tables in another schema, revoking the **SELECT ANY TABLE** privilege will invalidate the views or procedures.

Revoking system privileges can also be done in OEM. Use the same methodology as granting system privileges, but now select the privileges you want to remove from the list of granted privileges, choose the up arrow button, and click on Apply or OK.

Displaying System Privileges

The **DBA_SYS_PRIVS** view lists system privileges that have been granted in the database, including the grantee (the user or role receiving the grant), the system privilege granted, and a flag indicating the grant has been done **WITH ADMIN OPTION**. Here's an example of the data you might see in this view (the data has been reformatted to remove extraneous spaces):

```
SQL> SELECT * FROM dba_sys_privs
  2  WHERE grantee = 'JOAN';

GRANTEE     PRIVILEGE            ADM
----------  -------------------- ---
JOAN        CREATE SESSION       YES
JOAN        UNLIMITED TABLESPACE NO
```

Object Privileges

Object privileges allow a user to perform actions for a specific object, such as inserting, updating, or deleting data in tables or executing packages, procedures, or functions. The privileges that can be defined for the different objects are listed in Table 13.1.

Granting Object Privileges

The **GRANT** command is used to grant an object privilege. Here's an example:

```
SQL> GRANT select, insert, update(sal, job), delete
  2  ON emp TO joan WITH GRANT OPTION;

Grant succeeded.
```

This statement grants the **SELECT, INSERT, UPDATE,** and **DELETE** privileges on the **EMP** table to the user joan. Joan's update access is limited to the **SAL** and **JOB** columns. Make sure you grant update access to all mandatory columns if you restrict the update access like this (you can grant access to all columns instead if you need to). The **WITH GRANT OPTION** clause allows joan to pass on this grant to other users in the database. For security reasons, this ability should not be granted lightly.

In contrast to system privileges, if you pass on object privileges with the **WITH GRANT OPTION** clause, the user you grant the privilege to is not allowed to later remove the privilege from any user. (See the next section, "Revoking Object Privileges," for details on how to remove object privileges from a user.) Also unlike system privileges, users with the **SYSDBA** or **SYSOPER** privileges cannot by default grant access to another user's objects. If I want to use the statement just shown, I need to either be connected as the user who owns the **EMP** table, or

Table 13.1 Privileges that can be granted for different objects.				
Privilege	**Table**	**View**	**Sequence**	**Procedure**
ALTER	✓	✓		
DELETE	✓	✓		
EXECUTE				✓
INDEX	✓			
INSERT	✓	✓		
REFERENCES	✓			
SELECT	✓	✓	✓	
UPDATE	✓	✓		

I need to have been explicitly given access to the table with the **WITH GRANT OPTION** clause.

If I wanted to provide a privilege to any user who exists (or will exist) in the database, I would use the **PUBLIC** keyword instead of the username joan. Likewise, if I wanted to grant privileges through roles rather than directly to each user, I could use a role name rather than the username. (Roles are discussed in the "Creating, Altering, and Dropping Roles" section later in this chapter.) For reasons I discuss in that section, these are generally the preferred ways of granting privileges. I could also use the **ALL** keyword to grant all the different object privileges that make sense for the object in one simple statement.

You can also grant object privileges through OEM.

*Note: You can use OEM to grant object privileges for only those objects that you have been granted explicit access to with the **WITH GRANT OPTION** clause. If you attempt to grant access to any other objects, you will receive an ORA-01031 "insufficient privileges" error. The only other way I know to get around this is to define the user that owns the objects as an administrator in OEM. You can then connect as that user and perform the grants.*

To grant privileges using the OEM console, you need to follow the same steps that I mentioned before to get to the Edit User screen, but now click on the Object Privileges tab to see the screen shown in Figure 13.7.

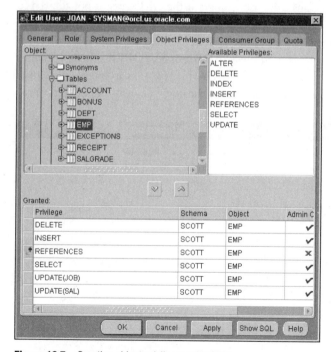

Figure 13.7 Granting object privileges with OEM.

In this screenshot, I have already chosen the schema **SCOTT** and the table **EMP**. I can now select the privileges I want to grant from the list of available privileges at the top right of the screen (you can press the Shift and Control keys to select multiple privileges in one statement if you like) and click on the down arrow button to move the privileges to the list of granted privileges. (Note that you have not actually granted the privileges yet.) If you want to grant update access to only particular columns, then click on the plus sign to the left of the **EMP** table to view a list of columns that you can choose from. If you want any of the privileges to be granted **WITH GRANT OPTION**, click on the cross in the Admin Option column, and it will turn into a checkmark. Now simply click on the Apply or OK button to grant the privileges. (The Apply button leaves you in this screen, ready to grant more privileges.)

Revoking Object Privileges

Revoking object privileges is done using the **REVOKE** command. Here's an example:

```
SQL> REVOKE select ON emp FROM joan;

Revoke succeeded.
```

To be able to revoke an object privilege, you must be connected as the user who performed the grant in the first place. If you aren't, you will get an error message, even if you're connected as a user who has been granted access **WITH GRANT OPTION**. The following example shows you what happens:

```
SQL> CONNECT scott/tiger
Connected.
SQL> GRANT select on emp TO joan;

Grant succeeded.

SQL> GRANT select ON emp TO system WITH GRANT OPTION;

Grant succeeded.

SQL> CONNECT system/manager
Connected.
SQL> REVOKE select ON scott.emp FROM joan;
REVOKE select ON scott.emp FROM joan
              *
ERROR at line 1:
ORA-01927: cannot REVOKE privileges you did not grant
```

```
SQL> CONNECT scott/tiger
Connected.
SQL> REVOKE select ON scott.emp FROM joan;

Revoke succeeded.
```

Note that you don't need any additional syntax to remove the **WITH ADMIN OPTION** clause; revoking the privilege also revokes the **WITH GRANT OPTION** clause. If you need to remove the ability to pass on grants from a user, you need to revoke the privilege completely and then grant it again but without the **WITH GRANT OPTION** clause. Also, in contrast to revoking system privileges, the **REVOKE** command *does* cascade. If user1 (who has been granted the ability to pass on object privileges to another user) grants user2 an object privilege and then user1's privilege is removed, user2 loses the object privilege as well.

You can also use the OEM Console to revoke object privileges. You'll use the same methodology as granting object privileges, but now you'll select the privileges you want to remove from the list of granted privileges, choose the up arrow button, and click on Apply or OK.

Displaying Object Privileges

Two data dictionary views are associated with object privileges:

➤ **DBA_TAB_PRIVS**—Lists object privileges that have been granted in the database at the object level (regardless of whether the object is a table or not), including the grantee (the user or role receiving the grant), the object privilege granted, and a flag indicating that the grant has been made **WITH GRANT OPTION**.

➤ **DBA_COL_PRIVS**—Lists all column object grants in the database, including the owner of the object, the grantor of the privilege, the grantee of the privilege, the column name, and a flag indicating that the grant has been made **WITH GRANT OPTION**.

Here's an example of the data you might see in these views. (The data has been reformatted slightly to meet the page-width requirements of this book.)

```
SQL> REM Table_name can also contain procedure names and so on.
SQL> REM The EXECUTE privilege shows us that this is a privilege
SQL> REM on a package, procedure or function.
SQL> SELECT owner, grantor, table_name, privilege, grantable
  2  FROM dba_tab_privs
  3  WHERE grantee = 'JOAN';
```

```
OWNER    GRANTOR      TABLE_NAME        PRIVILEGE    GRA
------   ----------   ---------------   ----------   ---
SYS      SYS          DBMS_SQL          EXECUTE      NO
SCOTT    SCOTT        EMP               DELETE       YES
SCOTT    SCOTT        EMP               INSERT       YES
SCOTT    SCOTT        EMP               SELECT       YES


SQL> SELECT owner, grantor, table_name,
  2          column_name, privilege, grantable
  3  FROM dba_col_privs
  4  WHERE grantee='JOAN';


OWNER    GRANTOR      TABLE_NAME        COLUMN_NAME   PRIVILEGE   GRA
------   ----------   ---------------   ------------- ---------   ---
SCOTT    SCOTT        EMP               JOB           UPDATE      YES
SCOTT    SCOTT        EMP               SAL           UPDATE      YES
```

Identifying Auditing Capabilities

Database auditing tracks the use of selected user activities in an audit trail, which can be located either in the operating system audit trail (if this is supported by your operating system) or in the database. Some auditing is always performed by the database: the use of certain privileged operations such as **STARTUP, SHUT-DOWN**, and connections as **SYSDBA**. These operations are audited at the operating system level. (Audit files are created in the $ORACLE_HOME/rdbms/audit directory on a Unix box.) Other auditing needs to be turned on specifically by the DBA. (For example, if you suspect someone is updating information that they should not be able to, you can turn on auditing for update statements.) This auditing does not keep the values for column changes, but just the fact that the change has taken place. If you need to track the old and new values for the changes, only auditing by an application can do this.

Using Database Auditing

To turn on database auditing, you need to set the initialization parameter **AUDIT_TRAIL** to either **DB** (tracks audit records in the database audit trail) or **OS** (tracks audit records in the operating system audit trail, if that is allowed). **NONE** is the default, which does not track any audit records.

You also need to specify what actions you are auditing, and whether audit records are generated every time an audited action occurs or only once per session, regardless of the number of times that the audited action occurs. SQL statements within a procedure or package are audited individually. The audit record is written at the execute phase (so entries are not produced for syntactically incorrect statements). If an action is rolled back, audit entries are not removed from the audit trail for that action. You can also audit successful executions of an operation, unsuccessful executions, or both. These options are useful for tracking when someone is attempting to hack into your database.

The **AUDIT** command is used to audit the use of types of statements, specific system privileges, or object privileges. Here are some examples:

```
SQL> REM First let's look at the use of certain types of
SQL> REM statements. In this example, let's look at the
SQL> REM USER statements. This command audits the use of
SQL> REM the DROP USER, CREATE USER or ALTER user commands:
SQL>
SQL> AUDIT user;

Audit succeeded.

SQL> REM Now let's look at the use of specific system privileges.
SQL> REM This example audits the use of the SELECT ANY TABLE
SQL> REM statement by the user JIM every time it is used - BY
SQL> REM ACCESS (this is the default for DDL privileges. I could
SQL> REM also use the BY SESSION clause to create a single audit
SQL> REM trail record per session, regardless of how many times
SQL> REM a privilege is used.
SQL>
SQL> AUDIT select any table BY jim BY ACCESS;

Audit succeeded.

SQL> REM Now let's look at auditing a specific object. In this
SQL> REM case I only want to track unsuccessful attempts to
SQL> REM insert into the EMP table. I could say WHENEVER
SQL> REM SUCCESSFUL to only track successful inserts (the
SQL> REM default is to track both)
SQL>
SQL> AUDIT insert ON scott.emp BY ACCESS WHENEVER NOT SUCCESSFUL;

Audit succeeded.
```

Statement and privilege auditing apply only to sessions that log on after the command is issued, not to current ones. By contrast, object-level auditing is performed for both existing and new sessions.

To disable auditing, you need to use the **NOAUDIT** command to match the **AUDIT** command you issued, except that **BY SESSION** or **BY ACCESS** are not allowed. Here are the commands to turn off the auditing I turned on in the previous examples:

```
SQL> NOAUDIT user;

Noaudit succeeded.

SQL> NOAUDIT select any table BY jim;

Noaudit succeeded.

SQL> NOAUDIT insert ON scott.emp WHENEVER NOT SUCCESSFUL;

Noaudit succeeded.
```

Auditing Guidelines

You should follow a number of guidelines when using auditing:

➤ Audit generally to identify suspicious activity, and then restrict the auditing. This is recommended because you may take up too much space storing audit records if you audit generally.

➤ As an extension of the previous guideline, monitor the space consumed by the audit trail to ensure that sufficient space exists. If you fill up the audit trail, operations that are being audited will fail.

➤ Protect the audit trail. There's little point in auditing information if users can delete that information from the audit trail. At the very least, if you turn on auditing, ensure that you audit deletes from the audit trail. Audit entries produced in this way cannot be deleted unless you have the **DELETE_CATALOG_ROLE** role.

➤ If you are using the database to store the audit trail, move the audit trail table (**AUD$**) to another tablespace. By default, **AUD$** is located in the SYSTEM tablespace, and auditing can cause fragmentation issues.

Displaying Auditing Information

Quite a number of data dictionary views are associated with auditing. These include:

➤ **DBA_AUDIT_OBJECT**—Contains audit trail records for all objects being audited in the database, including the username for the user who created the audit record, the timestamp for the creation of the record, the privilege used to perform the action, Oracle return codes, and so on.

➤ **DBA_AUDIT_SESSION**—Contains audit trail records for connects and disconnects.

➤ **DBA_AUDIT_STATEMENT**—Contains audit trail records for **GRANT, REVOKE, AUDIT, NOAUDIT,** and **ALTER SYSTEM** statements used in the database.

➤ **DBA_AUDIT_TRAIL**—Lists all audit trail records, including the username, the timestamp for the audit record entry, the privileges being used, and so on.

➤ **DBA_OBJ_AUDIT_OPTS, DBA_PRIV_AUDIT_OPTS,** and **DBA_STMT_AUDIT_OPTS**—Contain information for the objects, privileges, and statements being audited, respectively.

Here's an example of the material that goes into the audit trail. (To generate this entry, I connected as user jim and attempted to insert data into **SCOTT**'s **EMP** table, which I did not have access to.)

```
SQL> SELECT username, owner,
  2  to_char(timestamp, 'DD/MM/YY HH:MI') AS time, returncode
  3  FROM dba_audit_trail;

USERNAME   OWNER TIME           RETURNCODE
---------  ---- -------------- ----------
JIM        SCOTT 26/06/01 01:49      2004
```

Creating, Altering, and Dropping Roles

Although it's useful to be able to grant system and object privileges at a very granular level as I've been discussing, it's even more useful to be able to group those privileges together and grant them as a group to individual users, rather than having to specifically grant each privilege individually. That's what roles are used for. A role can be simply defined as a way of grouping a set of system and object privileges. Roles can also be granted to a user or to another role, thus simplifying the management of privileges.

Some of the characteristics of roles include:

➤ Roles are granted and revoked from users or other roles using syntax that is very similar to that for granting and revoking system privileges.

➤ Roles can be enabled or disabled on a user-by-user basis.

➤ Roles are not owned by any user.

➤ The definition of a role is stored in the data dictionary.

➤ Roles may be granted to any user or to another role, except to itself (including indirectly—that is, a role cannot be granted to a second role and then have the second role granted to the first one).

➤ Roles can require that a password be provided before they can be enabled.

Roles have a number of benefits, the largest of which is that roles reduce the number of privileges you need to grant in the database. For example, without roles, if you had a set of 10 privileges to grant to 10 users, you would need to issue 100 grant statements. If you use a role to define that group of privileges, you need only 10 grant statements to grant the privileges to the role, and another 10 to grant the role to the users, resulting in a total of 80 fewer grant statements to make. Other benefits of roles include:

➤ *Dynamic privilege management*—If you modify the privileges that a role has been granted, the modifications immediately apply to the users who are granted the role.

➤ *Selective availability of privileges*—By disabling a role, you can ensure that the privileges for the role are not available for use. Using this mechanism, privileges can be temporarily turned on and off without having to revoke the privileges and grant them again.

Creating a Role

To create a role, you use the **CREATE ROLE** command. You can specify that the role is protected by either the operating system (using the **IDENTIFIED EXTERNALLY** clause) or by a password (using the **IDENTIFIED BY** *password* clause). The default is to use neither. Here's an example:

```
SQL> CREATE ROLE my_connect;

Role created.
```

Note that the role name used in the **CREATE ROLE** command (**my_connect** in the example) must be different from any other role name or username.

You can also create a role in OEM. To do this, start the OEM Console, select the Databases folder, click on the database you want to add the role to, and click on the Security folder. Next, either right-click on the Roles folder and choose Create from the pop-up menu, or simply click on the Roles folder and choose Create Role from the context-sensitive Navigator menu, then click on the Create button. In either case, you'll see the screen shown in Figure 13.8.

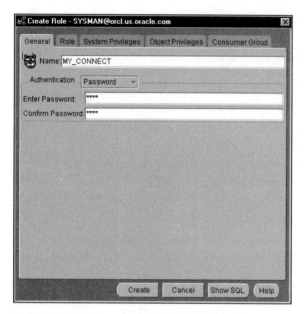

Figure 13.8 Creating a role with OEM.

Choose the authentication method you want to use, and then add the system and object privileges to the role by selecting the System Privileges and Object Privileges tabs as we did in previous examples. You can also use the Roles tab to grant roles to the role you are about to create.

Altering a Role

The **ALTER ROLE** command is used only to change a role's authentication method. For example, if you wanted to change a role's password, you could use a command such as:

```
SQL> ALTER ROLE my_connect IDENTIFIED BY ann;

Role altered.
```

If you want to change the privileges that a role has, you need to use the relevant **GRANT** and **REVOKE** commands, as discussed previously in this chapter.

You can also alter a role using OEM. Use the same path as before, but in this case, right-click on the role and select Edit from the pop-up menu (or simply click on the role to be altered and choose Edit Role from the context-sensitive Navigator menu). Doing so displays a screen very similar to that shown in Figure 13.8. You can now change whatever entries you wish and click on OK to apply the changes.

Granting and Revoking Roles to Users or Other Roles

The **GRANT** command is used to grant a role to a user or another role. Here's an example:

```
SQL> GRANT my_connect TO jim;

Grant succeeded.
```

As with system privileges, I could specify **WITH ADMIN OPTION** if I wanted to allow this user to pass on the grant to other users or roles. Users who are granted a role with the **WITH ADMIN OPTION** clause can also alter or drop the role. If you create a role, you are automatically granted the role **WITH ADMIN OPTION**.

You can also grant a role to a user or another role in OEM. If you want to grant a role to another user, navigate to the Users folder as discussed previously, bring up the Edit User screen, click on the Roles tab, and then click on the roles you want to add to the user in the list of available roles at the top of the screen. Then, click on the down arrow button, and then click on OK or Apply to add the new roles. (See Figure 13.9.)

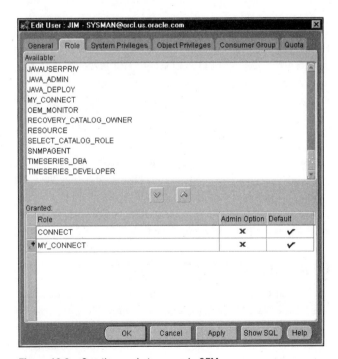

Figure 13.9   Granting a role to a user in OEM.

If you want to grant a role to another role, you need to open the Roles folder, then click on the role to bring up the Edit Role screen. Now you can click on the Roles tab and follow exactly the same steps as just described for adding a role to a user.

Revoking a role is done using the **REVOKE** command. Here's an example:

```
SQL> REVOKE my_connect FROM jim;

Revoke succeeded.
```

You can also revoke a role in OEM. This is done in the same way as granting a role, but now you need to click on the role you want to revoke from the list of granted roles, click on the up arrow button to move it to the list of available roles, and then click on OK or Apply.

Dropping A Role

You use the **DROP ROLE** command to remove a role from the database. Here's an example:

```
SQL> DROP ROLE my_connect;

Role dropped.
```

When you drop a role, Oracle automatically revokes it from all users as well. You have to have been granted the role **WITH ADMIN OPTION** or have the **DROP ANY ROLE** privilege to drop a role.

You can also drop a role in OEM. To do this, start the OEM Console, select the Databases folder, click on the database you want to add the role to, and then click on the Security folder. Next, click on the Roles folder and either right-click the role to be dropped and select Remove from the pop-up menu, or select the role you want to remove and choose Remove Role from the context-sensitive Navigator menu. In either case, you will be prompted with a screen that tells you the number of users that have been granted the role and asks if you're sure you want to remove it. If you select Yes, the role will be removed.

Controlling Availability of Roles

An individual user can be granted access to any number of roles, up to the value of the **MAX_ENABLED_ROLES** initialization parameter. When a role is granted to a user, it is automatically created as a default role. Default roles are those roles that are automatically enabled when a user connects to the database. You can change the default roles for a user using the **ALTER USER** command.

Here's an example:

```
SQL> ALTER USER jim DEFAULT ROLE ALL EXCEPT my_connect;

User altered.
```

In this example, I've changed jim's default roles to all the roles that he has been granted access to except the **MY_CONNECT** role. If I wanted to turn off all roles as defaults, I could change the clause **ALL EXCEPT my_connect** to the keyword **NONE**. If a default role has been secured by a password, the password is not needed when the user logs on.

You can also use OEM to set a role to be a default role for a user. To do this, simply click on the Default column in the Edit User screen. (Refer back to Figure 13.9.) When you grant a new role to a user in this screen, OEM automatically sets it as a default role.

Enabling and Disabling Roles

Disabling a role is a good way of temporarily removing privileges from a user. Roles are enabled at the session level, so if you disable a default role for a user, the user will have the role enabled again when he or she next connects to the database.

The **SET ROLE** command is used to enable or disable a role. If a role is protected by a password, you need to specify the password when it is enabled. If you want to disable a role for a user, you can't selectively disable one role and leave another role active. You need to first disable all roles and then reenable the ones that you want to keep active. Here are some examples:

```
SQL> SET ROLE NONE;

Role set.

SQL> SET ROLE my_connect IDENTIFIED BY ann;

Role set.
```

If you want to enable all roles, the **SET ROLE** command can be used with the **ALL EXCEPT** syntax described previously.

Using Predefined Roles

A number of predefined roles are defined automatically in the Oracle database. The main ones are described in Table 13.2.

Table 13.2 Predefined roles.	
Role	**Description**
AQ_ADMINISTRATOR_ROLE	Used to administer Advanced Queuing.
AQ_USER_ROLE	Used to enqueue and dequeue messages in Oracle8. Shouldn't be used anymore (available only for backward compatibility to version 8).
CONNECT	Used for backward compatibility to version 6. Provides the ability to connect to the database, as well as the ability to create simple objects.
DBA	Used for backward compatibility to version 6. Provides DBA level privileges. Use **SYSDBA** or **SYSOPER** instead.
DELETE_CATALOG_ROLE	Provides delete access to data dictionary tables. Be very careful to whom you grant this.
EXECUTE_CATALOG_ROLE	Provides execute privileges for the standard packages Oracle provides.
EXP_FULL_DATABASE	Allows you to perform a full export of the database.
IMP_FULL_DATABASE	Allows you to perform a full import of the database.
RESOURCE	Used for backward compatibility to version 6. Provides developers with the privileges that they need to perform their role.
SELECT_CATALOG_ROLE	Provides select access to the data dictionary tables.

Although these roles are defined in the database, you should not rely on them because there is no guarantee that Oracle will continue to support them in later releases. This is particularly the case for the **CONNECT, RESOURCE,** and **DBA** roles. Also, they are no one-to-one mappings with the equivalent functionality in version 6. Users who are granted the **RESOURCE** role, for example, are also granted the **UNLIMITED TABLESPACE** privilege, which can result in uncontrolled space consumption.

Displaying Role Information from the Data Dictionary

A number of data dictionary views contain role information. These include:

➤ **DBA_ROLES**—Lists all roles that exist in the database and whether the role is enabled by a password.

➤ **DBA_ROLE_PRIVS**—Contains information regarding roles granted to users and roles, including the grantee, the role being granted, and whether it's a default role.

➤ **DBA_SYS_PRIVS**—Lists system privileges granted to users and roles, including the grantee, the privilege granted, and whether the grant can be passed on.

➤ **ROLE_ROLE_PRIVS**—Describes roles that are granted to other roles, including the names of the two roles and whether the grant can be passed on. The information here pertains only to roles that you have access to.

➤ **ROLE_SYS_PRIVS**—Lists system privileges granted to roles, including the role name and the privilege name. The information here pertains only to roles that you have access to.

➤ **ROLE_TAB_PRIVS**—Provides information on object privileges granted to roles (including privileges to objects other than tables). The information here pertains only to roles that you have access to.

➤ **SESSION_ROLES**—Displays the roles that are currently enabled for the user you are connected as.

Here's an example of the information you can see in the **DBA_ROLES** view:

```
SQL> SELECT * FROM dba_roles;

ROLE                            PASSWORD
------------------------------- --------
CONNECT                         NO
RESOURCE                        NO
DBA                             NO
SELECT_CATALOG_ROLE             NO
EXECUTE_CATALOG_ROLE            NO
DELETE_CATALOG_ROLE             NO
EXP_FULL_DATABASE               NO
IMP_FULL_DATABASE               NO
RECOVERY_CATALOG_OWNER          NO
AQ_ADMINISTRATOR_ROLE           NO
AQ_USER_ROLE                    NO
...
```

Administering Profiles

A profile is a named set of resource and password limits that is associated with a user or group of users (profiles cannot be assigned to roles) to control resource utilization and passwords. Profiles can control the following limits:

➤ Amount of CPU time used

➤ Number of I/O operations performed

➤ Number of concurrent sessions

➤ Length of idle time

➤ Length of time a session is connected

➤ Amount of memory space (only for the private SQL areas in MTS configurations)

➤ Password aging and expiration

➤ Password complexity functions

➤ Password history

➤ Account locking

Profiles are assigned to a user with either the **CREATE USER** or **ALTER USER** command. Oracle provides a **DEFAULT** profile with all limits initially set to unlimited. You can change these limits, as you can for any other profile. (I'll cover how to do this later in this section.)

Creating a Profile

The syntax for the **CREATE PROFILE** command to administer resource settings is as follows:

```
CREATE PROFILE profile_name LIMIT
  [SESSIONS_PER_USER max_value]
  [CPU_PER_SESSION max_value]
  [CPU_PER_CALL max_value]
  [CONNECT_TIME max_value]
  [IDLE_TIME max_value]
  [LOGICAL_READS_PER_SESSION max_value]
  [LOGICAL_READS_PER_CALL max_value]
  [COMPOSITE_LIMIT max_value]
  [PRIVATE_SGA max_bytes]
```

The meaning for each of these keywords is covered in the section "Controlling Resource Usage with Profiles" later in this chapter. Any keywords not specified in the **CREATE PROFILE** command receive their values from the **DEFAULT** profile.

You can also create a profile using OEM. To do this, start the OEM console, choose the Databases folder, select the database you want to add the profile to, then either right-click on the Profiles folder and choose Create from the pop-up menu, or simply click on the Profiles folder, select Create Profile from the context-sensitive Navigator menu, and click on the Create button. In either case, you'll see the screen shown in Figure 13.10.

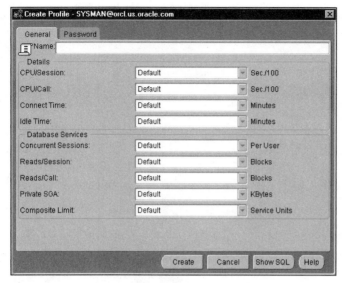

Figure 13.10   Creating a profile using OEM.

The syntax for the **CREATE PROFILE** command to administer password settings is:

```
CREATE PROFILE profile_name LIMIT
  [FAILED_LOGIN_ATTEMPTS max_value]
  [PASSWORD_LIFE_TIME max_value]
  [{PASSWORD_REUSE_TIME | PASSWORD_REUSE_MAX} max_value]
  [ACCOUNT_LOCK_TIME max_value]
  [PASSWORD_GRACE_TIME max_value]
  [PASSWORD_VERIFY_FUNCTION {function|NULL|DEFAULT}]
```

The meaning for each of these keywords is covered in the section "Managing Passwords Using Profiles" later in this chapter. Any keywords not specified in the **CREATE PROFILE** command receive their values from the **DEFAULT** profile.

You can also use OEM to set the password settings for a profile. Use the same path as previously but, this time, click on the Password tab to see the screen shown in Figure 13.11.

Altering a Profile

Profiles are altered using the **ALTER PROFILE** command. Any of the profile settings can be altered with this command, and the syntax for the various settings is the same as it is in the **CREATE PROFILE** command. Sessions that are currently connected that are using the profile will not be affected by the changes.

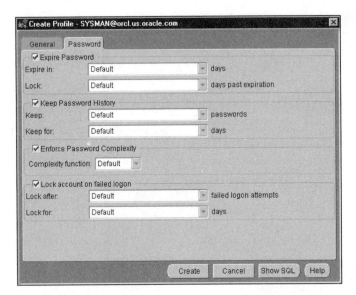

Figure 13.11   Administering password settings for a profile using OEM.

You can also use OEM to alter a profile. Using the same path mentioned previously, either right-click on the profile to be altered and choose Edit from the pop-up menu, or click on the profile and choose Edit Profile from the context-sensitive Navigator menu. A screen very similar to that shown in Figure 13.10 appears. Change the values you want to edit, and click on the OK button.

Dropping a Profile

You can drop profiles with the **DROP PROFILE** command. If you want to drop a profile that is allocated to existing users, you need to add the keyword **CASCADE**. Users who are currently allocated the profile will have their profile switched to the **DEFAULT** profile when they log on next. You cannot drop the **DEFAULT** profile. Here's an example of the command:

```
SQL> DROP PROFILE my_profile CASCADE;

Profile dropped.
```

You can also drop a profile using OEM. Use the same path to get to the profile as mentioned previously, but this time, choose either Remove from the pop-up menu or Remove Profile from the context-sensitive Navigator menu. You will be warned if the profile is allocated to users; otherwise, you will simply be asked if you are sure you want to drop the profile. Select Yes to drop the profile.

Managing Passwords Using Profiles

Profiles allow you to enforce stricter security in your database by controlling passwords. Password management allows you to control the following items:

➤ *Password aging and expiration*—Allow you to set the lifetime for a password in days and enforce expiration after a certain period (**PASSWORD_LIFE_TIME**). You can also set a password grace time (**PASSWORD_GRACE_TIME**) in days, which starts after the password lifetime is reached. Users are warned that they need to change their password until the grace time is reached, at which point the password expires.

➤ *Password complexity functions*—Allow you to configure a function to enforce a level of complexity in a password (**PASSWORD_VERIFY_FUNCTION**). For example, you can set up a password function to ensure that a password contains at least one letter, one number, and one special character. Oracle provides a default password complexity function that is created by running the utlpwdmg.sql script found under $ORACLE_HOME/rdbms/admin on Unix boxes and %ORACLE_HOME%\rdbms\admin on NT boxes. (The default function ensures that a password has a length of at least four characters; that it is different from the username; that it contains at least one letter, one number, and one special character; and that it differs by at least three letters from the previous password.) However, you can also create your own password function. If you do, it still needs to meet a certain specification as far as parameters are concerned, it must be owned by SYS, and it needs to return **TRUE** for success or **FALSE** for failure.

➤ *Password history*—Allows you to configure passwords so that passwords cannot be reused for a specific time (**PASSWORD_REUSE_TIME**) or a specific number of password changes (**PASSWORD_REUSE_MAX**). These settings are mutually exclusive: You use one or the other.

➤ *Account locking*—Allows you to specify the maximum number of invalid attempts to log in as a user before locking the account (**FAILED_LOGIN_ATTEMPTS**). You can also specify either that the account is locked for a certain time (**PASSWORD_LOCK_TIME**), after which it is automatically unlocked, or that it can be unlocked only manually. This helps to secure the database from hackers. You can also specifically lock an account with the **ALTER USER** command.

Controlling Resource Usage with Profiles

To enable resource usage to be controlled with profiles, you need to set the **RESOURCE_LIMIT** initialization parameter to **TRUE**. (This isn't necessary to enable password control.) This can be done either dynamically with the **ALTER SYSTEM** command or manually by editing the parameter file and bouncing the database.

Resources can be controlled at either the session level or the call level. The following resources are controlled at the session level:

➤ **CPU_PER_SESSION**—Sets, in hundredths of a second, the amount of CPU usage that a user can consume in a session.

➤ **LOGICAL_READS_PER_SESSION**—Sets, in blocks, the amount of both logical and physical I/O that a user can consume in a session.

➤ **IDLE_TIME**—Sets, in minutes, how long a session can be left idle before being disconnected. This is measured at the server side only, so you need to take into account whether the application is doing intensive client-side work.

➤ **CONNECT_TIME**—Sets, in minutes, how long a session can be connected before being disconnected.

➤ **PRIVATE_SGA**—Sets, in bytes, the amount of private space in the system global area (SGA) that a user can consume when connected through multithreaded server connections.

When a session-level resource limit is exceeded, an error message is returned and the user is disconnected.

The following resources are controlled at the call level:

➤ **CPU_PER_CALL**—Sets, in hundredths of a second, the amount of CPU usage that a user can consume in a single SQL call.

➤ **LOGICAL_READS_PER_CALL**—Sets, in blocks, the amount of both logical and physical I/O that a user can consume in a single SQL call.

When a call level limit is exceeded, Oracle rolls back the offending transaction and returns an error message to the user. However, the user is left connected to the database and can enter new SQL statements.

You can also use the **COMPOSITE_LIMIT** keyword to control a weighted sum of the **CPU_PER_SESSION, LOGICAL_READS_PER_SESSION, CONNECT_TIME**, and **PRIVATE_SGA** limits.

Obtaining Information about Profiles, Password Management, and Resources

Information about profiles, password management, and resources is kept in two main data dictionary tables:

➤ **DBA_USERS**—Contains information about the users in the database, including the profiles that they have been allocated.

➤ **DBA_PROFILES**—Contains information about profiles defined in the database, including profile name, resource name, resource type (password or kernel), and limit.

Here's an example of the data in these views:

```
SQL> SELECT p.profile, p.resource_name, p.limit
  2  FROM dba_users u, dba_profiles p
  3  WHERE p.profile=u.profile
  4  AND username='JIM'
  5  AND p.resource_type='KERNEL';
PROFILE           RESOURCE_NAME              LIMIT
--------------    -------------------------  --------
MY_PROFILE        COMPOSITE_LIMIT            DEFAULT
MY_PROFILE        SESSIONS_PER_USER                5
MY_PROFILE        CPU_PER_SESSION             100000
MY_PROFILE        CPU_PER_CALL               DEFAULT
MY_PROFILE        LOGICAL_READS_PER_SESSION  DEFAULT
MY_PROFILE        LOGICAL_READS_PER_CALL     DEFAULT
MY_PROFILE        IDLE_TIME                       60
MY_PROFILE        CONNECT_TIME               DEFAULT
MY_PROFILE        PRIVATE_SGA                DEFAULT
```

Practice Questions

Question 1

Which one of the following choices is a system privilege?

○ a. **INSERT**

○ b. **SELECT ANY TABLE**

○ c. **REFERENCES**

○ d. **EXECUTE**

Answer b is correct. **SELECT** is an object privilege, but **SELECT ANY TABLE** is a system privilege. Answers a, c, and d are incorrect because they are all object privileges.

Question 2

Which command would cause this condition?

```
ERROR:
ORA-28000 the account is locked
Warning: You are no longer connected to Oracle
```

○ a. **DROP USER**

○ b. **ALTER USER QUOTA**

○ c. **ALTER USER ACCOUNT LOCK**

○ d. **DROP USER CASCADE**

○ e. **ALTER USER QUOTA UNLIMITED**

Answer c is correct. A user account can be locked by changing a user's password or by locking the account with the **ALTER USER ACCOUNT LOCK** command. Answer a is incorrect because **DROP USER** eliminates the account from Oracle. Answer b is incorrect because **ALTER USER QUOTA** changes a user's quota on a tablespace. Answer d is incorrect because **DROP USER CASCADE** removes a user from the database and all the user's objects. Answer e is incorrect because **ALTER USER QUOTA UNLIMITED** gives the user unlimited usage of space on a tablespace.

Question 3

Which would be user Paul's default tablespace?

```
CREATE USER paul IDENTIFIED BY kilroy
TEMPORARY TABLESPACE temp01
QUOTA 20M ON data01;
```

- ○ a. TEMP01
- ○ b. USERS
- ○ c. DATA01
- ○ d. SYSTEM

Answer d is correct. If the **DEFAULT TABLESPACE** clause is not used when a user is created, the user's default tablespace is the SYSTEM tablespace. Answer a is incorrect because TEMP01 is set as the temporary tablespace for the user. Answer b is incorrect because USERS is not referenced in the **CREATE USER** command. Answer c is incorrect because Paul is given a quota of 20MB of space on the tablespace named DATA01, but it is not defined as the default tablespace.

Question 4

Why would you query **SESSION_ROLES**?
- ○ a. To display all roles in the database
- ○ b. To determine the roles granted to a user
- ○ c. To display the roles currently enabled for a user
- ○ d. To display information about system privileges granted to roles

Answer c is correct. **SESSION_ROLES** displays the roles currently enabled for a user. Answer a is incorrect because the **DBA_ROLES** view displays all roles in the database. Answer b is incorrect because the **DBA_ROLE_PRIVS** view displays roles granted to a user. Answer d is incorrect because the **ROLE_SYS_PRIVS** view displays system privileges granted to roles.

Question 5

Which view would you query to display information about password expiration, locking dates, and account status for a user?

○ a. **DBA_USERS**

○ b. **DBA_TABLES**

○ c. **DBA_OBJECTS**

○ d. **DBA_PASSWORDS**

Answer a is correct. **DBA_USERS** displays information about password expiration, locking dates, and account status for all the database users. Answer b is incorrect because **DBA_TABLES** displays information about tables. Answer c is incorrect because **DBA_OBJECTS** displays information about database objects. Answer d is incorrect because **DBA_PASSWORDS** is not a valid data dictionary view name.

Question 6

How do you enable the default password verification function?

○ a. Use the **ORAPWD** utility.

○ b. Execute the catproc.sql script in the **SYS** schema.

○ c. Execute the utlpwdmg.sql script in the **SYS** schema.

○ d. Set the **PASSWORD_VERIFY** initialization parameter to **TRUE**.

Answer c is correct. The utlpwdmg.sql script enables the **VERIFY_FUNCTION** function and alters the **DEFAULT** profile. Answer a is incorrect because the **ORAPWD** utility creates a password file for users granted the **SYSDBA** or **SYSOPER** privilege. It does not check the password for every user. Answer b is incorrect because the catproc.sql script sets up the database to use PL/SQL. Answer d is incorrect because **PASSWORD_VERIFY** is not an initialization parameter.

Question 7

Which **CREATE USER** command clause would you use to give a user the ability to use 20MB on the USERS tablespace?

○ a. **QUOTA**

○ b. **PROFILE**

○ c. **DEFAULT TABLESPACE**

○ d. **TEMPORARY TABLESPACE**

Answer a is correct. The **QUOTA** clause defines the amount of space that a user can use to create and maintain objects in a specified tablespace. Answer b is incorrect because the **PROFILE** clause assigns a profile to a user. Answer c is incorrect because **DEFAULT TABLESPACE** assigns a default tablespace for a user, but it does not define space usage. Answer d is incorrect because **TEMPORARY TABLESPACE** assigns a temporary tablespace to a user for temporary segments.

Question 8

If it has never been altered, what is the setting for **SESSIONS_PER_USER** in the **DEFAULT** profile?

○ a. 0

○ b. 1

○ c. 5

○ d. 10

○ e. **UNLIMITED**

Answer e is correct. User profiles can be created to limit the amount of system and database resources for a user. If a user is not assigned a profile, then the default database profile is used, giving unlimited access to resources. Answers a, b, c, and d are all incorrect because the default value is **UNLIMITED**.

Question 9

Which predefined role has all the system privileges?

- ○ a. **DBA**
- ○ b. **CONNECT**
- ○ c. **RESOURCE**
- ○ d. **IMP_FULL_DATABASE**
- ○ e. **DELETE_CATALOG_ROLE**

Answer a is correct. The **DBA** role is granted all the system privileges with the **WITH ADMIN OPTION**. All the other answers are incorrect because not all system privileges are granted to these roles. Answer b is incorrect because the **CONNECT** role allows users to establish sessions with the database and to create objects. Answer c is incorrect because the **RESOURCE** role only assigns privileges needed by developers and the **UNLIMITED TABLESPACE** system privilege. Answer d is incorrect because the **IMP_FULL_DATABASE** role assigns only the privileges needed to do a full import. Answer e is incorrect because **DELETE_CATALOG_ROLE** does not grant any system privileges.

Question 10

Which object privilege do you need to grant privileges on an object that's not in your schema?

- ○ a. **PUBLIC**
- ○ b. **REFERENCES**
- ○ c. **WITH GRANT OPTION**
- ○ d. **WITH ADMIN OPTION**

Answer c is correct. To grant an object privilege to another user, you must have been granted the privilege **WITH GRANT OPTION**. Answer a is incorrect because **PUBLIC** is not a privilege; it is a special user account. Answer b is incorrect because **REFERENCES** is used for defining a foreign key integrity constraint on tables only. Answer d is incorrect because **WITH ADMIN OPTION** is used for system privileges, not object privileges.

Question 11

Which statement is true about a role?

○ a. It is owned by **DBA**.

○ b. It can be granted to itself.

○ c. It can consist only of object privileges.

○ d. It can be granted to any role, except that it cannot be granted to itself, even circularly.

Answer d is correct. A role can be granted to a user, to another role, or to **PUBLIC**. Answer a is incorrect because roles aren't owned by anyone. Answer b is incorrect because a role cannot be granted to itself. Answer c is incorrect because roles can contain system and object privileges as well as other roles.

Need to Know More?

 Loney, Kevin, and Marlene Theriault. *Oracle8i DBA Handbook*. Oracle Press, Berkeley, CA, 1999. ISBN 0-07212-188-2. This book is a comprehensive guide and a must-have for all DBAs. See Chapter 9 for information on database security and auditing.

 See the Oracle documentation that is provided on CD with the Oracle RDBMS software. The following documents specifically pertain to this chapter:

Baylis, Ruth, and Joyce Fee. *Oracle8i Administrator's Guide*. Oracle Corporation, Redwood City, CA, 1999. This is the complete documentation of database administration tasks. Chapters 21 through 24 cover material pertaining to this chapter, including security policies, managing users and resources, managing privileges and roles, and auditing database use.

Leverenz, Lefty, Diana Rehfield, and Cathy Baird. *Oracle8i Concepts*. Oracle Corporation, Redwood City, CA, 1999. This is the complete documentation of Oracle concepts. Chapters 26 through 28 cover material pertaining to this chapter, including controlling users, roles, and privileges, and auditing database use.

Lorentz, Diana. *Oracle8i Reference*. Oracle Corporation, Redwood City, CA, 1999. Here you'll find specific details on initialization parameters, data dictionary views, and database limits.

 technet.oracle.com is Oracle's technical repository of information for clients.

 www.revealnet.com is the site where RevealNet Corporation provides Oracle administration reference software.

Using National Language Support

Terms you'll need to understand:

✓ Database character set
✓ National character set
✓ Single-byte character sets
✓ Multibyte character sets
✓ Unicode
✓ **NLS_LANGUAGE**
✓ **NLS_TERRITORY**
✓ **ORA_NLS33**
✓ **NLS_DATE_FORMAT**

Techniques you'll need to master:

✓ Choosing the database character set and national character set for a database
✓ Specifying language-dependent behavior using initialization parameters, environment variables, and the **ALTER SESSION** command
✓ Using the different types of National Language Support (NLS) parameters
✓ Obtaining information about NLS usage

National Language Support (NLS) is the functionality in Oracle databases that allows you to store, process, and retrieve data in languages other than English. It allows you to configure the database so that conventions such as date, time, sort orders, monetary formats, numeric formats, calendars, and error messages reflect the native language and environment. As the Internet continues to have a larger effect on everyday life, it's becoming more likely that the databases we manage will be used globally. Thus, it is increasingly important for you to understand how to take advantage of this functionality.

 Many DBAs have ignored NLS functionality and just use the defaults for the settings for NLS parameters. For the exam, however, you cannot afford to ignore NLS. Each time I have taken these exams, I found more questions on NLS than I thought were warranted (at least in proportion to the number of other questions). If you've never used NLS before, pay close attention to the information that's covered in this chapter.

Choosing the Database Character Set and the National Character Set

When you enter data into a database, the data is in a form that makes sense—that is, you can read the characters as they are typed. Computers, however, don't store the data in this way. Instead, each character is changed to an encoded numerical equivalent. So, when you create a database, you need to specify the database character set and the national character set that tell Oracle which languages can be represented in the database. The **CHARACTER SET** parameter in the **CREATE DATABASE** statement tells Oracle the database character set—that is, the character set that the database uses to store data—and the **NATIONAL CHARACTER SET** parameter tells Oracle which national character set to use specifically for **NCHAR, NVARCHAR2**, and **NCLOB** columns.

Oracle provides a number of different classes of character encoding sets for you to choose from. These include single-byte character sets (7- or 8-bit), multibyte character sets (varying width and fixed width), and Unicode character sets (UTF8 and AL24UTFFSS). Let's look at each of these in more detail:

➤ *Single-byte character sets*—Each character in a single-byte character set occupies one byte. A 7-bit, single-byte character set such as US7ASCII can contain up to 128 characters, whereas an 8-bit, single-byte character set such as WE8ISO8895P1 can contain up to 256 characters.

➤ *Multibyte character sets*—A varying-width multibyte character set such as CGB2312-80 uses one or more bytes to store each character. Varying-width multibyte character sets use space more efficiently than do fixed-width multibyte character sets. Fixed-width multibyte character sets such as

JA16EUFIXED provide similar functionality to the varying-width multibyte character sets except that each character takes up a fixed number of bytes. You can specify a fixed-width multibyte character set only for the national character set, not for the database character set. Fixed-width multibyte character sets can perform better for string operations than varying-width multibyte character sets. Multibyte character sets are normally used to support Asian languages.

➤ *Unicode character sets*—Unicode is an international standard for character encoding that can support any characters needed by a computer, including technical symbols. Oracle7 supported only Unicode 1.1, but Oracle8 also supports Unicode 2.0.

I mentioned that you specify the database character set, and optionally the national character set, when the **CREATE DATABASE** command is issued. These parameters cannot be changed without re-creating the database, so you need to ensure that the character sets you choose contain all of the characters that you are likely to need for the life of the database.

Specifying Language-Dependent Behavior

You can specify NLS parameters in three different ways:

➤ You can set the default values for the database as initialization parameters. (This will have no effect on the client-side settings, just the server side.)

➤ You can override the default settings for the server by setting environment variables at the client.

➤ You can override both the default settings and the environment variable settings with an **ALTER SESSION** command.

Let's look at each of these methods in a bit more detail.

Database Default Settings

Although many initialization parameters provide the database default settings for language-dependent behavior, most are derived from two parameters: **NLS_LANGUAGE** and **NLS_TERRITORY**.

NLS_LANGUAGE sets the values of language-dependent behavior such as the language of Oracle error messages. The parameters that are derived from it include **NLS_DATE_LANGUAGE** (day and month names and their abbreviations, and the equivalents of A.M., P.M., AD, and BC), and **NLS_SORT** (the default sorting sequence for character data).

NLS_TERRITORY sets the values of territory-dependent behavior such as the default date format, the decimal character and thousands separator, and currency symbols. The parameters that are derived from it include **NLS_CURRENCY** (the local currency symbol), **NLS_ISO_CURRENCY** (the ISO currency symbol), **NLS_DATE_FORMAT** (the default date format), and **NLS_NUMERIC_CHARACTERS** (the decimal character and the thousands separator). For those countries that use the Euro, an additional parameter (**NLS_DUAL_CURRENCY**) can be used to set an alternative currency symbol.

Environment Variable Settings

The most important environment variable to be aware of is the **ORA_NLS33** environment variable. If this is not configured (it should point to $ORACLE_HOME/ocommon/nls/admin/data on Unix boxes and %ORACLE_HOME%/ocommon/nls/admin/data on NT boxes), you can set the database character set to US7ASCII only.

The **NLS_LANG** environment variable can be used to override the default behavior for the database. The format of this environment variable is *language_territory.characterset* (where *language* overrides **NLS_LANGUAGE**, *territory* overrides **NLS_TERRITORY**, and *characterset* specifies the character encoding scheme used by the terminal where data is being entered).

All of the other initialization parameters can be specified as environment variables, along with a number of others that I won't detail here because they're not covered on the exam. For more details, refer to the *Oracle8i National Language Support Guide* (full bibliographic details are given in the "Need to Know More?" section at the end of this chapter).

How environment variables are set varies from operating system to operating system. On Unix systems, it depends on which shell you are using. On NT systems, these values are Registry keys, though they can overridden at the command prompt if necessary.

Session Settings

All of the preceding parameters can be used in an **ALTER SESSION** command. In fact, this is what happens if you set the parameters as environment variables and then connect to SQL*Plus. (SQL*Plus will issue implicit **ALTER SESSION** commands for you.) You can also use the **DBMS_SESSION.SET_NLS** procedure to do the same thing. The following example shows how to do this explicitly and provides the results of the command:

```
SQL> ALTER SESSION SET NLS_DATE_FORMAT = 'DD/MM/YYYY';

Session altered.

SQL> SELECT sysdate FROM dual;

SYSDATE
----------
29/06/2001
```

Using the Different Types of NLS Parameters

Some SQL functions allow you to specify NLS parameters explicitly in the function, and thus override the settings that you've specified in any of the three ways I just covered. Here's an example:

```
SQL> SELECT empno, ename,
  2          to_char(hiredate, 'DD/MON/YYYY',
  3                  'NLS_DATE_LANGUAGE=GERMAN') AS "Hire Date"
  4  FROM emp
  5  ORDER BY ename;

    EMPNO ENAME      Hire Date
---------- ---------- ----------
      7876 ADAMS      23/MAI/1987
      7499 ALLEN      20/FEB/1981
      7698 BLAKE      01/MAI/1981
      7782 CLARK      09/JUN/1981
      7902 FORD       03/DEZ/1981
      7900 JAMES      03/DEZ/1981
      7566 JONES      02/APR/1981
      7839 KING       17/NOV/1981
      7654 MARTIN     28/SEP/1981
      7934 MILLER     23/JAN/1982
      7788 SCOTT      19/APR/1987
      7369 SMITH      17/DEZ/1980
      7844 TURNER     08/SEP/1981
      7521 WARD       22/FEB/1981

14 rows selected.
```

The settings of the NLS parameters also can have an effect on the way in which data is loaded into the database using the Import and SQL*Loader utilities. During an import, data will be automatically converted to the value set by the

NLS_LANG parameter, and then converted again into the value defined by the database character set. It obviously makes sense from a performance perspective for these two settings to be the same.

The effect on SQL*Loader depends on whether data is being loaded in conventional or direct path. For conventional path loads, the behavior is the same as that just described for the Import utility. For direct path loads, data is converted directly into the database character set, ignoring the value set for **NLS_LANG**.

Obtaining Information about NLS Usage

The two main data dictionary views that provide information about NLS usage for the database are:

➤ **NLS_DATABASE_PARAMETERS**—Lists the database default settings for NLS parameters.

➤ **NLS_SESSION_PARAMETERS**—Lists the session settings for the NLS parameters, through both environment variables and **ALTER SESSION** commands.

Here's an example of the data in these views:

```
SQL> REM First let's change a parameter at the session level
SQL> ALTER SESSION SET NLS_DATE_FORMAT = 'DD/MON/YYYY';

Session altered.

SQL> REM This change isn't reflected in NLS_DATABASE_PARAMETERS
SQL> SELECT * FROM NLS_DATABASE_PARAMETERS;

PARAMETER                      VALUE
------------------------------ ------------------------------------
NLS_LANGUAGE                   AMERICAN
NLS_TERRITORY                  AMERICA
NLS_CURRENCY                   $
NLS_ISO_CURRENCY               AMERICA
NLS_NUMERIC_CHARACTERS         .,
NLS_CHARACTERSET               WE8ISO8859P1
NLS_CALENDAR                   GREGORIAN
NLS_DATE_FORMAT                DD-MON-RR
NLS_DATE_LANGUAGE              AMERICAN
NLS_SORT                       BINARY
NLS_TIME_FORMAT                HH.MI.SSXFF AM
NLS_TIMESTAMP_FORMAT           DD-MON-RR HH.MI.SSXFF AM
NLS_TIME_TZ_FORMAT             HH.MI.SSXFF AM TZH:TZM
```

```
NLS_TIMESTAMP_TZ_FORMAT          DD-MON-RR HH.MI.SSXFF AM TZH:TZM
NLS_DUAL_CURRENCY                $
NLS_COMP                         BINARY
NLS_NCHAR_CHARACTERSET           WE8ISO8859P1
NLS_RDBMS_VERSION                8.1.7.0.0

18 rows selected.

SQL> REM The change is reflected in NLS_SESSION_PARAMETERS
SQL> SELECT * FROM NLS_SESSION_PARAMETERS;

PARAMETER                        VALUE
------------------------------   ---------------------------------
NLS_LANGUAGE                     AMERICAN
NLS_TERRITORY                    AMERICA
NLS_CURRENCY                     $
NLS_ISO_CURRENCY                 AMERICA
NLS_NUMERIC_CHARACTERS           .,
NLS_CALENDAR                     GREGORIAN
NLS_DATE_FORMAT                  DD/MON/YYYY
NLS_DATE_LANGUAGE                AMERICAN
NLS_SORT                         BINARY
NLS_TIME_FORMAT                  HH.MI.SSXFF AM
NLS_TIMESTAMP_FORMAT             DD-MON-RR HH.MI.SSXFF AM
NLS_TIME_TZ_FORMAT               HH.MI.SSXFF AM TZH:TZM
NLS_TIMESTAMP_TZ_FORMAT          DD-MON-RR HH.MI.SSXFF AM TZH:TZM
NLS_DUAL_CURRENCY                $
NLS_COMP                         BINARY
```

Practice Questions

Question 1

> Which of the following keywords need to be set when the database is created? [Choose two]
>
> ❏ a. **CHARACTER SET**
>
> ❏ b. **NLS_LANGUAGE**
>
> ❏ c. **NLS_TERRITORY**
>
> ❏ d. **NATIONAL CHARACTER SET**

Answers a and d are correct. The keywords **CHARACTER SET** and **NATIONAL CHARACTER SET** are set when the database is created. **CHARACTER SET** specifies the database character set, and **NATIONAL CHARACTER SET** specifies the national character set for **NCHAR, NVARCHAR2,** and **NCLOB** columns. Answers b and c are incorrect because **NLS_LANGUAGE** and **NLS_TERRITORY** are initialization parameters that can be changed at any time and don't need to be specified when the database is created.

Question 2

> Which data dictionary view would you use to see the value of an NLS parameter that has been changed at the session level?
>
> ○ a. **NLS_DATABASE_PARAMETERS**
>
> ○ b. **NLS_SESSION_PARAMETERS**
>
> ○ c. **V$SESSION**
>
> ○ d. **V$PARAMETER**

Answer b is correct. **NLS_SESSION_PARAMETERS** lists session-level settings for NLS parameters. Answer a is incorrect because **NLS_DATABASE_PARAMETERS** lists database-level settings for NLS parameters, and changes at the session level are not reflected here. Answer c is incorrect because, although **V$SESSION** lists session information for each session connected to the database, it doesn't list NLS parameters. Answer d is incorrect because **V$PARAMETER** lists information about initialization parameters. It includes NLS parameters, but session-level parameter settings are not reflected here.

Question 3

Which environment variable needs to be set before you can create a database that uses a character set other than US7ASCII?

- ○ a. **NLS_LANG**
- ○ b. **NLS_TERRITORY**
- ○ c. **ORA_NLS33**
- ○ d. **CHARSET**

Answer c is correct. If the **ORA_NLS33** environment variable has not been set, the only kind of database that you can create is one that uses the US7ASCII character set. Answer a is incorrect because **NLS_LANG** overrides the default language, territory, and character set for the database. Answer b is incorrect because **NLS_TERRITORY** sets the value of territory-dependent behavior, such as currency symbols and the default date format. Answer d is incorrect because **CHARSET** is not a valid environment variable.

Question 4

If you are performing a direct path load using SQL*Loader, what character set will be used?

- ○ a. None. Character sets are ignored when using SQL*Loader in direct path mode.
- ○ b. The value of the **NLS_DATABASE** environment variable.
- ○ c. The value of the **NLS_LANG** environment variable.
- ○ d. The database character set with which the database was defined.

Answer d is correct. The database character set with which the database was defined will be used, regardless of the value of the **NLS_LANG** environment variable. Answer a is incorrect because character sets are not ignored when using SQL*Loader in direct path mode. Answer b is incorrect because **NLS_DATABASE** is not a valid environment variable. Answer c is incorrect because **NLS_LANG** is used with only conventional path SQL*Loader, not direct path.

Question 5

> Which data dictionary view lists the database character set?
>
> ○ a. **NLS_DATABASE_PARAMETERS**
> ○ b. **NLS_SESSION_PARAMETERS**
> ○ c. **V$DATABASE**
> ○ d. **V$INSTANCE**

Answer a is correct. **NLS_DATABASE_PARAMETERS** displays the database-level settings for NLS parameters, including the database character set. Answer b is incorrect because **NLS_SESSION_PARAMETERS** displays session-level information about NLS parameters, it and doesn't include the database character set. Answer c is incorrect because **V$DATABASE** displays information about the database from the control file, and it does not include the database character set. Answer d is incorrect because **V$INSTANCE** displays the current state of the instance, and it does not include the database character set.

Question 6

> How would you change the NLS date format to French for a single SQL statement?
>
> ○ a. You can't. **NLS_DATE_FORMAT** is set at the session level or higher.
> ○ b. Use **'NLS_DATE_LANGUAGE=FRENCH'** as the third argument to the **TO_CHAR** function.
> ○ c. Use **'NLS_DATE_FORMAT=FRENCH'** as the third argument to the **TO_DATE** function.
> ○ d. Use **'NLS_DATE_FORMAT=FRENCH'** as the third argument to the **TO_CHAR** function.

Answer b is correct. You use a string like **TO_CHAR(hiredate, 'DD-MON-YY', 'NLS_DATE_LANGUAGE=FRENCH')** to change the NLS date format for a single SQL statement. Answer a is incorrect because you can change the NLS date format at the individual SQL call level. Answers c and d are incorrect because **NLS_DATE_FORMAT** is not a valid format at the individual SQL statement level. Another reason answer c is incorrect is that the **TO_CHAR** function, not the **TO_DATE** function, is used to put a format mask on a date field.

Question 7

At which of the following levels can NLS parameters be set? [Choose two]

❑ a. The database level

❑ b. The instance level

❑ c. The environment variable level

❑ d. The database user level

Answers a and c are correct. NLS values can be set at either the database level or the environment variable level. Answer b is incorrect because NLS parameters are not set at the instance level. Answer d is incorrect because NLS parameters are not set at the user level. (Although they can be set at the session level, this is not the same as setting them at the user level.)

Need to Know More?

 See the Oracle documentation that is provided on CD with the Oracle RDBMS software. Specifically pertaining to this chapter are:

Lane, Paul. *Oracle8i National Language Support Guide*. Oracle Corporation, Redwood City, CA, 1999. This guide is the complete documentation of National Language Support configuration and use.

Lorentz, Diana. *Oracle8i Reference*. Oracle Corporation, Redwood City, CA, 1999. The document provides specific details on initialization parameters, data dictionary views, and database limits.

 technet.oracle.com is Oracle's technical repository of information for clients.

 www.revealnet.com is the site where RevealNet Corporation provides Oracle administration reference software.

Sample Test

Question 1

What does the **IDENTIFIED BY** clause do in the following command?

```
ALTER USER john IDENTIFIED BY doe;
```

○ a. Specifies an alias for user john.

○ b. Specifies a new username for user john.

○ c. Specifies a new password for user john.

○ d. Specifies the current tablespace for user john.

Question 2

Carol granted **SELECT** on the **DISTRICT** table **WITH GRANT OPTION** to Penny. Penny granted the privilege to Mark. If Penny's privilege is revoked, who will lose his or her privileges?

○ a. No one will lose his or her privileges

○ b. Only Penny

○ c. Both Penny and Mark

○ d. Only Mark

Question 3

Which statement about **CASCADE** in the following statement is true?

```
ANALYZE TABLE location
   VALIDATE STRUCTURE CASCADE;
```

- ○ a. It re-creates all indexes.
- ○ b. It verifies any tables referenced by **REF** pointers in the table.
- ○ c. It re-creates any dropped indexes.
- ○ d. It validates the structure of indexes associated with the table.

Question 4

If you set the **LOG_CHECKPOINT_INTERVAL** initialization parameter to 25, how frequently will a log switch occur?

- ○ a. Every 25 seconds
- ○ b. Every 25 minutes
- ○ c. After LGWR writes 25 Oracle data blocks
- ○ d. After LGWR writes 25 operating system blocks

Question 5

How can you show the current locations of the control files using SQL*Plus? [Choose three]

- ❑ a. Use the **SHOW SGA** command.
- ❑ b. Query **V$CONTROLFILE**.
- ❑ c. Use the **DESCRIBE** command.
- ❑ d. Query **V$PARAMETER**.
- ❑ e. Query **V$SYSTEM_PARAMETER**.
- ❑ f. Use the **SHOW PARAMETER** command.

Question 6

Which view would you query to find out the names of the tables and the columns included in a cluster?

○ a. **DBA_CLUSTERS**

○ b. **DBA_CLU_COLUMNS**

○ c. **DBA_OBJECTS**

○ d. **DBA_CATALOG**

Question 7

Which requirement must be met for the following command to execute?

```
create database "HII4"
controlfile reuse
maxinstances 8
maxlogfiles  32
maxlogfiles  32
maxlogmembers 5
maxdatafiles 1022
maxloghistory 800
datafile
'/u02/oradata/HII4/system01.dbf' size 200M
logfile
'/u05/oradata/HII4/redo01a.dbf' size 100M,
'/u05/oradata/HII4/redo02a.dbf' size 100M,
'/u05/oradata/HII4/redo03a.dbf' size 100M,
'/u05/oradata/HII4/redo04a.dbf' size 100M;
```

○ a. All the log files must exist.

○ b. The datafile must exist.

○ c. The control files specified in the parameter file must exist.

○ d. The user must have the **SYSOPER** privileges to create the log files and datafiles.

Question 8

When an instance fails, which type of segment is used to recover uncommitted transactions?

○ a. Table

○ b. Index

○ c. Rollback

○ d. Temporary

Question 9

Which environment variable needs to be set before a database can be created using a database character set other than US7ASCII?

○ a. **ORA_NLS33**

○ b. **NLS_LANG**

○ c. **NLS_LANGUAGE**

○ d. **NLS_TERRITORY**

Question 10

Which keywords are used to allow existing data in a table to violate a constraint while enforcing the constraint for new data?

○ a. **ENABLE VALIDATE**

○ b. **DISABLE NOVALIDATE**

○ c. **ENABLE NOVALIDATE**

○ d. **DISABLE VALIDATE**

Question 11

Which data dictionary view can you use to determine if an index is valid?

○ a. **DBA_TABLES**

○ b. **DBA_INDEXES**

○ c. **DBA_SEGMENTS**

○ d. **DBA_IND_COLUMNS**

Question 12

Which privilege do you need to audit objects in another user's schema?

○ a. **AUDIT ANY**

○ b. **ANALYZE**

○ c. **AUDIT**

○ d. **CREATE ANY AUDIT**

Question 13

Which **CREATE INDEX** clause ensures that redo generation will not affect performance when the index is created?

○ a. **NOSORT**

○ b. **UNIQUE**

○ c. **NOSTORAGE**

○ d. **LOGGING**

○ e. **MINTRANS**

○ f. **NOLOGGING**

Question 14

You have set the **REMOTE_LOGIN_PASSWORD_FILE** initialization parameter to **EXCLUSIVE**. Which view would you query to determine which users have been granted the **SYSOPER** privileges?

○ a. **V$DATABASE**

○ b. **V$INSTANCE**

○ c. **V$PARAMETER**

○ d. **V$PWFILE_USERS**

Question 15

Which characteristic describes a role?

- ○ a. It can be disabled for each authorized user.
- ○ b. It always requires a password.
- ○ c. It is enforced by database triggers.
- ○ d. It is stored in a schema.

Question 16

What would happen if you tried to start an Oracle instance and open a database with different database names in the parameter file and the control file?

- ○ a. An instance would not start.
- ○ b. An instance would start, but the database would not be mounted.
- ○ c. The database would open without using the parameter file.
- ○ d. An instance would start and the database would be mounted, but would not be opened.

Question 17

Which view shows the **SORT EXTENT POOL** status?

- ○ a. **V$SORT_SEGMENT**
- ○ b. **V$SORT_USAGE**
- ○ c. **V$SESSION**
- ○ d. **V$INSTANCE**

Question 18

If you want to find out if a role has a password, which view would you query?

- ○ a. **SESSION_ROLES**
- ○ b. **DBA_SYS_PRIVS**
- ○ c. **DBA_ROLES**
- ○ d. **DBA_ROLE_PRIVS**

Question 19

In the data buffer cache, which buffers are on the dirty list?

○ a. Empty buffers

○ b. Null buffers

○ c. Buffers currently being accessed

○ d. Buffers waiting to be written to disk

Question 20

Why would you use direct-load inserts when loading data into a table? [Choose two]

❑ a. Redo is generated in case of failure.

❑ b. Indexes are created to speed the data load.

❑ c. It loads data below the high-water mark to reclaim disk space.

❑ d. Other rows in the same table can be concurrently modified by other users.

❑ e. Data can be quickly copied from one table into another within the same database because it bypasses the buffer cache.

Question 21

Which of the following operations can be taken on a constraint? [Choose three]

❑ a. **ALTER**

❑ b. **CREATE**

❑ c. **DELETE**

❑ d. **DISABLE**

❑ e. **DROP**

❑ f. **ENABLE**

Question 22

Into which part of a database block is a new row inserted?

○ a. Header area

○ b. Table directory

○ c. Free space

○ d. Row directory

Question 23

How would you drop a redo log member from an active group when archiving is enabled?

○ a. After the group is archived, issue the **ALTER DATABASE DROP LOGFILE MEMBER** command.

○ b. Before the group is archived, issue the **ALTER DATABASE DROP LOGFILE MEMBER** command.

○ c. Issue the **ALTER SYSTEM SWITCH LOGFILE** command, then issue the **ALTER DATABASE DROP LOGFILE MEMBER** command.

○ d. Before the group is archived, issue the **ALTER SYSTEM SWITCH LOGFILE** command, then issue the **ALTER DATABASE DROP LOGFILE MEMBER** command.

Question 24

What is the maximum number of control files that you can specify in the **CONTROL_FILES** parameter?

○ a. 2

○ b. 4

○ c. 8

○ d. 16

○ e. 32

○ f. Unlimited

Question 25

Which script is used to create the data dictionary views?

○ a. catalog.sql

○ b. catproc.sql

○ c. dbmsutil.sql

○ d. sql.bsq

Question 26

Which data dictionary view contains the names of all the data dictionary views?

○ a. **DB_VIEWS**

○ b. **DBA_VIEWS**

○ c. **DICTIONARY**

○ d. **DBA_VIEW_DATA**

Question 27

Your database has a log group with three members. Two of the three members have become corrupted. What will happen when the database tries to write to this log group?

○ a. The database will hang.

○ b. LGWR will write to the available member.

○ c. The instance will crash.

○ d. Oracle will reformat the corrupt members.

Question 28

Where does Oracle store the database creation timestamp?

○ a. Database file header

○ b. Control file

○ c. Parameter file

○ d. Redo log files

○ e. Rollback segment

Question 29

Which parameter would you use to control the space reserved in each data block for updates of existing rows?

○ a. **INITRANS**

○ b. **MAXTRANS**

○ c. **PCTFREE**

○ d. **PCTUSED**

Question 30

Which of the following methods can be used to enable automatic extension for an existing datafile?

○ a. Use the **ALTER TABLESPACE AUTOEXTEND** command.

○ b. Drop the datafile and re-create it.

○ c. Use OS commands to autoextend existing files.

○ d. Use the **ALTER TABLESPACE RENAME DATAFILE** command to rename the datafile to a larger file.

Question 31

Which is the correct sequence of steps to move a datafile to a new location?

○ a. Take the tablespace offline, issue the **ALTER TABLESPACE RENAME DATAFILE** command, move the files using OS commands, and bring the tablespace back online.

○ b. Issue the **ALTER TABLESPACE RENAME DATAFILE** command, take the tablespace offline, move the files using OS commands, and bring the tablespace back online.

○ c. Take the tablespace offline, move the files using OS commands, bring the tablespace back online, and issue the **ALTER TABLESPACE RENAME DATAFILE** command.

○ d. Take the tablespace offline, move the files using OS commands, issue the **ALTER TABLESPACE RENAME DATAFILE** command, and bring the tablespace back online.

Question 32

Which privilege do you need to execute the **ALTER SYSTEM ENABLE RESTRICTED SESSION** command?

○ a. **RESTRICTED SESSION**

○ b. **ALTER SYSTEM**

○ c. **ALTER DATABASE**

○ d. **ALTER RESOURCE COST**

○ e. **ENABLE RESTRICTED SESSION**

Question 33

When you create a user, which clause would you use to control the amount of space that the user can use in a tablespace?

○ a. **DEFAULT TABLESPACE**

○ b. **PROFILE**

○ c. **QUOTA**

○ d. **TEMPORARY TABLESPACE**

Question 34

If you want to deallocate some but not all of the unused space in a table, which option of the **ALTER TABLE** command would you use?

○ a. **KEEP**

○ b. **CACHE**

○ c. **DEALLOCATE UNUSED**

○ d. **MODIFY**

Question 35

You have a set of users who need to view the DBA data dictionary views. Which of the following roles would you use to give them this access?

○ a. **DBA**

○ b. **EXECUTE_CATALOG_ROLE**

○ c. **RESOURCE**

○ d. **EXP_FULL_DATABASE**

○ e. **PLUSTRACE**

○ f. **SELECT_CATALOG_ROLE**

Question 36

What clause of the **CREATE TABLE** command can you use to control how extents are allocated to a table?

○ a. **PCTFREE**

○ b. **EXTENT**

○ c. **STORAGE**

○ d. **LOGGING/NOLOGGING**

○ e. **DEFAULT**

Question 37

Which view shows the constraint definitions for all tables in a database?

○ a. **ALL_CONSTRAINTS**

○ b. **DBA_CONSTRAINTS**

○ c. **DBA_CATALOG**

○ d. **USER_CONSTRAINTS**

Question 38

During which stage of starting an instance is the control file read?

○ a. **MOUNT**

○ b. **NOMOUNT**

○ c. **OPEN**

○ d. **RESTRICTED SESSION**

Question 39

Which of the following is not part of an Oracle instance?

○ a. Shared pool

○ b. Redo log buffer

○ c. User process

○ d. Data buffer cache

Question 40

What mode should a tablespace be in before it is transported to another tablespace?

○ a. Offline

○ b. Read-write

○ c. Read-only

○ d. Tablespaces can be transported without problems in any mode.

Question 41

Which of the following commands can be used to specify the default role for a user?

○ a. **CREATE ROLE**

○ b. **ALTER USER**

○ c. **ASSIGN ROLE**

○ d. **SET ROLE**

Question 42

You want to list all of the users with the **ALTER ANY ROLE** command. Which view would you use to create the list?

○ a. **DBA_ROLES**

○ b. **ALL_COL_PRIVS_RECD**

○ c. **USER_SYS_PRIVS**

○ d. **DBA_SYS_PRIVS**

Question 43

Which category of data dictionary views does not have an **OWNER** column?

○ a. **ALL_**

○ b. **DBA_**

○ c. **USER_**

Question 44

When are extents that are allocated to a sort segment released and the space returned to the temporary tablespace if that tablespace is defined as type **TEMPORARY**?

○ a. Never

○ b. When the instance is shut down

○ c. When the user process requesting the sort segment ends

○ d. When the sorting operation ends

Question 45

Which view would you query to determine if any database user is close to exceeding his/her space limit on a tablespace?

○ a. **USER_TS_QUOTAS**

○ b. **USER_TABLESPACES**

○ c. **DBA_TABLESPACES**

○ d. **DBA_TS_QUOTAS**

○ e. **DBA_USERS**

Question 46

What will happen to a user's tables if the quota for the tablespace containing the tables is altered to zero?

- ○ a. The tables will be truncated.
- ○ b. The tables will become inaccessible.
- ○ c. No new extents can be allocated to the table.
- ○ d. The tables will be dropped automatically when the quota is changed.

Question 47

Why does Oracle create temporary segments?

- ○ a. For sorting that cannot be performed in memory
- ○ b. So users can store tables in tablespaces that have been taken temporarily offline
- ○ c. To store tables that are created without specifying a tablespace
- ○ d. To roll back a sort operation

Question 48

Which view would you used to determine if a constraint is enabled?

- ○ a. **DBA_TABLES**
- ○ b. **DBA_CATALOG**
- ○ c. **PUBLIC_DEPENDENCY**
- ○ d. **DBA_CONSTRAINTS**
- ○ e. **DBA_CONS_COLUMNS**

Question 49

Which schema owns the data dictionary tables?

- ○ a. **SYS**
- ○ b. **SYSTEM**
- ○ c. **SYSDBA**
- ○ d. **SYSOPER**

Question 50

Which view would you use to find out the sequence number of the current redo log group?

○ a. **V$DATABASE**

○ b. **V$INSTANCE**

○ c. **V$THREAD**

○ d. **V$LOGFILE**

Question 51

What is the order in which objects are imported into a database from an export file?

○ a. Table data, integrity constraints, triggers, bitmap indexes, indexes on the table, table definitions

○ b. Table definitions, table data, indexes on the table, integrity constraints, triggers, bitmap indexes

○ c. Indexes on the table, integrity constraints, triggers, bitmap indexes, table definitions, table data

○ d. Table definitions, table data, integrity constraints, triggers, bitmap indexes, indexes on the table

○ e. Table definitions, integrity constraints, triggers, bitmap indexes, indexes on the table, table data

Question 52

Which Oracle utility could you use to re-create Oracle tables and their associated objects under a new schema name and move the associated data from the previous schema to the new tables?

○ a. SQL*Loader

○ b. Direct-load insert

○ c. Oracle Enterprise Manager Console

○ d. Export/import utilities

Question 53

When you created the temporary tablespace, the **PCTINCREASE** was set to zero. How will this affect the size of new extents in the temporary tablespace?

- ○ a. The second and all other extents will be the size of the **NEXT** parameter for the tablespace.
- ○ b. All extents will be the size of the **INITIAL** parameter for the tablespace.
- ○ c. The extents will be sized by the SQL*Plus **CREATE TEMPORARY SEGMENT** command.
- ○ d. No new extents can be allocated because **PCTINCREASE** is zero.

Question 54

Which of the following could be determined by the **DBA_FREE_SPACE** view?

- ○ a. The owner of a table
- ○ b. The date an extent was created
- ○ c. The amount of free space in a tablespace
- ○ d. The amount of used space in a tablespace

Question 55

Which SQL*Loader file specifies the database tables to be loaded?

- ○ a. Log file
- ○ b. Discard file
- ○ c. Control file
- ○ d. Bad file

Question 56

Which two views could you query to list the names and locations of the control files? [Choose two]

- ❑ a. **V$DATABASE**
- ❑ b. **V$DATAFILE**
- ❑ c. **V$INSTANCE**
- ❑ d. **V$PARAMETER**
- ❑ e. **V$CONTROLFILE**

Question 57

Which command would you use to change the weights for each session's resource limit?

- ○ a. **ALTER DATABASE**
- ○ b. **ALTER RESOURCE COST**
- ○ c. **ALTER SYSTEM**
- ○ d. **UPDATE RESOURCE COST**
- ○ e. **ALTER SESSION LIMITS**

Question 58

What is the order of precedence for storage clauses?

- ○ a. Extent level, segment level, tablespace level
- ○ b. Segment level, tablespace level, Oracle Server default
- ○ c. Tablespace level, segment level, Oracle Server default
- ○ d. Oracle Server default, tablespace level, segment level

Question 59

You have a table that has a data segment of 10,000 blocks, and 7,000 blocks of the table were actually used for data. All the rows were recently deleted. Where is the high-water mark for this table?

○ a. 0 blocks

○ b. 10,000 blocks

○ c. 3,000 blocks

○ d. 7,000 blocks

Question 60

Which background process writes changed buffers in the data buffer cache to the datafiles?

○ a. SMON

○ b. PMON

○ c. ARC*n*

○ d. LGWR

○ e. DBW*n*

Question 61

What is the recommended number of transactions per rollback segment?

○ a. 4

○ b. 8

○ c. 16

○ d. 32

Question 62

Which command would you use to drop a constraint?

○ a. **DELETE CONSTRAINT**

○ b. **REMOVE CONSTRAINT**

○ c. **ALTER CONSTRAINT DROP**

○ d. **ALTER TABLE**

Question 63

The database parameter **REMOTE_LOGIN_PASSWORDFILE** is set to **SHARED**.
Which Oracle users will the password file recognize? [Choose two]

❑ a. SYS

❑ b. Any user with DBA privileges

❑ c. SYSTEM

❑ d. INTERNAL

Question 64

Which files are examined to ensure that the log sequence number in each is
the same when the database is started? [Choose two]

❑ a. Datafiles

❑ b. Redo log files

❑ c. Parameter files

❑ d. Control files

Question 65

Which of the following operations is not performed by the SMON process?

○ a. Coalescing contiguous free space in tablespaces

○ b. Releasing resources held by failed transactions

○ c. Recovering an instance after instance failure

○ d. Cleaning up temporary segments

16

Answer Key

1. c	18. c	34. a	50. c
2. c	19. d	35. f	51. b
3. d	20. d, e	36. c	52. d
4. d	21. d, e, f	37. b	53. a
5. b, d, f	22. c	38. a	54. c
6. b	23. c	39. c	55. c
7. c	24. c	40. c	56. d, e
8. c	25. a	41. b	57. b
9. a	26. c	42. d	58. b
10. c	27. b	43. c	59. d
11. b	28. b	44. b	60. e
12. a	29. c	45. d	61. a
13. f	30. a	46. c	62. d
14. d	31. d	47. a	63. a, d
15. a	32. b	48. d	64. a, d
16. b	33. c	49. a	65. b
17. a			

Question 1

Answer c is correct. The **IDENTIFIED BY** clause of the **ALTER USER** command changes the user's password. Answer a is incorrect because usernames do not have aliases. Answer b is incorrect because the **ALTER USER** command cannot change a username. Answer d is incorrect because no existing command sets the current tablespace.

Question 2

Answer c is correct. Object privileges that are granted **WITH GRANT OPTION** have their privileges revoked because the revoke cascades. Answers a and b are incorrect because the revoke affects Penny and cascades to Mark. Answer d is incorrect because Penny loses her privileges as well.

Question 3

Answer d is correct. When you use the **ANALYZE TABLE** command on a table with indexes, the structures of the indexes are validated. Answer a is incorrect because the **ANALYZE** command does not create indexes. Answer b is incorrect because the **ANALYZE** command analyzes only the table specified, not referenced tables. Answer c is incorrect because, once an index is dropped, it can be re-created only by a **CREATE INDEX** statement.

Question 4

Answer d is correct. **LOG_CHECKPOINT_INTERVAL** specifies the number of OS blocks written by LGWR that will trigger a log switch. Answers a and b are incorrect, because **LOG_CHECKPOINT_TIMEOUT** specifies the number of seconds between checkpoints and the time period for checkpoints. Answer c is incorrect because **LOG_CHECKPOINT_INTERVAL** uses OS blocks, not Oracle blocks, for its value.

Question 5

Answers b, d, and f are correct. Using SQL*Plus, you show the current locations of the control files by querying the **V$CONTROLFILE** or **V$PARAMETER** view, or by executing the **SHOW PARAMETER** command. Answer a is incorrect because the **SHOW SGA** command displays information about the current instance's system global area. Answer c is incorrect because you cannot use the

DESCRIBE command on a control file. Answer e is incorrect because the **V$SYSTEM_PARAMETER** view contains information on system parameters, but it does not include the control file location.

Question 6

Answer b is correct. **DBA_CLU_COLUMNS** displays the names of the columns included in the cluster and their corresponding table column. Answer a is incorrect because the **DBA_CLUSTERS** view contains a description of the storage information on all clusters in the database. Answer c is incorrect because the **DBA_OBJECTS** view lists all objects in the database. Answer d is incorrect because the **DBA_CATALOG** view lists all database tables, views, synonyms, and sequences.

Question 7

Answer c is correct. Because the **CREATE DATABASE** command uses the **CONTROLFILE REUSE** option, the control files listed in the parameter file will be reused. For this command to execute successfully, the control files listed in the parameter file must exist. Answer a is incorrect because the log files must not exist for the command to succeed as written. Answer b is incorrect because the datafile must not exist for the command to succeed as written. Answer d is incorrect because users with the **SYSOPER** privilege cannot create a database. (**SYSDBA** is the correct privilege to use here.)

Question 8

Answer c is correct. Transaction recovery occurs after an instance failure. All uncommitted transactions are rolled back using the redo log files and the before images stored in rollback segments. Answer a is incorrect because tables are made up of data segments, and this type of segment is not used for recovery. Answer b is incorrect because indexes are made up of index segments, which also are not used for recovery. Answer d is incorrect because temporary segments are used for sorting and are not used for recovery.

Question 9

Answer a is correct. The **ORA_NLS33** environment variable needs to be set before a database can be created with a database character set that is not US7ASCII. Answer b is incorrect because **NLS_LANG** overrides the default language, territory, and character set for the database. Answer c is incorrect because **NLS_LANGUAGE** sets the values of language-dependent behavior, such as the language for the Oracle error messages. Answer d is incorrect because **NLS_TERRITORY** sets the value of territory-dependent behavior, such as currency symbols and default date format.

Question 10

Answer c is correct. The **ENABLE NOVALIDATE** keywords allow existing data to violate a constraint, but new data must meet the constraint criteria. Answer a is incorrect because existing data must meet the constraint criteria if **ENABLE VALIDATE** is specified. Answer b is incorrect because constraints are not enforced for existing or new data when **DISABLE NOVALIDATE** is specified. Answer d is incorrect because the constraint is disabled and no new data is allowed to be entered when a constraint is in the **DISABLE VALIDATE** state.

Question 11

Answer b is correct. **DBA_INDEXES** displays the status of each index, as well as the name, owner name, type, table name, uniqueness, tablespace name, and more. Answer a is incorrect because the **DBA_TABLES** view contains descriptions of all tables in the database. Answer c is incorrect because the **DBA_SEGMENTS** view contains information about storage allocated for all database segments. Answer d is incorrect because the **DBA_IND_COLUMNS** view contains descriptions of the columns that make up the indexes on all tables and clusters.

Question 12

Answer a is correct. To enable auditing, you must own the objects to be audited, or you must have the **AUDIT ANY** privilege. Answer b is incorrect because the **ANALYZE** command is used to collect statistics about schema objects used by the optimizer and to store them in the data dictionary. Answer c is incorrect because **AUDIT ANY** is a privilege, but **AUDIT** is not. Answer d is incorrect because **CREATE ANY AUDIT** is an invalid privilege.

Question 13

Answer f is correct. The **NOLOGGING** clause does not generate redo and increases the speed of the **CREATE INDEX** command. Answer a is incorrect because the **NOSORT** clause indicates to Oracle that the rows are stored in the database in ascending order; therefore, Oracle does not have to sort the rows when creating the index. Redo information is still created, however. Answer b is incorrect because **UNIQUE** specifies that the value of the column, or combination of columns, in the table being indexed must be unique. Answer c is incorrect because **NOSTORAGE** is an invalid SQL parameter. Answer d is incorrect because **LOGGING** specifies that redo information will be generated. Answer e is incorrect because **MINTRANS** is not a **CREATE INDEX** option.

Question 14

Answer d is correct. When password file authentication is enabled, **V$PWFILE_USERS** displays the names of users with the **SYSDBA** or **SYSOPER** privileges. Answer a is incorrect because the **V$DATABASE** view contains database information from the control file. Answer b is incorrect because the **V$INSTANCE** view displays the state of the current instance. Answer c is incorrect because the **V$PARAMETER** view lists information about initialization parameters.

Question 15

Answer a is correct. A role can be enabled or disabled for an individual user who has been granted the role. Answer b is incorrect because, although roles can have a password, they aren't required to. Answer c is incorrect because database triggers are used to enforce business rules and have nothing to do with roles. Answer d is incorrect because roles are not owned by any schema.

Question 16

Answer b is correct. The instance would start, but when the control file was read to open the database, the mismatch in database names would stop the database from mounting. The database could not open or mount because of the name mismatch. Answer a is incorrect because the instance would start without any problems. Answer c is incorrect because the database could not be mounted, let alone opened, with the mismatch in database names. Answer d is incorrect because the database cannot be mounted when there is a mismatch in database names.

Question 17

Answer a is correct. **V$SORT_SEGMENT** displays the status of the sort extent pool for the current instance. Answer b is incorrect because the **V$SORT_USAGE** view describes sort usage, but not the **SORT EXTENT**

POOL status. Answer c is incorrect because the **V$SESSION** view lists session information for each current session. Answer d is incorrect because the **V$INSTANCE** view displays the state of the current instance.

Question 18

Answer c is correct. **DBA_ROLES** displays the names of all the roles in the database and indicates whether they require a password. Answer a is incorrect because the **SESSION_ROLES** view lists the roles that are currently enabled to the user. Answer b is incorrect because the **DBA_SYS_PRIVS** view lists system privileges granted to users and roles. Answer d is incorrect because the **DBA_ROLE_PRIVS** view lists roles granted to users and roles.

Question 19

Answer d is correct. Buffers waiting to be written to disk are on the dirty list and cannot be overwritten. Answer a is incorrect because empty buffers are ready for use and do not need to be written to disk. Answer b is incorrect because the concept of a null buffer doesn't exist. Answer c is incorrect because buffers currently being accessed are on the least recently used (LRU) list and have not yet been moved to the dirty list.

Question 20

Answers d and e are correct. During a direct-load insert, users can be concurrently modifying existing data in the table. Also, the buffer cache is bypassed to speed up the insert. Answer a is incorrect because redo information is not generated during a direct-load insert. Answer b is incorrect because direct-load insert does not create any indexes. Answer c is incorrect because data is loaded above the high-water mark, not below it.

Question 21

Answers d, e, and f are correct. The **DROP, ENABLE,** and **DISABLE** can be taken on a constraint. Answer a is incorrect because an **ALTER CONSTRAINT** command does not exist; constraints are changed by the **ALTER TABLE** command. Answer b is incorrect because the **CREATE CONSTRAINT** command does not exist; constraints are created through the **CREATE TABLE** or **ALTER TABLE** command. Answer c is incorrect because constraints cannot be deleted—they must be dropped. This question is a little tricky because, although the behavior of constraints can change and constraints can obviously be created, the commands that perform these tasks are taking action on a table and not on the constraint directly.

Question 22

Answer c is correct. In a database block, row data is stored in the bytes allocated for free space, which then becomes part of the data space. Answer a is incorrect because the header contains general block information, such as the block address and the type of segment (for example, data, index, or rollback). Answer b is incorrect because the table directory holds information about the tables having rows in this block. Answer d is incorrect because the row directory contains information about the actual rows in the block.

Question 23

Answer c is correct. To drop a redo log member from an active group, cause a log switch first by using the **ALTER SYSTEM SWITCH LOGFILE** command, and then use the **ALTER DATABASE DROP LOGFILE MEMBER** command after the archiving of the logfile is complete. You must cause a log switch so the log group is not active. Answer a is incorrect because the log group must be archived before you use the **ALTER DATABASE DROP LOGFILE MEMBER** command. Since the question specifically says the log member to be dropped is part of the active group, it cannot have been archived yet. Answers b and d are incorrect because, if the database is in **ARCHIVELOG** mode, you cannot drop an online member until it has been archived. If the group is active, you must force a log switch before dropping one of its members.

Question 24

Answer c is correct. You can specify a maximum of eight control files in the **CONTROL_FILES** parameter.

Question 25

Answer a is correct. The catalog.sql script creates the data dictionary views to decode and summarize the data in the base tables. Answer b is incorrect because the catproc.sql script runs required scripts for PL/SQL use in the database. Answer c is incorrect because the dbmsutil.sql script creates the **DBMS_ TRANSACTION, DBMS_SESSION, DBMS_DDL, DBMS_UTILITY, DBMS_APPLICATION_INFO, DBMS_SYSTEM, DBMS_SPACE,** and

DBMS_ROWID packages. Answer d is incorrect because the sql.bsq script creates the base data dictionary tables.

Question 26

Answer c is correct. The **DICTIONARY** data dictionary view provides an overview for all the data dictionary views. Answer a is incorrect because **DB_VIEWS** is not a dictionary table. Answer b is incorrect because the **DBA_VIEWS** view contains the text of all views in the database. Answer d is incorrect because **DBA_VIEW_DATA** is not a dictionary table or view.

Question 27

Answer b is correct. If at least one member of the current group is accessible, the Oracle Server ignores the corrupt members. Answer a is incorrect because the database can write to the available log member, so the database will not hang. Answer c is incorrect because the instance will not crash unless all log members are corrupted. Answer d is incorrect because Oracle will not reformat corrupted log members.

Question 28

Answer b is correct. The control file records the structure of the database, including the time that the database was created. Answer a is incorrect because there is no concept of database file headers in Oracle. Tablespaces have datafiles headers, which have information about the datafile and the last checkpoint. Answer c is incorrect because Oracle does not write back to parameter files. Parameter files contain parameter settings used for performance tuning, administration, and file locations, but not the database creation timestamp. Answer d is incorrect because the redo log files contain information for recovery. Answer e is incorrect because rollback segments keep before images of all changed data that is not committed.

Question 29

Answer c is correct. **PCTFREE** determines the percentage of space in each block that is reserved for updates. Answer a is incorrect because **INITRANS** specifies the initial number of transaction entries allocated within each data block allocated to the table. Answer b is incorrect because **MAXTRANS** is the limit of concurrent transactions allowed in a data block. Answer d is incorrect because **PCTUSED** is the amount of space that Oracle maintains in each data block for inserts.

Question 30

Answer a is correct. The **AUTOEXTEND** clause can be used with the **ALTER TABLESPACE** command to enable automatic extension of an existing datafile. Answer b is incorrect because datafiles can be dropped only if the tablespace is dropped. Answer c is incorrect because you cannot extend Oracle datafiles by using OS commands. Answer d is incorrect because when a datafile is being moved, the file in the new location must be an exact copy of the original file; it cannot be made larger.

Question 31

Answer d is correct. The correct sequence of steps to move a datafile is to take the tablespace offline, move the files using OS commands, issue the **ALTER TABLESPACE RENAME DATAFILE** command and then bring the tablespace back online. Answer a is incorrect because you must move the datafile before using the **ALTER TABLESPACE** command. Answer b is incorrect because the datafile must be offline before you use the **ALTER TABLESPACE** command. Answer c is incorrect because the **ALTER TABLESPACE** command should be executed before the tablespace is brought back online.

Question 32

Answer b is correct. You need the **ALTER SYSTEM** privilege to use the **ALTER SYSTEM** command. Answer a is incorrect because the **RESTRICTED SESSION** privilege allows users to connect to a database that has been started (or altered to be) in restricted mode. Answer c is incorrect because the **ALTER DATABASE** privilege allows you to add datafiles to the database, but it does not give you the privilege to put a database into restricted mode. Answer d is incorrect because the **ALTER RESOURCE COST** privilege allows you to set costs for resources used in a session, but it does not give you the ability to put a database into restricted mode. Answer e is incorrect because **ENABLE RESTRICTED SESSION** is a clause of the **ALTER SYSTEM** command, not a privilege.

Question 33

Answer c is correct. The **QUOTA** clause defines the amount of space that a user can use to create objects in a specified tablespace. Answer a is incorrect because the **DEFAULT TABLESPACE** clause specifies the tablespace to be used if a tablespace is not provided in a **CREATE** or **ALTER** statement. Answer b is incorrect because the **PROFILE** clause can be used to manage resources such as CPU, session idle time, or logical reads per session, but not space allocation in tablespaces. Answer d is incorrect because the **TEMPORARY TABLESPACE** clause specifies the tablespace to be used for temporary segments.

Question 34

Answer a is correct. To deallocate unused space while keeping a specified number of bytes above the high-water mark, use the **KEEP** option as follows:

```
ALTER TABLE table_name DEALLOCATE UNUSED KEEP integer K/M;
```

Answer b is incorrect because the **CACHE** option is used to control how rows from the table are placed on the least recently used (LRU) list in the buffer cache during a full-table scan. Answer c is incorrect because **DEALLOCATE UNUSED** deallocates all unused space above the high-water mark unless the **KEEP** option is used. Answer d is incorrect because **MODIFY** is used to change the definition of existing columns.

Question 35

Answer f is correct. The **SELECT_CATALOG_ROLE** role allows users to query the DBA data dictionary views. Answer a is incorrect because although the **DBA** role gives users the ability to query the DBA data dictionary views, it also gives complete administrative capabilities to the database. The question states that you just want the users to be able to view the DBA dictionary views. This option makes this question tricky to answer. Answer b is incorrect because the **EXECUTE_CATALOG_ROLE** grants execute privileges on package procedures supplied with the database. Answer c is incorrect because the **RESOURCE** role grants **CREATE CLUSTER, CREATE PROCEDURE, CREATE SEQUENCE, CREATE TABLE,** and **CREATE TRIGGER** to users. Grantees of **RESOURCE** also get a separate grant of **UNLIMITED TABLESPACE**. Answer d is incorrect because the **EXP_FULL_DATABASE** role allows users to do an export of the database with the **FULL** option. Answer e is incorrect because the **PLUSTRACE** role gives users the privilege to use the **AUTOTRACE** function in SQL*Plus.

Question 36

Answer c is correct. The **STORAGE** clause includes the **INITIAL, NEXT, PCTINCREASE,** and **MAXEXTENTS** values, which control how extents are allocated to a table. Answer a is incorrect because **PCTFREE** specifies the percentage of space in each data block of the table that is reserved for future updates to the table's rows. Answer b is incorrect because **EXTENT** is an invalid option of the **CREATE TABLE** command. Answer d is incorrect because **LOGGING/NOLOGGING** controls the logging of the **CREATE** statement to the redo log file. Answer e is incorrect because **DEFAULT** is used to provide a default value for a column when a row is inserted without a value for the column.

Question 37

Answer b is correct. **DBA_CONSTRAINTS** displays the names and types of constraints in the database. Answer a is incorrect because **ALL_CONSTRAINTS** lists constraint definitions only on tables accessible to the user. Answer c is incorrect because **DBA_CATALOG** lists all database tables, views, synonyms, and sequences. Answer d is incorrect because **USER_CONSTRAINTS** lists constraint definitions on only the current user's tables.

Question 38

Answer a is correct. Because the control file records the database structure, the control file is read when a database is mounted by an instance. Answer b is incorrect because the control file for the database will not be read if the instance is started with the **NOMOUNT** option; **NOMOUNT** only starts the instance. Answer c is incorrect because the database will mount before it is opened, so the control file will have already been read before the database is opened. Answer d is incorrect because **RESTRICTED SESSION** controls access to the database and has no effect on when the control file is read.

Question 39

Answer c is correct. User processes are not part of an Oracle instance. Answers a, b, and d are incorrect because the shared pool, redo log buffer, and data buffer cache are all part of the instance's system global area (SGA).

Question 40

Answer c is correct. A tablespace should be in read-only mode to ensure that no changes are made while the tablespace is being prepared for transport. Answer a is incorrect because a tablespace does not need to be offline to be transported. Answer b is incorrect because transporting a tablespace in read-write mode runs the risk of data inconsistency between the time of starting the transportation and the time of ending it. Answer d is incorrect because tablespaces should be transported in read-only mode.

Question 41

Answer b is correct. The **ALTER USER** command is used to specify the default roles for a user. Answer a is incorrect because the **CREATE ROLE** command is used to create new roles. Answer c is incorrect because **ASSIGN ROLE** is an invalid command. Answer d is incorrect because **SET ROLE** is used to enable a role that a user has been granted but that is not being used.

Question 42

Answer d is correct. **DBA_SYS_PRIVS** displays system privileges granted to all users and roles. Answer a is incorrect because **DBA_ROLES** lists all roles that exist in the database. Answer b is incorrect because **ALL_COL_PRIVS_RECD** lists grants on columns for which the user or **PUBLIC** is the grantee. Answer c is incorrect because **USER_SYS_PRIVS** lists system privileges granted to the currently connected user only.

Question 43

Answer c is correct. **USER_** views provide information on objects owned by the user, so they do not contain the **OWNER** column, because this would be redundant. Answer a is incorrect because **ALL_** views have an **OWNER** column, providing information on all objects accessible by the user. Answer b is incorrect because **DBA_** views provide information on all the objects in the database and have an **OWNER** column.

Question 44

Answer b is correct. Temporary sort segment extents are released when the database is shut down. Otherwise, they are reused for the next sort request, so answers a, c, and d are all incorrect.

Question 45

Answer d is correct. **DBA_TS_QUOTAS** displays the names of tablespaces that any database user has a quota on, the number of bytes and blocks used, and the user's quota in bytes and blocks. Answer a is incorrect because the **USER_TS_QUOTAS** view lists information about tablespace quotas for the user performing the query. Answer b is incorrect because the **USER_TABLESPACES** view lists descriptions of accessible tablespaces. Answer c is incorrect because the

DBA_TABLESPACES view lists descriptions of all tablespaces. Answer e is incorrect because the DBA_USERS view lists information about all users of the database, but it does not contain quota information.

Question 46

Answer c is correct. The objects created by the user remain, but no new extents can be allocated to the objects. Answer a is incorrect because altering a user's quota does not truncate tables. Answer b is incorrect because altering a user's quota has no effect on table accessibility. Answer d is incorrect because altering a user's quota does not drop tables.

Question 47

Answer a is correct. Oracle creates temporary segments when sorting cannot be done in memory. Answer b is incorrect because tables cannot be created in tablespaces that have been taken offline. Answer c is incorrect because tables that are created without a specified tablespace are created in the user's default tablespace. Answer d is incorrect because there is no need to roll back a sort operation.

Question 48

Answer d is correct. The DBA_CONSTRAINTS view displays the names and types of all the constraints in the database and their current status. Answer a is incorrect because the DBA_TABLES view lists descriptions of all tables in the database. Answer b is incorrect because the DBA_CATALOG view lists all database tables, views, synonyms, and sequences. Answer c is incorrect because the PUBLIC_DEPENDENCY view lists dependencies to and from objects, by object number. Answer e is incorrect because the DBA_CONS_COLUMNS view lists information about accessible columns in constraint definitions.

Question 49

Answer a is correct. The data dictionary tables are created in the SYS schema. Answer b is incorrect because SYSTEM is a user that owns some of the data dictionary views that database users query, but not the base data dictionary tables. Answers c and d are incorrect because SYSDBA and SYSOPER are roles granted to a user and do not own any tables.

Question 50

Answer c is correct. The **V$THREAD** view displays the current redo log group, the number of online redo log groups, and the current sequence number. Answer a is incorrect because the **V$DATABASE** view lists database information, including the log mode, but not the current log group or the sequence number. Answer b is incorrect because the **V$INSTANCE** view lists the state of the current instance and does not contain any log group information. Answer d is incorrect because the **V$LOGFILE** view lists information about redo log files, but it does not include the sequence number.

Question 51

Answer b is correct. The order of import is table definitions, table data, indexes on the table, integrity constraints, triggers, bitmap indexes.

Question 52

Answer d is correct. Export/import utilities are used to move tables, their associated objects, and their data from one user to another. Answer a is incorrect because SQL*Loader is used to load data from external files into Oracle tables. Although it can be used to move data from one user to another, it can't create the tables as well. Answer b is incorrect because direct-load insert writes data directly into Oracle datafiles without using the buffer cache. Answer c is incorrect because the Oracle Enterprise Manager (OEM) Console can be used to create, edit, and examine schema objects, but it cannot move data from one schema to another.

Question 53

Answer a is correct. Because **PCTINCREASE** is always zero, the second and all other extents will always be the size of **NEXT**. Answer b is incorrect because the **INITIAL** parameter is used only for the initial extent. Answer c is incorrect because SQL*Plus has no **CREATE TEMPORARY SEGMENT** command. Answer d is incorrect because a **PCTINCREASE** of zero will not stop extents from being allocated.

Question 54

Answer c is correct. **DBA_FREE_SPACE** displays the tablespace name, relative file number, file ID, block ID, and size of the extent in Oracle blocks. Answers a and b are incorrect because the **DBA_FREE_SPACE** view does not contain any table information or extent creation dates. Answer d is incorrect because **DBA_FREE_SPACE** contains information about the free space, not the used space, in a tablespace.

Question 55

Answer c is correct. The control file used by SQL*Loader specifies the tables to be loaded. Answer a is incorrect because the log file holds information about the load, such as the number of records loaded/rejected, errors, and so forth. Answer b is incorrect because the discard file contains records that did not meet the specified selection criteria. Answer d is incorrect because the bad file holds records that are rejected because of incorrect data.

Question 56

Answers d and e are correct. **V$PARAMETER** lists the information about the initialization parameters, including the control file name and location. **V$CONTROLFILE** lists the names and locations of the control files and their status. Answer a is incorrect because the **V$DATABASE** view lists database information from the control file, but not the location of the control file. Answer b is incorrect because the **V$DATAFILE** view lists datafile information from the control file, but not information about the control file. Answer c is incorrect because the **V$INSTANCE** view lists the state of the current instance.

Question 57

Answer b is correct. To specify the weights assigned to each limit, use the **ALTER RESOURCE COST** command. Answer a is incorrect because, although the **ALTER DATABASE** command is used for many DBA tasks, it cannot change weights for resource limits. Answer c is incorrect because the **ALTER SYSTEM** command can enable or disable resource limits, but it cannot set or change the weighting. Answers d and e are incorrect because **UPDATE RESOURCE COST** and **ALTER SESSION LIMITS** are invalid SQL commands.

Question 58

Answer b is correct. The segment storage clause has the highest priority. If storage parameters were not specified at the segment level, then the tablespace parameters are used. If the storage parameters were not specified at the segment or tablespace level, then the Oracle Server default values are used. Therefore, answers c and d are incorrect. Answer a is incorrect because storage clauses aren't specified at the extent level.

Question 59

Answer d is correct. The high-water mark in a table is the last block ever used by the table, so 7,000 blocks is correct. Answers a, b, and c are all incorrect because they don't match the last block ever used.

Question 60

Answer e is correct. DBWn writes changed buffers to the datafiles. Answer a is incorrect because SMON performs instance recovery at instance startup. Answer b is incorrect because PMON performs process recovery when a user process fails. Answer c is incorrect because ARCn copies the online redo log files to archival storage when they are full. Answer d is incorrect because LGWR writes redo log entries to disk.

Question 61

Answer a is correct. Oracle recommends that you use four transactions per rollback segment for optimal performance and configuration.

Question 62

Answer d is correct. The **ALTER TABLE** command is used to drop a constraint. Answers a, b, and c are incorrect because they are invalid commands.

Question 63

Answers a and d are correct. If you use the **SHARED** option, the password file recognizes only users SYS and INTERNAL. Answers b and c are incorrect because other DBA accounts, including SYSTEM, will not be able to connect as **SYSDBA** or **SYSOPER**.

Question 64

Answers a and d are correct. The log sequence number in the control file is compared to the log sequence numbers in the headers of the datafiles to ensure they are the same before the database can be started. Answers b and c are incorrect because redo log files and parameter files are not used for comparing log sequence numbers. The parameter file doesn't store the log sequence number at all, and the log sequence number in the redo log files doesn't need to match that of the control files or the datafiles to start a database.

Question 65

Answer b is correct. Releasing resources held by failed transactions is the responsibility of PMON. SMON performs all the remaining tasks specified in the answers.

Glossary

ALTER
A Data Definition Language (DDL) command that changes database objects.

analysis
The step in the system development process at which the users' needs are gathered and analyzed to produce the documentation that is used to design a program system.

ANALYZE
A Data Definition Language (DDL) command that is used to gather statistics for clusters, tables, or indexes, or to validate the structure of these objects.

archive log
An archive copy of the redo log. The archive log is used to recover to an earlier point in time or to roll forward from a backup to the present time. Also known as "archived redo log."

authentication
The process by which Oracle determines if a user should be allowed access to a database.

bad file
A file that contains records that were rejected either by SQL*Loader or by Oracle.

block
The smallest unit of input/output (I/O) that an Oracle database can perform. Once defined for the database, the block size cannot be changed without re-creating the database.

buffer cache
An Oracle memory area that holds data, redo, or Structured Query Language (SQL) statement information. Buffers are specified using the DB_BLOCK_BUFFERS, DB_BLOCK_SIZE, LOG_BUFFER, and SHARED_POOL_SIZE initialization parameters.

cardinality

A term used in relational analysis to show how two objects relate; it tells how many. For example, "A person may have zero or one nose" shows a cardinality of zero or one. "A person may have zero, one, or many children" shows a cardinality of zero through many. And "A person has one or many cells" shows a cardinality of one or many. In reference to indexes, cardinality shows how many rows in an indexed table relate back to the index value. A low-cardinality index, such as a person's sex (M or F), should be placed in a bitmapped index if it must be indexed, whereas a high-cardinality value, such as a person's Social Security number or employee ID, should be placed in a standard B-tree index.

COMMIT

A command that marks a transaction as completed successfully and causes data to be written first to the redo logs and, once DBW*n* writes, to the disk. A **COMMIT** isn't complete until it receives word from the disk subsystem that the redo log write is complete. (Committed data cannot be rolled back using the **ROLLBACK** command and must be removed using more Data Manipulation Language (DML) commands.) Commits are issued either explicitly using the **COMMIT** command or implicitly as the result of a Data Definition Language (DDL) command.

CONNECT

A SQL*Plus command that enables a user to connect to the local or remote database.

control file

An Oracle file that contains information on all database files. The control file must be present and current for the database to start up properly.

conventional path load

The most commonly used form of the SQL*Loader database load utility. A conventional path load uses Data Manipulation Language (DML) statements to load data from flat operating system (OS) files into Oracle tables.

CREATE

A Data Definition Language (DDL) command that allows the creation of database objects or the database itself.

database

The logical and physical structures used to store and retrieve information.

database administrator (DBA)

A person responsible for the operation, maintenance, performance, availability, and recoverability of an Oracle database.

data buffer cache

The part of the system global area (SGA) that is used to store copies of data in memory to reduce input/output (I/O) requirements.

Data Definition Language (DDL)

A category of Structured Query Language (SQL) statements used to create or manipulate database structures. Examples are the **CREATE**, **ALTER**, and **DROP** commands.

data dictionary

A collection of C structs, tables, and views that contain the database metadata (information about the database's data). The data dictionary is used to store information used by all database processes to find out about database data structures.

datafile
An operating system (OS) file created by an Oracle database. A tablespace consists of one or more physical datafiles. A datafile can be associated with only one tablespace.

Data Manipulation Language (DML)
A category of Structured Query Language (SQL) statements that query, insert, update, and delete data in an Oracle database. The SQL commands that make up DML are **SELECT, INSERT, UPDATE**, and **DELETE**.

data segment
A unit that holds all the data in every cluster, nonclustered table, index, or partition in an Oracle database.

DBA
See *database administrator (DBA)*.

DBMS_TTS
A package that is used to check whether a transportable tablespace set is self-contained.

DDL
See *Data Definition Language (DDL)*.

deferred constraint
A constraint that is checked at the end of a transaction rather than on completion of every statement.

DELETE
A Data Manipulation Language (DML) command that removes data

by rows (generally speaking) from database tables.

DESCRIBE
A SQL*Plus command that retrieves information about database structure. Any stored object (except triggers and indexes) can be described.

dictionary-managed tablespace
A tablespace for which Oracle manages free space using data dictionary tables.

direct-load insert
A method of inserting data without logging redo or undo entries that significantly improves the insert performance. A direct-load insert loads records above the current high-water mark (HWM) and can waste space.

direct path load
A way of using the SQL*Loader data loading utility that inserts data directly into the table by prebuilding and then inserting data blocks. Because triggers, some constraints, and indexes are disabled during the load, a direct path load will generally be much faster than a conventional path load.

discard file
A file that contains records that were filtered out of a SQL*Loader load because they did not match any of the record-selection criteria specified in the control file.

DML
See *Data Manipulation Language (DML)*.

DROP

A Data Definition Language (DDL) command that removes database objects.

Export

A utility that extracts the object definitions and table data from an Oracle database and stores them in an Oracle binary-format export dump file.

extended ROWID

ROWID format introduced in Oracle8, composed of the data object number, the relative file number, the block number, and the row number.

extent

A logical unit of database storage space allocation composed of a number of contiguous data blocks.

foreign key

A value or set of values mapped from a primary or parent table into a dependent or child table and used to enforce referential integrity. A foreign key must be either NULL or exist as a primary or unique key in a parent table.

function

One of several structures. An implicit function is one that is provided as a part of the Structured Query Language (SQL), whereas an explicit function is one that is created by the user using PL/SQL. A function must return a value and must be named. As a part of the SQL standard, a function cannot change a database's or package's state, but can act on only external variables and values.

GRANT

A command used to grant object-level and system-level privileges to users and roles.

High-water mark (HWM)

An indication of the highest level of a database table being utilized. A table can reclaim empty space between currently filled blocks and the HWM only through a rebuild or truncation process. To get an accurate reading on how much space is actually used in a table, you must count the blocks used, not simply perform a count of used extents, because used extents are counted up to the HWM.

HWM

See *high-water mark (HWM)*.

Import

Utility that reads the dump file produced by the Export utility and inserts the data objects into the database.

index

A structure that enhances data retrieval by providing rapid access to frequently queried column values. Indexes can be either B-tree structured or bitmapped. Two general types of indexes exist: unique and nonunique. A unique index forces all values entered into its source column to be unique, whereas a nonunique index allows for repetitive and null values to be entered into its source column. Generally speaking, a column with high cardinality should be indexed using a B-tree type index (standard, default type of index), whereas low-cardinality values should be indexed using a bitmapped index.

INITIAL

A storage parameter that sets the size in bytes (no suffix in Oracle), kilobytes ("K" suffix), or megabytes ("M" suffix) of the initial extent allocated to a table, index, rollback segment, temporary segment, or cluster.

INITRANS

A storage parameter that reserves space in the block header for the transaction records associated with a table's blocks.

INSERT

A Data Manipulation Language (DML) command that enables users to place new records into a table.

instance

The system global area (SGA) and the background processes make up an Oracle instance.

locally managed tablespace

A tablespace in which extent management is handled by a bitmap in the header of the data file.

MAXEXTENTS

A parameter that sets the maximum number of extents an object can grow into. The default value for **MAXEXTENTS** is based on block size. Since version 7.3 of Oracle, this value can be set to **UNLIMITED**.

MAXTRANS

A companion to the **INITRANS** storage parameter, **MAXTRANS** sets the maximum number of transactions that can concurrently access a block.

MTS

See *multithreaded server (MTS)*.

multithreaded server (MTS)

Oracle allows multiplexing of database connections through MTS configuration. MTS consists of a listener process, one or more dispatcher processes, and multiple shared server processes. The server processes serve multiple user connections to the database. This multiplexing of database connections allows more users than would normally be serviced to use the database. It is especially useful on systems that are short on physical memory.

NEXT

A storage parameter that specifies the size in bytes (no suffix in Oracle), kilobytes ("K" suffix), or megabytes ("M" suffix) of the **NEXT** extent allocated to a table, index, rollback segment, temporary segment, or cluster. The **NEXT** parameter is used with the **PCTINCREASE** parameter to determine the size of all extents after the **INITIAL** and **NEXT** extents.

OEM Console

See *Oracle Enterprise Manager (OEM) Console*.

Oracle Enterprise Manager (OEM) Console

A graphical user interface (GUI) that allows you to manage multiple databases through a single interface.

ORAPWD

A generalized term for the Oracle password utility that creates and maintains the external password file. The external password file tells Oracle Enterprise Manager (OEM) and SQL*Plus who is authorized to perform database administrator (DBA) functions against a specific database.

OSDBA

A role assigned to users who are authorized to create and maintain Oracle databases. A user given the **OSDBA** role is authenticated by the operating system (OS).

OSOPER

A role assigned to users who are authorized to maintain Oracle databases. A user given the **OSOPER** role is authenticated by the operating system (OS).

package

A stored PL/SQL construct made of related procedures, functions, exceptions, and other PL/SQL constructs. Packages are called into memory when any package object is referenced. They are created or dropped as a unit.

PCTFREE

A parameter used in an Oracle block to determine the amount of space reserved for future updates. A **PCTFREE** that is too low can result in row migration and/or possibly row chaining for frequently updated tables, and a value that's too high requires more storage space.

PCTINCREASE

A parameter determining the percentage by which each subsequent extent after **INITIAL** and **NEXT** grows over the previously allocated extent. Not valid for rollback segments.

PCTUSED

A parameter determining when a block is placed back on the free block list. When used space in a block drops below **PCTUSED**, the block can be used for subsequent new row insertion.

PGA

See *program global area (PGA)*.

primary key

In a relational database, the unique identifier for a table. A primary key must be unique and not null. A primary key can either be natural (derived from a column or columns in the database) or artificial (drawn from a sequence).

procedure

A stored PL/SQL object that can—but isn't required to—return a value. Procedures are allowed to change a database or package state. Procedures can be placed into packages.

profile

A set of resource allocations that can be assigned to a user. It limits idle time, connect time, memory, and CPU usage, as well as enables password verification.

program global area (PGA)

The memory area allocated to each process that accesses an Oracle database.

read-only tablespace

A tablespace that has been placed in read-only mode, allowing queries but no writes to the tablespace.

RECOVER
A command used in SQL*Plus to explicitly perform database recovery operations.

redo
Records generated in the online redo logs that record all changes to the database.

redo log buffer cache
A memory structure inside the system global area (SGA) that buffers writes to the redo logs. The redo log buffer cache is sized by the LOG_BUFFERS parameter.

referential integrity
The process by which a relational database maintains record relation-ships between parent and child tables via primary key and foreign key values.

rejected record
In SQL*Loader, a record that does not meet load criteria for the table being loaded, either due to value, datatype, or other restrictions.

restricted ROWID
The ROWID format used in Oracle7, composed of three elements: the block number, the row number, and the file number.

role
A group of system and/or object privileges that can be granted directly to users or to other roles.

ROLLBACK
A command that undoes uncommit-ted database changes.

rollback segment
A database object that contains records used to undo database transactions. Whenever a parameter in the database refers to UNDO, it is actually referring to rollback segments.

row chaining
An action that occurs when a row is too large to fit into one data block when it is first inserted. It is thus stored in more than one data block reserved for that segment.

ROWID
The unique identifier that identifies each row in an Oracle database.

row migration
An action that occurs when a row that originally fit into one data block is updated so that the row length increases and not enough free space exists for the update in the current block. When this happens, Oracle migrates the data for the entire row to a new data block. A pointer is maintained in the original row piece of the migrated row to point to the new block containing the migrated row. Thus, the ROWID of the migrated row does not change.

segment
A set of extents that contains all the data for a specific logical storage structure within a tablespace.

SELECT
A Data Manipulation Language (DML) command that retrieves values from a database.

SET
A SQL*Plus command that changes the values of SQL*Plus environment parameters, such as line width and page length.

SGA

See *system global area (SGA)*.

shared pool

Part of the system global area (SGA), used to store the data dictionary cache and the library cache. Sized by the **SHARED_POOL_SIZE** initialization parameter.

SHOW

A SQL*Plus command that shows the value of a variable set with the **SET** command.

SHUTDOWN

The command that shuts down the database. This command has four modes: **NORMAL** prohibits new connections, waits for all users to log off, and then shuts down; **TRANS-ACTION AL** prohibits new connections, waits to the end of existing transactions, logs users off, and then shuts down; **IMMEDIATE** prohibits new connections, backs out uncommitted transactions, logs users off, and then shuts down; **ABORT** shuts down immediately and not gracefully.

SPOOL

A SQL*Plus command that sends output to either a printer or a file.

SQL

See *Structured Query Language (SQL)*.

SQL*Loader

A utility to load raw data into an Oracle database.

SQL*Loader control file

A file that specifies how to interpret data to be loaded, the tables and columns to insert the data into, and,

optionally, input datafile management information.

STARTUP

A command used to start up a database. A database can be started in one of several modes: **NOMOUNT, MOUNT, OPEN, EXCLUSIVE,** or **PARALLEL.**

STORAGE

The clause that Oracle uses to determine current and future settings for an object's extents. If a storage clause isn't specified, the object's storage characteristics are taken from the tablespace's **DEFAULT STORAGE**clause. If there is no **DEFAULT STORAGE** clause for the tablespace, the database's defaults are used.

Structured Query Language (SQL)

The standard language used to access and process data in a relational database.

SYSDBA

A role that has the same privileges as the **OSDBA** role. Users assigned the **SYSDBA** role are authenticated through the Oracle password file.

SYSOPER

A role that has the same privileges as the **OSOPER** role. Users assigned the **SYSOPER** role are authenticated through the Oracle password file.

system global area (SGA)

The database buffers, shared pool, and queue areas that are globally accessible by all database processes. The SGA is used to speed Oracle processing by providing for caching of data and structure information in memory.

table
The structure used to store data in an Oracle database. Entities map to tables in relational databases.

table mode export
An export that makes only a logical copy of one or more tables and their related objects, such as triggers, constraints, indexes, and grants.

table mode import
An import that inserts tables and their related objects into an Oracle database from an export file.

tablespace
A logical storage unit in an Oracle database, made up of one or more physical data files. (The database can have multiple tablespaces.)

temporary segment
A temporary workspace that the database uses for intermediate stages of Structured Query Language (SQL) statement parsing and execution. It is typically used for sorts that cannot be done in memory.

temporary table
A table that is used to hold session-private data that exists only for the duration of a transaction or a session.

temporary tablespace
A tablespace that is used for temporary (sort) segments only. A permanent tablespace can contain either permanent or temporary segments, whereas a tablespace that has been designated by either the **CREATE TABLESPACE** or **ALTER TABLESPACE** command as a temporary tablespace can contain only temporary segments.

transportable tablespace
A way of moving an entire tablespace or set of tablespaces from one Oracle database into another.

trigger
A stored PL/SQL program that executes whenever a particular Data Manipulation Language (DML) statement (**INSERT, UPDATE,** or **DELETE**) is executed.

TRUNCATE
A Data Definition Language (DDL) statement that removes all rows from a table. Because it is a DDL statement, it cannot be rolled back.

UGA
See *user global area (UGA)*.

UPDATE
A Data Manipulation Language (DML) command that allows data inside tables to be changed.

user global area (UGA)
The area used to store user-specified variables and stacks.

view
A preset query against one or more tables that is stored in a database and has no physical representation. Also known as a "virtual table."

Index

Bold page numbers indicate sample exam questions.

A

ABORT option, SHUTDOWN command. *See* SHUTDOWN ABORT command.
Account locking, 319, **322**
ADMINISTER DATABASE TRIGGER privilege, 122
Administration
    DBA Management Pack, 46, 52
    managing sessions, 80–82, **358**
    Oracle Enterprise Manager. *See* OEM.
    OS authentication, 42, 43–44, **56**
    password file authentication, 44–45, **56**, 96
    Server Manager, 45, 69, 72–74, **85**
    SQL*Plus, 45–46, 69, **85**, **86**, 332
    SYS and SYSTEM accounts, 42–43, **56**
Administrative scripts, 117–118, **123**
Advanced queuing, 27, 28
Alert file, initialization parameters, 82, **84**
Alert log, 25, 82–83, **84**, **85**
Alerts tab, Events pane, 50
ALL_* data dictionary views, 110, **124**
ALL_OBJECTS data dictionary view, 120
ALL_SOURCE data dictionary view, 119
ALL_TRIGGERS view, 122
ALTER ANY PROCEDURE privilege, 120
ALTER ANY ROLE command, **354**

ALTER command, 120
ALTER DATABASE command, 26, 72, 74, 143, 146, 167, 173
ALTER DATABASE ARCHIVELOG command, 138
ALTER DATABASE BACKUP CONTROLFILE command, 168
ALTER DATABASE CLEAR LOGFILE command, 140, **157**
ALTER DATABASE CLOSE command, 74
ALTER DATABASE DISMOUNT command, 74
ALTER DATABASE DROP LOGFILE MEMBER command, **348**
ALTER DATABASE MOUNT command, 72
ALTER DATABASE OPEN command, 72, **86**
ALTER DATABASE RENAME FILE command, 145, **157**
ALTER INDEX command, 246, 247
ALTER INDEX ALLOCATE EXTENT command, 246
ALTER INDEX DEALLOCATE EXTENT command, 247
ALTER INDEX REBUILD command, 247
ALTER PACKAGE command, **126**
ALTER privilege, 301
ALTER PROFILE command, 317
ALTER RESOURCE COST command, **358**

ALTER ROLE command, 310
ALTER ROLLBACK SEGMENT
  command, 203, 206, 209, **220**
ALTER SESSION command, 78, 79,
  142, 331, 334
ALTER SYSTEM command, 26, 63, 78,
  79, 80, 81, **87**, 215, 320
ALTER SYSTEM CHECKPOINT
  command, 137, 142
ALTER SYSTEM DEFERRED
  command, 78, **87**
ALTER SYSTEM DISABLE
  RESTRICTED SESSION command,
  80, 82
ALTER SYSTEM ENABLE
  RESTRICTED SESSION command,
  80, 81, **351**
ALTER SYSTEM FLUSH
  SHARED_POOL command, 23
ALTER SYSTEM KILL SESSION
  command, 81
ALTER SYSTEM SWITCH
  LOGFILE command, 137, 142, 145,
  149, **348**
ALTER SYSTEM privilege, **351**
ALTER TABLE command, 225,
  232–233, 235, **258**, **351**, **360**
ALTER TABLESPACE command,
  169, 170, 171, 173, **176**
ALTER TABLESPACE ALLOCATE
  EXTENT command, 235
ALTER TABLESPACE
  AUTOEXTEND command, **350**
ALTER TABLESPACE MINIMUM
  EXTENT command, **178**
ALTER TABLESPACE RENAME
  DATAFILE command, **176**, **350**
ALTER USER command, 294, 312, 316,
  319, **353**
ALTER USER ACCOUNT LOCK
  command, **322**
ALTER USER privilege, 294
ALWAYS_ANTI_JOIN parameter, 64
ALWAYS_SEMI_JOIN parameter, 64
ANALYZE command, 22, 241
AQ_ADMINISTRATOR_ROLE
  role, 314
AQ_TM_PROCESSES parameter,
  28, 64
AQ_USER_ROLE role, 314
Architecture, 14–29, 30–38

ARCHIVELOG mode, 98, 138, 146
Archive redo log files, 138
Archiver processes. *See* ARC*n* processes.
Archiving, 26, 138, **348**
ARCHIVING_LOG_START
  parameter, 26, 139
ARC*n* processes, 26, 138
AUDIT command, 306
Audit files, 305
Auditing, 305–308, **345**
Audit trail table, 307
Authentication, 43, **56**, 290
  OS authentication, 42, 43–44, **56**
  password file authentication, 44–45,
    56, 96
AUTOEXTEND clause, 99, 160, 165,
  166, 167

B

BACKGROUND_DUMP_DEST
  parameter, 64, 82, **84**
Background processes, 14, 18, 23–28, **32**,
  82, **85**, **359**
Backups, 138
Bad file, SQL*Loader, 264, **285**
Base data dictionary tables, 108–109
Bitmap indexes, 186, 244–245, **256**
Blocking sessions, 215
Block size, 16, 20
Bootstrap segment, 189
Bounce, 63
B-tree indexes, 186, 242–245
BUFFER_POOL clause, 21
BUFFER_POOL_KEEP parameter,
  21–22, 64
BUFFER_POOL_RECYCLE
  parameter, 22, 64
Buffer pools, data buffer cache, 21

C

CACHE clause, 21
Cache hit, 20
Cache miss, 20
Cache segment, 189
Call level limit, error messages, 320
catalog.sql script, 109, 117, **126**
cataudit.sql script, 118, **125**
catexp.sql script, **125**
catnoaud.sql script, 118
catno*.sql scripts, 118
catproc.sql script, 117, 120, **125**, **126**
cat*.sql scripts, 118, **123**

Change vectors, 15
Character encoding set, 330
CHARACTER SET keyword,
98, 330, **336**
Character sets, 95, 330
Checkpoint process. *See* CKPT process.
Checkpoints, 137, 142, **177**
CKPT process, **32–34**, 131, 137
Clock frequency, dirty buffers and, 21
Cluster key, 185
Clusters, 185
COMMIT command, 203
Commit processing, 28–29, 30, 30–34
Common services, 46, 51
COMPATIBLE parameter, 65
Composite indexes, 186, 242
COMPRESS parameter, 283
Concatenated indexes, 242, **257**
CONNECT role, 314
CONNECT_TIME parameter, 320
Constraints, 249–250, **258–259**, 344, 346,
352, 355, 360
        data dictionary views, 254, 352, 355
        deferred constraint checking, 250,
        259
        disabling, **258**
        dropping, **360**
        enforcement modes, 250
CONTROLFILE REUSE clause,
98, **103**
Control files, 15–16, **35**, **36**, **101**,
153–155, 343, 346, 349, 358, 360
        contents, 130–131
        creating, 130
        dynamic performance views,
        132–135
        location, **153**, **342**
        managing, 130
        mirroring, 131–132
        multiplexing, 131–132
        naming, **153**
        nonreusable section, 130
        reusable section, 130
        SQL*Loader, 264, **282**, **357**
        uses of, 130
CONTROL_FILES parameter, 58, 65,
96, 98, 99, **101–102**, 132, **153**, **154**
Conventional path loads, SQL*Loader,
264–265
CORBA components, 52
CORE_DUMP_DEST parameter, 84
CPU_PER_CALL parameter, 320

CPU_PER_SESSION parameter, 320
CREATE ANY PROCEDURE
        privilege, 298
CREATE ANY TABLE privilege, 298
CREATE ANY TRIGGER
        privilege, 122
CREATE_BITMAP_AREA_SIZE
        parameter, 246
CREATE CONTROLFILE command,
130, 168
CREATE DATABASE command, 96,
97–100, **102–105**, 108, 130, 330, **343**
CREATE GLOBAL TEMPORARY
        TABLE command, 230
CREATE INDEX command, **345**
CREATE PROCEDURE privilege, 298
CREATE PROFILE command,
316, 317
CREATE PUBLIC ROLLBACK
        SEGMENT command, 203, 205
CREATE ROLE command, 309
CREATE ROLLBACK SEGMENT
        command, 203, 205, **217**
CREATE SESSION privilege, 298
CREATE TABLE command, 187, 224,
228–230, **352**
CREATE TABLE privilege, 298
CREATE TABLESPACE command,
160–165
CREATE TABLESPACE privilege, 298
CREATE TEMPORARY
        TABLESPACE command, 168
CREATE TRIGGER privilege, 121
CREATE USER command,
291–294, 316
CREATE USER privilege, 298

D

Data
        Export utility, 270–276, 279, **283**,
        284, **286**, 356
        Import utility, 270–271, 276–279,
        282, **284**, **285**, 356
        loading, 262–270
        transportable tablespaces,
        279–281, **286**
Database. *See* Oracle database.
Database auditing, 305–308, **345**
Database buffer, 19
Database buffer cache, 19, 20, **35**, 359
Database character set, 95, 330–331, **337**

Database Configuration Assistant.
    See DBCA.
Database event trigers, 121–122
Database files, location, 92
Database triggers, 121, 249
Database Writer. *See* DBW*n* process.
Data blocks, 16–17, 189–191
Data buffer cache, 20–22, 24, **30–32**
Data Definition Language commands.
    See DDL commands.
Data dictionary, 14, 23, 108, **349**
    querying, 110–111, 119–120, **124**
    read-only, 108
    SYS account, 42
    SYSTEM account, 43
    updating, **124**
    uses of, 109–110
Data dictionary cache, 22, 23, **31**
Data dictionary tables, 43, 108, 125,
    321, **355**
Data dictionary views, 108, **349**
    ALL_*, 110, 119, 120
    archive log files, 138–139
    auditing, 307–308
    constraints, 254, **352, 355**
    constructing, 108–109
    control file names and locations, **358**
    DBA_*, 110–116, 119, 120
    indexes, 248–249, **256, 344**
    National Language Support (NLS),
        334–335, **336, 338**
    object privileges, 304–305, **326**
    profiles, 320
    redo log group, **356**
    roles, 314–315
    rollback segments, 213
    storage, 191–194, **196**
    system privileges, 300
    tables, 240–241, **343**
    tablespaces, 175
    USER_*, 110, 119, 120, **354**
    users, 297, 321
DATAFILE clause, 99
Datafiles, 14, 24, **35, 36, 350, 360**
    checkpoint, 137
    location, 131
    moving, **176, 350**
    naming, 131
    renaming, **84**
Data files, SQL*Loader, 264, **282–285**
Data integrity constraints, 249–254,
    258–259, 344, 346

Data segment, 17, **196, 359**
DBA accounts, 42–43
DBA_ANALYZE_OBJECTS view, 111
DBA_AUDIT_OBJECT view, 307
DBA_AUDIT_SESSION view, 308
DBA_AUDIT_STATEMENT view, 308
DBA_AUDIT_TRAIL view, 308
DBA_BLOCKERS view, 111
DBA_CLU_COLUMNS view, **343**
DBA_CLUSTERS view, 111
DBA_COL_PRIVS view, 111, 304
DBA_COL_TYPES view, 111
DBA_CONS_COLUMNS view, 111, 254
DBA_CONSTRAINTS view, 111, 254,
    352, 355
DBA_DATA_FILES view, 111, **123,**
    175, 191, 192
DBA_DB_LINKS view, 111
DBA_DDL_LOCKS view, 111
DBA_DEPENDENCIES view, 111
DBA_DIMENSIONS view, 111
DBA_DIRECTORIES view, 112
DBA_DML_LOCKS view, 112
DBA_ERRORS view, 112
DBA_EXTENTS view, 112, 191, 193
DBA_FREE_SPACE view, 109, 112,
    191, 194, **199, 357**
DBA_INDEXES view, 112, 248, **256,**
    344
DBA_IND_COLUMNS view, 112, 248
DBA_IND_PARTITIONS view, 112
DBA_IND_SUBPARTITIONS view,
    112
DBA_JOBS view, 112
DBA_JOBS_RUNNING view, 112
DBA_LIBRARIES view, 112
DBA_LOB_PARTITIONS view, 112
DBA_LOBS view, 113
DBA_LOCKS view, 113
DBA Management Pack, 46, 52
DBA_MVIEWS view, 113
DBA_OBJ_AUDIT_OPTS view, 308
DBA_OBJ_PRIVS view, **57**
DBA_OBJECTS view, 113, 120, **124,** 241
DBA_OBJECT_TABLES view, 113
DBA_OUTLINES view, 113
DBA_PART_HISTOGRAMS view, 113
DBA_PART_INDEXES view, 113
DBA_PART_TABLES view, 113
DBA_POLICIES view, 113
DBA_PRIV_AUDIT_OPTS view, 308
DBA_PROFILES view, 113, 321

DBA_QUEUES view, 113
DBA_QUEUE_TABLES view, 113
DBA_REFRESH view, 114
DBA_REFS view, 114
DBA_REPAIR_TABLE view, 114
DBA role, 42, 314, **326**
DBA_ROLE_PRIVS view, 114, 314
DBA_ROLES view, 114, 314, **346**
DBA_ROLLBACK_SEGS view, 114,
   213, 215, **217–218**
DBA_RSRC_CONSUMER_GROUPS
   view, 114
DBA_RSRC_PLANS view, 114
DBA_SEGMENTS view, 114, **124**, 191,
   192–193, 194, **196**, 209, 241
DBA_SEQUENCES view, 114
DBA_SNAPSHOTS view, 114
DBA_SOURCE view, 115, 119
DBA_STMT_AUDIT_OPTS view, 308
DBA_SYNONYMS view, 115
DBA_SYS_PRIVS view, **57**, 115, 315, **354**
DBA_TAB_COLUMNS view, 115
DBA_TAB_HISTOGRAMS view, 115
DBA_TABLES view, 110, 115, 194, 241
DBA_TABLESPACES view, 115, 175,
   191, 192
DBA_TAB_PARTITIONS view, 115
DBA_TAB_PRIVS view, 115, 305
DBA_TAB_SUBPARTITIONS
   view, 115
DBA_TEMP_FILES view, 115, 175
DBA_TRIGGERS view, 115, 122, **125**
DBA_TS_QUOTAS view, 115, **297**, **354**
DBA_TYPES view, 116
DBA_UNUSED_COL_TABS view, 241
DBA_USERS view, 116, **297**, 321, **324**
DBA_* views, 110–116, **124**
DBA_VIEWS view, 116, **123**
DBA_WAITERS view, 116
DB_BLOCK_BUFFERS parameter,
   20, 65
DB_BLOCK_LRU_LATCHES
   parameter, 24
DB_BLOCK_SIZE parameter, 20,
   65, 96
DBCA, 92–94, 100, 108, 135
DB_FILES parameter, 28, 65
DBMA_SESSION.SET_NLS
   procedure, 332–333
DBMS_ALERT package, 118
DBMS_APPLICATION_INFO
   package, 118

DBMS_AQADM package, 118
DBMS_AQ package, 118
DBMS_DDL package, 118
DBMS_DEFER package, 118
DBMS_DEFER_QUERY package, 118
DBMS_DEFER_SYS package, 118
DBMS_DESCRIBE package, 118
DBMS_JOB package, 27, 118
DBMS_LOB package, 118
DBMS_LOCK package, 118
DBMS_LOGMNR package, 118
DBMS_LOGMNR.ADD_LOGFILE
   procedure, 151
DBMS_LOGMNR_D.BUILD
   procedure, 150–151
DBMS_LOGMNR.END_LOGMNR
   procedure, 151
DBMS_LOGMNR.NEW procedure, 151
DBMS_LOGMNR.START_LOGMNR
   procedure, 151
DBMS_OUTPUT package, 118
DBMS_PIPE package, 118
dbms*.plb scripts, 118
DBMS_RANDOM package, 118
DBMS_REFRESH package, 119
DBMS_REPCAT package, 119
DBMS_REPCAT_ADMIN package, 119
DBMS_RESOURCE_MANAGER
   package, 119
DBMS_ROWID package, 119, 226–227
DBMS_SESSION package, 119
DBMS_SHARED_POOL package, 119
DBMS_SNAPSHOT package, 119
DBMS_SPACE package, 119, 120
DBMS_SQL package, 119
dbms*.sql scripts, 118, **123**
DBMS_STATS package, 119
DBMS_TRANSACTION package, 119
DBMS_UTILITY package, 119
dbmsutil.sql script, **126**
DB_NAME parameter, 65, 96, 98,
   104, 130
DBW*n* process, 14, 24, 26, 29, **32–34**,
   137, **359**
DBWR_IO_SLAVES parameter, 23, 24
DB_WRITER_PROCESSES
   parameter, 24, 65
DDL commands, 108
DEFAULT buffer pool, 21
Default space, 290
DEFAULT STORAGE clause,
   25, 172, **178**. *See also* **STORAGE** clause.

Deferred constraint checking, 250, **259**

DEFERRED option, **ALTER SYSTEM** command. *See* **ALTER SYSTEM DEFERRED** command.

Deferred rollback segments, 203, **221**

Deferred write model, 24

DELETE_CATALOG_ROLE role, 307, 314

DELETE privilege, 301

Dependency tree, 120

DESCRIBE command, 85, 120

DICT_COLUMNS data dictionary view, 111

Dictionary cache, **30**

Dictionary file, 150–151

Dictionary-managed tablespaces, 25

DICTIONARY view, 110–111, **123**, **349**

Direct-load inserts, 262–263

Direct path loads, SQL*Loader, 264–266

Dirty buffers, 20–21, **31**, **32**, 137

Dirty list, 20

Dirty read, 188, 202

DISABLE NOVALIDATE keyword, 249

DISABLE VALIDATE keyword, 250

Discard file, SQL*Loader, 264

Discover Nodes, 51

Discovery Services, 51

Disk contention issues, 149

Dispatcher processes. *See* D*nnn* processes.

Dispatchers, 27

DISTRIBUTED_TRANSACTIONS parameter, 27

DML statement, 250

D*nnn* processes, 26

DROP ANY ROLE privilege, 312

DROP PROFILE command, 318

DROP ROLE command, 312

DROP ROLLBACK SEGMENT command, 211

DROP STORAGE clause, 238, **257**

DROP TABLE command, 239–240

DROP TABLESPACE command, 174–175, **177**

DROP USER command, 296

Dynamic initialization parameters, 78–80

Dynamic performance tables, 116

Dynamic performance views, 74, 116
  control files, 132–135
  list, 74–78
  rollback segments, **219**

E

Edit Redo Log Group screen, 140–141

EJB components, 52

ENABLE NOVALIDATE keyword, 250, **258**, **344**

ENABLE VALIDATE keyword, 250, 251

Enterprise Manager. *See* OEM.

Environmental variables, 95, 332, **337**, **339**, **344**

Error messages, 82, 83
  account lock, **322**
  call level limit, 320
  ORA-00028, 82
  ORA-01545, 211
  ORA-01546, 215
  ORA-01555, **220**
  ORA-28000, **322**
  read-consistency errors, 214–215
  resizing datafiles, 167
  rollback segment, 211, **218**
  session-level resource limit, 320
  "snapshot too old," 214–215, **220**
  tablespace with active rollback segments, 215

Event Management System, 46, 51

Event notifications, 50

EVENT parameter, 65

Events pane, OEM, 47, 50

Exam. *See* Oracle OCP exam.

EXECUTE_CATALOG_ROLE role, 314

EXECUTE command, 120

EXECUTE privilege, 301

EXP_FULL_DATABASE role, 314

Export utility, 270–276, 279, **283**, **284**, **286**, **356**

Export Wizard, 274–276

exq command, 273

Extended **ROWID** format, 225

Extent boundary, 215

Extents, 17, **198**, **199**, 204, 235, **354**, **355**

F

FAILED_LOGIN_ATTEMPTS parameter, 319

Fast commits, 29, **33–34**

FAST_START_IO_TARGET parameter, 137, 142

File management, 131

Firing, triggers, 121–122

Fixed views, 74

Fixed-width multibyte character sets, 330–331

FORCE option, **STARTUP** command. *See* **STARTUP FORCE** command.

Fragmented tablespaces, **197**

Free buffers, 20–21, **35**

FREELISTS parameter, 190

Function-based indexes, 242

G

GRANT command, 120, 298, 301, 310, 311

Group commits, 29

Group pane, OEM, 47, 48, 50

H

HASH_AREA_SIZE parameter, 65

Hash clusters, 185

HASH_JOIN_ENABLED parameter, 65

Heap-organized table, 188

Heap table, 188

High-water mark, 236–238, **359**

History tab, Events pane, 50

Hot backups, 138

I

IDENTIFIED BY clause, **341**

IDENTIFIED EXTERNALLY clause, CREATE USER command, 293

IDLE_TIME parameter, 320

IFILE parameter, 63, 66

IMMEDIATE option, SHUTDOWN command. *See* **SHUTDOWN IMMEDIATE** command.

imp command, 276

IMP_FULL_DATABASE role, 314

Import utility, 270–271, 276–279, **282, 284, 285, 356**

Index clusters, 185

Indexes, 186–187, **256–257, 342**
    bitmap indexes, 186, 244–245, **256**
    B-tree indexes, 186, 242–245
    composite indexes, 186, 242
    concatenated indexes, 242, **257**
    creating, 243–246, **345**
    data dictionary views, 248–249, **256, 344**
    function-based indexes, 242
    LOB indexes, 187
    logical classifications, 242
    partitioned indexes, 186–187, 243
    physical classifications, 242–243
    rebuilding, 247–248
    reorganizing, 246–248
    reverse key indexes, 186, 243
    single-column indexes, 242
    space usage, 189
    storage, 242–249
    unique indexes, 242

Index-organized tables. *See* IOT.

INDEX privilege, 301

Index segments, 17, **198**

Initialization file, 16

Initialization parameters, 62
    alert file, 82, **84**
    changing, 63–64
    list, 64–68
    NLS, 332
    setting dynamically, 78

INITIALLY DEFERRED keyword, 251

INITIALLY IMMEDIATE keyword, 251

INITIAL parameter, ALTER TABLE command, 232

init.ora, 62

INITRANS parameter, 189–190, 233

INSERT privilege, 301

INSERT statement, 250, 262

Installer. *See* Oracle Universal Installer.

Instance. *See* Oracle instance.

Instance Manager tool, 52, **54, 55, 57**

Instance recovery, 25, **87, 156**

Integrity constraints, 249–254, **258–259, 344, 346**

Integrity rule, 249

Intelligent Agent, 46, **54**

Interinstance locking, 28

IOT, 187–188

ITEMS table, 184, 185

J

JAVA_POOL_SIZE parameter, 66

JOB_QUEUE_PROCESSES parameter, 27, 66

Job Scheduling System, 46, 51

Jobs pane, OEM, 47, 50–51, **54**

Jserver management, 52

K

KEEP buffer pool. *See* **BUFFER_ POOL_KEEP** parameter.

KEEP option, 21, **351**

Kernel, migrating to another version, 271

KILL SESSION command, 81–82

L

Large objects. *See* LOBs.
Large pool, 19, 23
LARGE_POOL_SIZE parameter, 23, 66
LCK*n* processes, 28
Least recently used list. *See* LRU list.
LGWR processes, 25, 29, 30, 32, 34,
    136–137, **342, 349**
Library cache, 22, 31
LMD, 28
LOAD parameter, **283**
LOB index clause, CREATE TABLE
    statement, 187
LOB indexes, 187
LOBs, 185
LOB segments, 185
Local partitioned indexes, 187
Lock Manager Daemon. *See* LMD.
LOG_ARCHIVE_DEST parameter,
    66, **84**
LOG_ARCHIVE_FORMAT
    parameter, 66
LOG_ARCHIVE_MAX_PROCESSES
    parameter, 26
LOG_ARCHIVE_START parameter,
    66, 138, 139
Log buffer cache, 19, 25, **31**, 137
LOG_BUFFER parameter, 66
LOG_CHECKPOINT_INTERVAL
    parameter, 137, 142, **342**
LOG_CHECKPOINT_TIMEOUT
    parameter, 137
LOGFILE clause, 98, 99, **102, 104**
Log files, SQL*Loader, 264, **284**
LOG_FILES parameter, 136
LOGGING operations, 161
Log groups, 143, **349**
Log history, 131
LOGICAL_READS_PER_CALL
    parameter, 320
LOGICAL_READS_PER_SESSION
    parameter, 320
Logical structure, 16–18
Log members, adding, 143
LogMiner utility, 150–152
Log sequence number, 26, 131, **360**
Log switches, 137, 142, **342**
Log Writer processes. *See* LGWR
    processes.
LRU list, 20
LRU algorithm, 21, 22

M

MAX* clause, 98
MAX_DUMP_FILE_SIZE parameter,
    66, 82
MAX_ENABLED_ROLES parameter,
    67, 312
MAXEXTENTS keyword, **179**, 204,
    205, 208, 214, **219**, 229, 232
MAXLOGDATAFILES parameter,
    98, **101**, 103
MAXLOGFILES parameter, 98, **104**, 136
MAXLOGHISTORY parameter, **104**
MAXLOGMEMBERS parameter,
    98, **104**, 136
MAXTRANS parameter, 189, 190, 233
Media recovery, 149, 150
Millsap, Cary, 41
MINEXTENTS, 205, 208, 215, **220**,
    229, 232
MINIMUM EXTENT keyword,
    161, 172, **178**, 179
Mirroring
    control files, 131–132
    redo log files, 15, 131
Monitoring
    alert and trace files, 82–83, **84, 85**
    Group pane, 50
MOUNT option, STARTUP command.
    See STARTUP MOUNT command.
MTS architecture, 19, 22, 26
MTS_DISPATCHERS parameter, 27
MTS_MAX_DISPATCHERS
    parameter, 27
MTS_MAX_SERVERS parameter, 27
MTS_SERVERS parameter, 27
Multibyte character sets, 330
Multiplexing
    control files, 131–132
    redo log files, 143
Multithreaded server architecture.
    See MTS architecture.

N

National character set, 330–331
NATIONAL CHARACTER SET
    keyword, 98, 330, **336**
National Language Support. *See* NLS.
Navigator pane, OEM, 47–48, 49, 134,
    140, 147, 162, 175
Nested tables, 184–185
Net8 files, 16

NEXT parameter, ALTER TABLE command, 232
NLS, 95, 330–335, **336–339**
  database character set, 330–331, **337**
  database default settings, 331–332
  data dictionary views, 334–335, **336, 338**
  environment variable settings, 332, **337, 339, 344**
  national character set, 330–331
  parameters, 331–334
  session settings, 332–333, **339**
NLS_CURRENCY parameter, 332
NLS_DATABASE_PARAMETERS view, 334, **338**
NLS_DATE_FORMAT parameter, 332
NLS_DATE_LANGUAGE parameter, 331, **338**
NLS_DUAL_CURRENCY parameter, 332
NLS_ISO_CURRENCY parameter, 332
NLS_LANG environmental variable, 332, **337**
NLS_LANGUAGE parameter, 331, 334
NLS_NUMERIC_CHARACTERS parameter, 332
NLS_SESSION_PARAMETERS view, 334, **336**
NLS_SORT parameter, 331
NLS_TERRITORY parameter, 331, 332
NOARCHIVELOG mode, 98
NO AUDIT command, 307
NOLOGGING clause, 262, **345**
NOLOGGING operations, 161
NOMOUNT option, STARTUP command. See STARTUP NOMOUNT command.
Nonreusable section, control file, 130
Non-SYSTEM rollback segment, 203
NORMAL option, SHUTDOWN command. See SHUTDOWN NORMAL command.
NT systems. See Windows NT systems.

O

Object-level auditing, 306
Object privileges, 290, 301–305, **326**
OEM, 40, 46–52, **54–55, 57**
  adding log groups or log members, 143–145
  altering role, 310

altering user, 295
changing storage settings, 172
common services, 46, 51
control files, 134
creating new user, 291–293
creating profile, 316–317
creating roles, 309–310
creating rollback segments, 206–207
creating tablespace, 162–165
dropping redo log groups, 147
dropping tablespace, 175
dropping user, 296–297
Events pane, 47, 50
exporting data, 274–276
extending data files, 166
first tier, 46, 47–51
granting object privileges, 302–303
granting role, 311
Group pane, 47, 48, 50
importing data, 278–279
Jobs pane, 47, 50–51, **54**
Navigator pane, 47–48, 49, 134, 140, 147, 162, 185
OEM Console, 46, 47–51
OEM Repository, 46, 52
Oracle Management Server (OMS), 46, 51
password settings, 317, 318
redo logs, 140
renaming or relocating datafiles, 174
renaming or relocating redo log files, 145
resizing datafiles, 167
revoking role, 312
rollback segments, 211
second tier, 46, 47, 51–52
SQL*Loader, 268–269
tablespace from read-only to read-write, 171
tablespace taken offline, 170
table storage parameters, 234
temporary tablespace, 169
third tier, 46, 47
OEM Console, 46, 47–51
  closing a dtabase, 72–74
  initialization parameters, 63
  opening a database, 69
OEM Repository, 46, 52
OFA, 41–42
OLTP, 16

OMS, 46, 51
ON COMMIT DELETE ROWS
clause, **CREATE GLOBAL
TEMPORARY TABLE** command,
230
ON COMMIT PRESERVE ROWS
clause, **CREATE GLOBAL
TEMPORARY TABLE** command,
230
Online redo log files, 135–138
multiplexing and maintaining, 143
planning, 148–149
Online redo logs, analyzing, 150
Online transaction processing. *See* OLTP.
OPEN_CURSORS parameter, 67
OPEN_LINKS parameter, 28
OPEN option, **STARTUP** command. *See*
STARTUP OPEN command.
Operating system, migrating to new, 271
Operating system authentication.
See OS authentication.
Optimal Flexible Architecture. *See* OFA.
OPTIMAL parameter, 204–205, 208,
214, 215, **220**
OPTIMIZER_MODE parameter, 67
ORA-00028 error message, 82
ORA-01545 error message, 211
ORA-01546 error message, 215
ORA-01555 error message, **220**
ORA-28000 error message, **322**
Oracle
architectural components, 13–29,
30–38
certification page, 9–11
PL/SQL program units, 117–119
Oracle7 character sets, 331
Oracle8, Unicode, 331
Oracle8i, standard packages, 118–119
Oracle9i, 44
ORACLE_BASE, 95
Oracle database, 14–18, **348, 349**
auditing, 305–308
block size, 16
character set, 95
closing, 72–74
crash, 149
creating, 92–100, **101–105, 349**
DBCA, 92–94, 100, 108, 135
defined, 14, 62
dropping, 93, 100
dropping profile, 318
Export utility, 270–276, 279, **283,**
284, 286, 356

identifier, 130
Import utility, 270–271, 276–279,
282, 284, 285, 356
managing sessions, 80–82
manual creation, 94–100
moving data between databases, 271
naming, 95, 130
National Language Support (NLS),
95, 330–335, **336–339**
opening, 69–72, **154, 346**
"owner-manager," 80
planning, 92
PL/SQL, 117–119
read-only mode, 72
restricted mode, 80–81, 82
segments, 17–18
structure, 14–18
terminating sessions, 81–82
troubleshooting, 149
Oracle Enterprise Manager. *See* OEM.
ORACLE_HOME, 95
Oracle Homes, 41
Oracle instance, 14, 18–28, **31**, 62
background processes, 23–28
bouncing, 63
failure, 150, **344**
Instance Manager tool, 52, **54, 55, 57**
managing, 62–83, **84–88**
name, 95
recovery, 25, **87, 156**
SGA, 18, 19–23, **30**
shutting down, 72–74, 137, **157**
starting, 69–72, **154, 346, 353**
Oracle Management Server. *See* OMS.
Oracle OCP exam
checkboxes, 4, 5
exhibits, 5
guessing, 6, 8
multiple-choice questions, 3–5, 7
practice tests, 2, 6, 8–9, 10, **341–360**
radio buttons, 4
readiness for, 2
scoring, 3, 9
setting, 3–4
test layout and design, 3–5
test software, 6
test strategies, 6–9
time given, 3
Web site for, 9–11
Oracle Parallel Server, 14, 203
ORACLE_SID, 95, 96
Oracle Universal Installer. *See* OUI.

Oracle Wrap utility, 119
ORA_NLS33 environmental variable, 95, **337, 344**
ORAPWD utility, 44–45, **55, 324**
ORDERS table, 184, 185
OS authentication, 42, 43–44, **56**
OUI, 40–42

P

Parallel direct loads, SQL*Loader, 266
Parallel execution, 27
Parallel Query processes. *See* P*nnn* processes.
Parallel Server environment, 28
Parameter files, 62, **346**
  creating, 62–69
  editing, 62
  initialization parameters, 62–68
  location of, 62
  SQL*Loader, 264
  syntax rules, 68–69
Parameters
  dynamic initialization parameters, 78–80
  dynamic performance views, 74–78
  syntax for, 68–69
  values for, 74–80
Partitioned indexes, 186–187, 243
Partitioned tables, 184
Password file authentication, 44–45, **56**, 96
Password files, 44, 45, 96
Password file utility, 44
PASSWORD_GRACE_TIME parameter, 319
PASSWORD_LIFE_TIME parameter, 319
PASSWORD_LOCK_TIME parameter, 319
PASSWORD_REUSE_MAX parameter, 319
PASSWORD_REUSE_TIME parameter, 319
Passwords, **324, 341, 346**
  account locking, 319, **322**
  aging and expiration, 319
  changing, 294
  complexity functions, 319
  history, 319
  managing with profiles, 319

settings, 317, 318, **346**
SYS account, 42
SYSTEM account, 43
PASSWORD_VERIFY_FUNCTION parameter, 319
PCTFREE parameter, 190–191, **197**, 231, 233, 246, **350**
PCTINCREASE parameter, 229, 233, **255, 357**
PCTUSED parameter, 190–191, 231, 233
PFILE clause, **STARTUP** command. *See* **STARTUP PFILE** command.
PGA, 22, 28
Physical database structure, 14–16
PL/SQL stored program units, 117–119
PMON processes, 19, 20, 26, **32–34, 82**
P*nnn* processes, 27
Point-in-time recoveries, 138
Predefined roles, 313–314
PRIVATE_SGA parameter, 320
Privilege auditing, 306
Privileges, 290, **322, 341**
  auditing, 306, **345**
  object privileges, 290, 301–305, **326**
  SYSDBA privilege, 42–43, 44, **56, 57**
  SYSOPER privilege, 44, **56, 57, 103, 345**
  system privileges, 290, 297–300
PROCESSES parameter, 67
Process global area. *See* PGA.
Process Monitor processes. *See* PMON processes.
Profiles, 315–321
  altering, 317–318
  controlling resource usage with, 320
  creating, 316–317
  data dictionary views, 320
  defined, 315
  password management, 319
Program global area. *See* PGA.
prvt*.plb scripts, 118, **123**
PUBLIC role, 109
Public synonyms, 109

Q

QMN*n* processes, 27–28
Queue Monitor processes. *See* QMN*n* processes.
QUOTA clause, **325, 351**

R

RBS tablespace, 18
Read-consistency, rollback segments, 188, 202–203
Read-consistency errors, 214–215
Read-only data dictionary, 108
Read-only mode, 72, **353**
Read-only transaction, 202
Read-write tablespace, 170
RECOVER command, 71
Recoverer (RECO) processes, 19, 20, 27
RECOVER option, **STARTUP** command. *See* **STARTUP RECOVER** command.
Recovery
    instance recovery, 25, **87, 156**
    media recovery, 149, 150
    rollback segments, 188, 202
    transactions, **218**
Recovery Manager. *See* RMAN.
RECYCLE buffer pool, 21, 22
Redo log buffer, 19
Redo log buffer cache, 19
Redo log entries, **35, 36**
Redo log files, 15, **155–157, 348**
    adding, 143
    archiving, 138, **348**
    clearing, 147–148
    creating, 130, 135
    dropping, 146–147
    instance recovery, **156**
    location, 149
    managing, 130
    mirroring, 15, 131
    multiplexing and maintaining, 143
    number of, 148
    online, 135–138
    planning, 148–149
    relocating, 145
    renaming, 145–146
    size for, 148–149
    troubleshooting, 149–150
    uses, 135–137
    writing to, 136
Redo log group, 15, **356**
Redo log member, 15, **348**
Redo logs, 15, 25, **34**
    analyzing, 150–152
    ARC*n* process, 26
    format, 150
    LogMiner, 150–152
    mirroring, 15, 131

REFERENCES privilege, 301
Refresh All Nodes, 51
REMOTE_LOGIN_PASSWORD_FILE parameter, 43, 45, **56**, 67, **345, 360**
Replication management, 52
RESIZE command, 167
Resizing, of datafiles, 162–164
RESOURCE_LIMIT parameter, 67, 320
Resource limits, 290, **358**
RESOURCE role, 314, **354**
Resource usage, controlling with profiles, 320
RESTRICTED SESSION privilege, 70, 80, 82
RESTRICT option, **STARTUP** command. See **STARTUP RESTRICT** command.
Reusable section, control file, 130
REUSE option, **SIZE** clause, **102**
REUSE STORAGE clause, 238
Reverse key indexes, 186, 243
REVOKE command, 120, 300, 304, 310, 312
RMAN, 16
Roles, 308–315, **323, 326, 327, 346, 352, 353**
    altering, 310
    avaibility of, 312–313
    benefits, 309
    characteristics, 308–309, **346**
    creating, 309–310
    data dictionary views, 314–315
    dropping, 312
    enabling and disabling, 313
    granting, 311–312
    predefined, 313–314
    revoking, 312
ROLLBACK command, 188, 203
Rollback recovery, 25
Rollback segments, 17, 188, **198–199**, 202, **344, 359**
    adding to tablespace, **55**
    changing storage parameters, 208
    creating, 205–207
    data dictionary views, 213
    deallocating unused space, 208–209
    deferred rollback segments, 203, **221**
    dropping, 211
    dynamic performance views, **219**
    growth of, 204
    maintaining, 208–211
    managing, **54**, 202–216, **217–221**

Non-SYSTEM rollback
  segment, 203
number, 212
offline, 209–210, 215–216
online, **217**
planning, 212–213
read-consistency, 188, 202–203
recovery, 188, 202
shrinkage of, 204–205
size, 212–213, **220**
SYSTEM rollback segment, 203
troubleshooting, 214–216
types, 203
with transactions, 204
ROLLBACK_SEGMENTS parameter,
  67, 203, 206, 207, 209
Rollforward recovery, 25
ROLL_ROLL_PRIVS view, 315
ROLL_SYS_PRIVS view, 315
ROLL_TAB_PRIVS view, 315
Row chaining, 232
Row directory, 17, 189
ROWID_BLOCK_NUMBER, 227
ROWID format, 225–226
ROWID_OBJECT, 227
ROWID_ROW_NUMBER, 227
ROWIDs, 225–228, 244, **255**
ROWID_TO_ABSOLUTE_FNO, 227
ROWID_TO_EXTENDED, 227
ROWID_TO_RESTRICTED, 227
Row migration, 232
Rows, **350**
  ROWIDs, 225–228, 244, **255**
  structure of, 224–225

S

Schema Manager tool, 52, **54, 55, 57**
Schema triggers, 121
SCN, 29, **30**, 202
Scripting, line-mode tools for, 45–46
Scripts, 117–118, **123, 125, 126**
Security. *See also* Users.
  account locking, 319, **322**
  auditing, 305–308, **345**
  authentication, 42–45, **56,** 290
  managing, 290–321, **322–327**
  passwords, 42–45, **56,** 96, 317–319,
    322, 324, 341, 346
  privileges, 290, 297–305, **341**
  profiles, 315–321
  roles, 308–315, **346**
  Security Manager tool, 52, **54, 55, 57**

SYS account, 42–43
SYSTEM account, 42–43
Security Manager tool, 52, **54, 55, 57**
Security Services, 51
Segments, 17–18, 184–189, **354**
  bootstrap segment, 189
  cache segment, 189
  data segments, 17, **196**
  extents, 17, **198, 199,** 204, 235,
    354, 355
  hash clusters, 185
  index clusters, 185
  indexes, 186–187, **198**
  index-organized tables (IOT),
    187–188
  LOB segments, 185
  nested tables, 184–185
  partitioned tables, 184
  rollback segments, 17, **54, 55,** 188,
    198–199, 202–216, **217–221, 344**
  separating, 194–195
  tables, 184
  temporary segments, 17, 188–189, **355**
SELECT_ANY_TABLE privilege,
  124, 322
SELECT_CATALOG_ROLE role,
  109, 314, **352**
SELECT privilege, 301
SELECT statement, 28, 192–193, 248
Server Manager, 45, 69, 72–74, **85**
Server processes, 19, 20
Session-level resource limit, 320, **358**
SESSION_ROLES view, 315, **323**
Sessions
  auditing, 306
  blocking, 215
  managing, 80–82, **358**
  NLS settings, 332–333, **339**
SESSIONS parameter, 67
SESSIONS_PER_USER parameter, **325**
SET ROLE command, 313
SET TRANSACTION READ ONLY
  command, 202
SET TRANSACTION
  SERIALIZABLE command, 203
SGA, 18, 19–23, **30**
Shared global area, 19
Shared pool, 19, **30, 31**
SHARED_POOL_SIZE parameter,
  22, 23, 68
Shared Server processes.
  See S*nnn* processes.

SHOW PARAMETER command, 74, 77, 85, 342

SHOW SGA command, **85**

SHUTDOWN command, 45, 73–74, 86, 87

SHUTDOWN ABORT command, 74, **88**, 137, 138

SHUTDOWN IMMEDIATE command, 73, 74, **86**, 87–88

SHUTDOWN NORMAL command, 73, 74, **86**, 87, 132

SHUTDOWN TRANSACTIONAL command, 73, **86**, 87

SID value, 95

Single-byte character sets, 330

Single-column indexes, 242

SIZE clause, **102**

SMON processes, 19, 20, 25–26, 32–34, **360**

Snapshot processes. *See* SNP*n* processes.

"Snapshot too old" error, 214–215, **220**

"Snapshot too old" error message, 214–215, **220**

S*nnn* processes, 26

SNP*n* processes, 27

SORT_AREA_SIZE parameter, 189

Sort extent pool, 19

SORT_EXTENT_POOL parameter, **346**

sql.bsq script, **125**, **126**

sqlldr command, 273, 276

SQL*Loader, 263–270, **282–285**
   conventional path loads, 264–265
   direct path loads, 264–266
   executing, 266–269
   features, 263–264
   files used, 264, **282**, **284**, **285**, 357
   NLS parameters, 334, **337**
   parallel direct loads, 266
   usage guidelines, 270

SQL*Plus, 45–46, **85**, 86
   location of control files, **85**
   NLS, 332
   opening a database, 69

SQL scripts, 117–118, **123**, **125**, **126**

SQL statements, **31**, 178

SQL_TRACE parameter, 68, 82

STANDARD package, 119, **126**

Standard packages, 108, 118–119

STARTUP command, 45, 70–72, 86, **104–105**

STARTUP FORCE command, 71

STARTUP MOUNT command, 70, 72, 84, 86, **154**

STARTUP NOMOUNT command, 70, 72, 84, 97, **105**

STARTUP OPEN command, 70–71, 72, **86**

STARTUP PFILE command, 71, 97

STARTUP RECOVER command, 71

STARTUP RESTRICT command, 71, **154**

Statement auditing, 306

Storage, 184–195, **196–199**, 358
   data blocks, 16–17, 189–191
   data dictionary views, 191–194, **196**
   indexes, 242–249
   segments, 184–189
   tables, 224–241
   tablespaces, 171–172

STORAGE clause, **358**. *See also*
   DEFAULT STORAGE clause.
   CREATE ROLLBACK
      SEGMENT command, 205, 206
   CREATE TABLE command, 228–230, **352**

Storage Manager tool, 52, **54**, **55**, **57**

Storage objects, Storage Manager tool, 52, **54**, **55**, **57**

Stored program units, 117–119, 119

Striping, tablespaces, 167

Super administrator, 51

SYS account, 42–43, **56**

SYSDBA privilege, 42–43, 44, **56**, **57**

SYSOPER account, **56**

SYSOPER privilege, 44, **56**, **57**, **103**, **345**

SYSTEM account, 42–43, **56**

System change number. *See* SCN.

System global area. *See* SGA.

System identifier value. *See* SID value.

System Monitor processes.
   See SMON processes.

System privileges, 290, 297–300
   data dictionary views, 300
   displaying, 300
   granting, 298–299
   revoking, 300
   system privileges, 299–300

SYSTEM rollback segment, 17, 203

SYSTEM tablespace, 14, 18, 108, **217**, 294, 323

T

Table directory, 16–17, 189
Tables, 184, **255**, **342**, **348**, **351**
   creating, 224, 228–232
   data dictionary tables, 43, 108, 125,
     321, **355**
   data dictionary views, 240–241, **343**
   dropping columns from, 239–240
   heap-organized table, 188
   index-organized tables (IOT),
     187–188
   nested tables, 184–185
   relocating, 235–236
   rows, 224–228
   space used by, 232–235, **351**
   temporary tables, 230
   truncating, 238, **257**
Table segment, 184
TABLES keyword, **286**
TABLESPACE clause, **CREATE
  TABLE** command, 228–230
Tablespace quotas, 290
Tablespaces, 18, 160–175, **176–180**, 217,
  354, **355**, **357**
   adding new datafiles, 166
   changing size of, 165–167, **178**
   creating, 160–165
   data dictionary views, 175
   dropping, 174–175, **177**
   fragmented, **197**
   free space in, **357**
   naming, 131
   read-only mode, **353**
   read-write mode, 170
   relocating, 173–174
   storage settings, 171–172
   striping, 167
   SYSTEM tablespace, 14, 18, 108,
     217, 294, **323**
   taken offline, 170, **177**, 215–216, **350**
   temporary, 18, 290, **354**, **357**
   transportable tablespaces,
     279–281, **286**
Tcl script, 51
TEMPFILE keyword, 168
TEMPORARY clause, 168
Temporary segments, 17, 188–189, **355**
Temporary tables, 230
Temporary tablespace, 18, 290, **354**, **357**
Tickle script. *See* Tcl script.

TIMED_STATISTICS parameter, 68
Tool Command Language script.
  See Tcl script.
Touch count, dirty buffers and, 21
Trace file, 25
Trace files log, monitoring, 82, **85**
TRANSACTIONAL option,
  SHUTDOWN command. *See*
  SHUTDOWN TRANSACTIONAL
  command.
Transaction rollback, 188, 202
Transactions, 204, 214, **218–221**, 359
TRANSACTIONS parameter, 68
Transportable tablespace process,
  279–281, **286**
TRANSPORT_TABLESPACE
  keyword, 280, **286**
Triggers, 121–122, **286**
Troubleshooting
   read-consistency errors, 214–215
   redo log files, 149–150
   rollback segments, 214–216
   transactions, 214, **218**, **220**
TRUNCATE command, 236, 238, **257**

U

Unicode character sets, 330, 331
UNIFORM SIZE clause, 168
Unique indexes, 242
Unix systems
   alert log, 82
   auditing, 305
   background processes, 24
   catproc.sql script, 117
   creating a database, 93, 95
   data dictionary tables, 108, 109
   DBCA, 93
   environmental variables, 95, 332
   OFA, 42
   OS authentication, 43
   parameter file, 62, 68
   SQL*Loader, 266–267
UPDATE privilege, 301
UROWID format, 225, 228
USER_DATA data dictionary view, **124**
USER_* data dictionary views, 110, 119,
  120, **124**, **354**
USER_DUMP_DEST parameter,
  68, 82, **84**
User global area, 19
USER_OBJECTS data dictionary
  view, 120

User processes, 28, **31**, **353**
Users, **322**, **345**, **351**, **354**, **360**
   account locking, 319, **322**
   altering, 294–295
   auditing, 305–308, **345**
   creating, 291–294, **351**
   data dictionary views, 297, 321
   dropping, 296–297
   listing, **354**
   monitoring information about, 297
   profiles, 315–321, **325**
   roles, 308–315, **346**, **352**, **353**, **354**
   system privileges, 290, 297–300
USER_SEGMENTS view, **124**
User sessions. *See* Sessions.
USER_SOURCE data dictionary
   view, 119
USERS tablespace, 18, **325**
USER_TABLES data dictionary
   view, 110
USER_TRIGGERS view, 122
UTL_FILE_DIR parameter, 68, 150, 151
UTL_FILE package, 119
UTL_HTTP package, 119
utlpwdmg.sql script, **324**
utl*.sql scripts, 118, **123**
utltree script, 120
utlxplan.sql script, **125**

V

V$ACCESS view, 74
V$ARCHIVE view, 74, 134, 138
Varying-width multibyte character sets, 330
V$BACKUP view, 74, 134
V$BGPROCESS view, 74
V$BUFFER_POOL view, 74
V$CONTROLFILE_RECORD_
   SECTION view, 133
V$CONTROLFILE view, 74, 85, 132,
   155, 342, 358
V$DATABASE view, 75, 134, 139
V$DATAFILE view, 75, 116, 134, 175
V$DB_OBJECT_CACHE view, 75
V$DISPATCHER view, 75
V$FILESTAT view, 75
V$FIXED_VIEW_DEFINITION
   view, 75
Views. *See* Data dictionary views,
   Dynamic performance views.
V$INSTANCE view, 75, 82, 139
V$LATCH view, 75
V$LIBRARYCACHE view, 75

V$LOCK view, 75
V$LOG view, 75, 134, 139–140
V$LOGFILE view, 75, 134, 140
V$LOG_HISTORY view, 75, 134, 140
V$LOGMNR_CONTENTS view,
   151, 152
V$LOGMNR_DICTIONARY view,
   152
V$LOGMNR_PARAMETERS view,
   152
V$MTS view, 75
V$OPEN_CURSOR view, 75
V$OPTION view, 75
V$PARAMETER view, 75, 77, 80, **85**,
   133–134, **154**, **155**, **342**, **358**
V$PROCESS view, 76
V$PWFILE_USERS view, 45, **57**,
   76, **345**
V$RECOVER_FILE view, 76
V$ROLLNAME view, 213, 216, **219**
V$ROLLSTAT view, 76, 211, 213, **219**
V$SESSION view, 76, 81, 213, 216
V$SESSION_EVENT view, 76
V$SESSION_LONGOPS view, 76
V$SESSION_WAIT view, 76
V$SESSTAT view, 76
V$SGASTAT view, 76
V$SGA view, 76, 116
V$SHARED_SERVER view, 76
V$SORT_SEGMENT view, **346**
V$SQLAREA view, 76
V$SQL view, 76
V$STATNAME view, 76
V$SYSSTAT view, 76
V$SYSTEM_EVENT view, 76
V$SYSTEM_PARAMETER view,
   76, 80, **85**
V$TABLESPACE view, 175
V$TEMPFILE view, 77, 134, 175
V$THREAD view, 140, **156**
V$TRANSACTION view, 77, 213, 216
V$ views, 74, 116
V$WAITSTAT view, 77

W

Windows 2000 systems, background
   processes, 24
Windows NT systems
   alert log, 82
   auditing, 305
   background processes, 24

catproc.sql script, 117
creating a database, 93, 96
data dictionary tables, 108, 109
DBCA, 93
environmental variables, 332
OFA, 42
OS authentication, 43
parameter file, 62, 68
SQL*Loader, 266–267

WITH ADMIN OPTION, 44
Wrap, 204
Write-ahead protocol, 25

Z

O7_DICTIONARY_ACCESSIBILITY
    parameter, 67, 298